CREDITS

Project Editors
Kathleen McFadden
Jade L. Williams

Acquisitions Editor
Jody Kennen

Product Development Manager
Lindsay Sandman

Copy Editors
Jill Mazurczyk
Marylouise Wiack

Technical Editor
Erick Tejkowski

Editorial Manager
Rev Mengle

Permissions Editor
Laura Moss

Media Development Specialist
Gregory Stafford

Manufacturing
Allan Conley
Linda Cook
Paul Gilchrist
Jennifer Guynn

Production Coordinator
Nancee Reeves

Book Design
maranGraphics®

Layout
Carrie Foster
LeAndra Johnson
Joyce Haughey
Kristin McMullan
Heather Pope

Screen Artist
Jill A. Proll

Cover Illustration
David E. Gregory

Proofreader
Laura L. Bowman

Quality Control
John Tyler Connoley
Andy Hollandbeck
Angel Perez

Indexer
Joan Griffitts

Vice President and Executive Group Publisher
Richard Swadley

Vice President and Publisher
Barry Pruett

Composition Director
Debbie Stailey

TABLE OF CONTENTS

Unix for Mac:
Your visual blueprint to maximizing
the foundation of Mac OS X

5) WORK WITH TEXT EDITORS

6) CUSTOMIZE YOUR SHELL

7) WORK WITH PROCESSES

TABLE OF CONTENTS

Unix for Mac:
Your visual blueprint to maximizing
the foundation of Mac OS X

11) SYSTEM ADMINISTRATION COMMANDS ———

12) INSTALL UNIX APPLICATIONS ———

13) INSTALL AND USE INTERNET APPLICATIONS ——

TABLE OF CONTENTS

14) SERVE WEB PAGES WITH APACHE

15) WORK WITH PERL

Unix for Mac:
Your visual blueprint to maximizing
the foundation of Mac OS X

16) RUN THE X WINDOW SYSTEM

17) INSTALL X WINDOW SYSTEM SOFTWARE

18) DEVELOP UNIX APPLICATIONS

APPENDIX

INDEX

HOW TO USE THIS BOOK

Unix for Mac: Your visual blueprint to maximizing the foundation of Mac OS X uses straightforward examples to teach you how to get the most out of your Mac OS X system by fully using its Unix capabilities.

To get the most out of this book, you should read each chapter in order from beginning to end. Each chapter introduces new ideas and builds on the knowledge learned in previous chapters. After you become familiar with Unix for Mac, you can use this book as an informative desktop reference.

Who This Book Is For

If you are looking for a resource that will help you learn how to maximize the Unix underpinnings of Mac OS X, *Unix for Mac: Your visual blueprint to maximizing the foundation of Mac OS X* is the book for you.

No prior experience with operating systems is required, but familiarity with UNIX or Mac is an asset.

What You Need To Use This Book

To perform the tasks in this book, you need a power PC running Mac OS X v.10.2. or higher.

The Conventions In This Book

A number of typographic and layout styles have been used throughout *UNIX for Mac: Your visual blueprint to maximizing the foundation of Mac OS X* to distinguish different types of information.

Courier Font

Indicates the use of Unix commands, scripting commands such as shell or Perl commands, source code such as C or Java commands, and HTML.

Bold

Indicates information that must be typed by you.

Italics

Indicates a new term being introduced.

Apply It

An Apply It section usually contains a segment of code that takes the lesson you just learned one step further. Apply It sections offer inside information and pointers that can be used to enhance the functionality of your code.

Extra

An Extra section provides additional information about the task you just accomplished. Extra sections often contain interesting tips and useful tricks to make working with Mac OS X easier and more efficient.

The Organization Of This Book

UNIX for Mac: Your visual blueprint to maximizing the foundation of Mac OS X contains 18 chapters.

The first chapter, "Get Started with Unix," introduces you to the Unix features that are built directly into the operating system and constitute the foundation on which all Mac OS X applications run. You can access this foundation directly by using the terminal application.

Chapter 2, "Work with Files," illustrates how the Unix shell enables you to move through the file system and access parts of your hard drive that are unavailable through the Finder.

Unix for Mac:
Your visual blueprint to maximizing
the foundation of Mac OS X

Chapter 3, "Work with Directories," shows how you can create, delete, move, copy, change, and navigate files and directories.

Chapter 4, "Work with Text," demonstrates how you can extract, view, and compare text files, and to chain text commands together.

Chapter 5, "Work with Text Editors," illustrates how you can edit a text file in Unix, such as an application's configuration file, a Web page, or a Perl program. Mac OS X offers three text editors — pico, vi, and emacs — for editing text files.

Chapter 6, "Customize Your Shell," shows you how to configure your terminal shell to fit your preference.

Chapter 7, "Work with Processes," demonstrates how you can suspend, start, run, kill, list, and monitor processes.

Chapter 8, "Automate Shell Tasks," illustrates how a shell script containing a set of instructions is typed in a terminal window and executed to form a basic Unix program. You will also learn how to set scripts to execute at a specific time of day or date using cron.

Chapter 9, "Combine Unix and Aqua," demonstrates how you can best take advantage of running Aqua — OS X GUI — alongside the Unix command line.

Chapter 10, "Work with Internet Commands," shows how you can connect to another computer and execute commands or download files.

Chapter 11, "System Administration Commands," details how you can assign yourself as the system administrator of your system.

Chapter 12, "Install Unix Applications," guides you through the download and installation of programs, some free and some not, which run on Mac OS X. These are often downloaded via the Internet, and come as packages or archives.

Chapter 13, "Install and Use Internet Applications," lists some of the most popular programs that you can download and install for better access via the shell to the Internet.

Chapter 14, "Serve Web Pages with Apache," shows you how to use the Apache server on your computer to serve live pages on the Internet, or as your own test bed for Web site creation.

Chapter 15, "Work with Perl," shows you how to use Perl for a variety of tasks from system administration to Web pages. Mac OS X comes with Perl pre-installed.

Chapter 16, "Run the X Window System," shows you how to get the advantage of using both Mac and Unix graphical programs by running an X server with the Mac OS X GUI called Aqua.

Chapter 17, "Install X Window System Software," introduces you to free alternatives to expensive commercial software such as the GIMP that provides the functions of Photoshop, and Open Office.org that is a free equivalent of Microsoft Office.

The final chapter, "Develop Unix Applications," shows you how to create and run programs in other languages on Mac OS X.

What's On The CD-ROM Disc

The CD-ROM disc included in this book contains office tools, such as OpenOffice.org, Gimp, XFree, Fink, and other open source software. See the appendix for more information on software included on the companion CD.

INTRODUCTION TO UNIX

You can get full use out of your Mac OS X computer by learning the ins and outs of the Unix operating system. Even though you may not know it, you use Unix every time you turn on your Mac OS X computer, because at the core, Mac OS X is Unix.

For most users, the Unix foundation for Mac OS X operates behind the scenes; they may use Mac OS X for years without needing to directly access the Unix features described in this book. However, by understanding and using Unix, you can take full advantage of the power of Mac OS X.

THE HISTORY OF UNIX

The original version of UNIX was created in the 1960s in the Bell Labs of AT&T, by researchers who devised a multi-user operating system for large mainframe computers. The role of an operating system like Unix is to provide basic functions such as running programs, saving data, and sending output to a monitor or other device. On your Apple computer, these functions are provided by the Mac OS X operating system, a direct descendent of the original Unix operating system.

BSD Unix System

From AT&T, the Unix system spread to research universities, that quickly adopted it. The University of California, Berkeley, was one of the earliest adopters and developers of Unix. The staff and students at Berkeley added many more features to this ever-evolving operating system. The updated Berkeley version of Unix was known as Berkeley Software Distribution (BSD), and it forms a major branch of the operating system family tree. The BSD family tree must be an apple tree, because the most recent fruit is Mac OS X, which is based on the BSD Unix system from Berkeley.

Open Source

Computer programs begin as source code, written in a computer language by programmers. They are then transformed into applications that you can run through a process called compiling, which translates the source code into commands that a computer can understand.

You do not need the source code to run the program. However, if you have access to the source code, you can recreate the application, or change the application by modifying the source code. Many commercial companies do not make their source code public because, if they did, nobody would buy their software. Other groups make their source code freely available to the public; this is known as *open source*.

Free Operating Systems and Applications

The most famous open-source software is the free operating system known as Linux. A young, Finnish software developer named Linus Torvalds created Linux as a version of Unix that could run on Intel-style PCs, as well as other hardware. In addition to Linux, there are several free versions of BSD Unix, known as Free BSD, Open BSD, and Net BSD. Mac OS X is a cousin to these free BSD operating systems, but is not itself a free operating system.

The largest collection of open-source applications comes from the GNU project, developed by the Free Software Foundation. GNU is an acronym for GNU's Not Unix, and yes, that is self-referential. Many of the Unix applications that you run are based on GNU code.

MAC OS X AND UNIX

Up to and including Mac OS 9, the Apple operating system was not based on Unix. There was no Unix code at the core of Mac OS 9 or earlier systems; instead, they used an operating system that was developed within Apple Computer.

Darwin

When it was time to create the next version of Mac OS, Apple chose to base it on a BSD Unix foundation, modified for the specific needs of Apple. This version of BSD Unix was called Darwin. Darwin consists primarily of the Unix kernel, which is the program that runs and manages all the processes and shells of the operating system, along with associated programs and files that make the kernel run. The source code for Darwin is open and available on the Web from http://developer. apple.com/darwin/, although you will probably never need to use it.

Not all the Mac OS X operating system is open source; for example, the programs used to create the Mac OS X desktop and windows, known collectively as Aqua, are not available for free and are only distributed as compiled applications.

Shell Commands

The original computers that ran Unix were not graphical; windows, drop-down menus, desktops, and the point-and-click capabilities of the mouse were to come later. Early versions of Unix were entirely text-based, taking input solely from the keyboard and displaying only on the screen, or sometimes just on a printer. This meant that all Unix programs were text-based, and responded to keystrokes. Users accessed the operating system through commands given to an application called a shell.

The Unix operating systems of today can handle graphics with ease, but underneath the graphical windows, text still reigns supreme. Your Mac OS X computer is no exception. In Mac OS X, you enter shell commands through an application named Terminal.

Aqua

Each time you run Mac OS X on your computer, you are using Aqua. Aqua is the graphical user interface system that gives your Macintosh the distinctive look and feel of Mac OS X — the main menu at the top, the Dock, the desktop, the three colored buttons at the upper left corner of each window. The Aqua interface lets you point-and-click to run applications. In truth, Aqua is a group of applications that run atop the Mac OS X foundation of Unix; Aqua starts automatically to provide you with the familiar Mac OS X interface, designed for both keyboard and mouse.

X Window System

The X Window System is another graphical user interface system that is used on most computers running Unix; however, it does not come standard with Mac OS X. Although both the X Window System and Mac OS X contain the letter X, they are not related — the X in X Window System comes from its being a successor to an earlier window-based system named W, and the X in Mac OS X, of course, stands for the Roman numeral ten.

Because the X Window System is used on so many other computers, including Linux, BSD, and Solaris machines, there are a number of applications written for the X Window System, most of them open source and free. You can run X Window System applications on your Mac OS X computer by installing an application called an X server, which gives you access to a wide variety of X Window System software.

START THE TERMINAL APPLICATION

You can use the Mac OS X Terminal application to enter Unix shell commands and to run Unix applications. The name of the Terminal application refers back to the physical terminal devices that were connected to old Unix mainframes. Each terminal consisted of a keyboard for input and a screen for text output. The Terminal application provides the same function, allowing you to enter your commands through the keyboard and to view the output in the Terminal window.

The Terminal application comes with the Mac OS X operating system as a utility application. You can find it in the Utilities folder of the Applications folder, by using Finder. Because you are using the Terminal application to run the Unix commands in this book, you want to keep the Terminal handy by setting it to Keep In Dock. This allows you to launch a Terminal window from the Dock with a single mouse-click.

You can have several Terminal windows running at once. You can also switch between Terminal windows by using the keyboard shortcuts.

Each Terminal application runs a separate Unix shell. A shell is an application that sends your commands to the Unix system and provides you with the output of those commands. The shell starts by printing a welcome message, then provides a prompt and waits for you to type a command. The prompt contains the name of your computer and your short username, as follows:

```
[computer:~] user%
```

When a Unix shell command is completed, the prompt appears again. As you provide commands to the shell, the output of your commands moves down the Terminal window. Output that scrolls past the top of the window is not lost forever; you can access it by using the scroll bar on the right side of the Terminal window, or by using the page-up and page-down keys.

START THE TERMINAL APPLICATION

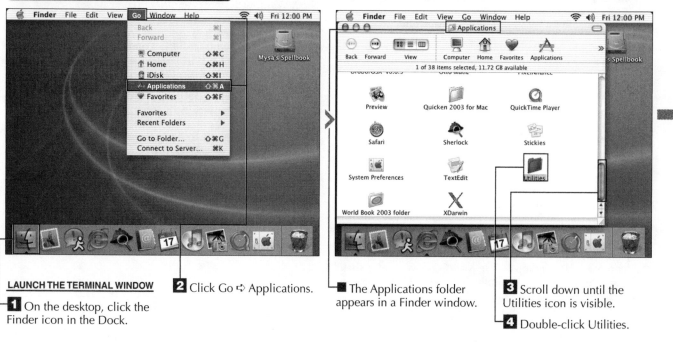

LAUNCH THE TERMINAL WINDOW

1 On the desktop, click the Finder icon in the Dock.

2 Click Go ➪ Applications.

■ The Applications folder appears in a Finder window.

3 Scroll down until the Utilities icon is visible.

4 Double-click Utilities.

Extra

You can have several Terminal windows running at once. To open a new Terminal window, press ⌘ + N. To switch between the Terminal windows, press ⌘ + ← or ⌘ + →.

If you use the scroll bars to scroll back and then type a command, the window snaps back to the current prompt, with the result that you can no longer see the scrolled text. The version of the Terminal application that comes with Mac OS X 10.2, Jaguar, lets you split your Terminal window so that you can keep scrolled text on-screen for reference.

To split the window, click the small icon that looks like a broken square in the upper-right corner of the Terminal window. A bar appears, separating the window into two panes. Each pane has a separate scroll bar, and only the lower pane scrolls when you type shell commands. You can change the relative sizes of the panes by clicking the separator bar and dragging it up or down.

To return the split windows to only one pane, click the square gray icon in the upper-right corner of the lower pane.

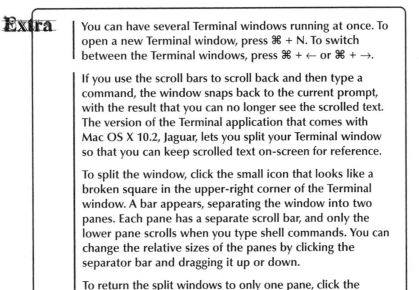

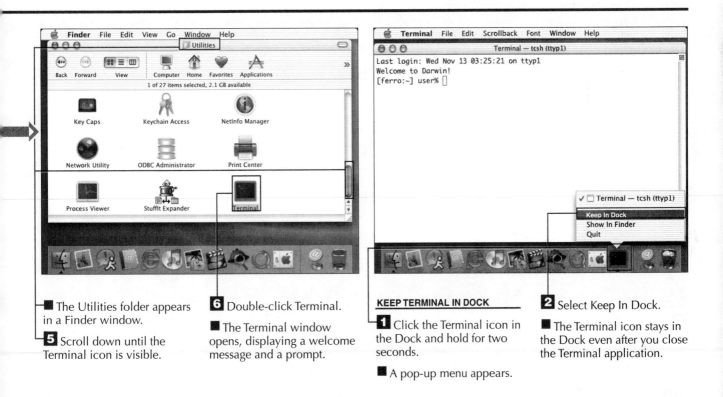

■ The Utilities folder appears in a Finder window.

5 Scroll down until the Terminal icon is visible.

6 Double-click Terminal.

■ The Terminal window opens, displaying a welcome message and a prompt.

KEEP TERMINAL IN DOCK

1 Click the Terminal icon in the Dock and hold for two seconds.

■ A pop-up menu appears.

2 Select Keep In Dock.

■ The Terminal icon stays in the Dock even after you close the Terminal application.

CONFIGURE THE TERMINAL APPLICATION

You can set the preferences and settings of the Terminal application to meet your particular needs. For example, you can give each Terminal a different name, such as Editing the Config File or Compiling the Server, to remind you of what you are doing in that Terminal; or, if you find the default font size too hard to read, you can enlarge it or change it to a different font.

You can access the Terminal application Preferences panel through the Terminal window. This panel allows you to change the command shell that executes when you start the Terminal application. For more information on using other shells, see Chapter 6.

You can change the appearance of the Terminal window by selecting the Window Settings option from the Terminal menu. The Terminal Inspector panel appears, allowing you to configure the settings for the current window. There are

seven groups of settings: Shell, Processes, Emulation, Buffer, Display, Color, and Window. You can switch between groups by selecting the group name at the top of the Terminal Inspector panel. Within each group, you can change a number of related settings; for example, the Window settings allow you to control the size of the Terminal window and the title at the top of the Terminal window.

Any changes that you make to the Window settings apply only to the current window. However, you can set the current values as the default for all future Terminal windows by clicking the Use Settings as Defaults button.

You can save your Window settings by selecting the Save, or Save As, option from the File menu; this creates a TERM file. You can load Window settings from a TERM file by using the Open command from the File menu, thus creating a new Terminal window with those settings.

CONFIGURE THE TERMINAL APPLICATION

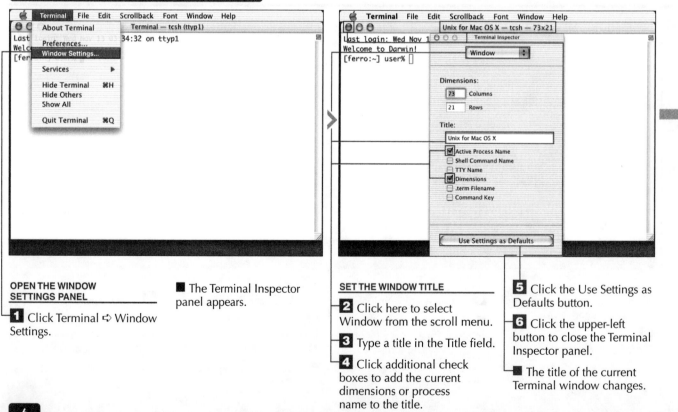

OPEN THE WINDOW SETTINGS PANEL

■ 1 Click Terminal ➪ Window Settings.

■ The Terminal Inspector panel appears.

SET THE WINDOW TITLE

2 Click here to select Window from the scroll menu.

3 Type a title in the Title field.

4 Click additional check boxes to add the current dimensions or process name to the title.

5 Click the Use Settings as Defaults button.

6 Click the upper-left button to close the Terminal Inspector panel.

■ The title of the current Terminal window changes.

Extra

The Shell and Processes settings let you determine whether the Terminal window closes when you quit the shell application, and they also help you to avoid accidentally closing windows with active Unix shell commands running. The Emulation settings allow fine-tuning of input and output controls to better emulate, or mimic, a physical terminal device. The Buffer settings control the number of lines that the shell saves as scroll back, and which you can access by using the scroll bars.

The Display settings control the appearance of the cursor and the text in the Terminal window. You can change the font or font size, or you can set the text to be anti-aliased. Anti-aliasing uses shades of gray to make the text easier to read, but it can also slow down the display of Unix shell commands.

You can change the color of the Terminal window and text by using the Color settings. The Window settings affect the dimensions of the window and the title that appears in the top bar of the Terminal window. You can set the title to a specific name, or to reflect the current size or running commands of the Terminal window.

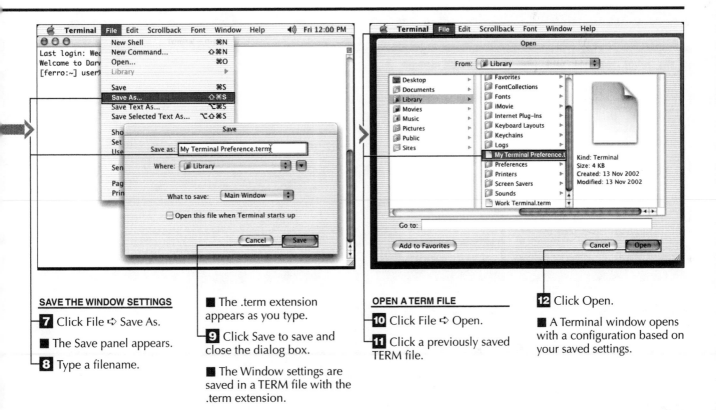

SAVE THE WINDOW SETTINGS

7 Click File ⇨ Save As.

■ The Save panel appears.

8 Type a filename.

■ The .term extension appears as you type.

9 Click Save to save and close the dialog box.

■ The Window settings are saved in a TERM file with the .term extension.

OPEN A TERM FILE

10 Click File ⇨ Open.

11 Click a previously saved TERM file.

12 Click Open.

■ A Terminal window opens with a configuration based on your saved settings.

ENTER UNIX SHELL COMMANDS

You can execute Unix shell commands by typing them directly at the prompt in the Terminal window. These commands allow you to run Unix applications from the shell. You can also run commands that tell you the current state of your shell commands, such as which programs are running or the current location of your Terminal shell in the file folder hierarchy.

After typing each command, you must press the Return key to tell the shell that you are done typing. The shell does not run your command until you press Return. This allows you to go back and edit the command before the shell runs it. If you make a typing mistake, you can use the Delete key to back up and erase your mistake, then retype the command and press Return.

If you do not notice your mistake before pressing Return, you may get an error message. If you type a non-existent command, such as mistake, Unix returns the following:

mistake: Command not found.

You can recall your last command by pressing the up-arrow key; the exact command you typed appears after the prompt. You can edit the line using the Delete key and then press Return when you have corrected the mistake. This is also a useful way to repeat commands. If you press the up-arrow key repeatedly, you can move either back or forward, respectively, through all the shell commands you have typed.

The easiest Unix command to type is the w command. This command shows you who is connected to your computer and how long they have been idle. Old Unix machines often had dozens or even hundreds of users connected at once, but you see only one line for each Terminal window you have open.

ENTER UNIX SHELL COMMANDS

```
   Terminal   File   Edit   Scrollback   Font   Window   Help
  Terminal — ttyp1
Last login: Wed Nov 13 03:42:10 on ttyp1
Welcome to Darwin!
[ferro:~] user% w
 3:44AM  up  3:14, 3 users, load averages: 0.29, 0.29, 0.26
USER     TTY FROM              LOGIN@  IDLE WHAT
user     co  -               12:31AM  3:13 -
user     p1  -                3:44AM     0 -
user     p2  -                3:29AM    13 -
[ferro:~] user%
```

```
   Terminal   File   Edit   Scrollback   Font   Window   Help
  Terminal — ttyp1
Last login: Wed Nov 13 03:42:10 on ttyp1
Welcome to Darwin!
[ferro:~] user% w
 3:44AM  up  3:14, 3 users, load averages: 0.29, 0.29, 0.26
USER     TTY FROM              LOGIN@  IDLE WHAT
user     co  -               12:31AM  3:13 -
user     p1  -                3:44AM     0 -
user     p2  -                3:29AM    13 -
[ferro:~] user% e
e: Command not found.
[ferro:~] user% ww
ww: Command not found.
[ferro:~] user%
```

ENTER THE w COMMAND

1 Open the Terminal application.

2 Type the letter **w** and press Return.

■ The shell displays the users connected to your computer.

3 Type the letter **e** and press Return.

■ An error message appears because there is no UNIX shell command named e.

4 Type **ww** and press Return.

■ An error message appears because there is no UNIX shell command named ww.

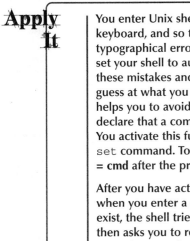

You enter Unix shell commands through a keyboard, and so they are susceptible to typographical errors. Fortunately, you can set your shell to automatically intercept these mistakes and to make a reasonable guess at what you are trying to type. This helps you to avoid error messages that declare that a command cannot be found. You activate this function by using the `set` command. To do this, type **set correct = cmd** after the prompt.

After you have activated the function, when you enter a command that does not exist, the shell tries to find a match. It then asks you to reply by typing a y for yes, **n** for no, **e** for edit, or **a** for abort.

TYPE THIS:

```
[darwin:~] user% ww
```

RESULT:

```
CORRECT>w (y|n|e|a)? yes
4:16AM  up  3:46, 2 users, load averages: 0.78, 0.80, 0.68
USER    TTY FROM               LOGIN@  IDLE WHAT
user    co  -                  4:01AM  3:45 -
user    p1  -                  3:53AM   0  -
```

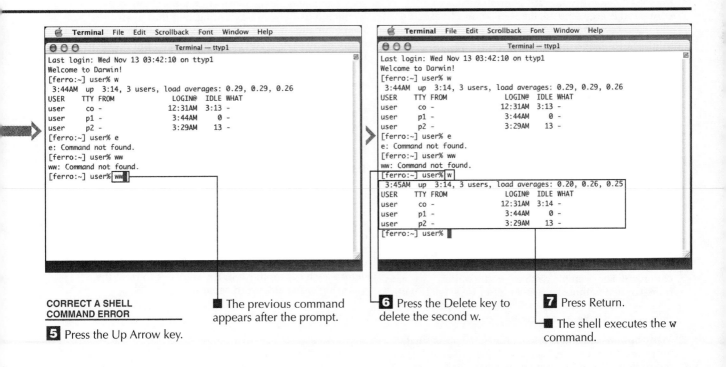

CORRECT A SHELL COMMAND ERROR

5 Press the Up Arrow key.

■ The previous command appears after the prompt.

6 Press the Delete key to delete the second w.

7 Press Return.

■ The shell executes the w command.

SHELL COMMAND CONCEPTS

S hell commands in Unix are often cryptic sets of letters strung together, apparently at random. To the uninitiated, they can appear arbitrary, but there are some general concepts that hold them together.

Shell commands execute as soon as you type them and press the Return key. The execution consists of two steps:

First, the shell interprets the command line you have typed and breaks it down into its constituent parts. Second, the shell uses those parts to determine whether a built-in command or an executable program should be run, and then passes the appropriate parameters to the command or executable program.

ANATOMY OF A SHELL COMMAND

Each shell command is composed of specific parts, including the command name, options, and arguments. These parts tell the shell which command to execute, how that command should be executed, and what other information on your computer it should use in the execution of the command. You can better understand how Unix reads shell commands by looking at the following example:

```
grep -i -C2 --line-number "Mac OS X"
Documents/to-do.txt
```

This command illustrates all of the components that comprise a shell command, and illustrates how to use multiword arguments by employing quotes.

Simple Command Name

The shell breaks down your command into words separated by spaces, and then interprets the commands one word at a time. The first word in the above command is grep, and so, the shell knows to execute the grep command.

To save on typing, Unix commands have traditionally been very short words. Some are not even pronounceable words in English, such as the ls, cd, rm, or pwd commands. The word grep can be pronounced, but it seems to have no meaning in English. This is because it is actually an acronym for *global regular expression print*. That may not help you much, but for now, it is enough to say that the grep command lets you search for text in a file.

Options

You can type a number of options after the command name; these are strings starting with a hyphen or dash, for example -i. You use these options to force Unix commands to change their behavior. Each command has a unique set of options that you can use with it, and the meanings of these options vary from command to command. For example, with grep the option -i means to match text without regard for letter case, while with rm — a command that deletes files — the option -i tells the shell to ask the user to confirm each file deletion.

Many options are single letters, but some are a single letter and then a value, such as -C2, which stands for the option -C and the numeric value 2. Longer options are often set off with two hyphens, as in --line-number.

Arguments

After the options in the command line, you can add arguments in the form of filenames or text. The shell command passes these arguments along to the command that you are executing, and they give the command such information as what file or information to look for, or where to store the results of the command when it is done. In the example above, the grep command has two arguments: "Mac OS X" and Documents/to-do.txt. The first argument to the grep command, "Mac OS X", is a specific piece of text that you want to find in a file, and the second argument, Documents/to-do.txt, is the name of that file.

Escaping Arguments

The quotation marks around the three words "Mac OS X" tell the shell to treat them as one argument rather than three. If the quotation marks are not used, the command line tells the grep command to look for the word *Mac* in files named OS, X, and Documents/to-do.txt. You can use quotation marks whenever you need to include multiword arguments or filenames in your Unix commands. Or, you can type a backslash (\) before each space; this tells the shell not to treat the following space as a word separator.

USING SHELL COMMANDS

Executable Files

Most commands that you enter on the command line are requests to run a program of some kind. The command may be a compiled program originally written in a language such as C++ and now saved on disk as a binary file. It may be a script written in Perl, or it may be a shell script. To be run, a file must be executable. *Executable* refers to both the contents and the attributes of a file.

The shell locates the executable by searching through a set of locations on your hard drive called your *path*. The path is a list of folders, also called directories. If you type the name of an executable within one of those folders and press Return, you are running that file as a shell application. By default, your path contains a reasonable set of directories, but you can add other file locations.

Built-In Commands

Some of the commands you type are built directly into the shell application and do not exist as separate files. These functions include starting and stopping commands, setting shell variables, repeating commands, and moving through the file structure.

You can get a full list of the built-in shell commands by typing the command **builtins** at the shell prompt. One built-in command that is quite useful is the which command. The which command tells you whether a command is a built-in command or an executable file; if it is an executable file, the shell lists the location of that file.

which Command

You use the which command to determine whether a command is built-in or is an executable file.

TYPE THIS:

```
[darwin:~] user% which w
```

⌄

RESULT:

```
/usr/bin/w
```

You can see from this output that w is an executable file stored in the location /usr/bin/w.

TYPE THIS:

```
[darwin:~] user% which which
```

⌄

RESULT:

```
which: shell built-in c
```

This output tells you th
built directly into the s

TYPE THE MAN

1 At the Termina
prompt, type **man** an
space.

READ THE UNIX MANUAL

You can read the Unix manual pages by using the man command. These pages give you a basic summary of how to use a specific Unix command as well as detailed information on the types of parameters you can use with that command.

The simplest way to get information about a given command is to type **man commandname**. If there is such a command and if there is a manual page for that command, the shell displays the manual page. Because most manual pages are long, only the first screen of information displays in your Terminal window; to continue on to the next screen, you can press the Spacebar. You can continue pressing the Spacebar for each screen of information until you have read the entire manual page.

A manual page first lists the name of the command, and in parentheses, the section number of the manual where you can find that command. Some commands or terms appear

in several sections, and you can select from among them by including the section number before the term. After the name of the command, a synopsis of the syntax for the command appears. Parameters in brackets are optional, but if you use them, you must replace the underlined words with an appropriate value or filename when you type the command.

A manual page also includes a description of the command and often provides examples of how you can use it. Related commands also appear along with section numbers, and any files that relate to the command, such as configuration files, are shown. Extra bits of trivia, such as the history of the command or known bugs, may also appear.

READ THE UNIX MANUAL

```
 Terminal  File  Edit  Scrollback  Font  Window  Help
000                    Terminal — ttyp1
Last login: Wed Nov 13 03:44:11 on ttyp1
Welcome to Darwin!
[ferro:~] user% man w
```

```
 Terminal  File  Edit  Scrollback  Font  Window  Help
000                    Terminal — ttyp1
W(1)                System General Commands Manual              W(1)

NAME
     w - who present users are and what they are doing

SYNOPSIS
     w [-hin] [-M core] [-N system] [user]

DESCRIPTION
     The w utility prints a summary of the current activity on the system,
     including what each user is doing.  The first line displays the current
     time of day, how long the system has been running, the number of users
     logged into the system, and the load averages.  The load average numbers
     give the number of jobs in the run queue averaged over 1, 5 and 15 min-
     utes.

     The fields output are the user's login name, the name of the terminal the
     user is on, the host from which the user is logged in, the time the user
     logged on, the time since the user last typed anything, and the name and
     arguments of the current process.

     The options are as follows:

     -h       Suppress the heading.
```

COMMAND
window
a

2 Type the name of a command and press Return.

■ The shell displays the first screen of the manual page.

■ This area displays the name and section.

■ This area displays the Command syntax summary.

■ This area displays the Description of the command.

3 Press the Spacebar.

Extra

It is quite common for Unix computers to ship without a printed manual explaining the Unix shell commands, and your Mac OS X computer is no exception. Decades of Unix users have relied upon the `man` command for instructions on the proper use of Unix commands. As heir to their legacy, you may sometimes find yourself consulting the manual pages to decipher obscure error messages. Therefore, you should be familiar with how to use the `man` command.

You will find that only reading a manual page is not enough; you also need to understand what it is trying to tell you. This can be difficult, as most manual pages seem complex at first glance, having been written for a very technical audience of Unix system administrators. The key to understanding manual pages is to read enough of them so that you begin to absorb the concepts through familiarity. Use keyword searches and look up related commands and terms that you do not understand. Reading manual pages requires practice, but it is worth the effort.

You can become familiar with the `man` command by trying some of the commands.

Example:

```
[darwin:~] user% man man
[darwin:~] user% man apropos
[darwin:~] user% man whatis
[darwin:~] user% man manpath
[darwin:~] user% man tcshb
```

Some of the resulting man pages can be very opaque; so do not worry about anything you cannot immediately understand. For example, the man page for `tcsh` is extremely long.

Terminal File Edit Scrollback Font Window Help

Terminal — ttyp1

```
can be found, w prints ``-''.)

    The CPU time is only an estimate, in particular, if someone leaves a
    background process running after logging out, the person currently on
    that terminal is ``charged'' with the time.

    Background processes are not shown, even though they account for much of
    the load on the system.

    Sometimes processes, typically those in the background, are printed with
    null or garbaged arguments.  In these cases, the name of the command is
    printed in parentheses.

    The w utility does not know about the new conventions for detection of
    background jobs.  It will sometimes find a background job instead of the
    right one.

COMPATIBILITY
    The -f, -l, -s, and -w flags are no longer supported.

HISTORY
    The w command appeared in UNIX 3.0.

4th Berkeley Distribution        June 6, 1993        4th Berkeley Distribution
[ferro:~] user%
```

Terminal File Edit Scrollback Font Window Help

Terminal — ttyp1

```
[ferro:~] user% man -k manual
getNAME(8)                - get NAME sections from manual source for whatis/apro
pos data base
man(1)                    - format and display the on-line manual pages
perlxs(1)                 - s-1XSs0 language reference manual
route(8)                  - manually manipulate the routing tables
setkey(8)                 - manually manipulate the IPsec SA/SP database
[ferro:~] user%
```

■ The second screen of information appears.

4 Press the Spacebar and read each screen until you see the shell prompt.

■ You have now read the entire manual page for that term.

SEARCH THE MANUAL BY KEYWORD

5 Type **man -k** and a space.

6 Type a keyword and press Return.

■ The shell lists commands related to the keyword.

7 Press the Spacebar to read the list until you see the shell prompt.

EXIT THE TERMINAL WINDOW

When you are done typing Unix shell commands, you can exit your shell and close the Terminal window, or exit the Terminal application. To do this, you can simply click the red Close button in the upper left-hand corner of each Terminal window. Alternatively, you can choose Close Window from the Window menu or Quit Terminal from the Terminal menu. However, these are not necessarily the best ways to shut down a shell window.

This is because Unix shell commands can often continue to run in a Terminal window even if they do not appear on the screen, or seem to be doing nothing. When you close the window, you also terminate the shell application that started those commands, and as a result, you often terminate the commands as well.

For this reason, it is best to use the `exit` command to end a shell in a Terminal window. The `exit` command ends the shell, but leaves the Terminal open. After you quit the shell, you can close the window manually by clicking the red Close button in the upper left-hand corner of the Terminal window. You can change this behavior in the Window settings for Terminal by setting the windows to close automatically when the shell ends.

If you close a Terminal window without exiting the shell, you probably do not do any serious harm if no shell commands are running. The Terminal application tries to prevent problems by warning you if you close a window that contains a running command. You can choose to continue closing the window, or cancel the window closure.

EXIT THE TERMINAL WINDOW

EXIT FROM THE SHELL

1 Type **exit** in the Terminal window.

■ The shell terminates.

2 Click the red Close button.

■ The Terminal window closes.

ABORT WINDOW CLOSURE WHEN COMMANDS ARE RUNNING

■ A command such as `top` is currently running.

1 Click the red Close button.

■ A warning tells you that there are commands running.

2 Click Cancel to stop the window from closing.

■ The Terminal window remains open.

Extra

The Terminal application maintains a list of commands that it terminates if you close a Terminal window while those commands are running. Those commands are `rlogin`, `slogin`, `telnet`, and `ssh`. Each of these is an application that lets you connect to another computer and run commands as if you were sitting at that computer.

You can add or remove applications from the list of commands that the Terminal application automatically terminates when you close a window in the Terminal Inspector window; the list is found in the Processes group of settings. Click the name of the application and then click the Remove button. If you need to add an application to the list, simply click Add and type the name of the application. Be sure to click Use Settings as Defaults to save your Window settings. You can also set the Terminal application to prompt you each time you attempt to close a window without typing **exit** first; or you can set it to never ask you. If you often connect to another computer via telnet or ssh — secure shell — you may want to remove those applications from the list to avoid accidentally disconnecting.

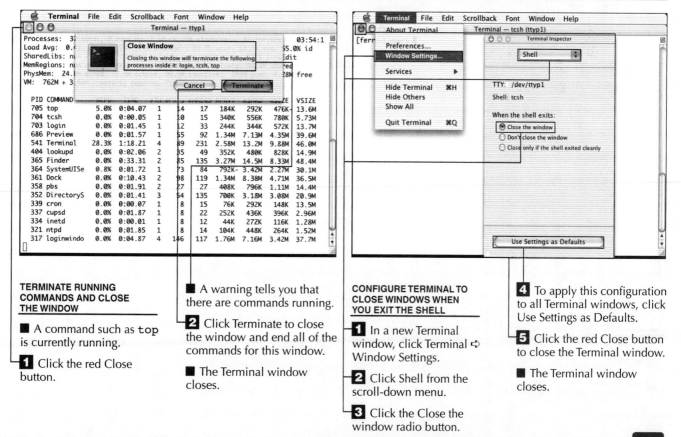

TERMINATE RUNNING COMMANDS AND CLOSE THE WINDOW

■ A command such as `top` is currently running.

1 Click the red Close button.

■ A warning tells you that there are commands running.

2 Click Terminate to close the window and end all of the commands for this window.

■ The Terminal window closes.

CONFIGURE TERMINAL TO CLOSE WINDOWS WHEN YOU EXIT THE SHELL

1 In a new Terminal window, click Terminal ⇨ Window Settings.

2 Click Shell from the scroll-down menu.

3 Click the Close the window radio button.

4 To apply this configuration to all Terminal windows, click Use Settings as Defaults.

5 Click the red Close button to close the Terminal window.

■ The Terminal window closes.

LIST FILES

When you are working in the Unix shell, everything is represented by a file within the file-based structure. The file structure is composed of directories, which are special types of files that can contain other files, including other directories. The commands you type are files as well — called executable files — with the exception of those commands built directly into the shell application. In fact, your shell itself is an executable file.

If you are familiar with the Mac OS X operating system, you are also familiar with the file-structure concept — everything is stored in folders. The folders of the Aqua interface are the directories of the shell interface — folders and directories are interchangeable terms. The term directory has it roots in Unix, while the word folder comes from the Mac OS graphical interface lineage.

Each file within a directory has a unique name. These names can contain letters, numbers, symbols, and even spaces, meaning you can have multiword filenames. However, if your filename contains spaces or punctuation symbols beyond a period, underscore, or dash, you need to place quotation marks around that filename when you specify it in a shell command.

When you open a Terminal window, your shell opens in a specific directory known as your Home directory. This is unique to each user on your computer, and Unix uses your Home directory to store the files, which you create using the various programs you run.

The command ls shows you the contents of the current directory in which you are working. You can use the option -F after the ls command to add an additional marker to indicate each type of file. A forward slash (/) after a filename indicates a directory and an asterisk (*) indicates an executable file.

LIST FILES

```
  Terminal  File  Edit  Scrollback  Font  Window  Help
○○○              Terminal — tcsh (ttyp1)
[ferro:~] user% ls
Desktop          Movies          Pictures        cute-puppy.jpg
Documents        Music           Public          my-dog.jpg
Library          Note To Mom.doc Sites           to-do.txt
[ferro:~] user%
```

```
  Terminal  File  Edit  Scrollback  Font  Window  Help
○○○              Terminal — tcsh (ttyp1)
[ferro:~] user% ls
Desktop          Movies          Pictures        cute-puppy.jpg
Documents        Music           Public          my-dog.jpg
Library          Note To Mom.doc Sites           to-do.txt
[ferro:~] user% ls -F
Desktop/         Movies/         Pictures/       cute-puppy.jpg
Documents/       Music/          Public/         my-dog.jpg
Library/         Note To Mom.doc Sites/          to-do.txt
[ferro:~] user%
```

SHOW FILE LIST

1 Open a Terminal window.

2 Type **ls** and press Return.

■ The shell displays a list of files.

LIST FILES WITH FILE TYPE

1 Type **ls -F** and press Return.

■ The shell displays a list of files.

■ A forward slash indicates a directory.

SHOW HIDDEN FILES

You can use the `-A` option with the `ls` command to list hidden files. Computers do not always display all files to the user. They do not do this to deceive you, but rather to help reduce the visual clutter in file listings. Hidden files are usually special files, set apart from the files that Unix users create and update. They may be configuration files or files that establish your shell environment. However, there are times that you may need to see a listing of all of your files, both hidden and normal, while working with Unix.

Unix hides files by giving them a filename starting with a period (.). Most commands, including the `ls` command, ignore these files. You cannot see them in a normal file listing. They also do not appear in the Mac OS X Finder. However, you can list them along with the visible files by using the `ls -A` command.

You can make it more obvious which files are directories by combining the `-A` option with the `-F` option. When you type the command `ls -A -F` to get a listing of all files, a forward slash (/) appears after each directory name. You can also combine these options together and type the command as `ls -AF`. This command lists hidden files and highlights directories at the same time.

You can run the `ls` command with an argument specifying the name of a file or directory. If you give a directory name, you see a listing of the contents of that directory. If the argument is an ordinary file, only the name of the file appears. If you specify a filename or directory that does not exist, the `ls` command tells you that there is no such file or directory.

SHOW HIDDEN FILES

```
 Terminal   File   Edit   Scrollback   Font   Window   Help
 ○ ○ ○                Terminal — tcsh (ttyp1)
[ferro:~] user% ls -A
.CFUserTextEncoding    Documents          Pictures
.DS_Store              Library            Public
.Trash                 Movies             Sites
.ssh                   Music              my-dog.jpg
Desktop                Note To Mom.doc    to-do.txt
[ferro:~] user% ls -A -F
.CFUserTextEncoding    Documents/         Pictures/
.DS_Store*             Library/           Public/
.Trash/                Movies/            Sites/
.ssh/                  Music/             my-dog.jpg
Desktop/               Note To Mom.doc    to-do.txt
[ferro:~] user%
```

```
 Terminal   File   Edit   Scrollback   Font   Window   Help
 ○ ○ ○                Terminal — tcsh (ttyp1)
[ferro:~] user% ls -AF Library
.DS_Store*             Keyboard Layouts/
.localized             Keychains/
Assistants/            Logs/
Audio/                 My Terminal Preference.term
Caches/                Preferences/
ColorPickers/          Printers/
Favorites/             Screen Savers/
FontCollections/       Sounds/
Fonts/                 Work Terminal.term
Internet Plug-Ins/     iMovie/
[ferro:~] user%
```

1 Type **ls -A** and press Return.

■ The shell displays hidden files.

2 Type **ls -A -F** and press Return.

■ The shell identifies the directories with a forward slash.

3 Type **ls -AF Library** and press Return.

■ The shell displays the contents of the Library directory, indicating hidden files and directories.

SHOW FILE ATTRIBUTES

You can show the attributes of each file, including the owner, permissions, and file size, by using the -l option with the ls command. Each file or directory has certain attributes that control who owns it and who can access it. All files have an owner, who is usually the user who created the file. For example, you are the owner of the files in your Home directory. You can also associate a file with a certain group; groups are collections of users to whom you can grant access privileges as a group.

When you type the ls -l command, you see one line for each file in the current directory, appearing in columns. The first column indicates the file mode; it looks like a series of dashes and seemingly random letters such as d, r, w, and x. The next column shows the number of other files or

directories that reference that file. These references, also called links, include the directory containing the file itself, so each file has at least one reference. For directories, the reference represents the number of files within each directory. The third and fourth columns show the user and group associated with the file. The fifth column shows the size of the file in characters or bytes. The sixth column shows the date and time the file was last modified. The final column shows the name of the file.

If you want to examine an individual file, you can give the filename as an argument to the ls -l command. Using the ls -l command on a directory lists the contents of the directory, although you can use the -d option to request the attributes of the directory without the directory contents.

SHOW FILE ATTRIBUTES

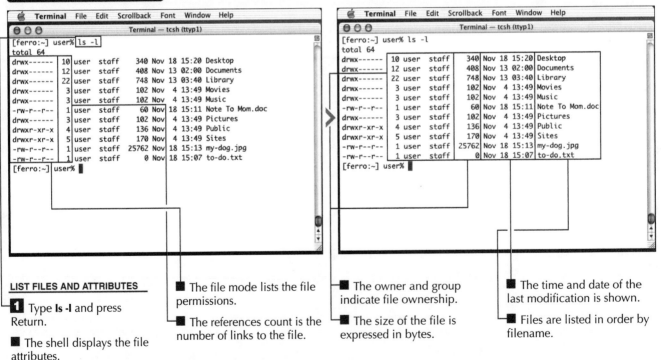

LIST FILES AND ATTRIBUTES

1 Type **ls -l** and press Return.

■ The shell displays the file attributes.

■ The file mode lists the file permissions.

■ The references count is the number of links to the file.

■ The owner and group indicate file ownership.

■ The size of the file is expressed in bytes.

■ The time and date of the last modification is shown.

■ Files are listed in order by filename.

Extra

The file mode indicates the file type and permissions. The first character is a d for a directory, or a dash for a normal file. The other nine letters are read in sets of three. The first set represents the permissions for the file owner, the middle set represents access by anyone in the file's group, and the last set is for all other users.

The first letter in each set, r, controls read access for the set of users. The second letter, w, controls write access. The last letter, x, designates execution access or, for a directory, access to directory files. Dashes in the mode field indicate that the corresponding permission is not set for the associated set. For example, rw- indicates that the users can read and write, but not execute the file.

Example:
```
drwxr-xr-x   5 user   staff   170 Nov  4 13:49 Sites
```

This directory can be read by the owner, the members of the group staff, and anyone else using the computer. Only the owner can write to the directory; however, anyone can move from directory to this directory.

Terminal File Edit Scrollback Font Window Help

Terminal — tcsh (ttyp1)

```
[ferro:~] user% ls -l my-dog.jpg
-rw-r--r--  1 user  staff  25762 Nov 18 15:13 my-dog.jpg
[ferro:~] user%
```

Terminal File Edit Scrollback Font Window Help

Terminal — tcsh (ttyp1)

```
[ferro:~] user% ls -l my-dog.jpg
-rw-r--r--  1 user  staff  25762 Nov 18 15:13 my-dog.jpg
[ferro:~] user% ls -ld Library
drwx------ 22 user  staff  748 Nov 13 03:40 Library
[ferro:~] user%
```

DISPLAY FILE ATTRIBUTES

1 Type **ls -l** and a space.

2 Type a filename and press Return.

■ The shell displays the file attributes.

SHOW THE ATTRIBUTES OF A DIRECTORY

1 Type **ls -ld** and a space.

2 Type a directory name and press Return.

■ The shell displays the directory attributes.

COPY A FILE

You can copy files with the `cp` command. This command allows you to save backups of important files or keep old versions of files while you edit them. Making copies of important files before editing them is a good practice because it assures that you can go back to the original.

To copy a file, you supply two arguments to the `cp` command: the first is the name of the original file, and the second is the name of the new file. You do not have to own the original file to copy it, but you must have permission to read it. You also need write permission in the directory to where you make the copy. Your `cp` command should look like this:

```
cp original-file copy-file
```

If `copy-file` is an existing directory, the copy will be placed in that directory and will be named the same as the `original-file`.

Copying a file can be dangerous if the file already exists with the same name you specify for the copy. In such a case, you write over the existing file with the new copy. The `cp` command does not automatically warn you, but copies the file, assuming that you want to overwrite the existing file.

To ensure that you do not accidentally write over a file, you can use the `-i` option with the `cp` command, so that it asks you to confirm that you want to write over the existing file. If you do, you can type **y** for yes and press Return; if you do not, you can press any key to cancel the process.

COPY A FILE

```
[ferro:~] user% ls -F
Desktop/        Movies/         Pictures/       my-dog.jpg
Documents/      Music/          Public/         to-do.txt
Library/        Note To Mom.doc Sites/
[ferro:~] user% cp my-dog.jpg cute-puppy.jpg
[ferro:~] user% ls -F
Desktop/        Movies/         Pictures/       cute-puppy.jpg
Documents/      Music/          Public/         my-dog.jpg
Library/        Note To Mom.doc Sites/          to-do.txt
[ferro:~] user%
```

```
[ferro:~] user% ls -F
Desktop/        Movies/         Pictures/       cute-puppy.jpg
Documents/      Music/          Public/         my-dog.jpg
Library/        Note To Mom.doc Sites/          to-do.txt
[ferro:~] user% cp -i my-dog.jpg to-do.txt
overwrite to-do.txt? n
[ferro:~] user%
```

CREATE A COPY

■1 Type **cp** and a space.

■2 Type the name of the original file, and a space.

■3 Type the name of the copy and press Return.

■ The shell copies the file.

COPY A FILE SAFELY

■1 Type **cp -i** *original-file* and press Return.

■ The shell asks you if you want to write over the file.

■2 Type your response and press Return.

■ The `cp` command either copies the file or abandons the operation, depending on your response.

DESIGNATE FILES BY PATHNAME

Y ou can include a pathname to indicate a location outside of your current directory when you give a filename as an argument to a command such as `cp`. The file system of your Mac OS X computer is set up as a hierarchy of folders containing files and other folders. Each of these folders corresponds to a directory. You can view the folders in the Mac OS X Finder application, or access them as directories through the Unix shell.

USING PATHNAMES

A pathname specifies the place in which you can find a file, just as an address tells you where to find someone in the physical world. For example, one might describe his current location by saying that he is on the planet Earth, in the country known as the United States of America, in the state of California, in the county of Orange, within the city of Fullerton, on Wilshire Avenue, in building number 110, on the Garden Level, in suite G-1, in the back office, at the desk of Kynn.

A file, on the other hand, might say that it is on a hard drive, in the Users directory, in the kynn subdirectory of the Users directory, in the Documents subdirectory of the kynn directory, and that it has the filename Chapter 02.doc. You can write that pathname as /Users/kynn/Documents/"Chapter 02.doc".

When writing the pathname, you must separate each directory name with a forward slash (/). In addition, because the filename contains a space, you must enclose it in quotation marks to refer to it in Unix.

Relative and Full Pathnames

The desk of Kynn is in an office that also contains the desk of Laura. If you are going to describe the location of Laura, you can just say the desk of Laura and not spell out everything starting with the planet Earth. This is a location relative to the desk belonging to Kynn. In the same way, you do not need to specify a full pathname if you are already in the same directory. For example, if you are working with files in the /Users/kynn directory and you want to copy the Chapter 02.doc file described above, you do not need to type the full pathname, only this:

```
[ferro:~] user% cp Documents/"Chapter
02.doc" backup-ch2.doc
```

This creates a copy of the file with the new name backup-ch2.doc. Note that this is in the /Users/kynn directory, not in the Documents directory.

The start of the Unix file system is the root directory, and you indicate it by an initial forward slash (/). A pathname beginning with a forward slash is therefore a full pathname, and is relative only to that root directory. Starting the pathname with the root directory is like starting with the planet Earth when telling someone where you are; the root directory corresponds to the Macintosh HD icon on your desktop in Finder. You use full pathnames to reference files that are outside of the directory in which you are currently working. For example, to copy a file in the /usr/share/dict directory to your own directory, you can type:

```
[ferro:~] user% cp /usr/share/dict/
propernames name-list.txt
```

Aliases for Special Pathnames

Three pathnames refer to special directories. The alias dot (.) refers to the current directory in which you are working. The alias dot-dot (..) refers to the parent directory — the directory which contains the current directory. The alias tilde (~) refers to your Home directory, where you store your personal files. If you give the name of another user immediately after the tilde, then it refers to the Home directory of that user.

RENAME A FILE

You can change the name of a file with the `mv` command. In Aqua, renaming files and moving files are two different functions. You move a file in Aqua by dragging it to a new location, and you rename it by clicking the name field of the file and typing a new name. However, within Unix, when you rename a file, you are simply moving the file to a new place within the file system; even if you are within the same directory, you are moving the file to a new name.

However, if you move a file to another file that already exists, you write over that second file. This is not a good practice unless you are certain that you want to overwrite the second file.

To avoid this problem, you can use the `-i` option with the `mv` command. If moving your file will overwrite another file, the shell asks you to confirm that you want to proceed. If you do, you can type **y** for yes, or any other key for no. To be safe, you should make a habit of using the `-i` option with the `mv` command. You can also set up a shell alias to automatically use the `-i` option with the `mv` command.

You can use the `mv` command to move a file from one location to another. When you move a file with a command such as `mv file /directory`, the resulting file retains its original name, but resides in a different directory. It is only when you move a file to both a new location and filename that you rename the file.

RENAME A FILE

```
   Terminal  File  Edit  Scrollback  Font  Window  Help

 O O O                   Terminal — tcsh (ttyp1)
[ferro:~] user% ls -F
Desktop/        Movies/         Pictures/       cute-puppy.jpg
Documents/      Music/          Public/         my-dog.jpg
Library/        Note To Mom.doc Sites/          to-do.txt
[ferro:~] user% mv cute-puppy.jpg big-dog.jpg
[ferro:~] user% ls -F
Desktop/        Movies/         Pictures/       big-dog.jpg
Documents/      Music/          Public/         my-dog.jpg
Library/        Note To Mom.doc Sites/          to-do.txt
[ferro:~] user%
```

```
   Terminal  File  Edit  Scrollback  Font  Window  Help

 O O O                   Terminal — tcsh (ttyp1)
[ferro:~] user% ls -F
Desktop/        Movies/         Pictures/       big-dog.jpg
Documents/      Music/          Public/         my-dog.jpg
Library/        Note To Mom.doc Sites/          to-do.txt
[ferro:~] user% mv -i big-dog.jpg to-do.txt
overwrite to-do.txt? n
[ferro:~] user%
```

RENAME A FILE

1 Type **mv** and a space.

2 Type the current filename and a space.

3 Type the new filename and press Return.

■ The shell renames the file.

RENAME A FILE SAFELY

1 Type **mv -i** *oldname newname* and press Return.

■ The shell asks you if you want to overwrite the file.

2 Type your response and press Return.

■ The **mv** command either renames the file or abandons the operation, depending on your response.

DELETE A FILE

Y ou can use the `rm` command to delete files you no longer want to keep. When you delete a file using the Mac OS X Finder in Aqua, the Finder does not immediately delete the file, but stores it in the Trash. However, when you delete a file using the `rm` command, the file completely and instantly disappears. This means that if you mistakenly delete a file from the shell, you cannot recover it by simply dragging it back out of the Trash.

As with the `cp` and `mv` commands, deleting files can be dangerous because people can make mistakes. You can use the `-i` option to tell the `rm` command to confirm that you want to delete a file; if you do, you can type **y** for yes, and press Return. If you do not, you can press any other key or simply the Return key.

By default, the `rm` command only removes ordinary files, although you can remove an empty directory with the `rmdir` command; for a directory containing files, you can use the `rm -r` command. You cannot remove directories unless they belong to you or you have write permission to the files. However, there is no special access permission required to delete a file.

It is possible to delete a file whose name begins with a dash, such as `-foo` or `-bar`. These are extremely hard to remove, because the `rm` command tries to interpret the filenames as an option, because options begin with dashes. In this situation, you can use the option `--` (a double dash). This means that the command does not check the rest of the line for more options, making this your last option flag.

DELETE A FILE

```
   Terminal   File   Edit   Scrollback   Font   Window   Help
 ⊙ ⊙ ⊙                  Terminal — tcsh (ttyp1)
[ferro:~] user% ls -F
Desktop/         Movies/          Pictures/        big-dog.jpg
Documents/       Music/           Public/          my-dog.jpg
Library/         Note To Mom.doc  Sites/           to-do.txt
[ferro:~] user% rm big-dog.jpg
[ferro:~] user% ls -F
Desktop/         Movies/          Pictures/        my-dog.jpg
Documents/       Music/           Public/          to-do.txt
Library/         Note To Mom.doc  Sites/
[ferro:~] user% ▊
```

```
   Terminal   File   Edit   Scrollback   Font   Window   Help
 ⊙ ⊙ ⊙                  Terminal — tcsh (ttyp1)
[ferro:~] user% ls -F
Desktop/         Movies/          Pictures/        my-dog.jpg
Documents/       Music/           Public/          to-do.txt
Library/         Note To Mom.doc  Sites/
[ferro:~] user% rm -i my-dog.jpg
remove my-dog.jpg? n
[ferro:~] user% ▊
```

DELETE A FILE

1 Type **rm** and a space.

2 Type the name of the file and press Return.

■ The shell deletes the file.

DELETE A FILE SAFELY

1 Type **rm -i** and a space.

2 Type the name of the file and press Return.

■ The shell asks you if you want to delete the file.

3 Type your response and press Return.

■ The `rm` command either deletes the file or abandons the operation, depending on your response.

CHANGE FILE PERMISSIONS

Y ou can change the permissions on files you own, allowing you to grant or withhold permission to others to read, write, or execute your files. There are two parameters for the chmod command, the first being the new mode, and the second being the file you want to change. You specify the mode change by indicating who the change affects, whether the change should be to add, remove, or set permissions, and what kind of permissions you want to set.

Unix uses letters to designate the users that your mode change affects: *u*, for the owner of the file, or user, *g*, for users in the file group, *o*, for others — users not in the group — or *a*, for all users. You can designate more than

one set of users by combining these designators together, such as go, to indicate users in the file group and users not in the file group, while omitting the file owner.

You can mark permission changes with a plus symbol (+) to add permissions, a minus symbol (-) to remove them, or an equal symbol (=) to set them. The possible permissions are the same as those shown by the ls -l command: r for read access, w for write access, and x for execute access.

You can make more than one change at a time to a given file by listing them with commas as separators. For example, to set the file example to be readable, writeable, and executable by you, readable and executable by those in the file group, and readable by those outside of the group, you can type **chmod u=rwx,g=rx,o=r example**.

CHANGE FILE PERMISSIONS

```
 Terminal   File   Edit   Scrollback   Font   Window   Help
 ○○○                    Terminal — tcsh (ttyp1)
[ferro:~] user% ls -l
total 64
drwx------  20 user   staff      680 Nov 18 15:24 Desktop
drwx------  12 user   staff      408 Nov 13 02:00 Documents
drwx------  22 user   staff      748 Nov 13 03:40 Library
drwx------   3 user   staff      102 Nov  4 13:49 Movies
drwx------   3 user   staff      102 Nov  4 13:49 Music
-rw-r--r--   1 user   staff       60 Nov 18 15:11 Note To Mom.doc
drwx------   3 user   staff      102 Nov  4 13:49 Pictures
drwxr-xr-x   4 user   staff      136 Nov  4 13:49 Public
drwxr-xr-x   5 user   staff      170 Nov  4 13:49 Sites
-rw-r--r--   1 user   staff    25762 Nov 18 15:13 my-dog.jpg
-rw-r--r--   1 user   staff        0 Nov 18 15:07 to-do.txt
[ferro:~] user% chmod og-r my-dog.jpg
[ferro:~] user% ls -la my-dog.jpg
-rw-------   1 user   staff    25762 Nov 18 15:13 my-dog.jpg
[ferro:~] user%
```

```
 Terminal   File   Edit   Scrollback   Font   Window   Help
 ○○○                    Terminal — tcsh (ttyp1)
[ferro:~] user% ls -l
total 64
drwx------  46 user   staff     1564 Nov 18 15:42 Desktop
drwx------  12 user   staff      408 Nov 13 02:00 Documents
drwx------  22 user   staff      748 Nov 13 03:40 Library
drwx------   3 user   staff      102 Nov  4 13:49 Movies
drwx------   3 user   staff      102 Nov  4 13:49 Music
-rw-------   1 user   staff       60 Nov 18 15:11 Note To Mom.doc
drwx------   3 user   staff      102 Nov 18 15:42 Pictures
drwxr-xr-x   4 user   staff      136 Nov  4 13:49 Public
drwxr-xr-x   5 user   staff      170 Nov  4 13:49 Sites
-rw-------   1 user   staff    25762 Nov 18 15:13 my-dog.jpg
-rw-r--r--   1 user   staff        0 Nov 18 15:07 to-do.txt
[ferro:~] user% chmod g+w to-do.txt
[ferro:~] user% ls -l to-do.txt
-rw-rw-r--   1 user   staff    0 Nov 18 15:07 to-do.txt
[ferro:~] user%
```

REMOVE READ ACCESS

1 Type **chmod** and a space.

2 Type **og-r** and a space.

3 Type the name of a file and press Return.

■ The shell indicates that only you can read the file.

ADD WRITE ACCESS

1 Type **chmod g+w** and a space.

2 Type the name of a file and press Return.

■ The shell indicates that anyone in the file group can change this file.

Apply It

You can change the permissions for an entire directory and its contents, including your Home directory, by using the -R option with the chmod command. The -R option dictates that modes should be changed recursively, which means that the changes apply to all files in that directory or in its subdirectories.

For example, if you want to make sure your Home directory is readable only by you and not by other users of your computer, you use the chmod -R command.

TYPE THIS:

```
[ferro:~] user% chmod -R go-rx ~
[ferro:~] user% ls -l
```

RESULTS:

```
drwx------   8 user   staff   272 Nov 13 13:57 Desktop
drwx------  12 user   staff   408 Nov 13 02:00 Documents
drwx------  22 user   staff   748 Nov 13 03:40 Library
drwx------   3 user   staff   102 Nov  4 13:49 Movies
drwx------   3 user   staff   102 Nov  4 13:49 Music
drwx------   3 user   staff   102 Nov  4 13:49 Pictures
drwx------   4 user   staff   136 Nov  4 13:49 Public
drwx------   5 user   staff   170 Nov  4 13:49 Sites
```

```
 Terminal  File  Edit  Scrollback  Font  Window  Help
                Terminal — tcsh (ttyp1)
[ferro:~] user% ls -l
total 64
drwx------  21 user  staff    714 Nov 18 15:25 Desktop
drwx------  12 user  staff    408 Nov 13 02:00 Documents
drwx------  22 user  staff    748 Nov 13 03:40 Library
drwx------   3 user  staff    102 Nov  4 13:49 Movies
drwx------   3 user  staff    102 Nov  4 13:49 Music
-rw-r--r--   1 user  staff     60 Nov 18 15:11 Note To Mom.doc
drwx------   3 user  staff    102 Nov  4 13:49 Pictures
drwxr-xr-x   4 user  staff    136 Nov  4 13:49 Public
drwxr-xr-x   5 user  staff    170 Nov  4 13:49 Sites
-rw-------   1 user  staff  25762 Nov 18 15:13 my-dog.jpg
-rw-rw-r--   1 user  staff      0 Nov 18 15:07 to-do.txt
[ferro:~] user% chmod a-x,u+x Sites
[ferro:~] user% ls -ld Sites
drwxr--r--  5 user  staff  170 Nov  4 13:49 Sites
[ferro:~] user%
```

```
 Terminal  File  Edit  Scrollback  Font  Window  Help
                Terminal — tcsh (ttyp1)
[ferro:~] user% ls -l
total 64
drwx------  22 user  staff    748 Nov 18 15:27 Desktop
drwx------  12 user  staff    408 Nov 13 02:00 Documents
drwx------  22 user  staff    748 Nov 13 03:40 Library
drwx------   3 user  staff    102 Nov  4 13:49 Movies
drwx------   3 user  staff    102 Nov  4 13:49 Music
-rw-r--r--   1 user  staff     60 Nov 18 15:11 Note To Mom.doc
drwx------   3 user  staff    102 Nov  4 13:49 Pictures
drwxr-xr-x   4 user  staff    136 Nov  4 13:49 Public
drwxr--r--   5 user  staff    170 Nov  4 13:49 Sites
-rw-------   1 user  staff  25762 Nov 18 15:13 my-dog.jpg
-rw-rw-r--   1 user  staff      0 Nov 18 15:07 to-do.txt
[ferro:~] user% chmod a=r "Note To Mom.doc"
[ferro:~] user% ls -l "Note To Mom.doc"
-r--r--r--  1 user  staff  60 Nov 18 15:11 Note To Mom.doc
[ferro:~] user%
```

SET EXECUTION PERMISSIONS

1 Type **chmod a-x,u+x** and a space.

2 Type the name of a file and press Return.

■ The shell indicates that only you can execute this file.

SET CUSTOM PERMISSIONS

1 Type **chmod a=r** and a space.

2 Type the name of a file and press Return.

■ The shell indicates the new permissions: the file is now read-only by everyone.

Note: You cannot alter this file without changing the permissions back.

SELECT FILES USING WILDCARDS

You can use wildcard characters to avoid having to type out the full name of each file you want to work with in Unix. This not only saves typing but also lets you refer to multiple files with similar names in a single command.

Unix shell wildcards are also called glob-patterns, and the use of these wildcards is known as *globbing* in Unix jargon. You can use these wildcards whenever you give a filename argument to a shell command.

The asterisk wildcard (*) matches any sequence of zero or more characters in a filename. The question mark (?) matches any single character. A range of characters in square brackets, such as [a-m], matches any single character within that range. Keep in mind that letters in filenames are case-sensitive, so while the letter d is a match for [a-m], the letter D is not, because it does not come between lowercase a and m.

A caret (^) at the start of a pattern or a range of characters indicates that the pattern should select those characters that do not match the given pattern. For example, if you want to use the ls -l command on all directories and files that begin with the letter P, you can type **ls -l P***. To remove all files beginning with A, followed by three letters, and ending in .doc, from your Documents directory, you can type **rm -i Documents/A???.doc**. You should always use the -i option with the rm command if you give it wildcard arguments, to avoid deleting the wrong files. A careless rm * command in the wrong directory can remove the contents of the directory.

Hidden files are resistant to being identified through wildcards. The command ls *, for example, does not list them while ls .* lists only hidden files.

SELECT FILES USING WILDCARDS

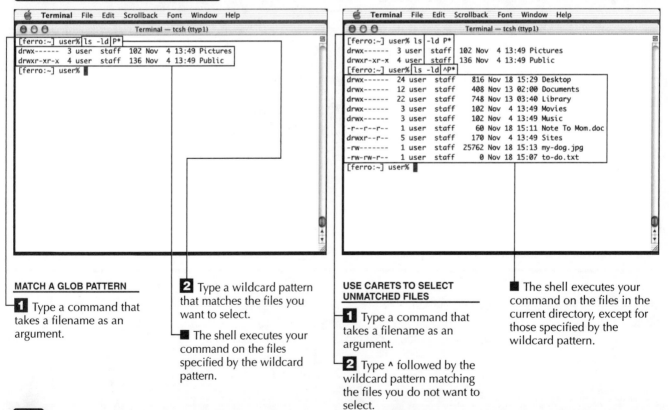

MATCH A GLOB PATTERN

1 Type a command that takes a filename as an argument.

2 Type a wildcard pattern that matches the files you want to select.

■ The shell executes your command on the files specified by the wildcard pattern.

USE CARETS TO SELECT UNMATCHED FILES

1 Type a command that takes a filename as an argument.

2 Type ^ followed by the wildcard pattern matching the files you do not want to select.

■ The shell executes your command on the files in the current directory, except for those specified by the wildcard pattern.

SELECT FILES USING COMPLETION

You can easily specify filename arguments by using command completion, which is a special function built into the shell. To use filename completion, you must type out the first part of the filename and then press the Tab key. If there is a file that matches the incomplete filename, the shell fills in the full filename for you.

If no file matches the filename, your shell program emits a beep, indicating that there is not a match. If more than one file matches, the shell program fills in as much as it can and then emits a beep, while waiting for you to enter more text to differentiate between the files that match the pattern up to that point and then differ. At this point, you can either type out the rest of the command line and press Return, or type enough of the command line to uniquely identify the file you want to access, and then press Tab again.

To see the results of an ambiguous match, you can press Control + D after the beep. Alternatively, you can type **set autolist**, which instructs your shell to list the remaining choice whenever file completion fails. This is a good command to save in your .tcshrc file, which ensures that this feature is set every time you start a Terminal window. Similarly, you can turn off autolist with **unset autolist**.

You can combine filename completion with full or relative pathnames as well; if you type a partial pathname and press Tab, the shell lists the options within that path. Using filename completion can save you a lot of typing as well as making it less likely that you mistype any characters.

SELECT FILES USING COMPLETION

```
   Terminal   File   Edit   Scrollback   Font   Window   Help
 ○ ○ ○                   Terminal — ttyp1
[ferro:~] user% set autolist
[ferro:~] user% ls -ld D
Desktop/    Documents/
[ferro:~] user% ls -ld D
```

```
   Terminal   File   Edit   Scrollback   Font   Window   Help
 ○ ○ ○                   Terminal — ttyp1
[ferro:~] user% set autolist
[ferro:~] user% ls -ld D
Desktop/    Documents/
[ferro:~] user% ls -ld Desktop/
drwx------  6 user   staff  204 Nov 18 16:34 Desktop/
[ferro:~] user%
```

1 Type **set autolist**.

2 Type a shell command that takes a filename as an argument.

3 Type the first few letters of the filename and press the Tab key.

■ A list of possible matches appears.

4 Type enough letters to make an unambiguous match.

5 Press the Tab key again.

■ The shell completes the filename.

6 Press Return.

■ The shell executes the command.

FIND FILES BY NAME

You can locate files by their names or other criteria by using the `find` command. This command tends to be faster than the Mac OS X Sherlock application for locating files, especially those that are used by the system or otherwise hidden from the Finder.

The `find` command is a complex and very powerful utility that lets you run many different types of searches and perform a variety of actions on the files that it finds. However, the most common use for the `find` command is simply to locate files with a certain name and print out their locations.

The basic syntax for the `find` command is:

```
find pathname -name filename -print
```

The first parameter, pathname, is the directory where you want to search. The filename is the name of the file for

which you are looking. The argument `-print` tells the `find` command to display the location of the file.

You can also give a wildcard pattern instead of a filename, and the `find` command lists all files that match that pattern. When you use wildcard patterns in this way you need to enclose them in quotation marks. For example, if you save a Word document but you do not keep track of what folder you save it in, you can use the `find` command to locate all the .doc files in your Documents directory:

```
find ~/Documents -name "*.doc" -print
```

This displays a list of all file locations matching the pattern. If you want to see a full file listing instead of the relative pathname for the files found, you can replace the `print` command with the `ls` command.

FIND FILES BY NAME

```
 Terminal   File   Edit   Scrollback   Font   Window   Help
 ○ ○ ○                Terminal — tcsh (ttyp1)
[ferro:~] user% ls -F
Desktop/        Movies/          Pictures/       to-do.txt
Documents/      Music/           Public/
Library/        Note To Mom.doc  Sites/
[ferro:~] user% find  .  -name my-dog.jpg
```

```
 Terminal   File   Edit   Scrollback   Font   Window   Help
 ○ ○ ○                Terminal — tcsh (ttyp1)
[ferro:~] user% ls -F
Desktop/        Movies/          Pictures/       to-do.txt
Documents/      Music/           Public/
Library/        Note To Mom.doc  Sites/
[ferro:~] user% find  .  -name my-dog.jpg -print
./Pictures/my-dog.jpg
[ferro:~] user% ▇
```

LOCATE FILES BY NAME

1 Type **find** and a space.

2 Type the pathname of a directory and a space.

3 Type **-name** and a space.

4 Type a filename.

5 Type **-print** and press Return.

■ The shell executes the `find` command and prints the file location.

Extra

In addition to searching by name or wildcard pattern, you can also search by other qualities of the file, such as the last time the file was changed, the owner of the file, or the permissions of the file. You control the search with the arguments you include after the pathname of the directory.

ARGUMENT	SEARCHES FOR
-group *groupname*	Files belonging to a certain group.
-iname *filename*	Like -name, but matches regardless of case.
-mmin *minutes*	Files modified within a certain number of minutes.
-mtime *days*	Files modified within a certain number of days.
-perm +*filemode*	Files that have specific permissions set.
-size *charsc*	Files that are an exact size in characters.

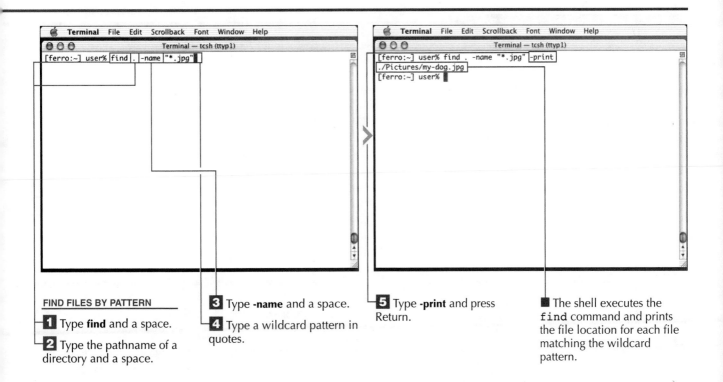

FIND FILES BY PATTERN

1 Type **find** and a space.

2 Type the pathname of a directory and a space.

3 Type **-name** and a space.

4 Type a wildcard pattern in quotes.

5 Type **-print** and press Return.

■ The shell executes the find command and prints the file location for each file matching the wildcard pattern.

CHANGE THE CURRENT DIRECTORY

Y ou can change your current directory by using the cd command. Each shell window operates in a specific location within the file structure, and you can view this location by typing the pwd command. The pwd command is Unix shorthand for print (display) working directory. The current working directory is the directory from which relative pathnames are computed and the default directory in which files are found or saved.

If you type **cd** alone, it returns you to your Home directory. If you provide the cd command with a pathname argument, either relative or full, you change to that directory. You can change your current directory to any directory that grants you execution access permissions. This allows you to explore nearly all of the directories on your hard drive, with the exception of a few system directories that are protected.

When your current directory changes, your prompt changes as well, to reflect the new location. Your prompt displays the names of up to three directories above your current location, or fewer if you are close to the root directory. For example, if you are in the directory /usr/share/tcsh/examples, on a computer named ferro, your prompt looks something like this:

```
[ferro:share/tcsh/examples] user%
```

You can use wildcards and filename completion with the cd command; it accepts special directory names such as cd .., to go up one directory level, and cd ~user, to change to the Home directory of the user user. You can also use the cd - command to return to the last directory in which you were working.

CHANGE THE CURRENT DIRECTORY

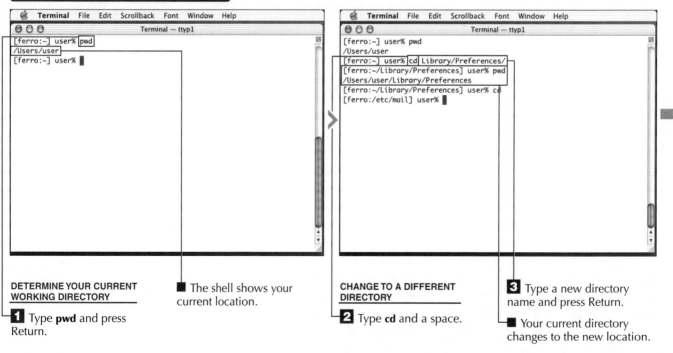

DETERMINE YOUR CURRENT WORKING DIRECTORY

■1 Type **pwd** and press Return.

■ The shell shows your current location.

CHANGE TO A DIFFERENT DIRECTORY

■2 Type **cd** and a space.

■3 Type a new directory name and press Return.

■ Your current directory changes to the new location.

Extra

You can move through the file system by using the directory stack. The stack is a list of directories of which the shell keeps track. You can list the stack by typing **dirs**.

To change to a new directory and add it to the directory stack, use the command `pushd pathname`. This command adds a new pathname to the stack, and prints the stack. You can use the directory stack by typing **popd** to remove the top directory from the stack and change to the next one down, or by typing **pushd** — with no arguments — to swap the top two stack entries and change to the new top directory. The directory stack is very useful if you are going to be switching between several directories in the same shell window.

Example:
```
[ferro:~/Documents] user% pushd /usr/lib
/usr/lib ~/Documents
[ferro:/usr/lib] kynn% pushd /etc
/etc /usr/lib ~/Documents
[ferro:/etc] kynn% popd
/usr/lib ~/Documents
[ferro:/usr/lib] kynn%
```

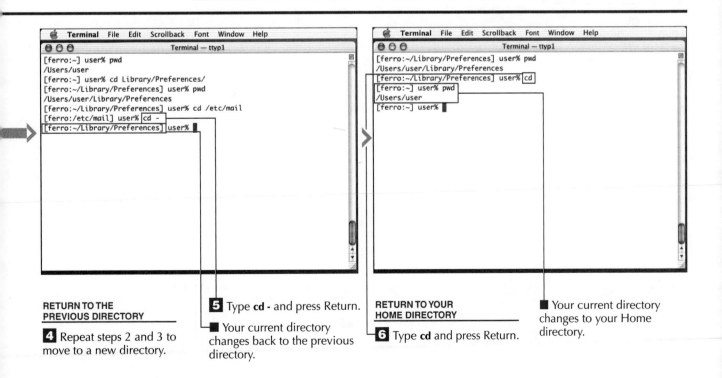

RETURN TO THE PREVIOUS DIRECTORY

4 Repeat steps 2 and 3 to move to a new directory.

5 Type **cd -** and press Return.

■ Your current directory changes back to the previous directory.

RETURN TO YOUR HOME DIRECTORY

6 Type **cd** and press Return.

■ Your current directory changes to your Home directory.

CREATE A DIRECTORY

You can use the `mkdir` command to create new directories. Directories are useful for organizing your files into a logical structure. When you create a directory in the Unix shell, you can access it through the Mac OS X Finder as a folder; conversely, when you create a folder in the Mac OS X Finder, you can access it as a directory in the Unix shell.

The arguments that you give to the `mkdir` command affect how the command creates new directories. When you create a directory with a space in the name, you must enclose it in quotation marks, unless you want to create several directories at once.

To create a directory, you need to have write permissions for the current directory or the directory in which you are creating the new directory. For example, if you want to

create the directory /usr/local/resp, you must have write access to the /usr/local directory. You can either change your working directory to the /usr/local directory using the `cd` command and type **mkdir resp**, or you can type **mkdir /usr/local/resp** from any current directory.

When you give a pathname, whether relative or full, the intervening directories must exist. If they do not, you receive an error message, and the directory is not created. You can tell the `mkdir` command to create any necessary directories by using the `-p` option. For example, to create the directory ~/Documents/by-date/2003/03, you can type **mkdir -p ~/Documents/by-date/2003/03**. This command creates the by-date and 2003 directories as well as the 03 directory if they do not already exist — presumably, the Documents directory already exists in your Home directory.

CREATE A DIRECTORY

```
[ferro:~] user% ls -F
Desktop/          Movies/           Pictures/         my-dog.jpg
Documents/        Music/            Public/           to-do.txt
Library/          Note To Mom.doc   Sites/
[ferro:~] user% mkdir Books
[ferro:~] user% ls -F
Books/            Library/          Note To Mom.doc   Sites/
Desktop/          Movies/           Pictures/         my-dog.jpg
Documents/        Music/            Public/           to-do.txt
[ferro:~] user%
```

```
[ferro:~] user% ls -F
Books/            Library/          Note To Mom.doc   Sites/
Desktop/          Movies/           Pictures/         my-dog.jpg
Documents/        Music/            Public/           to-do.txt
[ferro:~] user% mkdir Magazines Recipes Shows
[ferro:~] user% ls -F
Books/            Magazines/        Pictures/         Sites/
Desktop/          Movies/           Public/           my-dog.jpg
Documents/        Music/            Recipes/          to-do.txt
Library/          Note To Mom.doc   Shows/
[ferro:~] user%
```

CREATE A DIRECTORY

1 Type **mkdir** and a space.

2 Type the name of a new directory and press Return.

■ The shell creates the new directory.

CREATE SEVERAL DIRECTORIES AT ONCE

1 Type **mkdir** and a space.

2 Type the names of several directories you want to create and press Return.

■ The shell creates the new directories.

Extra

By default, anyone on the system can read and execute any directories you create, which means that all users of your computer can change to the new directories and list their contents. If you do not want universal access to your files or directories, you can change the directory permissions by using the chmod command, or you can instruct the mkdir command to set the file mode automatically by using the -m option.

When using the -m option, you follow it with the file mode you want to set, as with the chmod command.

Example:
```
[ferro:~] user% mkdir -m go-rwx Private
[ferro:~] user% ls -lad Private
drwx——  2 user  staff  68 Nov 20 17:03 Private
```

 Terminal File Edit Scrollback Font Window Help

```
○○○                    Terminal — ttyp1
[ferro:~] user% ls -F
Books/          Magazines/      Pictures/       Sites/
Desktop/        Movies/         Public/         my-dog.jpg
Documents/      Music/          Recipes/        to-do.txt
Library/        Note To Mom.doc Shows/
[ferro:~] user% mkdir "Class Assignments"
[ferro:~] user% ls -F
Books/          Movies/         Shows/
Class Assignments/  Music/       Sites/
Desktop/        Note To Mom.doc my-dog.jpg
Documents/      Pictures/       to-do.txt
Library/        Public/
Magazines/      Recipes/
[ferro:~] user% █
```

CREATE A DIRECTORY WITH A MULTIWORD NAME

1 Type **mkdir** and a space.

2 Type the name of your new directory in quotation marks, and press Return.

■ The shell creates the new directory.

 Terminal File Edit Scrollback Font Window Help

```
○○○                    Terminal — ttyp1
[ferro:~] user% cd Books
[ferro:~/Books] user% ls -F
[ferro:~/Books] user% mkdir -p "Unix for Mac"/Chapters/03
[ferro:~/Books] user% ls -F
Unix for Mac/
[ferro:~/Books] user% cd "Unix For Mac"
[ferro:~/Books/Unix For Mac] user% ls -F
Chapters/
[ferro:~/Books/Unix For Mac] user% cd Chapters
[ferro:~/Books/Unix For Mac/Chapters] user% ls -F
03/
[ferro:~/Books/Unix For Mac/Chapters] user% cd 03
[ferro:Unix For Mac/Chapters/03] user% ls -F
[ferro:Unix For Mac/Chapters/03] user% pwd
/Users/user/Books/Unix for Mac/Chapters/03
[ferro:Unix For Mac/Chapters/03] user% █
```

CREATE INTERVENING DIRECTORIES

1 Type **mkdir -p** and a space.

2 Type the pathname of your new directory, including intervening directories, which do not yet exist.

■ The shell creates the new directories.

DELETE A DIRECTORY

Y ou can remove unwanted directories by using the rmdir command. One use for this command is to remove extraneous directories that make it harder to locate files you actually need.

While you can use the rm command to delete normal files, you cannot use it to delete directories. This is a safety measure to prevent you from accidentally deleting a directory that might contain useful or important files. To delete a directory, you must use the rmdir command.

The argument given to the rmdir command is the name of the directory, or directories, that you want to remove. If that directory is empty, then the command removes it. If the directory is not empty, then a message appears, stating that you cannot remove the directory.

In such a case, you can go into the directory and remove any existing files using the rm command, or any

subdirectories using the rmdir command. You can now remove the directory. Sometimes apparently empty directories contain hidden files — such as .DS_Store, which is a Mac OS X system file — and you need to locate them with the ls -A command and remove them before removing the directory.

While you are not allowed to remove the current directory using the rmdir command, you may be able to remove it indirectly. For example, if you are in the subdirectory foo of your Home directory, you can type **rmdir ~/foo**. However, this is not generally a good idea, because you can end up stuck in an unresponsive non-directory where you cannot even use the ls command to list the directory contents. You can use the cd command, with no arguments, to return to your Home directory.

DELETE A DIRECTORY

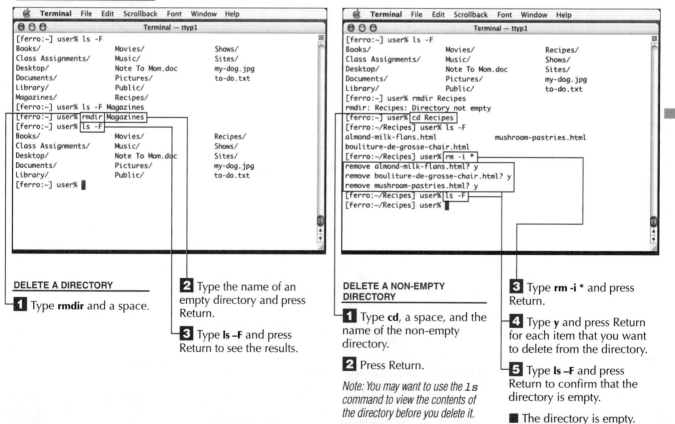

DELETE A DIRECTORY

1 Type **rmdir** and a space.

2 Type the name of an empty directory and press Return.

3 Type **ls –F** and press Return to see the results.

DELETE A NON-EMPTY DIRECTORY

1 Type **cd**, a space, and the name of the non-empty directory.

2 Press Return.

Note: You may want to use the ls command to view the contents of the directory before you delete it.

3 Type **rm -i *** and press Return.

4 Type **y** and press Return for each item that you want to delete from the directory.

5 Type **ls –F** and press Return to confirm that the directory is empty.

■ The directory is empty.

Extra

There is another way to remove an entire directory and its contents, hidden or otherwise, using the `rm` command. The `-r` option instructs the `rm` command to remove a directory and everything within it; the `-f` option instructs the `rm` command not to ask you about each deletion.

Although you can use the `rm -rf` command to delete an entire directory at once, you should be very careful about doing so, as a mistyped command could very easily wipe out important files, with no way to recover them.

Example:
```
[ferro:~] user% rm -rf Install/
[ferro:~] user% rm -rf ~/ Extra
[ferro:~] user% ls
ls: .: Permission denied
```

Note that in the second line above, the user probably means to type **~/Extra**, but accidentally puts a space before the word Extra. This is a costly mistake, as it means that the `rm` command deletes the Home directory of the user.

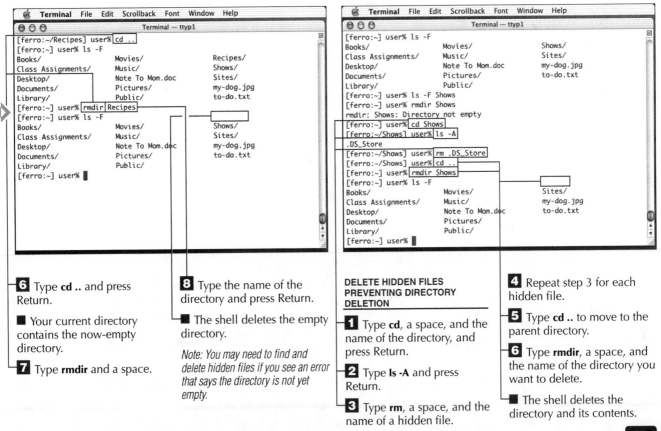

6 Type **cd ..** and press Return.

■ Your current directory contains the now-empty directory.

7 Type **rmdir** and a space.

8 Type the name of the directory and press Return.

■ The shell deletes the empty directory.

Note: You may need to find and delete hidden files if you see an error that says the directory is not yet empty.

DELETE HIDDEN FILES PREVENTING DIRECTORY DELETION

1 Type **cd**, a space, and the name of the directory, and press Return.

2 Type **ls -A** and press Return.

3 Type **rm**, a space, and the name of a hidden file.

4 Repeat step 3 for each hidden file.

5 Type **cd ..** to move to the parent directory.

6 Type **rmdir**, a space, and the name of the directory you want to delete.

■ The shell deletes the directory and its contents.

MOVE FILES INTO A DIRECTORY

You can move files into or out of a directory by using the mv command. This is the same as dragging a file in Finder to a new folder location. The mv command can rename a directory just as it renames a normal file, but it can also move the location of a file or directory within the file structure. You can use the mv command to move a file, or directory, by typing a command like this:

mv *file location*

The argument location must be a directory. Either this directory exists and is owned by you, or you must have permission to write files in the directory. If you type the name of a directory that does not exist, you will not see an error; the file will be renamed to the second name you typed. This can also happen if you mistype the name of the directory.

You can move multiple files using the mv command, however, they must all go into the same directory. To do this, you can simply type out each filename and specify the destination as the final argument, as follows:

mv *fileOne fileTwo fileThree andSoOn location*

This command moves all of the files that you list to the location that you specify. If that location does not exist as a directory, an error message appears, and the command does not execute.

Using the -i option with the mv command can prevent you from accidentally overwriting files when you move them.

MOVE FILES INTO A DIRECTORY

MOVE A FILE INTO A DIRECTORY

1 Type **mv** and a space.

2 Type the name of a file and a space.

Note: Use quotes around the filename only if it contains spaces.

3 Type the name of the destination directory and press Return.

4 Type **ls –F** and a space, followed by the name of the directory, and press Return.

■ The shell shows the file in the new directory.

MOVE MULTIPLE FILES INTO A DIRECTORY

1 Type **mv** and a space.

2 Type the names of the files separated by spaces.

3 Type the name of the destination directory and press Return.

4 Type **ls –F** and a space followed by the name of the directory, and press Return.

■ The shell shows the files in the new directory.

COPY A DIRECTORY

You can use the `cp` command to make a copy of a directory by using the `-R` option. Individual files can be copied using the `cp` command with no options, and as with the `mv` command, you can give a list of files and a destination directory in order to copy a number of files into the same directory:

```
cp fileOne fileTwo fileThree andSoOn location
```

You can use wildcards to copy files. For example, to copy all of your .doc files into your Documents directory, type **cp *.doc ~/Documents**.

When you copy files into a directory, the new versions of each file will be named with their original names. The directory needs to exist, as the `cp` command will not create a new directory for you. You can use the `mkdir` command to create the directory first.

However, if you try to copy a directory as you would copy a file, you see an error message because directories are not normal files:

```
[ferro:~] user% cp Documents "Backup of Docs"
cp: Documents is a directory (not copied).
```

To copy a directory, you must use the `-R` option, which tells the `cp` command to copy the directory and its contents to the new location. For example, to create a copy of the Documents directory, you can type **cp -R Documents "Backup of Docs"**.

This will copy the entire directory at once, creating the new directory and duplicating all of the files. The names of the original files will be the same, although the directory names will be different.

COPY A DIRECTORY

```
   Terminal   File   Edit   Scrollback   Font   Window   Help
 ○○○                        Terminal — ttyp1
[ferro:~] user% ls -F
Books/                Library/              Public/
Class Assignments/    Movies/               Sites/
Desktop/              Music/
Documents/            Pictures/
[ferro:~] user% ls -F Sites
images/                  www.cssin24hours.com/   www.unixformac.com/
index.html               www.kynn.com/
[ferro:~] user% cp -R Sites "Sites Archive 2002-11-20"
[ferro:~] user%
```

```
   Terminal   File   Edit   Scrollback   Font   Window   Help
 ○○○                        Terminal — ttyp1
[ferro:~] user% ls -F
Books/                          Music/
Class Assignments/              Pictures/
Desktop/                        Public/
Documents/                      Sites/
Library/                        Sites Archive 2002-11-20/
Movies/
[ferro:~] user% ls -F Sites
images/                  www.cssin24hours.com/   www.unixformac.com/
index.html               www.kynn.com/
[ferro:~] user% ls -F "Sites Archive 2002-11-20"
images/                  www.cssin24hours.com/   www.unixformac.com/
index.html               www.kynn.com/
[ferro:~] user%
```

1 Type **cp -R** and a space.

2 Type the name of the original directory and a space.

3 Type the name of the new copy of the directory and press Return.

4 Type **ls –F** and a space followed by the name of the original directory, and press Return.

5 Repeat the `ls –F` command in step 4 to show the contents of the new directory.

■ The new directory is a duplicate of the original directory.

DETERMINE DIRECTORY SIZE

You can use the du command to display the size and contents of a directory. The name of the du command stands for *disk usage*, and it tells you how much space each file or directory uses on your hard drive. This information is also available from the Finder using the Get Info menu option. When you use the ls -l command, you see a value for the size of the directory just as you do for other files. However, this value does not represent the size of the contents of the directory; it represents the size of the directory entry itself, a list of the files stored in the directory. To obtain the size of the contents of the directory, including subdirectories, you can use the du command.

If you type **du** alone, you get a listing of disk usage in the current working directory; if you give one or more arguments, you see the space taken up by each of those

directories or files. Additionally, the space used by all subdirectories also appears, along with subdirectories of subdirectories. This can make the output of the du command quite extensive and hard to read; if you want a single answer to summarize the size of a directory, you can use the option -s with the du command.

When the du command displays sizes for files and directories, it measures these sizes in disk blocks; a block on a Unix file system disk represents 512 characters. This is an easy number for computers to work with but somewhat difficult for us humans to grasp. You can use the option -k to make the du command list sizes in kilobytes, which are units of 1,024 bytes.

DETERMINE DIRECTORY SIZE

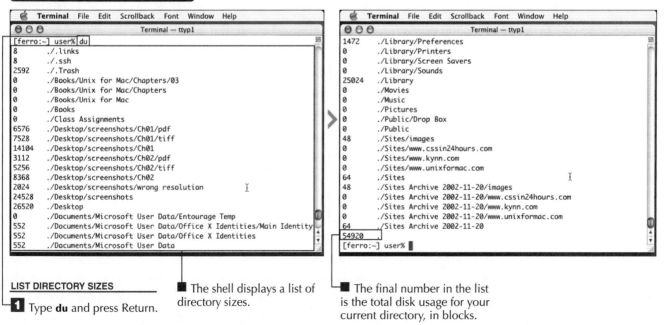

LIST DIRECTORY SIZES

1 Type **du** and press Return.

■ The shell displays a list of directory sizes.

■ The final number in the list is the total disk usage for your current directory, in blocks.

Extra

You can use the df command to check the total disk usage on your computer. Like du, df measures sizes in 512-character blocks, but you can use the -k option to make the results easier to read. The df -k command lists all file systems on your computer, and gives you a percentage indicating how full your disk is.

Example:

```
[ferro:~] user% df -k
Filesystem               1K-blocks      Used      Avail   Capacity       Mounted on
/dev/disk0s5               5865644   4027644    1779344        69%                /
devfs                           90        90          0       100%             /dev
fdesc                            1         1          0       100%             /dev
<volfs>                        512       512          0       100%            /.vol
automount -fstab [314]           0         0          0        00%  /Network/Servers
automount -static [314]          0         0          0       100%       /automount
```

The last five file systems in the above list correspond to internal systems used by the Unix operating system. You can safely ignore them and only look at the first listing. According to this listing, the above computer has a single disk that is 69 percent full.

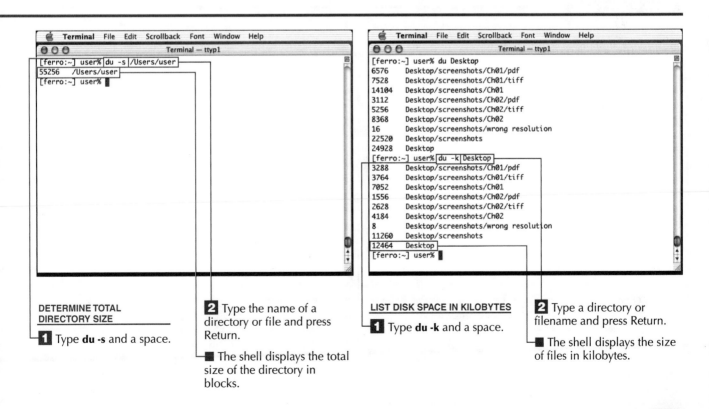

DETERMINE TOTAL DIRECTORY SIZE

1 Type **du -s** and a space.

2 Type the name of a directory or file and press Return.

■ The shell displays the total size of the directory in blocks.

LIST DISK SPACE IN KILOBYTES

1 Type **du -k** and a space.

2 Type a directory or filename and press Return.

■ The shell displays the size of files in kilobytes.

VIEW TEXT FILES

You can display the content of text files with the `cat` command. The name `cat` is short for *concatenate*, which means to join several things together into one. However, the `cat` command has additional functions beyond concatenation, one of which is to display files on-screen. You can display any file by typing this command:

`cat filename`

The screen displays the full contents of the file. If the file is longer than one screen, your Terminal window scrolls to display the whole file.

The two types of files that you can display using the `cat` command are text and binary files. A text file consists of ordinary letters, numbers, spaces, and punctuation, collectively known as *plain text*. If you are using a word-processing program and you save the file as text, you are creating a text file.

The other type of file that the `cat` command can display is a binary file. Binary files contain special characters that you cannot print, because the computer codes for these characters do not correspond to any printable symbols. The executable files that programmers create from compiled applications are often binary files, as are proprietary data formats such as Microsoft Word documents.

If you try to use the `cat` command to display a binary file, the best that you can expect is gibberish in your Terminal window. The worst result is that it resets the display format of your Terminal window, meaning that your prompt and any letters you type also appear as gibberish.

To display the contents of a binary file safely, you can use the `-v` option with the `cat` command. This command displays non-printable characters by showing a caret (^) before control characters, and M- before Meta characters.

VIEW TEXT FILES

```
⌘  Terminal  File  Edit  Scrollback  Font  Window  Help
000                  Terminal — ttyp1
[ferro:~] user% ls
Desktop          Movies          Pictures          my-dog.jpg
Documents        Music           Public            to-do.txt
Library          Note to Mom.doc Sites
[ferro:~] user% cat to-do.txt
My To-Do List

- Finish chapter 4
- Write tutorial for CSS site
- Email Vicki
- Work on accessibility proposal
[ferro:~] user%
```

```
⌘  Terminal  File  Edit  Scrollback  Font  Window  Help
000                  Terminal — ttyp1
[ferro:~] user% ls
Desktop          Movies          Pictures          my-dog.jpg
Documents        Music           Public            to-do.txt
Library          Note to Mom.doc Sites
[ferro:~] user% cat -v my-dog.jpg
M-^?M-XM-^?M-`^@^@PJFIF^@^A^A^A^@d^@d^@^@M-^?M-~^@M-^T^@^@^@^@^@^@^@^@^@^@^@
^@^@^@^@^@^@^@^@^@^@^@^@^@^@^@^@^@^@^@^@^@^@^@^@^@^@^@^@^@^@^@^@^@^@^@^@^@^@
@^@^@^@^@^@^@^@^@^@^@^@^@^@^@^@^@^@^@^@^@^@^@^@^@^@^@^@^@^@^@^@^@^@^@^@^@^@^@
^@^@^@^@^@^@^@^@^@^@^@^@^@^@^@^@^@^@^@^@^@^@^@^@^@^@^@^@^@^@^@^@^@^@^@^@^@^@^@
@^@^@^@^@^@^@^@^@^@^@^@^@^@^@^@^@^@^@^@^@^@^@M-^?M-[^@M-^D^@^L^H
    ^G^L

^M^L^L^N^R^^^S^R^P^P^R$^Z^[^U^^+&--*&*)06E:03A3)*<Q<AGIMNM.9TZTKZEKMJ^A^L
^M^M^R^O^R#^S^S#J1*1JJJJJJJJJJJJJJJJJJJJJJJJJJJJJJJJJJJJJJJJJJJJJJJJJJJM-^
?M-@^@^Q^H^AM-3^AM-^P^C^A!^@^B^Q^A^C^Q^AM-^?M-D^AM-"^@^@^A^E^A^A^A^A^A^A^A
@^@^@^@^@^@^@^@^@^A^B^C^D^E^F^G^H
^K^P^@^B^A^C^C^B^D^C^E^E^D^D^@^@^A}^A^A^B^C^@^D^Q^E^R!1A^F^SQa^G"q^T2M-^AM-
^QM-!^H#BM-1M-A^AURM-QM-p$3brM-^B
^V^A^W^A^X^A^Y^Z%&'()*456789:CDEFGHIJSTUVWXYZcdefghijstuvwxyzM-^CM-^DM-^EM-^FM-
^GM-^HM-^IM-^JM-^RM-^SM-^TM-^UM-^VM-^WM-^XM-^YM-^ZM-"M-#M-$M-%M-&M-'M-(M-
)M-*M-2M-3M-4M-5M-6M-7M-8M-9M-:M-BM-CM-DM-EM-FM-GM-HM-IM-JM-RM-SM-TM-UM-V
M-WM-XM-YM-ZM-aM-bM-cM-dM-eM-fM-gM-hM-iM-jM-qM-rM-sM-tM-uM-vM-wM-xM-yM-z^\
```

VIEW TEXT FILES

1 Type **cat** and a space.

2 Type the name of a text file and press Return.

■ The shell displays the contents of the file.

VIEW BINARY FILES

1 Type **cat -v** and a space.

2 Type the name of a binary file and press Return.

■ The shell displays the contents of the file, with non-printing characters shown.

■ This is an example of a Meta-Control-T character.

CREATE A SIMPLE TEXT FILE

Y ou can create a text file by using the `cat` command and redirecting the output to a file. If you type **cat** and press Return, the `cat` command appears to do nothing, but your prompt does not reappear. When you type something else and press Return, you just see whatever you typed echo back at you. This means that the `cat` command is letting you enter content. You are building a virtual file that only exists for the execution of the command. As long as you continue to type, you are adding content to that virtual file.

To indicate that you are finished entering text into the `cat` command, you must indicate the end of your virtual file. You do this by pressing Return and then pressing Control + D.

By itself, the ability to type text and see it reappear on-screen is not particularly useful. However, you can combine the `cat` command with output redirection to make simple text files. Output redirection means that you save the results of a command to a file instead of displaying them on-screen. To redirect the output of the `cat` command to a file, you can type the following:

```
cat > filename
```

This creates a new file called filename. For better compatibility with the Mac OS X Finder, you may want to name a text file with the extension .txt. This allows you to double-click the icon for the file in Finder and open it in the TextEdit application.

The contents of the new file are whatever you type after pressing Return. The file can contain multiple lines; just press Return at the end of each line. When you are done, you can press Control + D to create the file.

CREATE A SIMPLE TEXT FILE

Terminal   File   Edit   Scrollback   Font   Window   Help
Terminal — ttyp1
```
[ferro:~] user% cat > this-week.txt
```

Terminal   File   Edit   Scrollback   Font   Window   Help
Terminal — ttyp1
```
[ferro:~] user% cat > this-week.txt
Monday:  nothing planned
Tuesday:  work out at the gym
         class in the evening
Wednesday:  class in the evening
Thursday:  writers group
           work out at the gym
Friday:  nothing planned
[ferro:~] user% ls
Desktop          Movies          Pictures        my-dog.jpg
Documents        Music           Public          this-week.txt
Library          Note to Mom.doc Sites           to-do.txt
[ferro:~] user% cat this-week.txt
Monday:  nothing planned
Tuesday:  work out at the gym
         class in the evening
Wednesday:  class in the evening
Thursday:  writers group
           work out at the gym
Friday:  nothing planned
[ferro:~] user%
```

1 Type **cat** and a space.

2 Type a greater-than symbol and a space.

3 Type the name of the file you want to create, and press Return.

4 Type the text you want the file to contain.

5 Press Return.

6 Press Control + D.

■ The `cat` command creates a file containing the text you typed.

VIEW TEXT FILES AS PAGES

You can display long files one screen at a time using the less command. If you try to view a long file with the cat command, it quickly scrolls your Terminal window, and you must use the scroll bars to go back. The less command is an example of a pager command, a program that displays files one page at a time.

The less command displays a screen at a time, and waits for you to finish reading that screen before continuing. When you are ready to move ahead in the file, you can press the Spacebar.

You can also search ahead in the file for a specific text pattern by typing a forward slash (/) and then the text you want to find. This moves you ahead in the file to the next place that text appears.

If you try to use the less command on a binary file with unprintable characters, the less command warns you and asks if you want to continue. You can type **y**, for yes, and press Return, or simply press Return to cancel the less command.

You have already used the less command if you have used the man command; when you type **man**, you read a manual page by viewing it as you would with the less command.

The name of the less command makes sense when you know the history of pager commands in Unix. The original command for displaying a page at a time was named more, because, while waiting for you to read the page, it printed --More-- on the bottom line of the Terminal window. The less command was named as a natural successor to the more command, because it could do more than the more command could do.

VIEW TEXT FILES AS PAGES

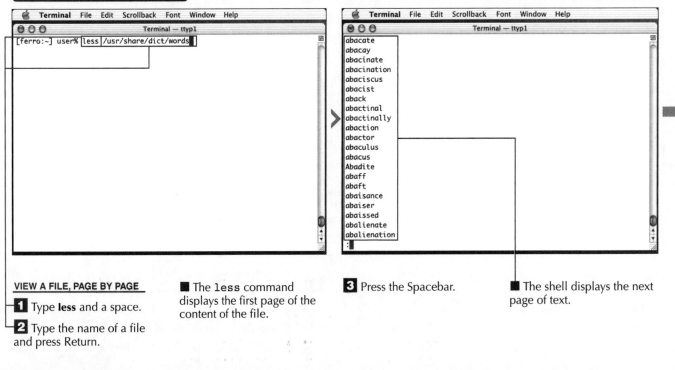

VIEW A FILE, PAGE BY PAGE

1 Type **less** and a space.

2 Type the name of a file and press Return.

■ The less command displays the first page of the content of the file.

3 Press the Spacebar.

■ The shell displays the next page of text.

Extra

In addition to pressing the Spacebar to page through a file using the `less` command, or the `man` command, you can also use other keystrokes to move through the file. For a full listing of keystrokes in `less`, type **man less** or type **h** while using the `less` command.

KEYSTROKE	MEANING
Return	Go forward one line.
Down arrow	Go forward one line.
Up arrow	Go back one line.
b	Go back one page.
?pattern	Search backwards in the file.
g	Go to the first line of the file.
G	Go to the last line of the file.
v	Open the file in a Unix text editor.
h	Read the `less` command help.
q	Quit immediately.

```
  Terminal   File   Edit   Scrollback   Font   Window   Help
○ ○ ○                    Terminal — ttyp1
A
a
aa
aal
aalii
aam
Aani
aardvark
aardwolf
Aaron
Aaronic
Aaronical
Aaronite
Aaronitic
Aaru
Ab
aba
Ababdeh
Ababua
abac
abaca
/pacif
```

```
  Terminal   File   Edit   Scrollback   Font   Window   Help
○ ○ ○                    Terminal — ttyp1
antipacifist
antipapacy
antipapal
antipapalist
antipapism
antipapist
antipapistical
antiparabema
antiparagraphe
antiparagraphic
antiparallel
antiparallelogram
antiparalytic
antiparalytical
antiparasitic
antiparastatitis
antiparliament
antiparliamental
antiparliamentarist
antiparliamentary
antipart
:
```

SEARCH AHEAD FOR A CERTAIN WORD

4 Type a forward slash.

■ The cursor appears in the lower-left corner of the Terminal window, beside the forward slash.

5 Type a word or phrase and press Return.

■ The `less` command skips ahead to that word or phrase and highlights it.

VIEW PORTIONS OF A TEXT FILE

You can display a portion of a text file by using the head and tail commands. To understand how the head and tail commands work, it is useful to visualize a text file as if it were a fish being chopped into head, tail, and body. The head command displays the portion of the fish containing its head, and the tail command shows the portion containing the tail of the fish. You can give additional options that indicate where along the body of the fish you want to cut.

Without any options, the head command shows the first ten lines of a specified file and the tail command shows the last ten lines. If the file has ten or fewer lines, the whole file displays.

You can change the number of lines that display in the following way:

```
head -linenumber filename
tail -linenumber filename
```

For example, type **head -3 /usr/share/dict/words** to see the first three lines of the file /usr/share/dict/words. Several Unix programs use this text file as a source of English words, so it makes a good example for text commands.

Typing **tail -3 /usr/share/dict/words** shows you the last three lines of this file. You can also tell the tail command to start a certain number of lines in from the beginning of the file by including a plus symbol:

```
tail +linenumber filename
```

If you want to view the tail of the words file starting at line 234,567 — it is a large file — you can type **tail +234567 /usr/share/dict/words**.

VIEW PORTIONS OF A TEXT FILE

```
[ferro:~] user% head /usr/share/dict/words
A
a
aa
aal
aalii
aam
Aani
aardvark
aardwolf
Aaron
[ferro:~] user%
```

```
[ferro:~] user% head -3 this-week.txt
Monday:   nothing planned
Tuesday:  work out at the gym
          class in the evening
[ferro:~] user%
```

VIEW THE BEGINNING OF A TEXT FILE

1 Type **head** and a space.

2 Type a filename and press Return.

■ The shell displays the first ten lines of the file.

3 Type **head** and a space.

4 Type a dash, the number of lines you want to display, and a space.

5 Type the filename and press Return.

■ The shell displays as many lines of the file as you specify.

Extra

You can also set the `tail` command to display any new lines added to the end of a file, by using the `-f` option.

The Mac OS X operating system maintains a number of files known as *log files*. These files record system activity, much of it invisible to the user, which you can use to diagnose problems or monitor processes. New lines are regularly appended to log files. You can find most of the important system logs in the /var/log directory.

You can monitor these log files by using the `tail -f` command. To stop monitoring these files, press Control + C.

Example:
```
[ferro:~] user% tail -5 -f /var/log/system.log
Dec  2 16:40:03 ferro configd[105]: executing
/System/Library/SystemConfiguration/Kicker.bundle/Resources/restart-AppleTalk
Dec  2 16:40:03 ferro lookupd[533]: lookupd (version 272) starting - Mon Dec
2 16:40:03 2002
Dec  2 16:40:05 ferro root: setting hostname to ferro.local.
Dec  2 16:40:05 ferro configd[105]: executing
/System/Library/SystemConfiguration/Kicker.bundle/Resources/set-hostname
Dec  2 16:40:06 ferro root: setting hostname to ferro.local.
^C
[ferro:~] user%
```

VIEW THE END OF A TEXT FILE

1 Type **tail** and a space.

2 Type the filename and press Return.

■ The shell displays the last ten lines of the file.

START IN THE MIDDLE OF A TEXT FILE

1 Type **tail** and a space.

2 Type a plus symbol, the number of the line you want to start from, and a space.

3 Type the filename and press Return.

■ The shell displays the file starting at the line you specify.

EXTRACT TEXT FROM A FILE

Y ou can find and display lines within a text file that match a specific pattern with the grep command. The grep command searches through a file to find lines that match a *regular expression*. Regular expressions, or *regexps*, are commonly used to match text patterns. Regular expressions are more powerful and flexible than normal glob patterns because they can match a variety of patterns and you can combine them to form very complex expressions.

The syntax for the grep command is:

```
grep 'pattern' filename
```

You do not need to enclose the regular expression pattern in single quotes. However, if you do not use the single quotes, the shell interprets the pattern as a glob pattern and matches it against files in the current directory. For this reason, it is always a good practice to use single quotes

around your regular expression pattern with the grep command.

Options for the grep command include -i, which makes grep consider upper- and lowercase letters the same for matching purposes; -v, which inverts the search and lists lines that do not match; and -l, which does not display matches but instead lists the names of files whose contents contain the regular expression pattern.

A simple but useful example of the power of the grep command is that it can help you with crossword puzzles or crossword-style games such as Scrabble. Using the list of English words in /usr/share/dict/words, you can display all lines matching a specific pattern. For example, if the first letter in a four-letter word is k, the third is n, and you do not know the rest, you can use this command to display all possible matches as show below:

```
grep -i '^k.n.$' /usr/share/dict/words
```

EXTRACT TEXT FROM A FILE

```
 Terminal  File  Edit  Scrollback  Font  Window  Help
 ○○○                    Terminal — ttyp1
[ferro:~] user% cat this-week.txt
Monday:  nothing planned
Tuesday:  work out at the gym
          class in the evening
Wednesday:  class in the evening
Thursday:  writers group
          work out at the gym
Friday:  nothing planned
[ferro:~] user% grep 'day' this-week.txt
Monday:  nothing planned
Tuesday:  work out at the gym
Wednesday:  class in the evening
Thursday:  writers group
Friday:  nothing planned
[ferro:~] user%
```

```
 Terminal  File  Edit  Scrollback  Font  Window  Help
 ○○○                    Terminal — ttyp1
[ferro:~] user% grep -i '^k.n.$' /usr/share/dict/words
kana
kang
kans
kend
keno
kent
kina
kind
king
kink
kino
kona
kung
kunk
[ferro:~] user%
```

EXTRACT TEXT USING THE GREP COMMAND

1 Type **grep** and a space.

2 Type a regular expression pattern enclosed in single quotes, and a space.

3 Type a filename and press Return.

■ The shell displays all lines in the file that match the pattern.

CHEAT ON CROSSWORD PUZZLES

1 Type **grep -i**, a space, a single quote, and a caret.

2 Type each letter you know, and type a period for each letter you do not know.

3 Type a dollar sign, a closing quote mark, a space, **/usr/share/dict/words**, and press Return.

■ The shell displays all words that might fit.

Extra

Regular expressions consist of ordinary text and characters with special meanings. The simplest regular expression is just plain text, such as Kynn. This matches any line that contains the word Kynn anywhere on the line.

To select matches at the beginning of a line, you can use the special character caret (^). The regular expression to match lines starting with Kynn is ^Kynn. Likewise, the dollar sign ($) indicates the end of a line, as with Kynn$, which only matches lines where Kynn is the final text of that line.

A period (.) matches any character. A set of characters in square brackets, such as [0123456789ABCDEF], matches any of those characters, and a range in brackets matches any character within that range, such as [a-zA-Z].

To match more than one character of the same type, you can use the plus symbol (+) after a special character, normal character, or range. To match zero or more of the preceding types of characters, use an asterisk (*). The regular expression '.*' matches anything, because it is zero or more of any character. A question mark (?) indicates zero or one repetition of the preceding character.

```
 Terminal  File  Edit  Scrollback  Font  Window  Help
                    Terminal — ttyp1
[ferro:~] user% cat this-week.txt
Monday:   nothing planned
Tuesday:  work out at the gym
          class in the evening
Wednesday:  class in the evening
Thursday:  writers group
          work out at the gym
Friday:  nothing planned
[ferro:~] user% grep -v 'day' this-week.txt
          class in the evening
          work out at the gym
[ferro:~] user%
```

```
 Terminal  File  Edit  Scrollback  Font  Window  Help
                    Terminal — ttyp1
[ferro:~] user% ls /usr/share/dict
README        connectives  propernames web2      web2a     words
[ferro:~] user% grep -l 'name' /usr/share/dict/*
/usr/share/dict/web2
/usr/share/dict/web2a
/usr/share/dict/words
[ferro:~] user%
```

INVERT A GREP SEARCH

1 Type **grep -v** and a space.

2 Type a regular expression pattern in quotes for lines you do not want to match, and a space.

3 Type a filename and press Return.

■ The `grep` command displays all lines that do not match your pattern.

LIST ALL FILES CONTAINING A PATTERN

1 Type **grep -l** and a space.

2 Type a regular expression pattern enclosed in single quotes, and a space.

3 Type an asterisk wildcard to search all files, and press Return.

■ The shell displays the names of all files that contain the pattern.

REDIRECT TEXT TO A FILE

You can save the text output of any shell command by redirecting the output to a file. Unix shell commands normally display their output in the Terminal shell window, immediately after you type the command. This display method is known as *standard output*. Using output redirection, you can change the destination of the standard output; it does not have to appear in the Terminal window.

To save the output of a command into a file, you can use a greater-than symbol (>):

```
command and arguments > output-file
```

For example, to save the output from the command grep 'Apple' CHANGES.txt into a file named apple-changes.txt, you can use this command:

```
grep 'Apple' CHANGES.txt > apple-changes.txt
```

You can use the grep command to record the output of a command for later processing, such as editing or printing the file. It is also an effective way of making a record of

information at any given time. For example, if you want to record your disk usage on a certain date, you can type **command du -s > du-2003-03-05**.

When you redirect text, the shell does not print any special messages on-screen; after you complete the command, you only see the prompt again. You can use other commands, such as cat, grep, or head, to examine the text file that you create.

You can combine output redirection with the cat command to create a new file from two or more files. You do this by using the following command:

```
cat filename1 filename2 filename3 > composite-file
```

The new composite-file consists of the text contained in each of the named files, in the order listed on the command line. You can concatenate as many files as you like.

REDIRECT TEXT TO A FILE

```
 Terminal   File   Edit   Scrollback   Font   Window   Help
 ○ ○ ○                    Terminal — ttyp1
[ferro:~] user% ls -l > ls-output.txt
[ferro:~] user%
```

```
 Terminal   File   Edit   Scrollback   Font   Window   Help
 ○ ○ ○                    Terminal — ttyp1
[ferro:~] user% ls -l > ls-output.txt
[ferro:~] user% ls
Desktop          Music          Sites           to-do.txt
Documents        Note to Mom.doc ls-output.txt
Library          Pictures       my-dog.jpg
Movies           Public         this-week.txt
[ferro:~] user% cat ls-output.txt
total 80
drwx------   21 user   staff     714 Dec  2 01:52 Desktop
drwx------    4 user   staff     136 Dec  2 01:36 Documents
drwx------   22 user   staff     748 Nov 13 03:40 Library
drwx------    3 user   staff     102 Nov  4 13:49 Movies
drwx------    3 user   staff     102 Nov  4 13:49 Music
-rw-------    1 user   staff      60 Nov 18 15:11 Note to Mom.doc
drwx------    3 user   staff     102 Nov 18 15:42 Pictures
drwxr-xr-x    4 user   staff     136 Nov  4 13:49 Public
drwxr-xr-x    8 user   staff     272 Nov 20 23:49 Sites
-rw-r--r--    1 user   staff       0 Dec  2 01:53 ls-output.txt
-rw-------    1 user   staff   25762 Nov 18 15:13 my-dog.jpg
-rw-r--r--    1 user   staff     200 Dec  2 01:40 this-week.txt
-rw-rw-r--    1 user   staff     111 Dec  2 01:36 to-do.txt
[ferro:~] user%
```

SAVE COMMAND OUTPUT

1 Type a Unix shell command that displays text output, and a space.

2 Type a greater-than symbol and a space.

3 Type the name of the file you want to create and press Return.

■ The shell saves the output in the file you create.

Extra

If you redirect output to an existing file, you overwrite that file with the new text output. This can be dangerous, because indiscriminately overwriting files can lead to loss of data.

You can instruct the shell to prevent output redirection from overwriting existing files by typing the command **set noclobber**. The shell prints an error message saying that the destination file exists, and the command does not execute.

If you have the `noclobber` command set and you need to overwrite an existing file, you can type an exclamation point (!), or *bang*, after the greater-than symbol. This causes the redirection to occur even if the file exists.

Example:
```
[ferro:~] user% head /var/log/system.log > log
[ferro:~] user% set noclobber
[ferro:~] user% tail /var/log/system.log > log
log: File exists.
[ferro:~] user% tail /var/log/system.log >! log
[ferro:~] user%
```

 Terminal   File   Edit   Scrollback   Font   Window   Help

```
Terminal — ttyp1
[ferro:~] user% ls
Desktop          Music          Sites          to-do.txt
Documents        Note to Mom.doc ls-output.txt
Library          Pictures       my-dog.jpg
Movies           Public         this-week.txt
[ferro:~] user% cat to-do.txt this-week.txt > my-schedule.txt
[ferro:~] user%
```

 Terminal   File   Edit   Scrollback   Font   Window   Help

```
Terminal — ttyp1
[ferro:~] user% ls
Desktop          Music          Sites          to-do.txt
Documents        Note to Mom.doc ls-output.txt
Library          Pictures       my-dog.jpg
Movies           Public         this-week.txt
[ferro:~] user% cat to-do.txt this-week.txt > my-schedule.txt
[ferro:~] user% cat my-schedule.txt
My To-Do List

- Finish chapter 4
- Write tutorial for CSS site
- Email Vicki
- Work on accessibility proposal
Monday:   nothing planned
Tuesday:  work out at the gym
          class in the evening
Wednesday:  class in the evening
Thursday:  writers group
          work out at the gym
Friday:  nothing planned
[ferro:~] user%
```

CONCATENATE TWO TEXT FILES

1 Type **cat** and a space.

2 Type the name of two or more files, separated by a space.

3 Type a greater-than symbol, a space, and the name of the file you want to create.

4 Press Return.

■ The `cat` command concatenates the file and saves the output in the file you create.

CHAIN TEXT COMMANDS TOGETHER

You can chain commands together by sending the output of one command as input to another. This is known as *piping*, and is an alternative way to use standard output. Instead of displaying on-screen or saving to a file, the standard output from one command becomes the standard input for another command. The second command runs using the output from the first command, and produces its own standard output, which you can then display, redirect to a file, or pipe to another command.

This technique gets its name from a special character called the vertical pipe (|). On Apple keyboards, you create this character by holding down the shift key and typing a backslash (\). The syntax for a pipe command looks like this:

```
first command and arguments | second command
and arguments
```

You can link together as many commands as you want to using pipes. Most commands that work with text, such as head, tail, grep, and others, automatically accept standard input if there is no filename given to the second

command. Some commands do not automatically read standard input. For those commands, you must read the manual pages, but the most common way to indicate that a command should read standard input is to use a single dash (-) as an argument.

Piping is similar to redirecting output to a temporary file and then applying a second command to that file, but it cuts out the middleman. For example:

```
[ferro:~] user% tail /var/log/system.log >
log.tmp
[ferro:~] user% grep 'ferro.local' log.tmp
Dec  2 16:40:06 ferro root: setting hostname
to ferro.local.
[ferro:~] user% rm log.tmp
[ferro:~] user%
```

You can accomplish the same result with a single command line:

```
tail /var/log/system.log | grep "ferro.local"
```

CHAIN TEXT COMMANDS TOGETHER

```
[ferro:~] user% ls -l |
```

```
[ferro:~] user% ls -l | grep '^d'
drwx------   26 user   staff    884 Dec  2 01:56 Desktop
drwx------    4 user   staff    136 Dec  2 01:36 Documents
drwx------   22 user   staff    748 Nov 13 03:40 Library
drwx------    3 user   staff    102 Nov  4 13:49 Movies
drwx------    3 user   staff    102 Nov  4 13:49 Music
drwx------    3 user   staff    102 Nov 18 15:42 Pictures
drwxr-xr-x    4 user   staff    136 Nov  4 13:49 Public
drwxr-xr-x    8 user   staff    272 Nov 20 23:49 Sites
[ferro:~] user%
```

CHAIN TEXT COMMANDS TOGETHER

1 Type a Unix shell command that displays text output.

2 Type a space, a vertical pipe character, and another space.

3 Type a second command to run on the output of the first command, and press Return.

■ The shell executes the first command and pipes the output to the second command as input.

Extra

You can chain together commands using the backtick (`` ` ``), a left-leaning single quote character found in the upper-left corner of your keyboard. You use the backtick to take the output of one command and provide it as an argument to another command. You write the second command normally, but where you want to insert the output of the first command, you enclose it within a pair of backticks. For example, to see the size and permissions of the executable file for the `less` command, you type **ls -l `which less`**.

This input executes the `which` command, which returns a full pathname to the `less` command, and then runs the `ls -l` command with that pathname as an argument.

To move all files containing the word obsolete to a subdirectory, type **mv -i `grep -l 'obsolete' *.txt` old-files/**

This input executes the `grep -l` command, which displays a list of files containing the search pattern, and that list is used as a set of arguments to the `mv` command.

```
 Terminal  File  Edit  Scrollback  Font  Window  Help
                    Terminal — ttyp1
[ferro:~] user% grep -i '^k' /usr/share/dict/words | grep -i '..n$'
Kabardian
Kabistan
Kachin
kachin
Kadayan
kadein
Kaffrarian
kafirin
kainyn
Kakan
Kalamian
Kalapooian
kaleidophon
kalian
Kalmarian
kalon
kalymmaukion
Kamasin
Kamchatkan
kameeldoorn
kameelthorn
```

```
 Terminal  File  Edit  Scrollback  Font  Window  Help
                    Terminal — ttyp1
[ferro:~] user% grep -i '^k.*n$' /usr/share/dict/words | less
Kabardiar
Kabistan
Kachin
kachin
Kadayan
kadein
Kaffrarian
kafirin
kainyn
Kakan
Kalamian
Kalapooian
kaleidophon
kalian
Kalmarian
kalon
kalymmaukion
Kamasin
Kamchatkan
:
```

MATCH TWO PATTERNS WITH GREP

1 Type **grep**, the first pattern, and the file you want to search.

2 Type a space, the vertical pipe character, and a space.

3 Type **grep** and the second pattern, and press Return.

■ The `grep` commands display lines of text matching both patterns.

PIPE OUTPUT THROUGH THE LESS COMMAND

1 Type a Unix shell command and a space.

2 Type a vertical pipe character and a space.

3 Type **less** and press Return.

■ The output of the command is piped to the `less` command for paging.

COMPARE TEXT FILES

You can compare two files by using the `diff` command, which shows you the differences between the files. You can compare three files by using the `diff3` command. You use the `diff` command if you want to compare two versions of the same file to see whether the file has changed. The syntax for the `diff` command is:

`diff first-file second-file`

The output from the `diff` command consists of those lines that are not the same in both files. If the files are identical, the `diff` command prints nothing; you only see the command line prompt again.

If there are differences, the `diff` command reports them in the following manner: The first line indicates the line numbers within each file, with a single letter between the

lines or range of lines. The letter tells whether an addition was made, a, a line was deleted, d, or a line was changed, c. The versions from each file then appear, preceded by a less-than symbol for lines in the first file, and a greater-than symbol for lines in the second file.

You can also use the `diff` command to compare non-text binary files; however, the `diff` command does not print the actual differences between files, because these are likely to be non-printable characters. Instead, `diff` returns you to the prompt if the files are identical, or prints a message saying that the binary files differ from each other.

The `diff` command only compares two files. If you need to compare three files, you can use the `diff3` command. Note that there is not a `diff4` command.

COMPARE TEXT FILES

```
[ferro:~] user% cat to-do.txt
My To-Do List

- Finish chapter 4
- Write tutorial for CSS site
- Email Vicki
- Work on accessibility proposal
[ferro:~] user% cat done.txt
My To-Do List

X Finish chapter 3
- Email Vicki
X Email Jade
[ferro:~] user% diff to-do.txt done.txt
3,4c3
< - Finish chapter 4
< - Write tutorial for CSS site
---
> X Finish chapter 3
6c5
< - Work on accessibility proposal
---
> X Email Jade
[ferro:~] user%
```

```
[ferro:~] user% cat to-do.txt
My To-Do List

- Finish chapter 4
- Write tutorial for CSS site
- Email Vicki
- Work on accessibility proposal
[ferro:~] user% cat done.txt
My To-Do List

X Finish chapter 3
- Email Vicki
X Email Jade
[ferro:~] user% diff to-do.txt done.txt
3,4c3
< - Finish chapter 4
< - Write tutorial for CSS site
---
> X Finish chapter 3
6c5
< - Work on accessibility proposal
---
> X Email Jade
[ferro:~] user%
```

COMPARE TWO TEXT FILES

1 Type **diff** and a space.

2 Type the name of one file and a space.

3 Type the name of a different file and press Return.

■ The shell displays the differences between the files.

■ The shell indicates that lines 3 and 4 have changed between the first and second files.

■ A less-than symbol indicates a line change in the first file.

■ A greater-than symbol indicates a line change in the second file.

Extra

If you use output redirection to save the output of the `diff` command into a file, the result is a diff file. You can use a diff file to record changes between text files. For example, you may want to update a Web page by saving a copy of the HTML text document and then changing a few lines. You can use the `diff` command to determine what changes you made, and save the results in a diff file.

The patch application uses a diff file to update an original file with the changes made to the diff file. This is useful if you are compiling new applications from updated source code. You can also use the patch application to update a configuration file or any other text file. The syntax for the `patch` command is

`patch original-file diff-file`

The original file, without the patches applied, is saved as original-file.orig.

You can use the output of the `diff` command with the `ed` command, a command line tool that lets you edit text. To make the output of the `diff` command into an instruction list, or ed script, that the `ed` command understands, use the `-e` option with the `diff` command.

```
 Terminal   File  Edit  Scrollback  Font  Window  Help
 ○ ○ ○              Terminal — tcsh (ttyp1)
[ferro:~/Pictures] user% ls
wwnkd_029.gif  wwnkd_030.gif  wwnkd_031.gif  wwnkd_032.gif
[ferro:~/Pictures] user% diff wwnkd_030.gif wwnkd_031.gif
Binary files wwnkd_030.gif and wwnkd_031.gif differ
[ferro:~/Pictures] user%
```

```
 Terminal   File  Edit  Scrollback  Font  Window  Help
 ○ ○ ○              Terminal — tcsh (ttyp1)
[ferro:~] user% diff3 to-do.txt done.txt last-week.txt
====
1:3,4c
  - Finish chapter 4
  - Write tutorial for CSS site
2:3c
  X Finish chapter 3
3:3,4c
  X Finish chapter 2
  - Finish chapter 3
====
1:6c
  - Work on accessibility proposal
2:5c
  X Email Jade
3:6c
  - Email Jade
[ferro:~] user%
```

COMPARE TWO BINARY FILES

1 Type **diff** and a space.

2 Type the name of one file, a space, and the name of another file, and press Return.

Note: If the files differ, the shell displays a message. If the files are identical, no message appears.

COMPARE THREE FILES

1 Type **diff3** and a space.

2 Type three filenames separated by spaces, and press Return.

■ The shell displays the differences between the files.

COUNT CHARACTERS, LINES, AND WORDS IN TEXT

Y ou can measure the number of lines, words, and letters in a file by using the wc command. The wc command, short for word count, also counts the number of lines and characters, or bytes, in a file. The output of the wc command looks like this:

```
lines     words     characters     filename
```

The *lines* value is the number of lines in the text. The *words* value is the number of words; a word, for this purpose, is any group of characters that does not contain a blank line or space. The *characters* value includes printed letters, numbers, and symbols, as well as blank lines and spaces.

You can tell the wc command to print only the lines, words, or characters by using the -l, -w, and -c options, respectively. If you do not specify any of these options, the wc command lists all three values.

The wc command can also count lines, words, and characters from standard output. You can use the wc command to count the results of other commands, such as the grep command.

For example, to count how many lines in a file contain a specific pattern, you can use this command:

```
grep 'pattern' filename | wc -l
```

Keep in mind that this counts the number of lines that the grep command returns, and not the number of times that the pattern appears in the file. A single line may have the pattern repeated many times; thus, this is not an accurate way to count the number of times a word, or pattern, appears in a text file.

To count the number of files in a directory, you can pipe the output of the ls command to the wc -l command.

COUNT CHARACTERS, LINES, AND WORDS IN TEXT

```
 Terminal  File  Edit  Scrollback  Font  Window  Help
                      Terminal — tcsh (ttyp1)
[ferro:~] user% ls -la my-schedule.txt
-rw-r--r--  1 user  staff  311 Dec  2 01:54 my-schedule.txt
[ferro:~] user% cat my-schedule.txt
My To-Do List

- Finish chapter 4
- Write tutorial for CSS site
- Email Vicki
- Work on accessibility proposal
Monday:  nothing planned
Tuesday:  work out at the gym
          class in the evening
Wednesday:  class in the evening
Thursday:  writers group
           work out at the gym
Friday:  nothing planned
[ferro:~] user% wc my-schedule.txt
     13      50      311 my-schedule.txt
[ferro:~] user%
```

```
 Terminal  File  Edit  Scrollback  Font  Window  Help
                      Terminal — tcsh (ttyp1)
[ferro:~] user% ls /usr/bin | wc -l
     548
[ferro:~] user%
```

COUNT WORDS AND LINES IN TEXT

1 Type **wc** and a space.

2 Type the name of a file and press Return.

■ The shell displays the number of lines, words, and characters, respectively.

COUNT THE NUMBER OF FILES IN A DIRECTORY

1 Type **ls** and a space.

2 Type the pathname of a directory and a space.

3 Type a vertical pipe character and **wc -l**, then press Return.

■ The shell displays the number of lines of output from the ls command.

ARRANGE TEXT IN COLUMNS

You can create neatly arranged columns of text by using the `column` command. It is easier to read long lists if they appear in multiple columns, as this allows you to see more of a file in the Terminal window. The `column` command arranges your text lists into columns, based on the width of your Terminal window. The syntax of the `column` command is:

```
column filename
```

You can also provide a list to the `column` command from another command by piping the output to the `column` command. For example, if you want to make columns from the output of the `grep` command, you can type the following:

```
grep 'pattern' filename | column
```

The maximum width of the lines in the input file determines the width of each column. If, for example, your Terminal window is 80 characters across and the maximum width of all lines within the file is 21, then you can have three columns. You cannot have four columns, because they would exceed the width of the Terminal window. If the longest line in the file is 50 characters wide, then you can only have one column, because you cannot have two columns of 50 characters each within an 80-character Terminal window.

The `column` command arranges the items in the list vertically in columns. The second item appears under the first item, and continues until you reach the bottom of the first column. The list then continues at the top of the second column. If you want your columns to run horizontally instead of vertically, you can use the `-x` option with the `column` command.

ARRANGE TEXT IN COLUMNS

FILL COLUMNS VERTICALLY

1 Type **column** and a space.

2 Type the name of the input file and press Return.

■ The shell displays the input file in columns.

FILL COLUMNS HORIZONTALLY

1 Type **column -x** and a space.

2 Type the name of the input file and press Return.

■ The shell displays the input file in columns, but in horizontal order.

SORTING TEXT

You can sort lines of text by using the `sort` command. You can eliminate duplicate lines in sorted text by using the `uniq` command. Sorted text is easier to read, especially when you are comparing values or locating a specific word in a list. The `sort` command makes it easy to do this automatically rather than manually.

You can control the `sort` command by using options, based on the type of list you want to sort. By default, the `sort` command uses character order. This seems sensible at first, except that computers sort uppercase and lowercase letters in a rather confusing manner. According to your computer, the alphabet consists of the uppercase letters A through Z, then the lowercase letters a through z. So the word Yellow comes before the word blue, in character order, because all capital letters come before lowercase letters.

You can instruct the `sort` command to use alphabetical order instead of character order with the `-f` option. This sorts blue to come before Yellow, because the letter b comes before the letter Y.

Neither way of sorting works well with numbers. All numbers beginning with 1 come first, and then numbers beginning with 2, and so on. So the number 111 comes before the number 28, because 111 starts with 1, and 28 starts with 2. To sort numerically, you can use the `-n` option with the `sort` command, which then sorts numbers correctly.

A similar command to the `sort` command is the `uniq` command. The `uniq` command takes sorted lines of text, either given as a command line argument or from standard input, and removes those lines that are duplicates. The command then displays all lines that are unique.

SORTING TEXT

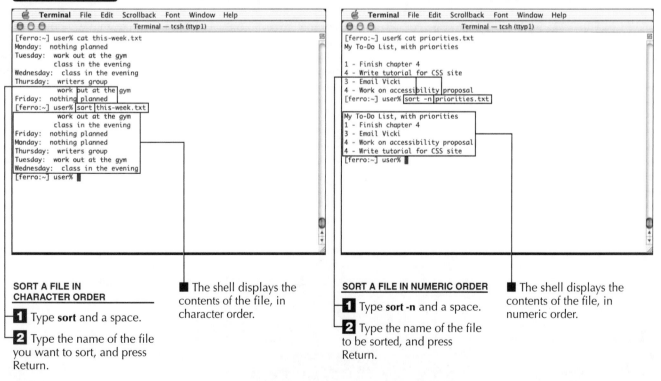

SORT A FILE IN CHARACTER ORDER

1 Type **sort** and a space.

2 Type the name of the file you want to sort, and press Return.

■ The shell displays the contents of the file, in character order.

SORT A FILE IN NUMERIC ORDER

1 Type **sort -n** and a space.

2 Type the name of the file to be sorted, and press Return.

■ The shell displays the contents of the file, in numeric order.

Extra

You can use the `sort` command with the `du` command to determine which of your subdirectories are taking up the most space. This can help you plan your use of disk space when it becomes limited.

The `du` command lists the size of each directory and subdirectory in blocks; if you prefer, you can use the `-k` option to show kilobytes. The first column of each line displays the size of the file, so you can use the `-n` option of the `sort` command to list the directory sizes in numeric order.

Example:
```
[ferro:~] user% du -k Documents | sort -n
0          Documents/Dogs/Sounds
4          Documents/Letters
28         Documents/Dogs
28         Documents/Dogs/Images
56         Documents/To Do Lists
88         Documents
[ferro:~] user%
```

The example shows that the smallest directory is the Sounds subdirectory of the Dogs directory, and the largest is the entire Documents directory itself.

SAVE SORTED TEXT

1 Type **sort** and a space.

2 Type the name of the file you want to sort, and a space.

3 Type a greater-than symbol and the name of a new file, and press Return.

■ The command sorts the contents of the file and saves the output in the new file.

ELIMINATE DUPLICATE ITEMS

1 Type **sort** and a space.

2 Type the name of the file you want to sort, and a space.

3 Type a vertical pipe, a space, then **uniq**, and press Return.

■ The command sorts the file and removes duplicate lines.

PRINT TEXT ON A PRINTER

You can print a file on your printer using the `lpr` command. You can format and print a file on a PostScript printer with the `enscript` command. The `lpr`, or line printer, command sends text directly to your printer. The printer simply outputs the lines, in the order that it receives them. The syntax for the `lpr` command is

`lpr filename`

The `lpr` command also prints text that is piped from the standard output of another command:

`another command | lpr`

If you do not connect a printer to your computer, the `lpr` command does not work, and you receive an error message.

If you try to print a non-text binary file, two things may happen: If the binary file is in a format known to the printing system, such as a JPEG image file, it prints on your printer. However, if it is an unknown file format, or an executable binary file, it may not print at all.

You can also use the `enscript` command, which converts your text file to PostScript. PostScript is a computer language understood by many printers; you should check your printer manual to see if it understands PostScript. If it does, you can use the `enscript` command to print text.

The `enscript` command produces better output than the `lpr` command, because PostScript lets you use special effects. For example, you can place a large, diagonal message, such as Top Secret, in light gray underneath your text. This is known as an *underlay*, and is set by the `--underlay=` option of the `enscript` command.

PRINT TEXT ON A PRINTER

```
 Terminal  File  Edit  Scrollback  Font  Window  Help
          Terminal — tcsh (ttyp1)
[ferro:~] user% lpr this-week.txt
[ferro:~] user%
```

```
 Terminal  File  Edit  Scrollback  Font  Window  Help
          Terminal — tcsh (ttyp1)
[ferro:~] user% ls -l | lpr
[ferro:~] user%
```

PRINT A FILE ON THE LINE PRINTER

■1 Type **lpr** and a space.

■2 Type the name of a file and press Return.

■ The printer outputs the file.

PRINT COMMAND OUTPUT

■1 Type a Unix shell command that displays text output, and a space.

■2 Type a vertical pipe and a space.

■3 Type **lpr** and press Return.

■ The printer outputs the text.

Extra

Additional options in the `lpr` and `enscript` commands give you even greater control over the appearance of your printed page. The `-o` option of `lpr` allows you to set specific printing options.

-O OPTION	PRINT EFFECT
`-o landscape`	Print in landscape, or wide, mode.
`-o media=Legal`	Print on legal-sized paper.
`-o media=A4`	Print on A4, European standard, paper.
`-o number-up=2`	Print two pages per sheet of paper.
`-o number-up=4`	Print four pages per sheet of paper.
`-o number-up=8`	Print eight pages per sheet of paper.
`-o number-up=16`	Print sixteen pages per sheet of paper.
`-o prettyprint`	Print a header with the date and filename.

The `enscript` command has even more options that you can use to generate or print PostScript output. For a more complete list, see the manual page for the `enscript` command by typing **man enscript**.

 Terminal   File   Edit   Scrollback   Font   Window   Help
Terminal — tcsh (ttyp1)

```
[ferro:~] user% enscript this-week.txt
[ 1 pages * 1 copy ] sent to printer
[ferro:~] user%
```

 Terminal   File   Edit   Scrollback   Font   Window   Help
Terminal — tcsh (ttyp1)

```
[ferro:~] user% enscript --underlay='DRAFT ONLY' this-week.txt
[ 1 pages * 1 copy ] sent to printer
[ferro:~] user%
```

PRINT A FILE ON A POSTSCRIPT PRINTER

1 Type **enscript** and a space.

2 Type the name of a file and press Return.

■ The printer prints the file.

PRINT AN UNDERLAY

1 Type **enscript --underlay=**.

2 Type the underlay text in single quotes, and a space.

3 Type the name of the file and press Return.

■ The printer outputs the file with the text running diagonally beneath it.

OPEN A FILE WITH PICO

Y ou can edit text files with Pico, a basic and easy-to-use text editor. The function of a text editor is to enable you to open, edit, and save plain-text files. Mac OS X provides several text editors for this purpose. Text editors are less complex than word processors; they do not allow you to select fonts, layouts, or other factors that affect the look of the printed page.

Three shell editors come with Mac OS X; they are Pico, vi, and emacs. Although they accomplish the same basic task of editing text, each one has its own strengths and limitations. Pico is the simplest to use, because all keystroke commands appear on-screen, and there are not many to learn. Because of its simplicity, Pico is a good choice for new users of the Mac OS X shell as well as experienced users who need to do simple text editing.

You start the Pico editor by typing **pico** at the command prompt, along with an optional filename as an argument. If the filename argument exists and is a text file, Pico opens the file for editing; if it does not exist, you start with a blank file.

The list of Pico commands appears at the bottom of the screen. A caret (^) before a letter means that you need to hold down the Control key while typing a key. For example, the notation ^X stands for Control + X.

You can use your keyboard to easily move around in a Pico document. You use the arrow keys to move to the position you want to insert text, and then start typing. You use the delete key to erase text to the left of the cursor.

OPEN A FILE WITH PICO

```
    Terminal   File   Edit   Scrollback   Font   Window   Help
  ● ● ●                    Terminal — ttyp9
[ferro:~/Documents] user% ls
Dogs            Letters         To Do Lists      my-schedule.txt
[ferro:~/Documents] user% pico my-schedule.txt

                          I
```

```
    Terminal   File   Edit   Scrollback   Font   Window   Help
  ● ● ●                    Terminal — ttyp9
  UW PICO(tm) 2.5                    File: my-schedule.txt

My To-Do List

- Finish chapter 4
- Write tutorial for CSS site
- Email Vicki
- Work on accessibility proposal
Monday:   nothing planned
Tuesday:   work out at the gym
           class in the evening
Wednesday:   class in the evening
Thursday:   writers group
           work out at the gym
Friday:  nothing planned




                      [ Read 13 lines ]
^G Get Help  ^O WriteOut  ^R Read File ^Y Prev Pg  ^K Cut Text  ^C Cur Pos
^X Exit      ^J Justify   ^W Where is  ^V Next Pg  ^U UnCut Text ^T To Spell
```

OPEN A FILE WITH PICO

■1 Type **pico** and a space.

■2 Type the name of a text file and press Return.

■ The Pico editor opens the file and displays it for you.

■ This area displays the filename.

■ This area displays the document.

■ This area displays Pico commands.

Extra

The basic keystrokes for Pico appear on-screen. The function of each keystroke is not immediately obvious, so this table summarizes the most useful Pico commands. Many of these commands are not intuitive, but the mnemonics may help. For example, to view the help screen you would press Control + G, not Control + H, so you might think of the command as getting help.

KEYSTROKE	MNEMONIC	FUNCTION
^C	Current location	Display the location of the cursor.
^D	Delete	Delete the character under the cursor.
^G	Get help	Display the program help screens.
^J	Justify	Reformat a paragraph.
^O	write Out	Save the current file.
^R	Read file	Insert the contents of another file.
^X	eXit	Quit Pico; save if necessary.
^W	Where is	Find text in the current file.
^V	-	Scroll down a page.
^Y	-	Scroll up a page.

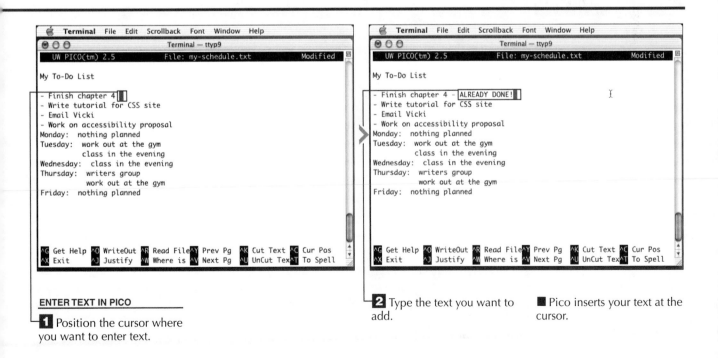

ENTER TEXT IN PICO

1 Position the cursor where you want to enter text.

2 Type the text you want to add.

■ Pico inserts your text at the cursor.

EDIT A FILE WITH PICO

You can edit text in the Pico editor, performing basic tasks such as finding specific text or saving a file. Pico is based on the text-editing functions of the Pine e-mail program, a shell application that allows you to compose, send, and read e-mail. You can learn more about installing and using the Pine e-mail program in Chapter 13.

If you edit a file with long lines, Pico does not automatically wrap the lines of text to fit the size of the window. Instead, Pico shows a dollar sign ($) at the right side of the Terminal window for each line that extends beyond the width of the window. You can view those lines by moving the cursor up or down with the arrow keys, and then using the right and left arrows to move through the line.

The Pico text editor has several command-line options that you can use when starting the editor. The -f option activates the function keys, although you should note that only the first four keys, F1 through F4, work in Mac OS X. The -v option opens a file in read-only mode, which means that you cannot make any changes in the file.

The most useful Pico editing commands are those that find and modify text, save a file, and then allow you to exit the text editor. For example, to locate a phrase or word, you can press Control + W. Saving a file is the same as writing an output file, so you can use the Control + O command to save your work. If you do not save your file, and you press Control + X, Pico asks you whether you want to save the file.

EDIT A FILE WITH PICO

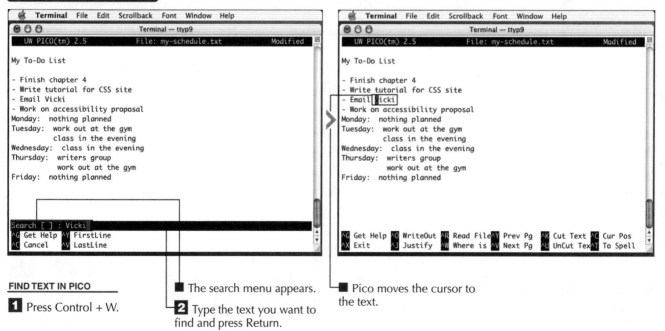

FIND TEXT IN PICO

1 Press Control + W.

■ The search menu appears.

2 Type the text you want to find and press Return.

■ Pico moves the cursor to the text.

Extra

You can move text within your file by using the cut-and-paste functions of Pico. Pico uses keyboard commands to mark, copy, delete, and move sections of text. Pico does not allow you to export text to other applications.

To cut a section of text in Pico, move the cursor to the start of the text you want to cut by using the arrow keys. Press Control + Shift + 6. Pico marks the beginning of the text block that you want to select by highlighting it in black. Using the arrow keys, move the cursor to the end of the text selection and press Control + K. Pico cuts the block from the file. This is an easy way to delete large sections of text.

To paste text into a new location, use the arrow keys to position the cursor where you want to move the deleted text and press Control + U. This command uncuts, or pastes, the text.

Terminal File Edit Scrollback Font Window Help
Terminal — ttyp9
UW PICO(tm) 2.5   File: my-schedule.txt   Modified

My To-Do List

- Finish chapter 4
- Write tutorial for CSS site
- Email Vicki
- Work on accessibility proposal
Monday: nothing planned
Tuesday: work out at the gym
          class in the evening
Wednesday: class in the evening
Thursday: writers group
          work out at the gym
Friday: nothing planned

File Name to write : my-schedule.txt
^G Get Help ^T To Files
^C Cancel

Terminal File Edit Scrollback Font Window Help
Terminal — ttyp9
UW PICO(tm) 2.5   File: my-schedule.txt   Modified

My To-Do List

- Finish chapter 4
- Write tutorial for CSS site
- Email Vicki
- Work on accessibility proposal
Monday: nothing planned
Tuesday: work out at the gym
          class in the evening
Wednesday: class in the evening
Thursday: writers group
          work out at the gym
Friday: nothing planned

Save modified buffer (ANSWERING "No" WILL DESTROY CHANGES) ?
                      Y Yes
^C Cancel   N No

SAVE A FILE WITH PICO

1 Press Control + O.

■ The Pico editor prompts you with the current filename.

Note: You can change the filename by using the Delete key or adding text.

2 Type the name of the file and press Return.

■ Pico saves the file.

QUIT PICO

1 Press Control + X.

■ The Pico editor asks whether you want to save your file.

2 Type **y** to save your file or **n** to exit without saving.

■ The Pico editor exits.

OPEN A FILE WITH VI

Y ou can use the vi editor to edit text files. The vi editor is more powerful than Pico and can perform many more text-editing functions. The name vi is short for *visual*; vi is a visual editor because you can edit the files on-screen as you see them, as opposed to using the command line as you would with sed, a stream editor. To begin using the vi editor, you can type **vi** at the command prompt with an optional filename argument:

```
vi file-name
```

If you do not specify a filename, the vi editor creates a temporary file for you and opens that temporary file for editing. The name of the temporary file consists of a seemingly random series of characters and numbers;

a sample filename with the full path would be /tmp/vi.Y8pi7R, because vi stores temporary files in the /tmp directory.

When vi displays a file, lines that are longer than the width of the Terminal screen continue on the next line. The vi editor breaks lines at the edge of the screen, which means that the first half of a word may appear at the end of one line, with the other half beginning on the next line. The word itself is still intact and whole; vi simply displays it this way for editing purposes.

The vi editor automatically uses the full Terminal window. If there are additional lines on the screen that vi does not use to display the file, a tilde (~) appears at the beginning of each of these lines. These are not part of your file; they simply indicate the end of the content of the file.

OPEN A FILE WITH VI

EDIT A FILE IN VI

1 Type **vi** and a space.

2 Type the name of a text file and press Return.

■ The vi editor opens and displays the file.

■ This area displays the filename.

■ This area displays the document.

3 Press Control + Shift + X to exit the file.

Extra

You can change the behavior of the vi editor by setting editor options. You do this by typing a colon (:), the word **set**, a space, and then the option name. For example, to turn on line numbers, type **:set number**. To turn off an option, type a colon, the word **set**, a space, the word **no**, and then — with no space before it — the name of the option. For example, to turn off line numbers, you type **:set nonumber**.

OPTION	FUNCTION
autoindent	Automatically indent new lines.
list	Display a $ symbol to indicate the end of each line.
number	Display line numbers on the left.
ruler	Display the current line number and character position.
showmode	Show the current mode, for example, insert, in the lower right corner.
verbose	Use wordy and informative warnings and messages.

You can see which options are currently set if you type **:set** and press Return. For a full list of all vi editor options, type **:set all**.

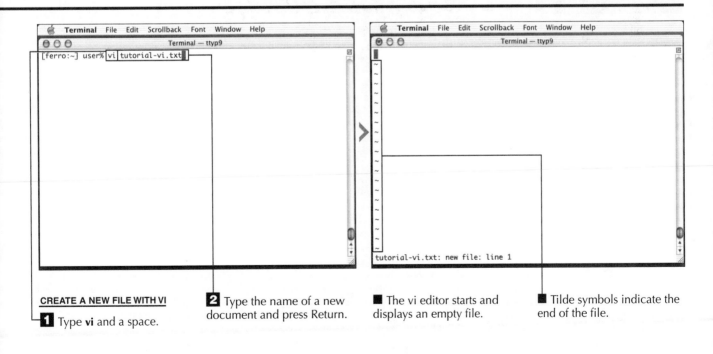

CREATE A NEW FILE WITH VI

1 Type **vi** and a space.

2 Type the name of a new document and press Return.

■ The vi editor starts and displays an empty file.

■ Tilde symbols indicate the end of the file.

MOVEMENT WITHIN VI

You can use single keystroke commands to move through a file in the vi editor. One feature that distinguishes the vi editor from the other visual editors is the concept of *modes*. The vi editor is always in one of two states, *Command mode* or *Input mode*. Command mode allows you to use keystroke commands to delete lines, move text, or save files. Input mode allows you to type text into the document at the location of the cursor. While in Command mode, you can use keystroke commands to change to Input mode.

The Command-mode keystrokes in the vi editor are usually a single letter, and, unlike the Pico editor commands, they are typed without holding down the Control key. However, the keystroke commands are case sensitive, which means that a is a different command than A. You need to use the Shift key, of course, to create the uppercase letters.

To move within a document in vi, the application must be in Command mode. The vi editor offers many ways to navigate the content of a file, some of which appear on the facing page. The easiest way is to use the arrow keys to move the cursor, as you would in Pico. You can also use the lowercase letters h, j, k, and l to move the cursor around on-screen.

The find command in vi is much like the find command in less. When you type a forward slash (/) and enter the word or phrase you are seeking, the vi editor automatically moves the cursor to the next occurrence of that text. If you type a question mark (?) instead of a forward slash, the search occurs backwards in the file from your current position.

MOVEMENT WITHIN VI

Terminal   File   Edit   Scrollback   Font   Window   Help

Terminal — ttyp9

```
The vi editor seems complex at first
but it is actually easy to use.  The
tricky part is the fact that there
are two MODES:

* The COMMAND MODE lets you type commands
  to move around

* The INPUT MODE allows you to enter text
  directly into the document

If you don't know what mode you are in, you
can press ESC a few times until vi beeps at
you
~
~
~
~
~
~
```

Terminal   File   Edit   Scrollback   Font   Window   Help

Terminal — ttyp9

```
The vi editor seems complex at first
but it is actually easy to use.  The
tricky part is the fact that there
are two MODES:

* The COMMAND MODE lets you type commands
  to move around

* The INPUT MODE allows you to enter text
  directly into the document

If you don't know what mode you are in, you
can press ESC a few times until vi beeps at
you
~
~
~
~
~
~
```

MOVING IN VI

1 With vi in Command mode, press Shift + H to move to the start of the file.

2 Press Shift + G to move to the end of the file.

3 Press Shift + 6 to move to the beginning of a line.

4 Press Shift + 4 to move to the end of the line.

Extra

The commands in the table below allow you to move quickly through a file in vi, repositioning the cursor and scrolling the screen when necessary.

KEYSTROKE	EFFECT
H	Move to the first line of the file.
G	Move to the last line of the file.
h	Move one character to the left.
j	Move down one line.
k	Move up one line.
l	Move one character to the right.
^	Move to the beginning of the current line.
$	Move to the end of the current line.
w	Move ahead one word.
/text	Find text from the cursor forward.
?text	Find text from the cursor backward.

Terminal File Edit Scrollback Font Window Help

Terminal — ttyp9

```
The vi editor seems complex at first
but it is actually easy to use.  The
tricky part is the fact that there
are two MODES:

* The COMMAND MODE lets you type commands
  to move around

* The INPUT MODE allows you to enter text
  directly into the document

If you don't know what mode you are in, you
can press ESC a few times until vi beeps at
you.
~
~
~
~
~
~
/document
```

Terminal File Edit Scrollback Font Window Help

Terminal — ttyp9

```
The vi editor seems complex at first
but it is actually easy to use.  The
tricky part is the fact that there
are two MODES:

* The COMMAND MODE lets you type commands
  to move around

* The INPUT MODE allows you to enter text
  directly into the document

If you don't know what mode you are in, you
can press ESC a few times until vi beeps at
you.
~
~
~
~
~
```

FINDING TEXT IN VI

1 Type /.

2 Type a word or phrase and press Return.

■ The vi editor moves the cursor to that word or phrase.

ENTER TEXT IN VI

Y ou can enter text into a document by switching to Input mode in vi. When you start the vi editor, it switches to Command mode by default, allowing you to move through the file or enter keystroke commands. If you try to enter text while in Command mode, you can produce some very strange results, because many characters correspond to keystroke commands in Command mode. It is therefore very important to know which mode you are in before you enter text.

The easiest way to determine your current mode is to enable the option showmode. You can do this by typing **:set showmode** while in Command mode. Your current mode appears in the lower right corner.

You can use a number of single keystrokes to switch to Input mode from Command mode. However, there is only one way to switch to Command mode from Input mode,

and that is to press the Esc (Escape) key, located on the upper-left corner of most keyboards. If you are not sure which mode you are in, you can press the Esc key to return to Command mode. Pressing the Esc key while in Command mode does nothing, so it is safe to press this key several times to make sure.

Many useful command-mode keystrokes appear in the table on the facing page. The most important keystrokes are i, which inserts text at the current cursor location, and o, which opens a new line below the current one and allows you to enter text directly. When you edit the text in your file, vi does not save your changes until you give the command to do so.

```
       Terminal   File   Edit   Scrollback   Font   Window   Help
  ⊙ ⊙ ⊙                      Terminal — ttyp9
  The vi editor seems complex at first
  but it is actually █asy to use.  The
  tricky part is the fact that there
  are two MODES:

  * The COMMAND MODE lets you type commands
    to move around

  * The INPUT MODE allows you to enter text
    directly into the document

  If you don't know what mode you are in, you
  can press ESC a few times until vi beeps at
  you.
  ~
  ~
  ~
  ~
  ~
  ~
```

```
       Terminal   File   Edit   Scrollback   Font   Window   Help
  ⊙ ⊙ ⊙                      Terminal — ttyp9
  The vi editor seems complex at first
  but it is actually somewhat █asy to use.  The
  tricky part is the fact that there
  are two MODES:

  * The COMMAND MODE lets you type commands
    to move around

  * The INPUT MODE allows you to enter text
    directly into the document

  If you don't know what mode you are in, you
  can press ESC a few times until vi beeps at
  you.
  ~
  ~
  ~
  ~
  ~
  ~
```

INSERT TEXT

1 Position the cursor where you want to enter text.

2 Type the letter **i**.

■ The vi editor switches to Input mode.

3 Type the text you want to insert.

4 Press Esc.

■ The vi editor switches to Command mode.

Extra

The keystroke commands that you use to switch to Insert mode appear in the table below. There are other modes that function like Insert mode, allowing you to type text into the file. As with Insert mode, you can leave these modes by pressing the Esc key to switch to Command mode.

KEYSTROKE	MODE ENTERED	FUNCTION
A	Insert	Append text at the end of the current line.
a	Insert	Append text after the current character.
I	Insert	Insert text at the beginning of the current line.
i	Insert	Insert text at the current location.
O	Insert	Insert a new line before the current line.
o	Insert	Insert a new line after the current line.
R	Replace	Replace existing text with the text you type.
r	Replace	Replace a single character with the text you type.
S	Change	Substitute the current line with one you type.
s	Change	Substitute a single character with the text you type.

 Terminal File Edit Scrollback Font Window Help

Terminal — ttyp9

```
The vi editor seems complex at first
but it is actually somewhat easy to use.  The
tricky part is the fact that there
are two MODES:

* The COMMAND MODE lets you type commands
  to move around

* The INPUT MODE allows you to enter text
  directly into the document


If you don't know what mode you are in, you
can press ESC a few times until vi beeps at
you.
~
~
~
~
~
```

 Terminal File Edit Scrollback Font Window Help

Terminal — ttyp9

```
The vi editor seems complex at first
but it is actually somewhat easy to use.  The
tricky part is the fact that there
are two MODES:

* The COMMAND MODE lets you type commands
  to move around

* The INPUT MODE allows you to enter text
  directly into the document
The modes are confusing at first.

If you don't know what mode you are in, you
can press ESC a few times until vi beeps at
you.
~
~
~
~
~
```

OPEN A NEW LINE OF TEXT

1 Position the cursor to the line above where you want to insert a new line.

2 Type the letter **o**.

■ The vi editor switches to Input mode and opens a new blank line.

3 Type the text you want to insert.

4 Press Esc.

■ The vi editor switches to Command mode.

DELETE TEXT IN VI

Y ou can delete text from a file using keystroke commands. If you press the Delete key while in Command mode, this generates the symbols, ^?, which do not correspond to any command known to vi, and an error message appears. In Command mode, the Delete key has no function. You can use other keystroke commands to delete text.

To delete content from your document, you must first move to the location of the unwanted text using the arrow keys or a movement command. Deletion commands use the current location of the cursor as the starting point of the deletion.

You can delete the character underneath the cursor by typing a lowercase x. If there is more text on the line, it shifts to the left to fill the space formerly occupied by the deleted character. A capital X deletes the character to the left of the cursor.

You can delete larger sections of text by typing the letter **d** and applying a movement command. For example, to delete from the current location to the beginning of the line, you can type **d^**, because the ^ keystroke moves the cursor to the beginning of the line. To delete the current line, you can type **dd.** If you want to delete everything from the current position to the end of the current line, you can type either **D** or **d$**. A list of deletion commands appears in the table on the facing page. When you edit the text in your file, vi does not save your changes until you give the command to do so.

DELETE TEXT IN VI

```
     Terminal   File   Edit   Scrollback   Font   Window   Help
  ● ○ ○                     Terminal — ttyp9
The vi editor seems complex at first
but it is actually somewh t easy to use.   The
tricky part is the fact that there
are two MODES:

* The COMMAND MODE lets you type commands
  to move around

* The INPUT MODE allows you to enter text
  directly into the document
The modes are confusing at first.

If you don't know what mode you are in, you
can press ESC a few times until vi beeps at
you.
~
~
~
~
~
~
```

```
     Terminal   File   Edit   Scrollback   Font   Window   Help
  ● ○ ○                     Terminal — ttyp9
The vi editor seems complex at first
but it is actually somewh t easy to use.   The
tricky part is the fact that there
are two MODES:

* The COMMAND MODE lets you type commands
  to move around

* The INPUT MODE allows you to enter text
  directly into the document
The modes are confusing at first.

If you don't know what mode you are in, you
can press ESC a few times until vi beeps at
you.
~
~
~
~
~
~
```

DELETE CHARACTERS

1 Position the cursor over the character you want to delete.

2 Type the letter **x**.

■ The vi editor deletes the character.

Extra

You can use these commands to remove text from the file you are editing. If you make a mistake, you can type the keystroke command u, which undoes the most recent change. You can use this command to undo insertions as well as deletions.

KEYSTROKES	EFFECT
D	Delete from current position to end of line.
dd	Delete current line.
dG	Delete from current position to end of file.
dw	Delete current word, from current position to end of word.
d^	Delete from current position to beginning of line.
d$	Delete from current position to end of line.
d/text	Delete from current position to next occurrence of text.
u	Undo last command that changed the file.
X	Delete character to left of cursor.
x	Delete character under cursor.

DELETE A LINE OF TEXT

1 Position the cursor on the line you want to delete.

2 Type **dd**.

■ The vi editor deletes the line.

EDIT TEXT WITH VI

You can edit text files using the multiline editing capabilities of the vi editor. While in Command mode, you activate the command line for editing purposes by first typing a colon (:). There are many useful commands that you can learn about, including the ex editor that provides the line edit commands. You can obtain more information from the vi manual by typing **man vi** or consulting online references or books about the vi editor.

To replace text, you can use the substitute command by typing :s. When you type commands that begin with a colon (:), they appear on the bottom line of the Terminal window. vi carries out the command after you type the full command and press Return.

There are many ways you can use the :s command, including:

```
:s/old/new/
:s/old/new/g
:%s/old/new/g
```

The first instance replaces a single occurrence of *old* with *new* on the current line. The second instance adds the flag g, which stands for global. This means that vi replaces all occurrences of *old* with *new* on that line, and not just the first occurrence. The third instance includes a range option, %, which tells vi to replace all instances of the word throughout the entire file.

To join two lines of text together onto one line, you can use the editing command J. This removes the line break at the end of the current line, and joins it to the next line. When you edit the text in your file, vi does not save your changes until you give the command to do so.

EDIT TEXT WITH VI

FIND AND REPLACE TEXT

1 Type :.

■ The cursor moves to the bottom of the screen following a colon.

2 Type **%s/** and the original word or phrase you want to replace.

3 Type a forward slash and the new word or phrase.

4 Type another forward slash, the letter **g**, and press Return.

■ The vi editor globally replaces the old text with the replacement text.

Extra

You can cut-and-paste text in vi by using the deletion keystroke commands and the p command. When you delete text, it is not completely lost; instead, vi stores it in a *paste buffer*. You can think of this as a container that holds the most recently deleted text.

You can paste the contents of the paste buffer into the current location of the cursor by typing the letter **p**. For example, to move a line, delete it by typing **dd** and move to the new location in the file. Type the letter **p**, and vi inserts the deleted line into the new location.

You can copy text into the paste buffer without deleting it by using the y command, which stands for *yank*. As with deletion commands, you must follow the y with a movement command that indicates how many lines you want to yank, or you can type yy to yank the current line.

To yank or delete a number of lines, you can precede the y or d keystrokes with a number. For example, to yank 12 lines, including the current one, type **12yy**.

 Terminal File Edit Scrollback Font Window Help

Terminal — ttyp9

```
The vi editor seems complex at first
but it is actually somewat easy to use.  The
are two MODES:

* The COMMAND MODE lets you type commands
  to move around

The INPUT MODE allows you to enter text
  directly into the document
The modes are confusing at first.

If you don't know what mode you are in, you
can press the escape key a few times until vi beeps at
you.
~
~
~
~
~
~
```

 Terminal File Edit Scrollback Font Window Help

Terminal — ttyp9

```
The vi editor seems complex at first
but it is actually somewat easy to use.  The
are two MODES:

* The COMMAND MODE lets you type commands
  to move around

* The INPUT MODE allows you to enter text directly into the document
The modes are confusing at first.

If you don't know what mode you are in, you
can press the escape key a few times until vi beeps at
you.
~
~
~
~
~
```

JOIN TWO LINES OF TEXT

1 Position the cursor to the first of two lines you want to join.

2 Press Shift + J.

■ The vi editor joins the two lines together.

SAVE A FILE WITH VI

When you finish editing a file with the vi editor, you can save your work. It is a good practice to use the `save` command any time you make changes that you do not want to lose. To save the current file, you can type **:w** and press Return. vi saves the file to your hard drive, and any changes you make become permanent. The vi editor displays the filename, the number of lines, and the number of characters in the file after you save it.

You can save the file with a different name by typing a filename before pressing Return. For example, to save the current file as my-update.txt, you can type **:w my-update.txt** and press Return. If you start vi without specifying a filename, you must remember to save with a new name, or else vi saves it in the /tmp directory with an arbitrary name such as vi.XW0hyP.

You may name your text file whatever you like, but for compatibility with Aqua applications, you should append text files with the file extension .txt. However, if you are creating a specific type of text file, such as an HTML file, a Cascading Style Sheets file, or an XML settings file, you must save it with the appropriate extension such as .html, .css, or .plist.

To exit the vi editor, you can type the `quit` command as **:q.** You can combine the `:w` and `:q` commands together as **:wq,** which saves the file and exits the vi editor, returning you to the shell. If you have made changes but do not want to save them, you can exit vi by appending an exclamation point (**!**) to the `:q` command.

SAVE A FILE WITH VI

```
     Terminal   File   Edit   Scrollback   Font   Window   Help
 ● ● ●                      Terminal — ttyp9
The vi editor seems complex at first
but it is actually somewat easy to use.   The
are two MODES:

* The COMMAND MODE lets you type commands
  to move around

* The INPUT MODE allows you to enter text directly into the document
The modes are confusing at first.

If you don't know what mode you are in, you
can press the escape key a few times until vi beeps at
you.
~
~
~
~
~
~
~
:w
```

```
     Terminal   File   Edit   Scrollback   Font   Window   Help
 ● ● ●                      Terminal — ttyp9
The vi editor seems complex at first
but it is actually somewat easy to use.   The
are two MODES:

* The COMMAND MODE lets you type commands
  to move around

* The INPUT MODE allows you to enter text directly into the document
The modes are confusing at first.

If you don't know what mode you are in, you
can press the escape key a few times until vi beeps at
you.
~
~
~
~
~
~
~
:w bad-tutorial.txt
```

SAVE A FILE WITH VI

1 Type **:**.

■ The cursor moves to the bottom of the screen following a colon.

2 Type the letter **w** and press Return.

■ The vi editor saves the file.

SAVE WITH A DIFFERENT FILENAME

1 Type **:**.

2 Type the letter **w** and a space.

3 Type a new filename and press Return.

■ The vi editor saves the file under the new name.

Extra

One file you may want to edit is the .exrc file. This is a file that you store in your Home directory and that vi editor reads when it starts up. vi automatically runs the commands in the file, so this makes it a good place to store your preferred editor options, such as showmode. Because the filename starts with a period, it is a hidden file, invisible to the ls command, but you can still list it by typing **ls -a**.

EXRC File Example:
```
set autoindent
set ruler
set verbose
set showmode
~
~
~
```

To use these settings, make sure you are in your Home directory by typing **cd**, and then type **vi .exrc**. Enter the lines above into the file, save it, and exit. The next time you start vi, it automatically applies these options.

Terminal File Edit Scrollback Font Window Help

Terminal — ttyp9

```
The vi editor seems complex at first
but it is actually somewat easy to use.  The
are two MODES:

* The COMMAND MODE lets you type commands
  to move around

* The INPUT MODE allows you to enter text directly into the document
The modes are confusing at first.

If you don't know what mode you are in, you
can press the escape key a few times until vi beeps at
you.
~
~
~
~
~
~
~
:wq
```

Terminal File Edit Scrollback Font Window Help

Terminal — ttyp9

```
The vi editor seems complex at first
but it is actually somewat easy to use.  The
are two MODES:

* The COMMAND MODE lets you type commands
  to move around

* The INPUT MODE allows you to enter text directly into the document
The modes are confusing at first.

If you don't know what mode you are in, you
can press the escape key a few times until vi beeps at
you.
~
~
~
~
~
~
:q!
```

SAVE AND EXIT VI

1 Open a file and add some text.

2 Type **:**.

3 Type **wq** and press Return.

■ The vi editor saves the file and exits.

EXIT VI WITHOUT SAVING

1 Type **:**.

2 Type **q!** and press Return.

■ The vi editor exits without saving.

OPEN A FILE WITH EMACS

You can use the emacs editor to edit text files. emacs is a very complex program that can do everything from editing simple text files to downloading and displaying Web sites.

Among advanced Unix users, there is a friendly rivalry between users of vi and users of emacs. This book gives greater coverage to vi because it is less complex than emacs. However, if you do not find vi to your liking or you prefer to use a very flexible and adaptable text editor, the emacs editor is an excellent choice.

The basic functions of the emacs editor are easy to use. To open a file, you can simply give the name of the file as an argument, as with other text editors. Unlike vi, emacs does not have different modes for Command and Input, so you do not have to switch between modes as you would with vi.

As with Pico, you can use the arrow keys to move around, and you can edit text directly.

You can execute commands in emacs by using either the Control or Meta key. When you type a character with the Control key, this corresponds to the prefix C- in emacs terminology; a character that you type with the Meta key corresponds to the prefix M-. For example, to search for text, you press Control + S (C-s), and to move to the end of a file, you press Esc + > (M->). Keep in mind that the prefix C- means that you must hold down the Control key while pressing another key, and M- means you must press and release the Esc key before typing the following key. You use the Esc key instead of the Meta key because Apple keyboards do not have a Meta key.

OPEN A FIILE WITH EMACS

OPEN A FILE WITH EMACS

1 Type **emacs** and a space.

2 Type the name of the file and press Return.

■ The emacs editor displays the file.

■ This area displays the filename.

■ This area displays the document.

■ This area displays the status line.

Extra

The following table is a summary of some of the most useful emacs commands for moving and finding text.

KEYSTROKES	COMMAND NAME	EFFECT
C-a	Beginning of line	Move to the start of the current line.
C-b	Backward char	Move one character to the left.
C-e	End of line	Move to the end of the current line.
C-f	Forward char	Move one character to the right.
C-n	Next line	Move down one line.
C-p	Previous line	Move up one line.
C-r	Search backward	Search backward for text.
C-s	Search forward	Search forward for text.
M-<	Beginning of buffer	Move to the start of the file.
M->	End of buffer	Move to the end of the file.

```
 Terminal  File  Edit  Scrollback  Font  Window  Help
                        Terminal — ttyp9
File Edit Options Buffers Tools Help
The vi editor seems complex at first
but it is actually somewat easy to use.   The
are two MODES:

* The COMMAND MODE lets you type commands
  to move around

* The INPUT MODE allows you to enter text directly into the document
The modes are confusing at first.

If you don't know what mode you are in, you
can press the escape key a few times until vi beeps at
you.



--1-:**-F1  bad-tutorial.txt      (Text)--L10--All-----
```

```
 Terminal  File  Edit  Scrollback  Font  Window  Help
                        Terminal — ttyp9
File Edit Options Buffers Tools Help
The vi editor seems complex at first
but it is actually somewat easy to use.   The
are two MODES:

* The COMMAND MODE lets you type commands
  to move around

* The INPUT MODE allows you to enter text directly into the document
The modes are confusing at first.

Emacs is much better because emacs doesn't have modes!!!!!
If you don't know what mode you are in, you
can press the escape key a few times until vi beeps at
you.



--1-:**-F1  bad-tutorial.txt      (Text)--L11--All-----
```

INSERT TEXT IN EMACS

1 Position the cursor where you want to insert text.

2 Type your text directly into emacs.

■ emacs adds the text to the file at the insertion point.

EDIT A FILE WITH EMACS

You can edit and save text files in emacs with keystroke commands that use the Control and Meta keys. You can also configure the Terminal application to allow the Option key to function as the Meta key.

There are literally hundreds of emacs commands that you can use, and you can even add additional extensions to emacs to increase this number. Many of the more esoteric commands in emacs are only of interest to serious Unix users. As a beginning user, you may want to type **C-h t** to read the emacs tutorial. To do this, you hold down the Control key and type the letter **h**, then release the Control key and type the letter **t**.

A short list of commands that let you edit your files appears on the facing page. As with other text editors, emacs does not make your changes permanent until you save the file.

To make it easier to type Meta keystroke commands, those indicated by the M- prefix, you can configure the Terminal application to use the Option key. You can activate this Window setting from the Terminal menu. It allows you to type Meta keystrokes by holding down the Option key while pressing the appropriate key, instead of pressing and releasing the Esc key before the following key.

You can also get emacs to recognize and work with your mouse, a capability that most shell applications do not possess. To do this, you enable the Terminal Window setting named Option click to position cursor; when you hold down the Option key and click your mouse, emacs moves the cursor to the current position of the mouse pointer.

EDIT A FILE WITH EMACS

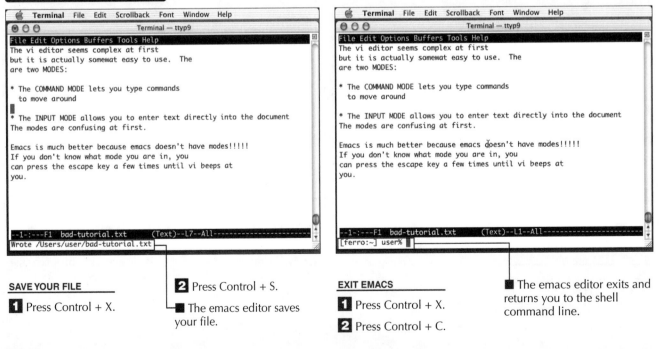

SAVE YOUR FILE

1 Press Control + X.

2 Press Control + S.

■ The emacs editor saves your file.

EXIT EMACS

1 Press Control + X.

2 Press Control + C.

■ The emacs editor exits and returns you to the shell command line.

Extra

The table below contains some emacs commands that you can use to edit text files and save your changes.

KEYSTROKES	COMMAND NAME	EFFECT
C-d	Delete char	Delete the current character.
C-k	Kill line	Delete the current line, current position to end of line.
C-t	Transpose chars	Transpose, or switch, two characters.
C-x C-c	Save buffer, kill emacs	Exit emacs.
C-x C-f	Find file	Open a new file for editing.
C-x C-s	Save file	Save the file.
C-x C-t	Transpose lines	Transpose, or switch, two lines.
C-x C-w	Write file	Save the file under a different name.
C-x u	Undo	Undo the last change to the file.
M-%	Query replace	Find and replace text, type y to confirm.
M-w	Transpose words	Transpose, or switch, two words.

Keep in mind that the prefix C- means to hold down the Control key while pressing another key, and M- means you must press and release the Esc key before typing the following key. You can also hold down the Option key to type M- keystrokes, if you have enabled the correct Terminal setting.

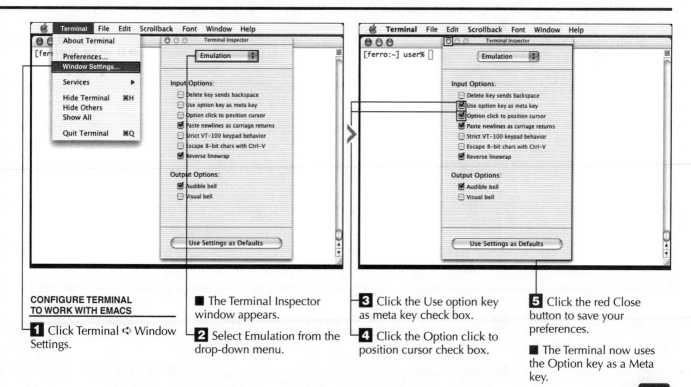

CONFIGURE TERMINAL TO WORK WITH EMACS

1 Click Terminal ➪ Window Settings.

■ The Terminal Inspector window appears.

2 Select Emulation from the drop-down menu.

3 Click the Use option key as meta key check box.

4 Click the Option click to position cursor check box.

5 Click the red Close button to save your preferences.

■ The Terminal now uses the Option key as a Meta key.

SET YOUR PROMPT

You can change your command line prompt by setting special shell variables. Changing your prompt lets you customize the information that the prompt displays to better suit your needs.

The prompt lets you know that you are entering text into the shell, rather than a program. When it reappears, this tells you that the last command has finished executing. You can set your shell prompt to contain whatever information you like using the following command:

```
set prompt = 'prompt formatting sequence'
```

A *prompt formatting sequence* is a series of letters, symbols, and special character codes that serves as your prompt. A list of the most useful special formatting codes appears on the facing page.

The default prompt is set to the name of the computer, the partial path, and your short username. This is useful on a

multi-user system, or if you frequently log on remotely to other computers. However, many users are only on one computer at a time — the one they are sitting in front of — and only as a single user. If this is true for you, you may want to set your prompt to the time, the number of commands entered, or the full path.

In addition to the shell command prompt, you can set several other prompts. You use the prompt2 setting if you end a command line with a backslash (\), indicating that the current command continues on the next line. You see the prompt3 message if you have auto correction on for misspelled commands. You see the rprompt message on the right side of the Terminal window for every command.

Prompt settings only last as long as the Terminal window in which they are set is open. To make them permanent, see "Edit Your .tcshrc File" in this chapter.

SET YOUR PROMPT

Terminal   File   Edit   Scrollback   Font   Window   Help

```
Terminal — ttyp8
[ferro:/usr/share] user% set prompt = '(%t #%h) %c%# '
(1:04am #13) share% pwd
/usr/share
(1:05am #14) share%
```

Terminal   File   Edit   Scrollback   Font   Window   Help

```
Terminal — ttyp8
(1:06am #18) share% set prompt2 = 'what else? '
(1:06am #19) share% cd \
what else? ~
(1:06am #20) ~%
```

CHANGE THE DEFAULT PROMPT

1 Type **set prompt =** and a space.

2 Type a prompt formatting sequence in single quotes, and press Return.

■ The prompt changes.

SET THE SECOND PROMPT

1 Type **set prompt2 =** and a space.

2 Type a prompt formatting sequence in single quotes, and press Return.

■ The second prompt changes.

Extra `set prompt = '[%m:%c3] %n%# '` is the standard shell prompt in Mac OS X. The formatting Code table explains the meanings of these and other special codes.

FORMATTING CODE	EXAMPLE	MEANING
%c	Documents	The current directory.
%d	Fri	The day of the week.
%D	06	The day of the month.
%cnumber	local/etc/httpd	A partial pathname.
%h	14	This is the 14th command.
%M	ferro.idyllmtn.com	The full name of the computer.
%m	ferro	The short name of the computer.
%n	user	Your short username.
%p	10:04:21pm	The precise time.
%t	10:04pm	The current time.
%w	Dec	The month of the year.
%W	12	The numerical month of the year.
%y	02	The year in two digits.
%Y	2003	The year in four digits.
%#	%	The % symbol, # if you are root.

 Terminal   File   Edit   Scrollback   Font   Window   Help
```
                          Terminal — ttyp8
(1:09am #36) ~% set prompt3 = 'Huh? How about %R? (y or n) '
(1:09am #37) ~% mf my-dog.jpg Pictures/

Huh? How about mv my-dog.jpg Pictures/? (y or n) yes
(1:09am #38) ~%
```

 Terminal   File   Edit   Scrollback   Font   Window   Help
```
                          Terminal — ttyp8
(1:10am #39) ~% set rprompt = '<-- %n@%m'
(1:10am #40) ~% ls                                    <-- user@ferro
Desktop    Images     Movies    Pictures  Sites
Documents  Library    Music     Public    Sounds
(1:11am #41) ~%                                       <-- user@ferro
```

SET THE THIRD PROMPT

1 Type **set prompt3 =** and a space.

2 Type a prompt formatting sequence in single quotes, and press Return.

■ The third prompt changes.

SET THE RIGHT-HAND PROMPT

1 Type **set rprompt =** and a space.

2 Type a prompt formatting sequence in single quotes, and press Return.

■ The right-hand prompt changes.

SET COMMAND ALIASES

You can save time and reduce typing by setting short aliases for long commands. You can use the `alias` command to define and list aliases. To create a new alias, you can use a command line like this:

```
alias short-alias 'longer command'
```

One commonly used alias is `ll`, which most Unix users define with the following command:

```
alias ll 'ls -l'
```

This alias allows you to type `ll` as a command and have it execute the `ls -l` command, which shows a long listing. You can insert additional arguments, such as a directory, after the `ll` command just as you can with the original `ls -l` command.

You can also redefine existing commands to be aliases. For example, if you are afraid that you may mistakenly delete an important file because you do not always remember to use the `-i` option with the `rm` command, you can set an alias as follows:

```
alias rm 'rm -i'
```

As a result, all of your `rm` commands automatically include the `-i` option.

If you redefine a command, such as the `rm` command, using an alias, and you need to use the original version, not the alias, you can do so by typing a backslash (\) before the command name. This bypasses aliases and invokes an executable program in your path or a shell built-in command.

To list all of your aliases, you can type **alias** without any arguments. If you need to remove an alias, you can use the `unalias` command.

Like other shell settings, your aliases only remain as long as your Terminal window is open. You can make your aliases permanent by saving them in your .tcshrc file. See "Edit Your .tcshrc File" in this chapter.

SET COMMAND ALIASES

```
  Terminal  File  Edit  Scrollback  Font  Window  Help
  ● ● ●                    Terminal — ttyp8
[ferro:~] user% alias ll 'ls -l'
[ferro:~] user%
```

```
  Terminal  File  Edit  Scrollback  Font  Window  Help
  ● ● ●                    Terminal — ttyp8
[ferro:~] user% alias ll 'ls -l'
[ferro:~] user% ll
total 0
drwx------  12 user  staff  408 Dec 11 01:12 Desktop
drwx------   6 user  staff  204 Dec  2 19:32 Documents
drwxr-xr-x   2 user  staff   68 Dec 11 01:08 Images
drwx------  22 user  staff  748 Nov 13 03:40 Library
drwx------   3 user  staff  102 Nov  4 13:49 Movies
drwx------   3 user  staff  102 Nov  4 13:49 Music
drwx------   8 user  staff  272 Dec 11 01:09 Pictures
drwxr-xr-x   4 user  staff  136 Nov  4 13:49 Public
drwxr-xr-x   8 user  staff  272 Nov 20 23:49 Sites
drwxr-xr-x   2 user  staff   68 Dec  2 19:36 Sounds
[ferro:~] user%
```

SET COMMAND ALIASES

1 Type **alias** and a space.

2 Type a short alias.

3 Type a long command in single quotes and press Return.

4 Type the short alias with any appropriate arguments and press Return.

■ The shell executes the long command.

Extra

Most advanced Unix users like to avoid typing unnecessary characters, and thus make extensive use of the `alias` command. Some of the most common and useful aliases appear in the following table. You can save these aliases by storing them in your .tcshrc file.

SHORT ALIAS	LONG COMMAND	DESCRIPTION
cd	pushd	Always maintain the directory stack.
cd..	cd ..	In case you forget the space.
cp	cp -i	Prevent cp from overwriting files.
home	cd ~	Return to Home directory.
ll	ls -l	Long file listing.
ls	ls -F	Always include file-type indicator.
print	lpr	It is easier to remember print than lpr.
rm	rm -i	Prompt for each file deletion.
..	cd ..	Change directory to the parent directory.

```
 Terminal   File   Edit   Scrollback   Font   Window   Help
 000                     Terminal — ttyp8
[ferro:~] user% alias
ll      ls -l
[ferro:~] user% alias ll
ls -l
[ferro:~] user%
```

```
 Terminal   File   Edit   Scrollback   Font   Window   Help
 000                     Terminal — ttyp8
[ferro:~] user% unalias ll
[ferro:~] user% ll
ll: Command not found.
[ferro:~] user%
```

LIST ALL CURRENT ALIASES

1 Type **alias** and press Return.

■ The shell lists all aliases.

2 Type **alias**, a space, then an alias, and press Return.

■ The shell lists the long command for that alias.

DELETE AN ALIAS

1 Type **unalias** and a space.

2 Type the name of an alias and press Return.

■ The alias is no longer defined.

83

SET SHELL VARIABLES

You can affect the way your shell functions by setting shell variables. A shell variable can either have a value or it can have no value — in which case the value is null. You can think of shell variables without values as simple on-or-off switches. If the variable is set, the shell functions as if the switch is on. If the variable is not set, the switch is off.

A shell variable with a value, on the other hand, acts like a blank line on an application that you can fill with the correct information. If you are applying for a job, for example, there is a line labeled Name on the application where you fill in your name, and another labeled E-mail where you write your e-mail address.

To set a variable, you use the set command:

```
set variable
set variable = 'value'
```

The first example sets the variable without giving it a value; it simply sets the switch to on. The second example sets the variable to a value, like filling in the blank on a job application.

If you type set by itself on a line, you see the list of your current shell variables. The shell automatically sets many of these either when you start up the Terminal window or when you type commands. In addition to these automatic variables, you can set a number of other variables that affect how your shell works. These appear in the table on the facing page.

Shell variables normally last as long as the Terminal window is open, although you can use the unset command to get rid of shell variables beforehand. To make your shell settings permanent, see "Edit Your .tcshrc File" in this chapter.

SET SHELL VARIABLES

LIST CURRENT SHELL VARIABLES

1 Type set and press Return.

■ The shell displays all shell variables.

■ This is an example of a Shell variable with no value.

■ This is an example of a Shell variable with a value.

SET A SHELL VARIABLE

1 Type set and a space.

2 Type a variable name and press Return.

■ The shell variable is set but has no value.

Extra

You can set any variables you want, as long as their names start with a letter and contain only letters, numbers, and the underline symbol. However, these variables only affect the shell if their name corresponds to the list of special variables understood by the shell. Some of the most useful special variables appear in the table below.

VARIABLE	SAMPLE VALUE	MEANING
autocorrect	No value	Correct command mistypings.
autologout	30	Exit the shell after 30 minutes of no activity.
complete	enhance	Use improved, case-insensitive, tab completion.
dunique	No value	Remove duplications in the pushd directory stack.
history	75	Show last 75 command lines.
nobeep	No value	Shell commands do not beep at you.
noclobber	No value	Redirection does not overwrite existing files.
path	(/bin /usr/bin)	Your path.
visiblebell	No value	Flash the Terminal window instead of beeping.

There are a number of variables that are automatically set by the shell such as version, uid, user, shlevel, term, and home. You should not change shell variables unless you know what effect they produce.

SET THE VALUE OF A SHELL

1 Type **set** and a space.

2 Type a variable name followed by an equal sign (=).

3 Type a variable value in quotes, and press Return.

■ The shell variable is set to the value.

UNSET A SHELL VARIABLE

1 Type **unset** and a space.

2 Type a name of a variable and press Return.

■ The shell variable is unset.

SET ENVIRONMENT VARIABLES

You can change values that applications inherit by setting environment variables. Environment variables are similar to shell variables. Any command that the shell runs can access environmental variable settings; the environment variables represent the environment in which you run commands. Depending on the command, the shell may or may not use an environment variable to affect the execution of the command.

For example, if you type a V in less, the less command uses the EDITOR environment variable, so that you can edit the file that displays. To set an environment variable, you use the setenv command:

setenv VARIABLE

setenv VARIABLE 'value'

The first example sets the variable without a value, that is, with a null value, and the second example gives a value to

the variable. Note that unlike the set command, the setenv command requires no equal sign. You should type environment variable names in all capital letters to distinguish them from shell variables.

You can get a listing of the current environment variables and their values by typing the printenv command. If you compare this listing to that of shell variables — viewed by typing set — you can see that there is some duplication. Pairs of variables such as HOME/home, TERM/term, and SHLVL/shlvl have the same names and values. This duplication allows the values to be accessed by the shell as well as by commands run within the environment of the shell. These variable pairs automatically link so that changing one changes the other.

If you need to unset an environment variable, you can use the unsetenv command. Your environment variables last only as long as the current Terminal window is open, unless you save the setenv commands in your .tcsrhc file.

SET ENVIRONMENT VARIABLES

LIST CURRENT ENVIRONMENT VARIABLES

1 Type **printenv** and press Return.

■ The shell displays all current environment variables.

SET AN ENVIRONMENT VARIABLE

1 Type **setenv** and a space.

2 Type an environment variable name and press Return.

■ The shell sets the environment variable, but with no value.

Extra

Applications are the primary users of environment variables. This means that each application may have a different set of environment variables that it looks for in order to affect its operation. To know which environment variables to set, you must consult the documentation for the programs you use. You can usually find this information on the manual page by using the man command.

Some environment variables are standard and are understood by many programs. Some of these are listed in the table below. Those marked with a plus symbol (+) are set by the system and should generally be left unchanged.

VARIABLE	SAMPLE VALUE	MEANING
EDITOR	/bin/vi	Your preferred text editor.
HOME (+)	/Users/kynn	Your Home directory.
LANG (+)	en_US	Your preferred language.
PATH	/bin:/usr/bin	Your path.
PWD (+)	/Users/kynn/Music	The current directory.
SHELL (+)	/bin/tcsh	The pathname of your shell.
TERM (+)	vt100	The Terminal application emulates a vt100.
USER (+)	kynn	Your short username.
VISUAL	/bin/vi	Your preferred text editor.

 Terminal   File   Edit   Scrollback   Font   Window   Help

Terminal — ttyp8

```
[ferro:~] user% setenv EDITOR '/usr/bin/pico'
[ferro:~] user% printenv
HOME=/Users/user
SHELL=/bin/tcsh
USER=user
LANG=en_US
PATH=/bin:/sbin:/usr/bin:/usr/sbin
__CF_USER_TEXT_ENCODING=0x1F8:0:0
TERM=vt100
TERMCAP=◆◆◆
TERM_PROGRAM=Apple_Terminal
TERM_PROGRAM_VERSION=81
LOGNAME=user
HOSTTYPE=macintosh
VENDOR=apple
OSTYPE=darwin
MACHTYPE=powerpc
SHLVL=1
PWD=/Users/user
GROUP=staff
HOST=ferro.local.
EDITOR=/usr/bin/pico
```

 Terminal   File   Edit   Scrollback   Font   Window   Help

Terminal — ttyp8

```
[ferro:~] user% unsetenv ARBITRARY
[ferro:~] user%
```

SET THE VALUE OF AN ENVIRONMENT VARIABLE

1 Type **setenv** and a space.

2 Type the name of an environment variable and a space.

3 Type a value in single quotes and press Return.

■ The shell sets the environment variable to the value.

UNSET AN ENVIRONMENT VARIABLE

1 Type **unsetenv** and a space.

2 Type the name of an environment variable and press Return.

■ The environment variable is unset.

SET YOUR PATH

You can change the directories where the shell searches for commands by setting your path variable. Changing your path is necessary if you install new command-line software on your computer.

The default path includes the directories /bin, /sbin, /usr/bin, and /usr/sbin because they are where Mac OS X stores the programs that come with the system. If you add new programs, they may install into other directories such as /usr/local/bin, /usr/local/sbin, or /sw/bin. If you do not change your path, then the only way to run those programs is to type out the full pathname before each, as in /usr/local/bin/vim filename.

You can set your path by typing out a list of pathnames in a set command. Because you are providing a list, you should use parentheses instead of single quotes. For example:

```
set path = (/bin /sbin /usr/bin /usr/sbin
/sw/bin)
```

This command immediately updates your path as well as the PATH environment variable. When you type the filename, it locates any executables stored in the new path; you can use the which command to confirm this.

If you already have a long path value, it may be difficult to retype or copy-and-paste the current path value. Instead, you can add new directories to the path by typing:

```
set path = ($path /new-directory)
```

$path tells the shell to insert the current value of the path variable before setting the value. You type the pathname of the new directory after $path to append it to your path.

Because path is a shell variable, any value that you set lasts only while the current Terminal window is open. To make the changes to your path permanent, you can store the command to set the path in your .tcshrc file.

SET YOUR PATH

Terminal File Edit Scrollback Font Window Help

Terminal — ttyp8

```
[ferro:~] user% set path = ( /bin /sbin /usr/bin /usr/sbin /sw/bin )
[ferro:~] user% which emacs
/sw/bin/emacs
[ferro:~] user%
```

Terminal File Edit Scrollback Font Window Help

Terminal — ttyp8

```
[ferro:~] user% set path = ( $path /usr/local/bin /usr/local/sbin )
[ferro:~] user% which lynx
/usr/local/bin/lynx
[ferro:~] user%
```

SET PATH TO DIRECTORY LIST

1 Type **set path =** and a space.

2 Type a list of directories within parentheses and press Return.

■ The shell sets your path to the directory list.

APPEND TO YOUR PATH

1 Type **set path =** and a space.

2 Type a left parenthesis, **$path**, and a space.

3 Type a list of directories and a right parenthesis, and press Return.

■ The shell adds the new directories to your path.

EDIT YOUR .TCSHRC FILE

Y ou can save the commands to set your prompt, your aliases, your shell variables, your environment variables, and your path so that each time you open Terminal, your shell is configured to your preferences.

You save these commands in a special file called .tcshrc that you create in your Home directory. The period, or dot, at the beginning of the name indicates that the file normally hides from the Mac OS X Finder and from the ls command, although you can still list it using the -a option with the ls command. It is common for Unix programs, such as the tcsh shell, to store their configuration settings in invisible dot-files in your Home directory. These files begin with a period and often end in rc.

The tcsh shell executes all commands in your .tcshrc file whenever you open a Terminal window or start a shell. To create your .tcshrc file, you can use any text editor, including Pico, vi, or emacs, and enter one command per line.

You can also use the example tcsh files that are located in the /usr/share/tcsh/examples directory on your computer. You can add a line at the very beginning of your .tcshrc file as follows:

```
source /usr/share/tcsh/examples/rc
```

The source command tells the shell to read the commands from a text file and run them as if they are being entered directly into the Terminal program. As a result, this command in your .tcshrc file tells the shell, upon starting, to run the commands stored in the /usr/share/tcsh/examples/ rc file. For more information, you can type less /usr/share/ tcsh/examples/README. You can also store your aliases, variables, and environment variables in separate files as described in the README file, although it is acceptable to set them all within your .tcshrc file.

EDIT YOUR .TCSHRC FILE

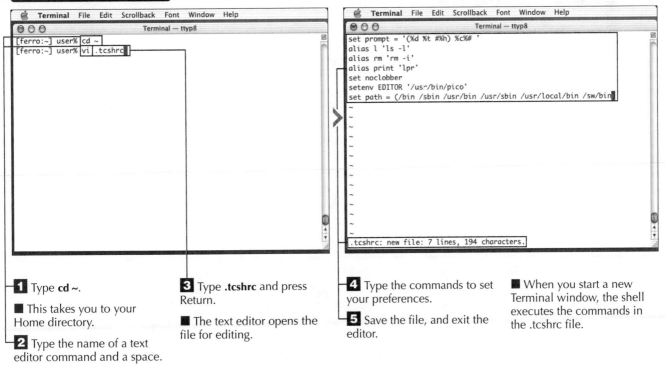

■1 Type cd ~.

■ This takes you to your Home directory.

■2 Type the name of a text editor command and a space.

■3 Type .tcshrc and press Return.

■ The text editor opens the file for editing.

■4 Type the commands to set your preferences.

■5 Save the file, and exit the editor.

■ When you start a new Terminal window, the shell executes the commands in the .tcshrc file.

RECALL YOUR COMMAND HISTORY

You can list the commands that you have typed before by using the `history` command. You can also use special characters to repeat or edit commands you have already typed.

The `history` command lists the commands you have typed since opening this Terminal window, along with the time at which each command was run. The `history` command lists the 100 most recent commands, provided that you have typed more than 100 commands into the current Terminal window.

You can repeat commands or portions of commands using the history recall built into the shell. You do this by typing an exclamation point (!), or bang, followed by a special code that indicates what information from your history you want to recall. There are a number of different history codes that you can use, the simplest being two exclamation points (! !); this code repeats the last command that you

typed. If you type an exclamation point and then some letters, the shell searches through the command history for the most recent command beginning with those letters, and repeats that command. In both cases, the shell displays the recalled command immediately before executing it. A list of other history codes appears on the facing page.

You can also edit the previous line by using a caret (^). This is a method to correct a mistake you may have made, or to change a command so that it applies to different files. You use the caret as follows:

```
^old-text^new-text
```

The command is repeated, but with the *old-text* replaced by the *new-text*. For example, if you have just typed **cd /usr/shrae** and you want to correct yourself, you can type **^shrae^share** and press Return.

RECALL YOUR COMMAND HISTORY

```
   Terminal   File   Edit   Scrollback   Font   Window   Help
   ● ● ●                  Terminal — ttyp8
[ferro:~/Images] user% history
    1  1:31      cd Pictures/
    2  1:31      ls
    3  1:31      mv my-dog.jpg ../Images/
    4  1:31      cd ../Images/
    5  1:31      ls
    6  1:31      history
[ferro:~/Images] user%
```

```
   Terminal   File   Edit   Scrollback   Font   Window   Help
   ● ● ●                  Terminal — ttyp8
[ferro:~/Images] user% ls -l my-dog.jpg
-rw-------  1 user  staff  25762 Nov 18 15:13 my-dog.jpg
[ferro:~/Images] user% !!
ls -l my-dog.jpg
-rw-------  1 user  staff  25762 Nov 18 15:13 my-dog.jpg
[ferro:~/Images] user%
```

LIST COMMAND HISTORY

1 Type **history** and press Return.

■ The shell lists all the commands you have typed into the current Terminal window.

REPEAT THE LAST COMMAND

1 Type **!!** and press Return.

■ The shell displays the previous command.

■ The shell executes the previous command.

Extra

The table below lists some of the most useful history codes. You can use these history substitutions anywhere in your command line. For example, if you have just moved a series of files with the `mv` command and you want to change their file permissions, you can type **chmod +r !!*** to use the `chmod` command on the arguments supplied to the `mv` command that you have just executed.

HISTORY CODE	MEANING
!!	The previous command.
!!*	The argument of the previous command.
!!^	The first argument of the previous command.
!!$	The last argument of the previous command.
!text	The last command beginning with text.
!?text?	The last command containing text.
!number	The command number from the history command.
!-3	The command three commands ago.

Terminal File Edit Scrollback Font Window Help

Terminal — ttyp8

```
[ferro:~/Documents/To Do Lists] user% history
   19  1:35   cd
   20  1:35   cd Documents
   21  1:35   ls
   22  1:35   cd "To Do Lists"
   23  1:35   ls
   24  1:35   wc priorities.txt
   25  1:35   wc k-words.txt
   26  1:35   grep -i '^ky' k-words.txt
   27  1:36   ls
   28  1:36   history
[ferro:~/Documents/To Do Lists] user% !wc
wc k-words.txt
   2220    2220   18874 k-words.txt
[ferro:~/Documents/To Do Lists] user%
```

Terminal File Edit Scrollback Font Window Help

Terminal — ttyp8

```
[ferro:~/Documents/To Do Lists] user% grap 'keep' k-words.txt
grap: Command not found.
[ferro:~/Documents/To Do Lists] user% ^grap^grep
grep 'keep' k-words.txt
keep
keepable
keeper
keeperess
keepering
keeperless
keepership
keeping
keepsake
keepsaky
keepworthy
[ferro:~/Documents/To Do Lists] user%
```

REPEAT A SPECIFIC COMMAND

1 Type !.

2 Type the first few letters of a previous command and press Return.

■ The shell executes the most recent command that begins with those letters.

CORRECT A MISTAKE IN THE LAST COMMAND

1 Mistype a command and press Return.

2 Type ^ and the mistyped portion of the command.

3 Type ^ and the corrected portion of the command.

4 Press Return.

■ The shell executes the last command with the correction in place.

START A NEW SHELL

You can start another shell by typing the pathname of the shell. Running commands in a sub-shell can preserve your shell settings or allow you to use a different shell program.

Each time you start a new shell, it executes the commands stored in your .tcshrc file — or the appropriate dot-file for the shell if it is not tcsh — and gives you a new prompt. Most shell variables are set to their initial default values, but environment variables remain set with any values they had in the original shell.

When the new shell starts up, it has a clean command history. If you type **history**, you see a very short list that does not include any of the commands executed in the original shell. Likewise, after you exit the new shell, the command history for that shell does not appear in the history of the original shell. You only see the command to start the newer shell.

If you are done using a new shell, you can close it by typing the `exit` command. This returns you to your original shell. If you changed your current directory in the new shell, you find yourself back in the original directory when the new shell exits.

Mac OS X comes with three shells installed. The tcsh shell is the default, and the one that this book assumes you are using. The Bourne-again shell, known as bash, is a popular alternative to the tcsh. The Z shell, zsh, offers many customization opportunities for Unix power users. The pathnames for these shells, respectively, are /bin/tcsh, /bin/bash, and /bin/zsh. For more information about the bash and zsh shells, see "Work with the Bourne-Again Shell" and "Work with the Z Shell" later in this chapter.

START A NEW SHELL

Terminal File Edit Scrollback Font Window Help

Terminal — ttyp8

```
[ferro:~] user% /bin/bash
bash-2.05a$ 
```

Terminal File Edit Scrollback Font Window Help

Terminal — ttyp8

```
bash-2.05a$ cd Pictures/
bash-2.05a$ ls -l
total 200
-rw-r--r--  1 user  staff  23287 Dec  2 02:11 wwnkd_029.gif
-rw-r--r--  1 user  staff  21614 Dec  2 02:11 wwnkd_030.gif
-rw-r--r--  1 user  staff  25167 Dec  2 02:11 wwnkd_031.gif
-rw-r--r--  1 user  staff  23046 Dec  2 02:11 wwnkd_032.gif
bash-2.05a$ cd ..
bash-2.05a$ pwd
/Users/user
bash-2.05a$ which pwd
/bin/pwd
bash-2.05a$ exit
exit
[ferro:~] user% 
```

START A SHELL PROCESS

■ A new shell process starts.

1 Type the full pathname of a shell you want to start.

EXIT THE NEW SHELL

1 Type **exit** and press Return.

■ The shell exits, returning you to your original shell.

■ The path remains what it was before you started the new shell.

CHANGE YOUR SHELL

You can change your default shell from tcsh to bash or zsh, so that the Terminal program automatically starts with your preferred shell. You may never want to change your shell; the tcsh shell is a very useful and user-friendly shell program. However, many people like the bash shell, especially those from a Linux background, and you may wish to use that shell instead. For more information about the different shells, see "Work with the Bourne-Again Shell" and "Work with the Z Shell" later in this chapter.

Changing your shell is a two-step process. The first step is to use the chpass command to change your shell record in the master password file. You can update this file, which is located at the pathname /etc/master.passwd, by typing the following:

```
chpass -s /path/to/shell
```

For example, *chpass -s /bin/zsh* makes your default shell the Z shell, and *chpass -s /bin/bash* changes your default shell to the Bourne-again shell.

After you update the master password file, you need to enter the changes into the NetInfo database. NetInfo is a database maintained by Mac OS X for keeping track of many things related to the operation of your computer, including default shells. To make your shell change take effect in NetInfo, type the following command exactly as it appears here:

```
sudo cat /etc/master.passwd | sudo niload -m
passwd /
```

This example uses the sudo command to allow you access to files and permissions you normally would not be able to change. For this reason, you must make sure that you do not make a mistake typing the command. After you press the Return key, you see a prompt asking you to enter a password. At this point, you can enter your normal user password and press Return.

CHANGE YOUR SHELL

1 Type **chpass -s** and a space.

2 Type the full pathname to a shell and press Return.

■ The chpass command updates the master password file.

3 Type the command to update the NetInfo database and press Return.

4 Enter your password and press Return.

■ This command updates the NetInfo database, and changes your shell.

WORK WITH THE BOURNE-AGAIN SHELL

You can use bash instead of tcsh as your primary shell, or you can start the bash shell from the command line. The Bourne-again shell is a popular alternative to tcsh, which is commonly used on Linux computers.

The original shell on early Unix systems, /bin/sh, is known as the Bourne shell after the programmer who wrote it, Steven Bourne. The bash shell takes its name from Bourne in a clever play on words. The Bourne-again shell is more compatible with the commands of the original /bin/sh program than the tcsh shell, which is based on the later C shell.

If you are a typical user, you may not see a great difference between the tcsh and bash shells. You can type commands as you normally would, redirect output, and perform most tasks without problems. The first obvious difference is a change in your prompt, letting you know that you are now running the bash shell.

You notice the second difference if you try to change your shell settings. The Bourne-again shell uses different commands to set variables. To set a variable, for either shell or environment, in the bash shell, you type the following:

```
variable-name=value
```

No set or setenv command is necessary, just the variable name and value, separated by an equal sign. All variables are automatically shell variables unless you export them as environment variables. To make the value of a variable available as an environment variable for use by other programs, you can type the command export *variable-name*.

Another important difference is that the bash shell does not run the commands in the .tcshrc file when you start a new shell. Instead, it executes the commands in the .bashrc file in your Home directory.

WORK WITH THE BOURNE-AGAIN SHELL

START BASH FROM TCSH

1 Type **/bin/bash** and press Return.

■ The shell starts a new bash shell.

SET AN ENVIRONMENT VARIABLE

1 Type a variable name, then **=**, and the value of the variable, and press Return.

2 Type **export**, a space, and the variable name, and press Return.

■ The variable is designated as an environment variable.

WORK WITH THE Z SHELL

I f you are an advanced user, you can write functions that perform shell tasks in the highly configurable Z shell. If you are new to Unix, this may be much more than you need.

The differences between shells are most apparent when you are writing shell scripts, as these scripts use the advanced features of the shell. The Z shell uses a number of functions that you can define in order to override or change default behavior.

The Z shell was created to be compatible with another early shell known as the Korn shell, or ksh. If you are going to be using your shell a great deal and want to become more familiar with shell customization, the Z shell may be a good choice for you.

Many of the built-in commands familiar from the tcsh shell have different command names and values in the zsh shell. For example, you can set zsh shell options — similar to shell

variables in tcsh — by using the command `setopt`, and you can set and export environment variables as you would in bash. Instead of running the contents of the .tcshrc file when a shell starts, the zsh shell executes commands in the .zshrc file in your Home directory. Aliases in the zsh shell must be set using the following syntax, which differs from the tcsh shell by the requirement of an equal sign:

```
alias short-alias='command and options'
```

You can take full advantage of the extensibility of the Z shell by creating specialized functions in your .zshrc file. A function creates a command, similar to an alias but with more flexibility and control. To learn about Z shell functions, you can see the manual pages for zsh by typing **man zsh**.

WORK WITH THE Z SHELL

```
  Terminal   File   Edit   Scrollback   Font   Window   Help
                        Terminal — ttyp8
[ferro:~] user% /bin/zsh
ferro% 
```

```
  Terminal   File   Edit   Scrollback   Font   Window   Help
                        Terminal — ttyp8
[ferro:~] user% /bin/zsh
ferro% function cp() { command cp -i "$@" }
ferro% which cp
cp () {
        command cp -i "$@"
}
ferro% cd Pictures
ferro% cp wwnkd_030.gif wwnkd_031.gif
overwrite wwnkd_031.gif? no
ferro% 
```

START ZSH FROM TCSH

1 Type **/bin/zsh** and press Return.

■ The shell starts a new zsh shell.

CREATE A SIMPLE Z SHELL FUNCTION

1 Type **function cp()**, a space, and then type **{**.

2 Type **command cp -i "$@"**, a space, and then type **}**.

3 Press Return.

■ The Z shell defines a new command named **cp**.

SUSPEND THE CURRENT PROCESS

You can suspend a process to regain control of the command line, and from that point, kill the process, move it into the background, or leave it suspended until you are ready to restart it. Just as almost everything that makes up a Unix system is a file, almost everything that a Unix system does is a *process*. The shell that responds to the commands you enter in a Terminal window is a process. Each command you enter is a process. When you ask the system what processes are currently running, that too is a process. Just as Unix makes little distinction between system files, application files, and personal files, it makes little distinction between system processes, applications, and the commands that you enter in a Terminal window. The activity of the system is implemented as a series of processes.

Unlike some operating systems, Unix systems like Mac OS X allow you to gather a lot of information about the processes that are running on your system. In fact, you can start, stop,

and suspend them if you have sufficient privileges. You can also move processes to the background so that you can issue other commands.

Every process has a *process ID* — a unique numeric identifier that the system assigns. While you enter a command in your shell, that shell is an active process. When you press Return, the command that you just entered starts running, and your shell is suspended until that process completes.

You can suspend a process by pressing Control + Z. When you suspend a process, it cannot run. It does not access files, accumulate run time, or task the CPU. A suspended process is also referred to as a *stopped job*.

SUSPEND THE CURRENT PROCESS

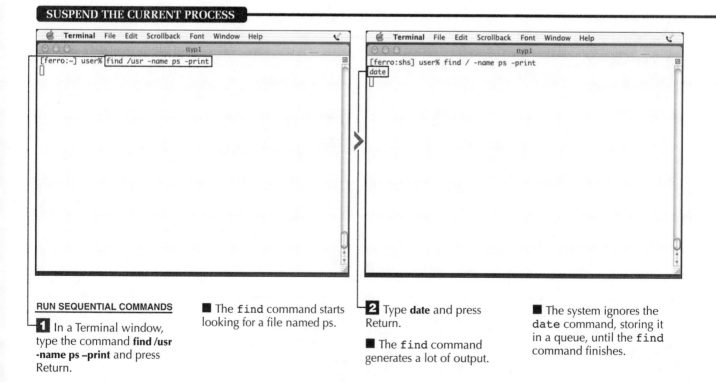

RUN SEQUENTIAL COMMANDS

1 In a Terminal window, type the command **find /usr -name ps –print** and press Return.

■ The find command starts looking for a file named ps.

2 Type **date** and press Return.

■ The find command generates a lot of output.

■ The system ignores the date command, storing it in a queue, until the find command finishes.

Extra

On a multiprocessing system such as Unix, many processes appear to be running at the same time. They are actually running in quick succession, taking turns using the system's CPU and memory. The system tracks the resources that each process requires and restores the process environment as needed each time a process gets its turn to run. At almost any instant in time, most processes are waiting for some resource, whether that resource is a response from the user, data from the disk, or simply a turn at the processor.

Processes change state frequently while they are running. Process states include running, sleeping, stopped, and terminated.

When you suspend a process, you essentially put it on hold so that you can run other commands. Similar to putting a caller on hold, suspending a process means that no progress is made as long as that process is suspended. The process is stopped, awaiting your instruction to start again or to terminate and release all of its resources.

You can open a second Terminal window when you are working on the system, but this is not an option if you are logged in remotely.

Terminal File Edit Scrollback Font Window Help

ttyp1

```
[ferro:~] user% man date
```

Terminal File Edit Scrollback Font Window Help

ttyp1

```
NAME
     date - display or set date and time

SYNOPSIS
     date [-nu] [-r seconds] [+format]
       [[[[[cc]yy]mm]dd]hh]mm[.ss]

DESCRIPTION
     date displays the current date and time when invoked without argumen
ts.
     Providing arguments will format the date and time in a user-defined
way
     or set the date.  Only the superuser may set the date.

     The options are as follows:

     -n      The utility timed(8) is used to synchronize the clocks on gr
oups
[1]  +   491 Suspended                      man date
[ferro:~] user%
[ferro:~] user%
```

SUSPEND A PROCESS

1 Type **man date** and press Return.

2 Press Control + Z to suspend the process.

3 Press Return.

■ Unix assigns a job number to the suspended process and displays its process ID.

■ The system responds with another prompt indicating that you have control of the shell.

RESTART A PROCESS

You can save some work by restarting a suspended process. Instead of running the job again, you can pick up where you left off when you suspended the process. In addition, restarting a suspended process frees resources tied up by that process.

All processes that you run, suspended or not, are associated with the particular shell in which they were started. If you suspend a single process in each of two Terminal windows, for example, each of these processes will have 1 as its job number. At the same time, each of these suspended processes will also have a unique process ID. Where each job number is related to the parent shell and only the parent shell, each process ID is related to the entire system. This means that you can refer to a process by its job number only in the shell in which it was started.

Job numbers are always small numbers like 1 or 4. While you can accumulate a large number of suspended jobs if you work at it, in practice this is never done. Process IDs are usually large numbers like 325 or 5234. The system assigns these numbers in some fashion, reusing the numbers as needed. If you see a process running today with the process ID 4321, you might not see this number used again for months. Process numbers that are small like 1 or 69 are assigned to system tasks.

To restart a suspended process, use the fg (foreground) command. If only one suspended process is in your current shell, that process restarts. If there are several suspended processes, the one most recently suspended will restart. To restart a particular suspended process, enter the fg command followed by its job number.

RESTART A PROCESS

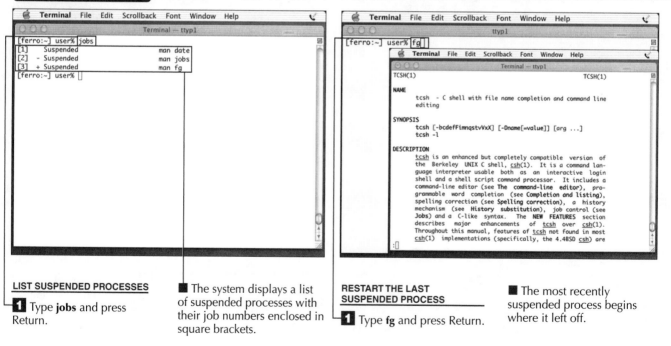

LIST SUSPENDED PROCESSES

1 Type **jobs** and press Return.

■ The system displays a list of suspended processes with their job numbers enclosed in square brackets.

RESTART THE LAST SUSPENDED PROCESS

1 Type **fg** and press Return.

■ The most recently suspended process begins where it left off.

Extra

You can only restart a process that has been suspended. You cannot restart a process that has run to completion or a process you have terminated. Each process has a life of its own. Even if you run the same command seven times in a row, each running is an independent process.

You can restart processes by bringing them back into the foreground, and they will then continue running as if they had not been suspended. You can also restart processes by sending them to the background and continue entering commands from the shell from which these processes were run.

If you press Control + D to exit a shell in which you have suspended processes, the shell alerts you to the suspended processes. The message "There are suspended jobs" appears. This warning ensures that you do not forget about commands that you suspended. You can still exit the shell by pressing Control + D again. If you exit the Terminal window by clicking the red button, no alert appears. The suspended processes are quietly killed when you close the window.

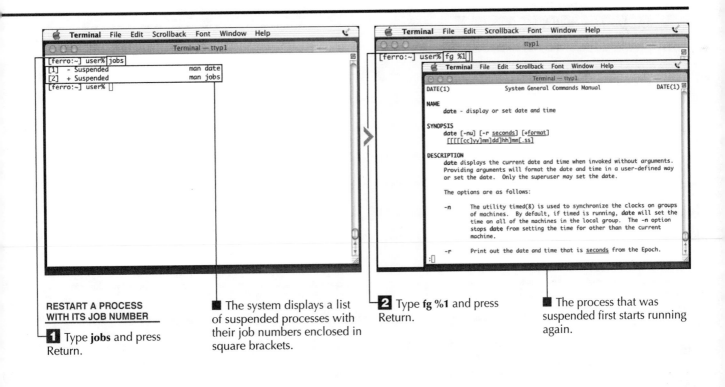

RESTART A PROCESS WITH ITS JOB NUMBER

1 Type **jobs** and press Return.

■ The system displays a list of suspended processes with their job numbers enclosed in square brackets.

2 Type **fg %1** and press Return.

■ The process that was suspended first starts running again.

RUN A PROCESS IN THE BACKGROUND

Running a command as a background process allows you to continue entering commands while that process runs. A process running in the background is not suspended; it continues to execute. When you run a command in the Terminal application, the output from the command appears on your screen. Until the command finishes, no other commands can run. This is called *foreground processing*. When the command finishes running, your command prompt returns.

Unix allows you to run commands in the foreground or in the background. Unlike commands in the foreground, commands run as background processes allow you to enter additional commands. Your shell continues prompting and you can continue entering commands.

The simplest way to run commands in the background is to start them in the background. You can run a command in the background by adding an ampersand (&) to the end of the command line. For example, if you enter a find

command, type an ampersand at the end of the line, and press Return, the find command continues processing and writes to your screen as it locates files that meet your search criteria. At the same time, you have control of the command line and can issue other commands while the find command continues to run.

Like suspended processes, jobs that run in the background have both a job number and a process ID. Both suspended processes and background processes appear in the listing when you use the jobs command. The important difference between a suspended process and a background process is that a background process continues to run while a suspended process is inactive.

Running commands as background processes allows you to get more work done in a single Terminal window. If you press Control + D to exit a shell while there are background processes running, the system issues a warning.

RUN A PROCESS IN THE BACKGROUND

1 Type **find / -name fg –print & ** and press Return.

■ The job number and process ID of the background process appears.

■ A message displays indicating that your find command cannot search some directories.

2 Type **date** and press Return.

■ The find command continues running in the background, while you enter the date command and get your output.

Apply It

You can place a process into the background by first suspending it with Control + Z and then using the `bg` (background) command to move it into the background. If you run a command, such as `find / -name findme -print`, and then suspend it by pressing Control + Z, you can restart it in the background with a `bg` command, such as `bg %3`. The command continues running and searching for your files while allowing you to enter other commands at the shell prompt.

TYPE THIS:

```
find / -name findme -print
control+Z
bg
pwd
date
```

RESULT:

```
/Users/user
Thu May  1 11:12:13 EDT 2003
```

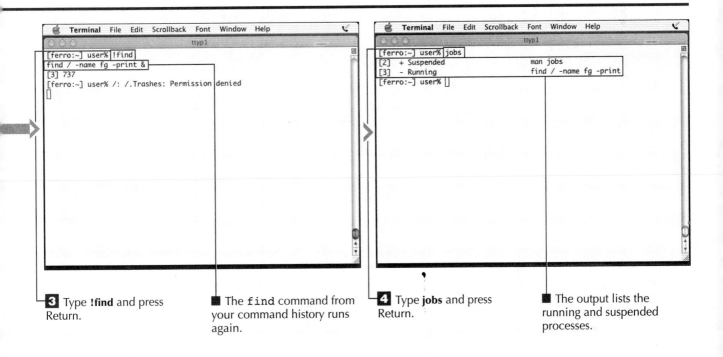

3 Type **!find** and press Return.

■ The `find` command from your command history runs again.

4 Type **jobs** and press Return.

■ The output lists the running and suspended processes.

KILL A PROCESS

You can use the `kill` command to stop a running or a suspended process. By halting a command that you mistyped, you can avoid wasting system resources or performing a process that you did not intend to run.

Stopping a process that is running on a Unix system is called *killing* it. To kill a running process, you use the `kill` command followed by the process ID of the process. For example, `kill 1234` would kill the process with process ID 1234. To kill a suspended process, you use the `kill` command followed by the job number. For example, `kill %2` would kill the second suspended process.

After you kill a process, you cannot restart it. You can run the same command again, but this action starts a new process.

You can kill a process by name. The variant of the `kill` command used for this purpose is called `killall`. If you enter `killall man`, you will kill all `man` commands, even

if they are running in other Terminal windows. When you issue the `killall` command, the system looks for commands you are running.

As a normal non-root user, you can only kill processes that you have started. As a root user, however, you can kill any process on the system. Unix provides little protection from making mistakes that can bring your system down. One of the worst mistakes that root users can make on a Unix system is to enter `kill 1` when they mean to enter `kill %1`. The user's intention is to kill a suspended process. Typing the command without the % kills a process known as `init` and will likely crash your system. For this reason, most disciplined system administrators avoid using the root account except when there is no other way to accomplish a job.

KILL A PROCESS

```
 Terminal   File   Edit   Scrollback   Font   Window   Help
                            ttyp1
[ferro:~] user% jobs
[2]  + Suspended                    man jobs
[ferro:~] user% kill %2
[ferro:~] user%
```

```
 Terminal   File   Edit   Scrollback   Font   Window   Help
                            ttyp1
[ferro:~] user% ps
  PID  TT  STAT      TIME COMMAND
  402 std  S      0:00.67 -tcsh (tcsh)
  457 p2   S+     0:00.27 -tcsh (tcsh)
  462 p2   S      0:00.01 man date
  463 p2   S      0:00.01 less -se /usr/share/man/cat1/date.1
  494 p3   S+     0:00.20 -tcsh (tcsh)
[ferro:~] user% kill 462
[ferro:~] user%
```

**KILL A PROCESS
BY JOB NUMBER**

1 Type **jobs** and press Return.

2 Type **kill** followed by a job ID number, such as %2, and press Return.

■ The second suspended process terminates.

KILL A PROCESS BY PROCESS ID

1 Type **ps** and press Return.

2 Type **kill** followed by a process ID from the list displayed and press Return.

■ The second suspended process terminates.

Apply It

You can use the `kill` command to send signals to running processes. The `kill` command is useful for terminating a process. Although most people talk about the `kill` command as if its sole function were to terminate processes, this is not the case. In fact, the `kill` command's real function is to send very short messages called *signals* to running processes to control the behavior of these processes. The default `kill` command — the command without an argument — sends a signal that asks the process to terminate. Systems people often refer to the default signal as a SIGTERM. Another common signal, referred to as a SIGHUP, for *hang up*, is most often used to tell a running process that it should go back and re-read its configuration file. Many system processes remain unaware that their configuration files have changed unless you send this signal to them. Another often-used signal is SIGKILL, a signal used to terminate a process that is not terminated with SIGTERM.

TYPE THIS:

```
[ferro:~] user% man kill
control+Z
[ferro:~] user% kill -KILL <type the process id>
[ferro:~] user% jobs
```

RESULT:

The process is killed.

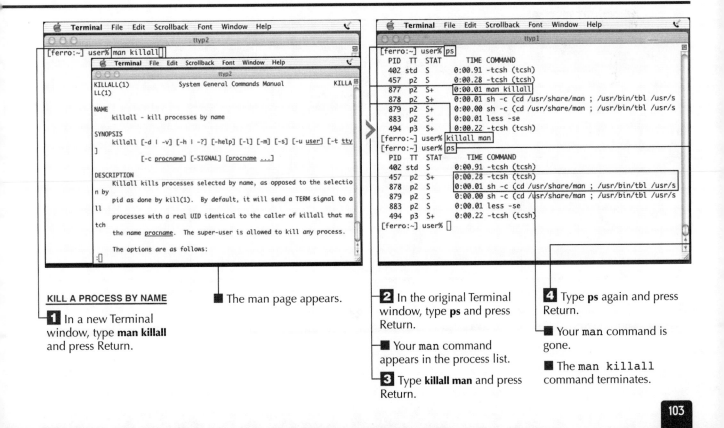

KILL A PROCESS BY NAME

1 In a new Terminal window, type **man killall** and press Return.

■ The man page appears.

2 In the original Terminal window, type **ps** and press Return.

■ Your `man` command appears in the process list.

3 Type **killall man** and press Return.

4 Type **ps** again and press Return.

■ Your `man` command is gone.

■ The `man killall` command terminates.

LIST ACTIVE PROCESSES

You can use the `ps` command to find out what processes are running on your system or to find the process ID for a job that you want to kill. To kill a process by its process ID, you obviously must know its process ID. Fortunately, Unix systems provide a command that displays information about running processes, including the process IDs. That command is `ps`.

You can also use the `ps` command to display a list of all processes that are running on your system. Depending on the arguments that you provide, this list can include information about the time each process started and who started each process.

The `ps` command by itself only displays a list of the commands you are running. To list system commands and the commands that other users are issuing, you add arguments to your `ps` command. The `ps -aux` command shows all processes running on the system and provides details on each one.

The `ps -a` command lists all users' processes. You will own some of these processes, while others start when the system boots.

The `ps -u` command adds information such as when each process started, as well as the how much CPU and memory each process is using.

The `ps -x` command adds processes that are not associated with a particular Terminal window, such as the processes started before you logged on.

The most commonly used `ps` command for Mac OS X users is `ps -aux`, combining the most useful command options.

By using the ps command followed by a vertical bar, commonly referred to in Unix as a *pipe*, you can restrict the output that it return to your specific interests. For example, `ps -aux | grep init` displays the init process and other processes that contain this string in their names.

LIST ACTIVE PROCESSES

```
Terminal  File  Edit  Scrollback  Font  Window  Help
ttyp1
[ferro:~] user% ps
  PID  TT  STAT    TIME COMMAND
  402 std  S     0:01.04 -tcsh (tcsh)
 1019 p2   S     0:00.23 -tcsh (tcsh)
 1024 p2   S     0:00.01 man ps
 1025 p2   S     0:00.01 sh -c (cd /usr/share/man ; /usr/bin/tbl /usr/s
 1026 p2   S     0:00.01 sh -c (cd /usr/share/man ; /usr/bin/tbl /usr/s
 1029 p2   S     0:00.00 /usr/bin/col
 1030 p2   S     0:00.01 less -se
 1038 p2   S+    0:00.08 python
[ferro:~] user% []
```

```
Terminal  File  Edit  Scrollback  Font  Window  Help
ttyp1
[ferro:~] user% ps -u
USER   PID %CPU %MEM    VSZ   RSS  TT STAT STARTED     TIME COMMAND
user   402  0.0  0.4   5912   980 std  S   8:05AM   0:01.07 -tcsh (
user  1019  0.0  0.4   5912   976  p2  S   1:09PM   0:00.23 -tcsh (
user  1024  0.0  0.1   1452   308  p2  S   1:09PM   0:00.01 man ps
user  1025  0.0  0.2   1828   460  p2  S   1:09PM   0:00.01 sh -c (
user  1026  0.0  0.1   1828   300  p2  S   1:09PM   0:00.01 sh -c (
user  1029  0.0  0.1   1300   308  p2  S   1:09PM   0:00.00 /usr/bi
user  1030  0.0  0.1   1392   340  p2  S   1:09PM   0:00.01 less -s
user  1038  0.0  0.6  15024  1496  p2  S+  1:09PM   0:00.08 python
[ferro:~] user%
```

1 In a Terminal window, type **ps** and press Return.

■ The screen displays a list of the processes you are running.

2 Type **ps -u** and press Return.

■ The screen displays a detailed list of the processes you are running.

Extra

The columns in the output of the `ps -aux` command provide a lot of information about running processes. This information can help you understand who is using your system, what is running, and sometimes why the systems is running slowly. Each of these columns is explained in the table below.

PS COLUMN	MEANING
USER	Username of the person running the process.
PID	Numeric process ID.
%CPU	Percentage of CPU resources the process is using.
%MEM	Percentage of memory the process is using.
VSZ	Virtual size of the process in kilobytes.
RSS	Size of process in memory.
TT	Associated control terminal, or ?? if there is no associated terminal.
STAT	Status of the process.
STARTED	Time, if started today, or date a process was started.
TIME	Accumulated run time.
COMMAND	Command that is running, complete with arguments.

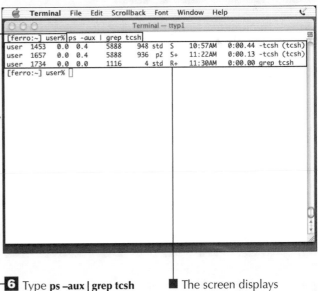

3 In the Terminal window, type **ps -aux** and a space.

4 Type a vertical bar (|) and a space.

5 Type **more** and press Return.

■ The screen displays details for all processes running on the system.

6 Type **ps –aux | grep tcsh** and press Return.

■ The screen displays information for each `tcsh` process, plus the `grep` command used to select these processes.

MONITOR THE TOP PROCESSES

You can use the top command to find out which processes are using the most resources on your system. This knowledge is especially useful when your system is running slowly. Although processes appear to be running simultaneously, they actually take turns using the CPU. This sharing happens at an extremely rapid rate, but you can view some process details using commands such as ps and top.

While the ps command allows you to view important statistics related to processes — such as how long they have been running or how much memory they are using — the ps output display order is somewhat random. To examine processes to determine how much demand they are placing on the system, another tool is more appropriate. That tool is top.

The top command orders its output to display the tasks using the bulk of the CPU time available at the top of the list. The columns in the top output are similar to those that

the ps command displays. In addition, the top command provides useful information about processes in general and system performance.

The information included in the top output for each process includes the process ID (PID), the simple command without arguments, and the percentage of CPU usage. It also includes information on threads and memory sizes.

Some of the information the top command displays tells you a lot about system performance. For example, if a system is more than 90 percent idle, you know that the system is not running more processes than it can handle and you can assume that performance is good. Another good indicator of performance is the system load. The top command has numerous options that you can use to alter its behavior. For more information on these options, type **man top** and press Return.

MONITOR PROCESSES WITH TOP

```
 Terminal   File   Edit   Scrollback   Font   Window   Help

                            ttyp1

[ferro:~] user% top
```

```
 Terminal   File   Edit   Scrollback   Font   Window   Help

                            ttyp1
Processes:  48 total, 2 running, 46 sleeping... 104 threads        1
Load Avg:  0.26, 0.19, 0.06      CPU usage:  2.8% user, 5.6% sys, 91.6
SharedLibs: num =     7, resident = 2.21M code, 136K data, 568K LinkEdit
MemRegions: num = 2683, resident = 22.5M + 6.80M private, 38.1M shared
PhysMem:  29.3M wired, 53.0M active, 62.8M inactive,  145M used,  111M f
VM: 1.01G + 3.62M    5331(0) pageins, 1(0) pageouts

  PID COMMAND     %CPU   TIME   #TH #PRTS #MREGS RPRVT  RSHRD  RSIZE  V
 1097 top         5.6%  0:00.71   1    14    18   228K   328K   524K  1
 1094 lookupd     0.0%  0:00.57   3    16    47   340K   512K   876K  1
 1047 tcsh        0.0%  0:00.22   1    10    17   508K   656K   976K  5
 1046 login       0.0%  0:00.81   1    12    33   248K   380K   576K  1
 1038 python      0.0%  0:00.08   1    11    20   516K  1016K  1.46M  1
 1030 less        0.0%  0:00.01   1     9    14    64K   384K   340K  1
 1029 col         0.0%  0:00.00   1     9    13   120K   304K   308K  1
 1026 sh          0.0%  0:00.01   1     8    13    56K   712K   296K  1
 1025 sh          0.0%  0:00.01   1     9    13    48K   712K   456K  1
 1024 man         0.0%  0:00.01   1     9    14    88K   324K   308K  1
 1019 tcsh        0.0%  0:00.23   1    10    16   504K   656K   972K  5
 1018 login       0.0%  0:00.81   1    12    33   244K   380K   572K  1
  417 Grab        0.0%  2:30.65   4   133   151  4.40M  8.07M  9.20M  6
[ferro:~] user%
```

1 In a Terminal window, type **top** and press Return.

2 Press Control + C.

■ The **top** command displays information about processes.

■ The **top** command stops processing.

Apply It

You can use the `top` command to determine how hard your system is working. The load averages that the `top` command displays tell you how many jobs, on average, were ready to run but were waiting for access to the CPU. Small load averages like those shown in the `top` output support the conclusion that the CPU on this particular system is not busy and that processes rarely have to wait for access to it. Load averages above four may indicate a system that is burdened. Load averaging higher than 10 indicates a system with excessive CPU contention.

You can use the `uptime` command to see how many users are logged on and to display load averages. This command tells you how long the system has been up, how many users are currently logged on (though it counts each Terminal as a separate logon), and the 1-minute, 5-minute, and 15-minute load averages.

TYPE THIS:	RESULT:
uptime	2:26 PM 4:18, 3 users, load averages: 0.03, 0.03, 0.01

Terminal   File   Edit   Scrollback   Font   Window   Help

ttyp1

```
[ferro:~] user% top -e
```

3 Type **top –e** and press Return.

Terminal   File   Edit   Scrollback   Font   Window   Help

ttyp1

```
Processes:  48 total, 2 running, 46 sleeping... 103 threads
Load Avg:  0.23, 0.17, 0.02    CPU usage:  2.7% user, 2.1% sys, 95.3
Networks:      1508 ipkts/177K            3136 opkts /2997K
Disks:      145707 reads/635732K        41968 writes/172599K
VM:            5331 pageins               1 pageouts

 PID COMMAND      %CPU   TIME    FAULTS  PAGEINS  COW_FAULTS MSGS_SENT
1107 top          1.9%  0:00.30  998     0        22         4241
1094 lookupd      0.0%  0:00.58  343     0        42         167
1047 tcsh         0.0%  0:00.24  493     0        79         74
1046 login        0.0%  0:00.81  282     0        50         145
1038 python       0.0%  0:00.08  474     0        70         58
1030 less         0.0%  0:00.01  182     0        24         42
1029 col          0.0%  0:00.00  168     0        22         41
1026 sh           0.0%  0:00.01  131     0        53         12
1025 sh           0.0%  0:00.01  152     0        23         30
1024 man          0.0%  0:00.01  109     0        12         38
1019 tcsh         0.0%  0:00.23  485     0        78         71
1018 login        0.0%  0:00.81  299     0        51         145
 417 Grab        50.0%  2:35.93  89853   285      189        212080
```

■ The `top` command displays processing events for the `top` processes.

WRITE A SIMPLE SHELL SCRIPT

You can place commands that you repeatedly execute in a file and execute these commands by entering the name of the file. A file of Unix commands that you execute is called a *shell script*. Writing shell scripts can save you a lot of work and make it unnecessary for you to remember complicated commands.

The Unix commands that you place in a script are commands that you might have entered in a Terminal window. When you run the script, the system executes the commands in the order entered. Shell scripting is a very basic form of Unix programming, although scripts can run the gamut from a simple list of commands to elaborate programs with looping, embedded functions, and complex data structures.

If you enter a command such as ls in a Terminal window, the shell passes the command to the kernel for execution. The result is a listing of your files. If you enter the same

command in a file and execute that file, you also get a listing of your files. While there is no advantage to executing a simple command such as ls using a script, the advantage to scripting becomes readily obvious when you need to execute complex commands or many commands in a certain order. In fact, script writing is so efficient that nearly everyone who manages a Unix system automates routine tasks by writing scripts.

You can write shell scripts that ask the person running them to supply some information or that make use of the user's shell variables. For example, one of the simplest shell scripts you can write greets a user when he or she executes it. If you place the command echo hello, $USER in a file, the user running the script sees a personalized message such as "hello, jdoe."

WRITE A SIMPLE SHELL SCRIPT

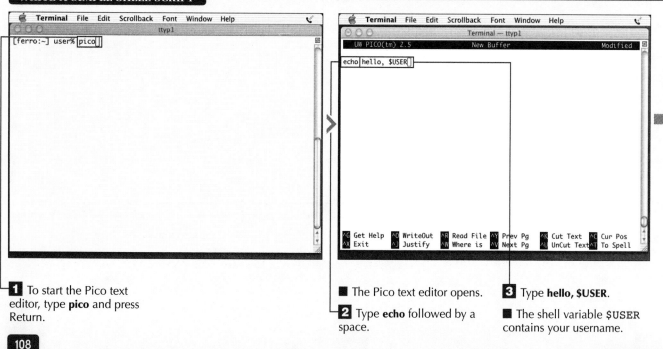

1 To start the Pico text editor, type **pico** and press Return.

■ The Pico text editor opens.

2 Type **echo** followed by a space.

3 Type **hello, $USER**.

■ The shell variable $USER contains your username.

You can write scripts that are easier to understand and maintain by adding comments that explain the complicated commands and describe how the scripts work. *Comments* are lines in scripts that the system ignores when it runs the script. Comments serve the function of explaining your script to others who read it so that complex commands are easier to understand and so other users do not have to read the entire script to know what it is supposed to do.

To turn a line of text in a script into a comment, insert a pound sign (#) in the first column. The shell ignores that line when it runs the script, so you can place anything you like in a comment. You can also add comments to the end of a line of code by adding # at the end of the Unix command and before the text of your comment. Always place at least one space or tab on each side of the #.

While it is a good idea to include some comments in a script to explain what the script does, you do not need to comment every line of code. Inserting one or two lines of comments at the beginning of a script is useful. Placing a comment on every other line is distracting. When you run this script, the shell ignores the comments.

TYPE THIS:

```
# this is a script that greets the user
echo hello, $USER        # address user by his username
```

RESULT:

```
hello, user
```

---

4 Press Control + O to write out the file.

5 Type a name for your new shell script.

6 Press Return.

7 Press Control + X to exit Pico.

RUN A SIMPLE SHELL SCRIPT

You can save yourself a lot of work and better remember complicated Unix commands by placing commands in scripts and running the scripts. When you run a script, you can execute a sequence of commands by typing no more than a single filename. After you turn a series of commands into a script, you can type the filename of that script just as if it were another Unix command. In fact, many Unix advocates like to think of scripts as extensions to the operating system. In a sense, when you create a script, you add a new command to your system.

You can execute a script in two ways. The first way is to type the command source, followed by the name of the script. When you use the source command, the shell reads and executes the file one line at a time just as if you were

typing each line in the Terminal window. The second way is to first make the script executable and then execute it by typing its name. See Chapter 2 for more information on file permissions.

For a script that you intend to run many times, changing the file permissions so that you can run it by entering only its name can save you time. If you use the chmod a+x command, other users can execute the script too.

The source command is especially handy when you want to run scripts that do not have execute permissions set. If you do not own a script and cannot change its permissions, you may still be able to run it by using the source command. You must have read permission, which enables you to read a file, to run it using the source command.

RUN A SIMPLE SHELL SCRIPT

```
 Terminal  File  Edit  Scrollback  Font  Window  Help
 Terminal — ttyp1
[ferro:~] user%  source greetme
hello, user
[ferro:~] user% 
```

```
 Terminal  File  Edit  Scrollback  Font  Window  Help
 Terminal — ttyp1
[ferro:~] user%  chmod a+x greetme
[ferro:~] user% 
```

1 Type **source** followed by a space.

2 Type the name of a script and press Return.

■ The shell runs the commands in the specified script.

3 Type **chmod** followed by a space.

4 Type **a+x** followed by a space.

5 Type the name of a script and press Return.

■ The chmod command adds execute permissions for all users.

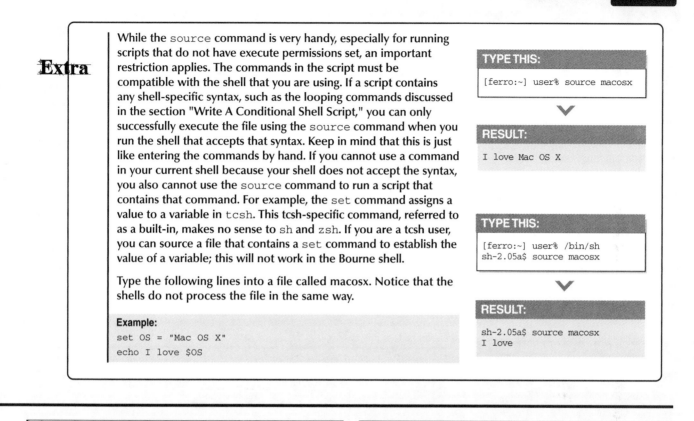

Extra

While the `source` command is very handy, especially for running scripts that do not have execute permissions set, an important restriction applies. The commands in the script must be compatible with the shell that you are using. If a script contains any shell-specific syntax, such as the looping commands discussed in the section "Write A Conditional Shell Script," you can only successfully execute the file using the `source` command when you run the shell that accepts that syntax. Keep in mind that this is just like entering the commands by hand. If you cannot use a command in your current shell because your shell does not accept the syntax, you also cannot use the `source` command to run a script that contains that command. For example, the `set` command assigns a value to a variable in `tcsh`. This tcsh-specific command, referred to as a built-in, makes no sense to `sh` and `zsh`. If you are a tcsh user, you can source a file that contains a `set` command to establish the value of a variable; this will not work in the Bourne shell.

Type the following lines into a file called macosx. Notice that the shells do not process the file in the same way.

Example:
```
set OS = "Mac OS X"
echo I love $OS
```

TYPE THIS:
```
[ferro:~] user% source macosx
```

RESULT:
```
I love Mac OS X
```

TYPE THIS:
```
[ferro:~] user% /bin/sh
sh-2.05a$ source macosx
```

RESULT:
```
sh-2.05a$ source macosx
I love
```

-◢ **6** Type **ls -l** followed by a space.

7 Type the name of a script and press Return.

■ The screen displays the script's file permissions.

-◢ **8** Type **./** followed by the name of a script and press Return.

■ The shell executes the commands in the script.

WRITE LOOPING SHELL SCRIPTS

Y ou can issue a command or a list of commands many times by placing a loop in your shell script. Adding a loop keeps you from having to run your script for every file in a directory or every value in a list.

When you want your script to loop through a series of files, numbers, or other values, you can use a looping command. To ensure that the proper shell is used when your script runs, you can add a line to the top of your script beginning with #! followed immediately by the full pathname for the particular script. For example, a script written to run in tcsh starts with #!/bin/tcsh.

For tcsh, you can use the foreach command to loop through a set of values. The command foreach number (4 5 6) runs three times, once for each of the numbers

listed. Each time through the loop, the next number is assigned to the variable $number. Following the foreach command, you can enter whatever commands you want to execute for each $number. You terminate your loop by entering the word end on a line by itself.

For some tasks, you want the number of times that you loop through a set of commands to depend on the value of a certain variable or some other condition. For example, if you want to write a script that adds two numbers, you can write it so that it adds the numbers until the person running the script stops entering numbers. In this case, you use a while loop. A while loop continues executing as long as the specified test condition is true.

WRITE LOOPING SHELL SCRIPTS

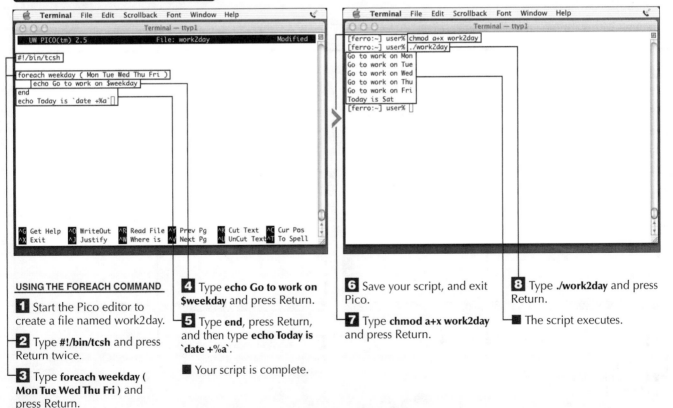

USING THE FOREACH COMMAND

1 Start the Pico editor to create a file named work2day.

2 Type **#!/bin/tcsh** and press Return twice.

3 Type **foreach weekday (Mon Tue Wed Thu Fri)** and press Return.

4 Type **echo Go to work on $weekday** and press Return.

5 Type **end**, press Return, and then type **echo Today is `date +%a`**.

■ Your script is complete.

6 Save your script, and exit Pico.

7 Type **chmod a+x work2day** and press Return.

8 Type **./work2day** and press Return.

■ The script executes.

Apply It

You can often reduce the lines in a script by placing repetitious commands in a loop. You can loop by using any of the shells provided with Mac OS X. The `foreach` and `while` commands are built-ins associated with `tcsh` and `csh`. You must use a different syntax if you are writing scripts in `bash`, `zsh`, or `sh`. The `for` command syntax for these shells uses the word `for`, followed by a variable name and the word `in`, followed by list of values. The words `do` and `done` mark the beginning and end of the commands to be executed in your loop. Make sure that you use `/bin/sh`, `/bin/bash`, or `/bin/zsh` when you run the following exercise that loops through the days of the week.

TYPE THIS:

```
[ferro:~] $user /bin/sh
sh-2.05a$ for weekday in Mon Tue Wed Thu Fri
> do
>   echo Go to work on $weekday
> done
```

RESULT:

```
Go to work on Mon
Go to work on Tue
Go to work on Wed
Go to work on Thu
Go to work on Fri
```

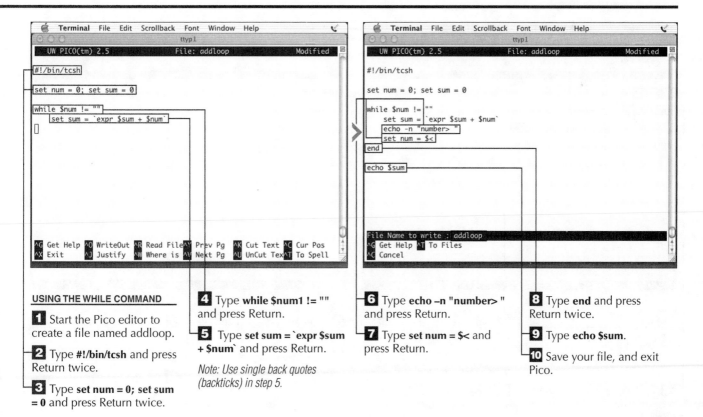

USING THE WHILE COMMAND

1 Start the Pico editor to create a file named addloop.

2 Type **#!/bin/tcsh** and press Return twice.

3 Type **set num = 0; set sum = 0** and press Return twice.

4 Type **while $num1 != ""** and press Return.

5 Type **set sum = `expr $sum + $num`** and press Return.

Note: Use single back quotes (backticks) in step 5.

6 Type **echo –n "number> "** and press Return.

7 Type **set num = $<** and press Return.

8 Type **end** and press Return twice.

9 Type **echo $sum**.

10 Save your file, and exit Pico.

WRITE A CONDITIONAL SHELL SCRIPT

Conditional statements make scripts more useful. You can use an `if` command to test conditions in shell scripts and proceed with different commands depending on the outcome of your test. This type of operation is called *conditional logic*. All Unix shells provide some form of conditional logic. However, like looping, the syntax depends on the shell. The `if` command is a built-in, so you cannot find a file if you enter the command `which if` in your Terminal window.

For `tcsh` and `csh`, you follow the `if` command with the condition you want to test enclosed in parentheses, followed by the word `then`. To test if a number is equal to 0, for example, your command is `if ( $number == 0 ) then`. To test whether a variable contains a particular string, enclose the string in quotes: `if ( $answer == "yes" ) then`.

You then enter a list of commands that you want to execute if the condition you specified is `true`. For readability, script writers usually indent these lines. After this list of commands, end your conditional statement with the word `endif` on a line by itself.

In `bash`, `sh`, and `zsh`, the `if` statement takes a different form. You follow the word `if` by a set of square brackets that enclose the test condition. Follow the brackets with a semicolon (`;`) and the word `then`. You can type the word `then` on the following line if you prefer. You terminate the list of commands to be executed with `fi`.

You can also specify a list of commands that should run if the specified conditions are *not* met. In both forms of `if` commands, you use the word `else` to begin this list. An `else` class must follow the `if` clause that it is related to.

WRITE A CONDITIONAL SHELL SCRIPT

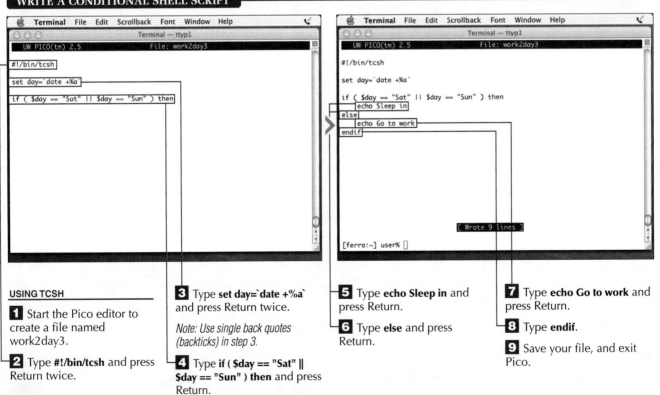

USING TCSH

1 Start the Pico editor to create a file named work2day3.

2 Type **#!/bin/tcsh** and press Return twice.

3 Type **set day=`date +%a`** and press Return twice.

Note: Use single back quotes (backticks) in step 3.

4 Type **if ($day == "Sat" || $day == "Sun") then** and press Return.

5 Type **echo Sleep in** and press Return.

6 Type **else** and press Return.

7 Type **echo Go to work** and press Return.

8 Type **endif**.

9 Save your file, and exit Pico.

Extra

It is often useful to collect information from the system by running a command and assigning its output to a variable. The work2day scripts in this chapter use backticks (`) for this. The output from the command enclosed in backticks is assigned to the variable and can then be displayed or tested.

You can use backticks to run almost any simple Unix command. However, you should always take care to consider the output that will be assigned to your variable. It may be different than you expect. Be sure you use tcsh or csh when you loop on the command line.

TYPE THIS:

```
[ferro:~] user% foreach FILE ( 'ls -l' )
foreach -> echo $FILE is a file
foreach -> end
```

RESULT:

```
total is a file
64 is a file
-rw-r-r- is a file
1 is a file
user is a file
staff is a file
134 is a file
May is a file
5 is a file
07:21 is a file
addloop is a file
```

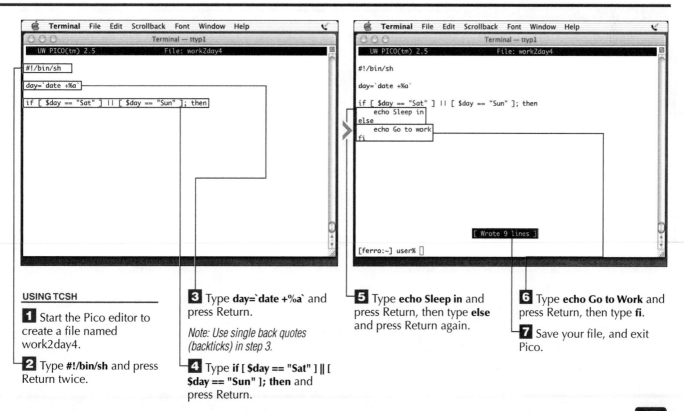

USING TCSH

1 Start the Pico editor to create a file named work2day4.

2 Type **#!/bin/sh** and press Return twice.

3 Type **day=`date +%a`** and press Return.

Note: Use single back quotes (backticks) in step 3.

4 Type **if [$day == "Sat"] || [$day == "Sun"]; then** and press Return.

5 Type **echo Sleep in** and press Return, then type **else** and press Return again.

6 Type **echo Go to Work** and press Return, then type **fi**.

7 Save your file, and exit Pico.

EXTRACT INFORMATION WITH AWK

Y ou can use the `awk` command to extract text from files or from the output of other commands. It is particularly useful for extracting a portion of each line. You can then use the output from `awk` for further processing.

Like many other Unix commands, `awk` works well with the concept of white space – any combination of spaces and tabs that might exist between strings of text and numbers. If you want to display the first or the third word on every line of a text file, `awk` is the tool to use. If you want to display the last word on each line, `awk` can handle that as well. If the information that you want to display is not separated by white space, you can still use `awk` to extract it.

You can use `awk` on the command line, or you can write scripts using nothing but `awk` commands. Though `awk` is a

programming language, it is most popularly used within shell scripts or on the command line to select data from files or the output of other commands.

Any command that you write for `awk` and `awk` scripts begins with an opening brace (`{`) and ends with a closing brace (`}`). The `awk` command processes lines of text one at a time and assigns each portion of a line to a variable such as `$1`, `$2`, and so on. The `awk` command language has some built-in variables such as `NF` and `NR` that represent the number of fields on each line and the record number of the current line. *Fields* are portions of text separated by white space or some other delimiter that you specify.

You can write many useful scripts and commands using awk. Awk is a scripting language that includes conditional tests and looping.

EXTRACT INFORMATION WITH AWK

USING AWK ON THE COMMAND LINE

1 Type **awk** followed by a space.

2 Type **'{print $1}'** followed by a space.

3 Type the name of a text file and press Return.

■ Awk prints the first word of every line of your file.

4 Type **ls -l** followed by a space.

5 Type **|** followed by a space.

6 Type **awk '{print $5}' |** and press Return.

■ Awk prints the size of each file in the current directory.

Apply It

Some features of the `awk` language give it a very different appearance than shell scripts. For example, variable names in `awk` do not start with a $. The variables $1, $2, and so on represent fields in the text being processed. If you use a variable name that has no value, `awk` ignores the command and continues processing.

The command to display lines of text in `awk` is `print`, not `echo`. You must include lines of text in single quotation marks. Awk uses { and } markers to begin and end blocks of code.

TYPE THIS:

```
[ferro:~] cat work2day | awk '{print NF}'
```

▼

RESULT:

```
1
0
9
6
1
5
```

TYPE THIS:

```
[ferro:~] cat work2day | awk '{print $NF}'
```

▼

RESULT:

```
#!/bin/tcsh

)
$weekday
end
+%a'
```

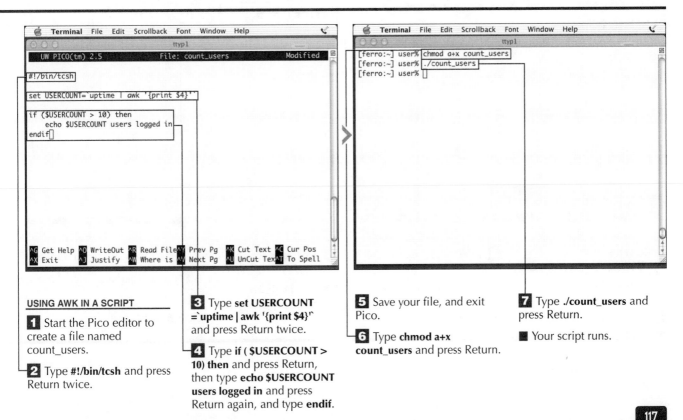

USING AWK IN A SCRIPT

1 Start the Pico editor to create a file named count_users.

2 Type **#!/bin/tcsh** and press Return twice.

3 Type **set USERCOUNT =`uptime | awk '{print $4}'`** and press Return twice.

4 Type **if ($USERCOUNT > 10) then** and press Return, then type **echo $USERCOUNT users logged in** and press Return again, and type **endif**.

5 Save your file, and exit Pico.

6 Type **chmod a+x count_users** and press Return.

7 Type **./count_users** and press Return.

■ Your script runs.

EXTEND SCRIPTS WITH SED

The sed command lets you modify the input or output of a Unix command or the content of a file without having to use a text editor. Sed is a special editor that is unlike Pico, emacs, and vi. It can change the contents of files or the output of other commands on the command line. Think of sed as a pipe into which you pour text and out of which modified text flows. The shape of this pipe, representing a set of editing commands that you specify, determines what text changes and how that text changes.

The simplest sed command replaces one string with another string. The command echo Please go to work today | sed "s/go to work/stay home/" prints "Please stay home today".

Sed changes one instance of the first string to the second on each line. If you want the same text to change every time it appears in a line, add the letter g to the end of the command. The command sed "s/a/z/g" changes every occurrence of the letter a in its input to the letter z in its output.

If you want to change a number of strings at the same time, create a file containing all of your substitutions. The command sed -f subs < infile > outfile looks for a series of change requests in the file subs, applies these changes while processing the file called infile, and writes the changed text to outfile.

If the text that you want to change includes a forward slash (/), you can see where sed might be confused as to what portion of text it needs to change. However, you can specify a different delimiter to separate the old and new text. The command sed "s:old:new:" works as well as sed "s/old/new/". Whichever delimiter you use, be sure to use three of them.

EXTEND SCRIPTS WITH SED

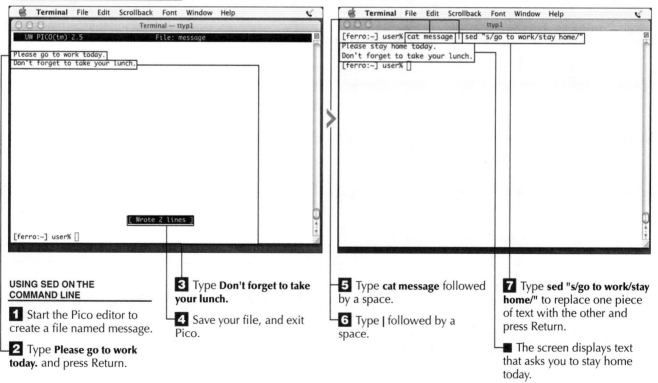

USING SED ON THE COMMAND LINE

1 Start the Pico editor to create a file named message.

2 Type **Please go to work today.** and press Return.

3 Type **Don't forget to take your lunch.**

4 Save your file, and exit Pico.

5 Type **cat message** followed by a space.

6 Type **|** followed by a space.

7 Type **sed "s/go to work/stay home/"** to replace one piece of text with the other and press Return.

■ The screen displays text that asks you to stay home today.

Extra

As with awk, you can use sed to create fairly complex scripts, but you most often use the command to extend shell scripts. Scripts written entirely in sed can be simple or extremely challenging. Try a simple sed script like that shown here. Enter this script in a file called `oneline` and make it executable. It joins lines of a file into a single line by removing linefeeds. Then, try the following commands.

TYPE THIS INTO A FILE NAMED ONELINE:

```
#!/bin/sed -nf
H
$ {
  x
  s/\n//g
  p
}
```

TYPE THIS:

```
[ferro:~] echo a > mytext; echo b > mytext; echo c > mytext
[ferro:~] user% ./oneline < mytext
```

RESULT:

abc

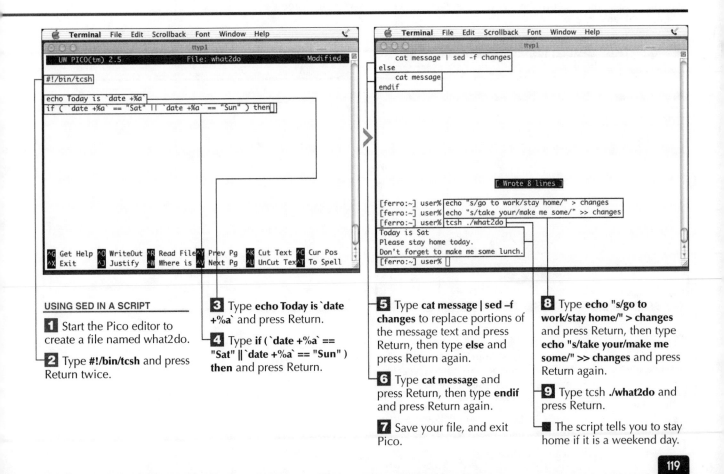

USING SED IN A SCRIPT

1 Start the Pico editor to create a file named what2do.

2 Type **#!/bin/tcsh** and press Return twice.

3 Type **echo Today is `date +%a`** and press Return.

4 Type **if (`date +%a` == "Sat" || `date +%a` == "Sun") then** and press Return.

5 Type **cat message | sed –f changes** to replace portions of the message text and press Return, then type **else** and press Return again.

6 Type **cat message** and press Return, then type **endif** and press Return again.

7 Save your file, and exit Pico.

8 Type **echo "s/go to work/stay home/" > changes** and press Return, then type **echo "s/take your/make me some/" >> changes** and press Return again.

9 Type tcsh **./what2do** and press Return.

■ The script tells you to stay home if it is a weekend day.

SCHEDULE SCRIPTS TO RUN AUTOMATICALLY

You can schedule scripts or other Unix commands to run automatically at a time you specify. This can keep you from forgetting to run routine scripts and can allow you to schedule big jobs to run when the system is not busy.

Use the `cron` command to schedule the execution of commands or scripts. Cron makes use of files called `crontab` files that specify what time commands and scripts are to be run. All `crontab` files have the following format:

```
min hr day month day-of-week command-to-run
```

The first field represents the minutes, and the second represents the hours. If you want a script to run at 2:15 p.m. every day, enter **15 14** for these fields. The entry **8 1** in the day and month fields means January 8th. The day-of-week field must be a number between 0 and 6; Sunday is 0, Monday is 1, and so on.

Time fields can include a string of comma-separated values or an asterisk (*). An asterisk indicates that every possible value for the field is valid. In the day-of-week field, for example, * tells `cron` to run the command every day of the week. Typing **0,30** in the minutes field tells `cron` to run the command on the hour and half hour. You can also specify values such as */10 in the minutes field to tell `cron` to run the command every ten minutes.

A job scheduled to run via `cron` only runs if all of the timing criteria are met. For example, the line 5 17 * * 5 /Users/user/bin/send_weekly runs the send_weekly script every Friday at 5:05 p.m.

To schedule jobs to run automatically, use the `crontab -e` command and add a line for each command or script you want to schedule.

SCHEDULE SCRIPTS TO RUN AUTOMATICALLY

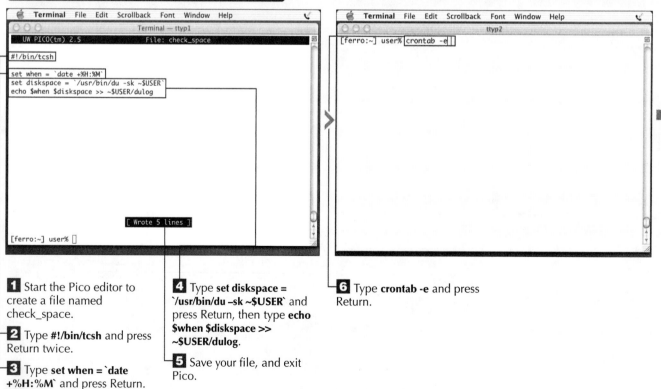

1 Start the Pico editor to create a file named check_space.

2 Type **#!/bin/tcsh** and press Return twice.

3 Type **set when = `date +%H:%M`** and press Return.

4 Type **set diskspace = `/usr/bin/du –sk ~$USER`** and press Return, then type **echo $when $diskspace >> ~$USER/dulog**.

5 Save your file, and exit Pico.

6 Type **crontab -e** and press Return.

Extra

Cron stores files in `/var/cron/tabs`, and each file is named after the user who owns it. The `cron` process starts when the system starts up and is one of the processes that runs all of the time. Such processes are referred to as *daemons*. The format of `crontab` entries is fairly rigid.

If you do not include the required five timing fields, the system does not set up your `cron` jobs and asks when you try to save the changes if you want to retry your edits. If you do not retry your changes, `cron` leaves your `crontab` file unchanged. You should never edit `cron` files except through the `crontab -e` command, and the system protects against this by setting the permissions of the `cron` files so that you can only edit them as root and, of course, the `crontab` process.

TYPE THIS IN YOUR CRONTAB FILE:

```
*/5 * * * 7 /bin/echo hello > /dev/ttyp1
```

RESULT:

Cron does not let you save the file. The 7 in the day-of-week field is invalid. Only a value between 0 (Sunday) and 6 (Saturday) is allowed in this field. Change it to the proper digit for the current day of the week and "hello" messages should appear in your Terminal window after a few minutes. To inactivate the line without removing it, use the `crontab -e` command again and type a pound sign (#) in column 1.

7 Type ***/5 * * * * /Users/user/check_space > /dev/null**, replacing user with your username.

8 Save your cron file, and exit the editor.

9 Type **chmod a+x check_space** and press Return.

10 Type **crontab -l** and press Return.

■ Your scheduled job appears.

OPEN AQUA APPLICATIONS FROM THE SHELL

Y ou can use the shell command open to open a file in an Aqua application such as TextEdit, Preview, Photoshop, or Microsoft Word. The file opens as if you had double-clicked it in the Mac OS X Finder. There are three ways to use the open command:

```
open filename
open -e filename
open -a Application-name filename
```

The first version of this command launches an Aqua application to open the designated filename. Mac OS X associates each document with information known as *metadata*. This metadata includes information such as which Aqua application created the file. The open command launches that application.

If the application that created the file is not listed in the metadata, then Mac OS X looks at the extension of the file. The extension is the last part of the filename that appears

from the period (.) on. For example, the filename my-dog.jpg has an extension of .jpg. Mac OS X uses the default application for opening .JPG files. This is the same method the Mac OS X Finder uses to determine which application to use when you double-click the icon of a document.

Not all Unix text files end with the .txt extension. An HTML file may be named about-cat.html. If you use open, the file opens in a Web browser, but if you want to edit it, you may want to use TextEdit. The second form of the open command, with the -e option, opens the file in TextEdit, which lets you edit text files not ending in the .txt extension, such as HTML pages or configuration files.

The third version of the command lets you specify which application to use. You can name any application located in the /Applications directory or its subdirectories. You can start the application with a blank file by omitting the filename argument.

OPEN AQUA APPLICATIONS FROM THE SHELL

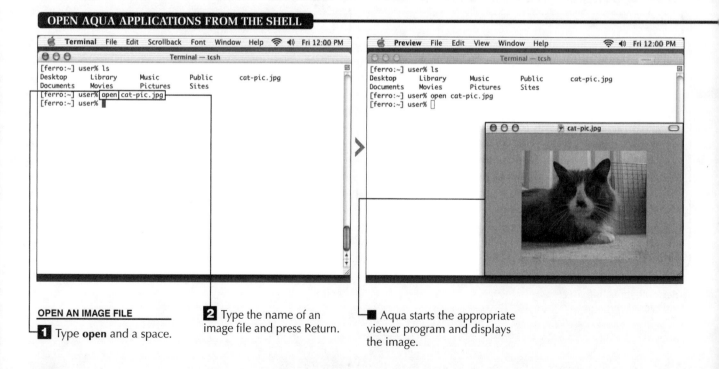

OPEN AN IMAGE FILE

1 Type **open** and a space.

2 Type the name of an image file and press Return.

■ Aqua starts the appropriate viewer program and displays the image.

Extra

The open command is not limited to only opening files. If you provide other arguments, the open command tries to display those arguments in the appropriate viewer or editor.

One of the most useful ways to employ open is to open directories in the Mac OS X Finder. This command creates a Finder folder window to open the current directory.

```
[ferro:~/Pictures] user% open
```

The open command can also open Web URLs in the default Web browser you have specified in your System Preferences on the Internet panel. To open, type your URL as the argument.

```
[ferro:~] user% open http://cssin24hours.com/
```

You may need to enclose the Web URL in quotation marks to prevent the shell from interpreting question marks and other special characters.

You can also send e-mail to an address by using a mailto: URL. This command starts your default mail program and sends mail to the specified address.

```
[ferro:~] user% open mailto:kynn@idyllmtn.com
```

OPEN A TEXT FILE IN TEXTEDIT

1 Type **open** and a space.

2 Type **-e** and a space.

3 Type the name of a text file and press Return.

■ The TextEdit application launches and opens the text file.

CAPTURE A SCREENSHOT FROM UNIX

You can create a screenshot of your current desktop and application windows by using the `screencapture` command. A *screenshot* is simply a graphics file that shows the state of your display at any given time. You can use a screenshot for troubleshooting or sharing what you see with someone else who does not have direct access to your computer. Screenshots are also useful for step-by-step instructions, such as those used extensively in this book.

You can create a screenshot at any time in Mac OS X by holding down the Shift + Command (⌘) keys while typing the number 3. This key sequence captures whatever is currently on the entire screen and saves it to a file in your Desktop directory. The file is named Picture 1.pdf and is in the Portable Document Format (PDF) developed by Adobe. The Mac OS X Preview application or the Adobe Acrobat Reader program can read PDF files. If you create more screenshots in this manner, they receive successive filenames, such as Picture 2.pdf and Picture 3.pdf.

The `screencapture` shell command gives you more control over your screenshots, allowing you to save them wherever you wish and with any filename. The syntax for this command is

`screencapture options filename.pdf`

If you use the `-m` option, the screenshot captures the entire main screen. The `-i` option puts the `screencapture` command into Interactive mode. In Interactive mode, you can define an area of the screen to capture by dragging the mouse. Typing a space in Interactive mode switches the selection from mouse selection to window selection; if you click a window in Window Selection mode, that entire window is captured.

CAPTURE A SCREENSHOT FROM UNIX

```
 Terminal  File  Edit  Scrollback  Font  Window  Help  🛜 ◀) Fri 12:00 PM
○ ○ ○                        Terminal — tcsh
[ferro:~/Desktop] user% screencapture -m '53730X Fg0905.pdf'
[ferro:~/Desktop] user% ls
53730X Fg0905.pdf
[ferro:~/Desktop] user%
```

```
 Terminal  File  Edit  Scrollback  Font  Window  Help  🛜 ◀) Fri 12:00 PM
○ ○ ○                        Terminal — tcsh
[ferro:~] user% ls -la
total 56
drwxr-xr-x  13 user  staff    442 Dec 24 17:22 .
drwxrwxr-t  10 root  wheel    340 Dec 23 14:34 ..
-rw-r--r--   1 user  staff      3 Dec 22 21:53 .CFUserTextEncoding
drwx------   2 user  staff     68 Dec 24 17:06 .Trash
drwx------   8 user  staff    272 Dec 24 17:22 Desktop
drwx------   3 user  staff    102 Dec 22 21:53 Documents
drwx------  19 user  staff    646 Dec 24 17:10 Library
drwx------   3 user  staff    102 Dec 22 21:53 Movies
drwx------   3 user  staff    102 Dec 22 21:53 Music
drwx------   3 user  staff    102 Dec 22 21:53 Pictures
drwxr-xr-x   4 user  staff    136 Dec 22 21:53 Public
drwxr-xr-x   5 user  staff    170 Dec 22 21:53 Sites
-rw-r--r--   1 user  staff  24301 Dec 24 17:13 cat-pic.jpg
[ferro:~] user% screencapture -i 'time-screenshot.pdf'
```

1 Type **screencapture** and a space.

2 Type **-m** and a space.

3 Type a filename ending in .pdf and press Return.

■ Your screenshot is saved in the PDF file.

CAPTURE A SECTION OF THE SCREEN

1 Type **screencapture -i** and a space.

2 Type a filename ending in .pdf and press Return.

■ The cursor becomes a crosshair pointer.

Extra

After you have captured a screenshot, you will probably want to edit it. The Mac OS X screen capture only saves files in Adobe's PDF format, which is usually not the best format for images. Many graphics applications do not open PDF files, and you cannot use a PDF file as an image in a Web page or word processing document.

There are two ways to deal with this inconvenient file format. The first is to use the Preview application, a standard Mac OS X application, to convert the screenshot to a different format. You can open the screenshot in Preview using the open command.

```
open -a Preview screenshot.pdf
```

The Export function is available through the File menu and allows you to choose a different format, such as TIFF, JPG, or BMP.

The other approach saves your screenshot directly to the Aqua paste buffer, using the -c option with the screencapture command.

```
screencapture -c -i
```

No filename is necessary because the captured portion of the screen is stored in your clipboard. You can paste it into a graphics application such as Photoshop or Preview and then save the file in whatever format you prefer.

3 Position the cursor over the corner that you want to capture.

4 Click and hold the mouse button.

5 Drag the mouse to indicate the section you want to capture.

6 Release the mouse button.

■ Your screenshot is saved in the PDF file.

ACCESS THE AQUA CLIPBOARD

You can copy and paste using the Aqua clipboard with the pbcopy and pbpaste commands. Mac OS X keeps temporary data in a special memory space known as the *clipboard* or *paste buffer*. When you use the Copy function of an Aqua application, whatever you copy replaces the contents of the clipboard. When you use the Paste function, you paste the contents of the clipboard into the document. The Copy and Paste functions are usually listed in an application's Edit menu, or you can use the shortcuts ⌘ + C for copy and ⌘ + V for paste.

The pbcopy command reads text from the standard input and places it into the Aqua clipboard buffer. You can use this command to read a file's content into the clipboard by using input redirection from a file or by piping the output from another command to the pbcopy command.

```
pbcopy < filename
shell-command | pbcopy
```

This action stores the contents of the file or the output of the command in the paste buffer, and you can paste it into other applications, such as TextEdit or Mail.

If you have copied text from another application, you can access the paste buffer's contents by using the pbpaste command. This command sends the contents of the clipboard to standard output, where you can redirect it to a file or pipe it to another command.

```
pbpaste > filename
pbpaste | shell-command
```

Typing **pbpaste** alone displays the current contents of the paste buffer. If you have forgotten what is on your clipboard, this is an easy way to check.

ACCESS THE AQUA CLIPBOARD

```
[ferro:~] user% pbcopy < /usr/share/calendar/calendar.usholiday
[ferro:~] user%
```

```
[ferro:~] user% ls -la
total 112
drwxr-xr-x  14 user   staff     476 Dec 24 17:23 .
drwxrwxr-t  10 root   wheel     340 Dec 23 14:34 ..
-rw-r--r--   1 user   staff       3 Dec 22 21:53 .CFUserTextEncoding
drwx------   2 user   staff      68 Dec 24 17:06 .Trash
drwx------  12 user   staff     408 Dec 24 17:29 Desktop
drwx------   3 user   staff     102 Dec 22 21:53 Documents
drwx------  19 user   staff     646 Dec 24 17:10 Library
drwx------   3 user   staff     102 Dec 22 21:53 Movies
drwx------   3 user   staff     102 Dec 22 21:53 Music
drwx------   3 user   staff     102 Dec 22 21:53 Pictures
drwxr-xr-x   4 user   staff     136 Dec 22 21:53 Public
drwxr-xr-x   5 user   staff     170 Dec 22 21:53 Sites
-rw-r--r--   1 user   staff   24301 Dec 24 17:13 cat-pic.jpg
-rw-r--r--   1 user   staff   26949 Dec 24 17:23 time-screenshot.pdf
[ferro:~] user% ls -la | pbcopy
[ferro:~] user%
```

COPY A TEXT FILE TO THE CLIPBOARD

1 Type **pbcopy** and a space.

2 Type < and a space.

3 Type a text file's filename and press return.

■ The clipboard now contains the file that you can paste into other programs.

COPY COMMAND OUTPUT TO THE CLIPBOARD

1 Type a command that outputs text and a space.

2 Type a vertical pipe character (|) and a space.

3 Type **pbcopy** and press Return.

■ The clipboard now contains the command output that you can paste into other programs.

Extra

You can combine the `pbpaste` and `pbcopy` commands by piping the commands together. This action allows you to insert a shell command to modify the contents of your paste buffer. For example, you could copy the following text from a Web site using your browser's Copy function:

```
Nying, a dog
Olorin, a cat
Kim, a dog
Angie, a dog
```

You can use the following command to sort the contents and then store the text in your clipboard:

```
[ferro:~] user% pbpaste | sort -bfi | pbcopy
```

If you paste the text into your word processor, the list of pets is sorted:

```
Angie, a dog
Kim, a dog
Nying, a dog
Olorin, a cat
```

You can extract a list of the dogs only with the following pipe through the `grep` command:

```
[ferro:~] user% pbpaste | grep 'dog' | pbcopy
```

🍎 **Terminal** File Edit Scrollback Font Window Help 🛜 ◀) Fri 12:00 PM

```
⊗ ⊖ ⊖                    Terminal — tcsh
[ferro:~] user% pbpaste > ls-la.txt
[ferro:~] user% cat ls-la.txt
total 112
drwxr-xr-x  14 user  staff     476 Dec 24 17:23 .
drwxrwxr-t  10 root  wheel     340 Dec 23 14:34 ..
-rw-r--r--   1 user  staff       3 Dec 22 21:53 .CFUserTextEncoding
drwx------   2 user  staff      68 Dec 24 17:06 .Trash
drwx------  12 user  staff     408 Dec 24 17:29 Desktop
drwx------   3 user  staff     102 Dec 22 21:53 Documents
drwx------  19 user  staff     646 Dec 24 17:10 Library
drwx------   3 user  staff     102 Dec 22 21:53 Movies
drwx------   3 user  staff     102 Dec 22 21:53 Music
drwx------   3 user  staff     102 Dec 22 21:53 Pictures
drwxr-xr-x   4 user  staff     136 Dec 22 21:53 Public
drwxr-xr-x   5 user  staff     170 Dec 22 21:53 Sites
-rw-r--r--   1 user  staff   24301 Dec 24 17:13 cat-pic.jpg
-rw-r--r--   1 user  staff   26949 Dec 24 17:23 time-screenshot.pdf
[ferro:~] user%
```

🍎 **Terminal** File Edit Scrollback Font Window Help 🛜 ◀) Fri 12:00 PM

```
⊗ ⊖ ⊖                    Terminal — tcsh
[ferro:~] user% pbpaste
total 112
drwxr-xr-x  14 user  staff     476 Dec 24 17:23 .
drwxrwxr-t  10 root  wheel     340 Dec 23 14:34 ..
-rw-r--r--   1 user  staff       3 Dec 22 21:53 .CFUserTextEncoding
drwx------   2 user  staff      68 Dec 24 17:06 .Trash
drwx------  12 user  staff     408 Dec 24 17:29 Desktop
drwx------   3 user  staff     102 Dec 22 21:53 Documents
drwx------  19 user  staff     646 Dec 24 17:10 Library
drwx------   3 user  staff     102 Dec 22 21:53 Movies
drwx------   3 user  staff     102 Dec 22 21:53 Music
drwx------   3 user  staff     102 Dec 22 21:53 Pictures
drwxr-xr-x   4 user  staff     136 Dec 22 21:53 Public
drwxr-xr-x   5 user  staff     170 Dec 22 21:53 Sites
-rw-r--r--   1 user  staff   24301 Dec 24 17:13 cat-pic.jpg
-rw-r--r--   1 user  staff   26949 Dec 24 17:23 time-screenshot.pdf
[ferro:~] user% pbpaste | wc
      15     128     793
[ferro:~] user%
```

PASTE THE CLIPBOARD INTO A TEXT FILE

1 Type **pbpaste** and a space.

2 Type **>** and a space.

3 Type a filename and press Return.

■ The file now contains the contents of the clipboard.

PASTE THE CLIPBOARD TO STANDARD OUTPUT

1 Type **pbpaste** and a space.

2 Type a vertical pipe character (|) and a space.

3 Type a command that reads standard input.

■ The contents of the clipboard are sent to the command.

COPY APPLE RESOURCE FORKS

You can copy a file and its resource fork using the ditto command. Mac OS X uses resource forks to store additional information about the file. A resource fork is a hidden file that accompanies another document. When you use Aqua applications, resource forks are created automatically but are kept invisible to both the Mac OS X Finder and the Unix shell. To list resource forks in your current directory, type this command:

```
[ferro:~] user% ls -l */rsrc
```

You see that your files are shadowed by smaller files of the same name with /rsrc appended. Each of these files contains encoded information about which application created the file and other types of metadata. Aqua applications use this information, but Unix shell commands ignore it.

The Unix cp command does not normally copy resource fork files because they are effectively invisible to most shell commands. If you copy a file or directory with cp, your copy does not have a resource fork. However, resource fork sizes are included in the disk usage totals provided by the du command; thus, your copy may not appear to be the same size as the original.

The ditto command is another way to copy files and directories. Unlike the cp command, ditto copies a directory and its contents automatically so you do not need to include an -r option as you would with cp. You do need to include the -rsrcFork option:

```
[ferro:~] user% ditto -rsrcFork original copy
```

This action produces a copy with the resource forks preserved.

COPY APPLE RESOURCE FORKS

COPY A FILE

1 Type **ditto** and a space.

2 Type **-rsrcFork** and a space.

3 Type the name of a file and a space.

4 Type the name of the destination file and press Return.

■ The **ditto** command copies the file and its resource fork.

Extra

Two other commands work with resource forks to ensure that the Mac OS X Finder has access to metadata. These commands are the CpMac and MvMac commands. CpMac is a version of cp that copies files along with resource forks, and MvMac is a version of mv that moves files while preserving resource forks.

The CpMac and MvMac commands are not automatically installed on all Mac OS X computers, but are on the Mac OS X Developer Tools CD-ROM. For more information on installing the Developer Tools, see Chapter 12.

The executable files for the CpMac and MvMac commands are stored in the /Developer/Tools directory. If you have not added that directory to your shell's path, you will have to type the full pathname to use these commands.

Example:
```
[ferro:~] user% du -s cat-pics/
48744    cat-pics/
[ferro:~] user% cp -r cat-pics/ cat-pics-cp
[ferro:~] user% du -s cat-pics-cp
37872    cat-pics-cp
[ferro:~] user% /developer/Tools/CpMac -r cat-pics/ cat-pics-CpMac
[ferro:~] user% du -s cat-pics-CpMac
48744    cat-pics-CpMac/
```

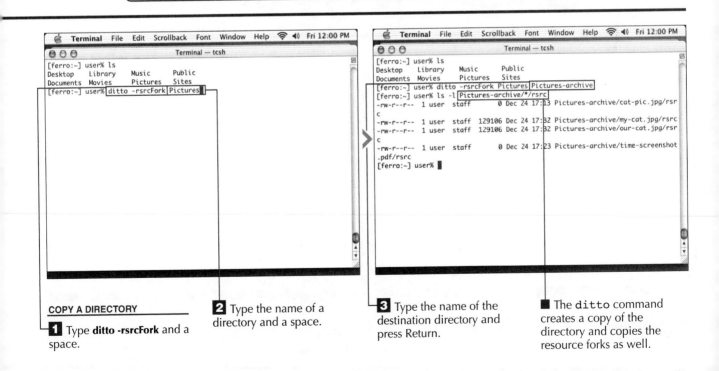

COPY A DIRECTORY

1 Type **ditto -rsrcFork** and a space.

2 Type the name of a directory and a space.

3 Type the name of the destination directory and press Return.

■ The ditto command creates a copy of the directory and copies the resource forks as well.

RUN APPLESCRIPT FROM THE SHELL

You can run Applescript commands or files from the command line, letting you access and control other Mac OS X applications. Applescript is a simple but powerful programming language built into the Mac OS X. It is relatively easy to read and understand because it uses a syntax similar to English. For example, to have the Finder application create a pop-up dialog box, you can use the following Applescript:

```
tell Application "Finder" to display dialog
"Good morning!"
```

The Applescript language follows the Open Scripting Architecture (OSA) standard, making it an OSA language. For a full list of OSA languages installed on your computer, you can type the osalang command. To execute scripts written in OSA languages from the command line, use the osascript command. There are two forms of this command:

```
osascript script-file
osascript -e 'one line of script'
```

The first version runs a file containing an OSA script language; you do not need to set the script-file executable. If you omit the script-file argument, the osascript command reads lines of script from the standard input.

The second version of the command reads and executes a single line of script that is specified on the command line. You can include multiple -e arguments if you want to execute more than one line of script at the same time.

The default scripting language for osascript is Applescript. If you have another OSA language installed, you can specify it by giving a -l option to osascript, followed by the name of the language.

You can use the Applescript language in many more ways than shown here. You can use Applescript to control most Mac OS X applications. To learn more about the Applescript language, www.apple.com/applescript for Apple's Web site.

RUN APPLESCRIPT FROM THE SHELL

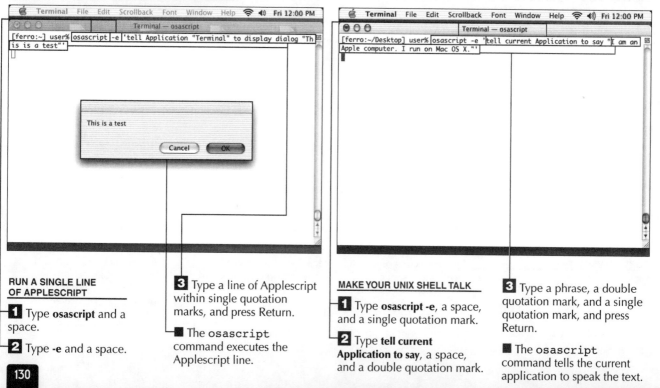

RUN A SINGLE LINE OF APPLESCRIPT

1 Type **osascript** and a space.

2 Type **-e** and a space.

3 Type a line of Applescript within single quotation marks, and press Return.

■ The osascript command executes the Applescript line.

MAKE YOUR UNIX SHELL TALK

1 Type **osascript -e**, a space, and a single quotation mark.

2 Type **tell current Application to say**, a space, and a double quotation mark.

3 Type a phrase, a double quotation mark, and a single quotation mark, and press Return.

■ The osascript command tells the current application to speak the text.

Apply It

You can use `osascript` to announce the new directory each time you use the `cd` command. It uses the special `tcsh` shell script `cwdcmd`, a command executed each time you change the current working directory.

1 Create a directory for storing scripts, such as `~/Library/OSAscript`.

2 Create a shell script in the directory named **say-dir.sh**, containing the following: `osascript -e 'tell current Application to say "New Dir: '$cwd'"'`

3 Add an `alias` command to your .tcshrc file that sets the `cwdcmd` alias: `alias cwdcmd 'source ~/Library/OSAscript/say-dir.sh'`

■ You can type **source .tcshrc** to run your .tcshrc file and add this alias, or you can type the `alias` command (in step 3) to set the alias for your current Terminal window.

When you change to a new directory, the `cwdcmd` alias executes. The `source` command reads in the shell script and runs it, calling the `osascript` command. The value of the current working directory is stored in the shell variable `$cwd`, and the new directory is announced because the value is used in the Applescript `say` command.

There is one hitch to using this script: You will change directories slowly because the `cd` command will not end until the full path is spoken.

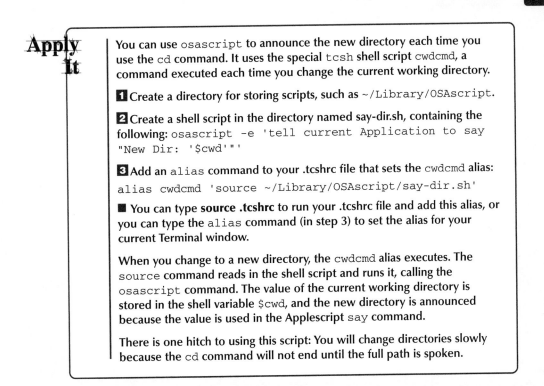

RUN AN APPLESCRIPT FILE

1 Create a text file containing your Applescript, using a text editor.

2 Type **osascript** and a space.

3 Type the name of the script file and press Return.

■ The `osascript` command executes the Applescript file.

CREATE CLICKABLE SHELL SCRIPTS

You can make shell scripts that you can run by double-clicking their icons in the Mac OS X Finder. A script is clickable if the name of the script file ends with the suffix .command.

Ordinary shell scripts are not clickable. Double-clicking a shell script's icon opens it in a text editor instead of running it. To make it clickable, you can make the script executable by using the chmod command and giving it a name ending in .command.

When you double-click the icon of a .command file, the Terminal program opens a new window and executes the command in that window. For example, if you want to run the top program in a shell window, you can write a shell script like this:

```
#!/bin/csh
# top.command:
# This script will start the top command
with the options
# you prefer.  It can be run by double-
clicking the file
# icon in the Finder.

top -u -s5    # sort by CPU, update every 5
seconds
```

If you save this file as top.command and set it as executable, you can double-click the icon to start the top command. You can also add a new icon using the Mac OS X Finder. You can make other types of executable programs clickable by renaming them to .command filenames as well.

CREATE CLICKABLE SHELL SCRIPTS

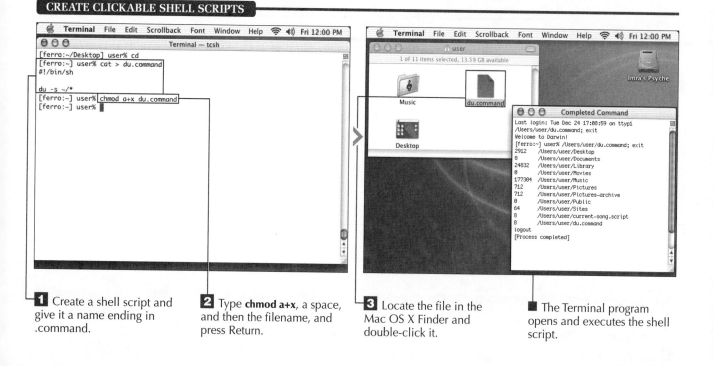

1 Create a shell script and give it a name ending in .command.

2 Type **chmod a+x**, a space, and then the filename, and press Return.

3 Locate the file in the Mac OS X Finder and double-click it.

■ The Terminal program opens and executes the shell script.

DRAG PATHNAMES TO THE TERMINAL WINDOW

Y ou can use any file found in the Mac OS X Finder by dragging the icon onto the Terminal window. The pathname of the file appears in the shell as if you had typed it. This capability is useful if you are deep within folders in the Finder and you want to use a shell command on a file you have found. You can save typing in this way and make it much less likely that you will mistype a pathname. For example, to get a long directory listing of a file, type a partial command and a space:

```
[ferro:~] user% ls -l
```

Then switch to Finder and locate the file. Click and hold the mouse button on the file's icon and then drag it to whatever part of your Terminal window is visible. You do not need to be able to see the full window, only a portion of it. When you

release the mouse button, the file is not moved, as it usually would be if you dragged the icon to a new folder. Instead, the file's full pathname is pasted onto your Terminal window:

```
[ferro:~] user% ls -l
/Users/user/Pictures/kitty/olorin1.jpg
```

You can then press the Return key and execute the command. This action works with any file, including folders, to paste the directory path of a dragged folder into the Terminal window.

You can drag multiple files to the Terminal if you are typing a command that takes several arguments, such as the diff shell command. You need to remember to type spaces between each file, or the pathnames will not be separated and will be read as one long pathname.

DRAG PATHNAMES TO THE TERMINAL WINDOW

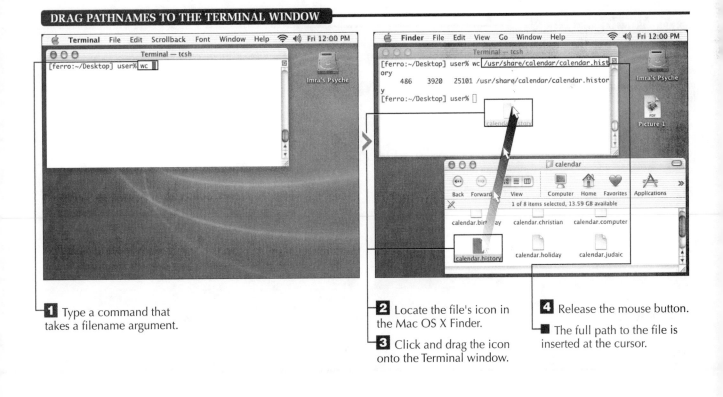

1 Type a command that takes a filename argument.

2 Locate the file's icon in the Mac OS X Finder.

3 Click and drag the icon onto the Terminal window.

4 Release the mouse button.

■ The full path to the file is inserted at the cursor.

CONNECT TO THE INTERNET

The Internet is a loose connection of systems and networks that spans the globe. This supernetwork makes it possible for people in New Jersey to send e-mail to people in Ethiopia, for teens in California to read their Pennsylvania grandmother's recipes on the Web, and for people to chat and form meaningful relationships with people they may never meet face to face.

Connecting a Mac OS X system to the Internet is relatively easy. You can establish dial-up, *digital subscriber line (DSL)*, and *local area network (LAN)* connections, depending on your resources and circumstances.

Unix systems were built to be networked. In fact, the first Unix systems and the first efforts to connect systems from different locations on the first internetworks started as contemporaries. Mac OS X is no exception. Mac OS X systems run the Internet networking protocols — a collection of protocols called *Transmission Control Protocol/Internet Protocol (TCP/IP)* — natively.

If your Macintosh is a home-based system, you will probably hook up to the network using a dial-up or DSL connection. If your Macintosh is on your desk at work, you will probably hook up to network wiring that is installed throughout your building. After you are connected, you can use all the services of the Internet from the classics, such as telnet and ftp, to Web surfing and more.

Home-based systems almost always rely on technology that automatically assigns an address to the system and directs it to a name server and router that allows it to reach other systems. Although these topics are not covered in depth in this chapter, you should know the names of these services. *Dynamic Host Configuration Protocol (DHCP)* dynamically assigns IP addresses to its client systems. *Domain Name System (DNS)* allows you to look up domain names, such as www.apple.com, and retrieve their IP addresses.

CONNECT TO THE INTERNET

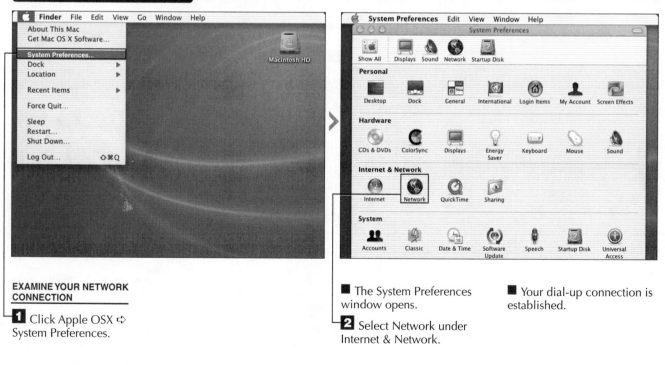

EXAMINE YOUR NETWORK CONNECTION

1 Click Apple OSX ⇨ System Preferences.

■ The System Preferences window opens.

2 Select Network under Internet & Network.

■ Your dial-up connection is established.

Extra

Connecting to the Internet allows you to take advantage of a wealth of information and services. Understanding the basics of how this connection works will make it easier for you to report on and resolve problems when they occur.

For dial-up accounts, you generally do not need to be concerned about the IP address, subnet mask, DNS server, or default router that your system will use. Although this information is critical to your network connection, your Internet service provider (ISP) assigns it when you connect. If your Macintosh is attached to a local area network, you might use a static IP address — one that is permanently assigned to your system — or one that a DHCP server assigns when you boot your system.

Regardless of how this information is assigned, your system requires a unique IP address to identify it as a member of a network, a subnet mask to allow the system to determine the extent of the local network, a default router to direct remote connections, and a DNS server to allow you to locate systems by name.

SET UP A NETWORK CONNECTION

1 Enter your IP Address and Subnet Mask on the TCP/IP tab.

2 Enter your DNS Servers and domains.

■ You will be prompted to save the information upon closing the form.

■ Check with your system administrator if you are unsure about these settings.

SET UP A DIAL-UP CONNECTION

1 Click the PPPoE tab.

2 Type the information provided to you by your ISP.

■ You will be prompted to save the information upon closing the form.

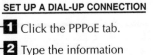

LOOK UP AN INTERNET ADDRESS

You can look up an IP address to verify that you can reach a system over the Internet. The command you use to look up an address is nslookup. To use this command effectively, you need to know about IP addresses and name translation.

A local area network might, for example, include all of the IP addresses between 128.2.10.1 and 128.2.10.254. On such a network, an address such as 128.2.10.13 functions much like a street address.

A subnet mask is a value of the form 255.255.255.0 that numerically marks the dividing line between the portion of an IP address that identifies the network and the portion that identifies a particular system or host. When a netmask contains only values of 255 and 0, this dividing line is easy to determine — it is the point at which the values change from 255 to 0. If the network portion of an address were the street, the host portion of the address would be the

house number. A subnet mask allows a system to determine when systems are on the same network and when they are not. When the network portions of two IP addresses are different, the systems are not on the same network. The default router is a system on the local network that forwards communications to remote systems — systems not on the local network.

While all of these addresses are essential for network connections, it is more convenient to use fully qualified domain names such as www.apple.com to communicate on the Internet instead of IP addresses such as 17.254.0.91. For this to be possible, you need to use a service that translates names into IP addresses and vice versa. The service that translates between domain names and IP addresses is called the *Domain Name System* and is generally referred to as *DNS*. The nslookup command allows you to make use of DNS services on the command line.

LOOK UP AN INTERNET ADDRESS

```
[ferro:~] user% nslookup
Default Server:  sys1a.coretel.net
Address:  162.33.160.100

> []
```

```
[ferro:~] user% nslookup
Default Server:  sys1a.coretel.net
Address:  162.33.160.100

> www.apple.com
Server:  sys1a.coretel.net
Address:  162.33.160.100

Non-authoritative answer:
Name:     www.apple.com.akadns.net
Address:  17.254.0.91
Aliases:  www.apple.com

> []
```

Note: You must be connected to the Internet for this task.

■ In the Terminal window, type **nslookup** and press Return.

■ The screen displays the name and/or address of the DNS server servicing your system.

■ Type a fully qualified host name and press Return.

■ The screen displays the IP address for that URL.

Extra

You can only use the Internet effectively if your system makes use of DNS. Servers are able to resolve domain names into IP addresses and IP addresses back into domain names only because records containing this information have been established and made available through the distributed lookup service known as DNS. If DNS records have not been established for a system, you will only be able to locate that system over the Internet if you know its IP address. A system that DNS knows about is said to be *registered*.

No DNS server knows about every system that is registered. Instead, each knows about locally registered systems for which it is said to be authoritative. However, DNS servers also know how to communicate with other DNS servers, so that lookup requests can be answered regardless of how remote the system and the DNS server might be.

Although few users are aware of the activity of DNS, they use the service every time they make a connection to a remote system or browse to a Web site. To examine where your system looks for DNS services, use the cat command to display the file /etc/resolv.conf where this information is stored.

TYPE THIS:

```
[ferro:~] cat /etc/resolv.conf
```

RESULT:

The content of the resolv.conf file showing DNS configuration data is displayed.

```
 Terminal  File  Edit  Scrollback  Font  Window  Help

                              ttyp1
[ferro:~] user% nslookup
Default Server:  sys1a.coretel.net
Address:  162.33.160.100

> www.apple.com
Server:  sys1a.coretel.net
Address:  162.33.160.100

Non-authoritative answer:
Name:    www.apple.com.akadns.net
Address:  17.254.0.91
Aliases:  www.apple.com

> 17.254.0.91
Server:  sys1a.coretel.net
Address:  162.33.160.100

Name:    www.apple.com
Address:  17.254.0.91

> □
```

```
 Terminal  File  Edit  Scrollback  Font  Window  Help

                              ttyp1
[ferro:~] user% nslookup
Default Server:  sys1a.coretel.net
Address:  162.33.160.100

> www.apple.com
Server:  sys1a.coretel.net
Address:  162.33.160.100

Non-authoritative answer:
Name:    www.apple.com.akadns.net
Address:  17.254.0.91
Aliases:  www.apple.com

> 17.254.0.91
Server:  sys1a.coretel.net
Address:  162.33.160.100

Name:    www.apple.com
Address:  17.254.0.91

> exit
[ferro:~] user% □
```

3 Type the returned IP address and press Return.

■ The screen displays the domain name of the IP address you entered.

4 Type **exit** and press Return.

■ Your **nslookup** session terminates.

LOOK UP DOMAIN INFORMATION

You can gather quite a bit of information about a domain by using the `nslookup` or the `whois` commands. These commands provide information that can be helpful if you want to know how to reach someone responsible for a domain. Such information can also be useful in troubleshooting.

The primary function of DNS is to return IP addresses in exchange for fully qualified domain names such as www.apple.com. The secondary function is to return fully qualified domain names in exchange for IP addresses. These, however, are only the most obvious services that DNS provides to the systems that use the service around the clock and around the globe. DNS also provides several other useful functions. For example, DNS maintains and can provide information about a domain and its registration.

You can retrieve information about a domain by requesting the statement of authority (SOA) record with the `nslookup` command. The SOA record includes a statement about the

server's zone of authority — what information it can vouch for — and usually provides a point of contact. It also contains the serial number and information about when zone information expires.

The DNS mail exchanger (MX) record identifies the mail servers for the domain. These records determine which systems are contacted when another system needs to deliver e-mail to someone with an address at that domain. You can also get this information using the `nslookup` command.

The `whois` command looks up information in the Network Information Center (NIC) database. This information includes the registrar and the name servers responsible for the registration. If you are curious about a domain that has a name similar to your own or you want to determine whether you can buy it, the `whois` command will provide you with some basic information.

LOOK UP DOMAIN INFORMATION

Note: You must be connected to the Internet for this task.

1 Type **whois** followed by a space.

2 Type the name of a domain and press Return.

■ The screen displays the NIC information for the specified domain.

Extra

DNS records include those defined in the table below.

RECORD TYPE	FUNCTION
A	Maps a domain name to an IP address
CNAME	Provides an alternate name or alias for a system
PTR	Maps an IP address to a domain name
MX	Identifies a mail exchanger for a domain
SOA	Provides information about the domain as a whole

There is not necessarily a one-to-one correspondence between fully qualified domain names and IP addresses. A single fully qualified domain name can resolve into multiple IP addresses. This indicates that connections to these systems are being distributed in such a way that each system in the set is responding to a share of the overall traffic.

A single system may have virtually any number of fully qualified domain names, and this is, in fact, often the case with ISPs that provide Web site support for hundreds or thousands of customers. For this to work, each of these domain names must resolve to the same IP address.

```
                        Terminal  File  Edit  Scrollback  Font  Window  Help
                                          ttyp1
[ferro:screenshots] user% nslookup
Default Server:  sys1a.coretel.net
Address:  162.33.160.100

> set querytype=SOA
> www.apple.com
Server:  sys1a.coretel.net
Address:  162.33.160.100

Non-authoritative answer:
www.apple.com   canonical name = www.apple.com.akadns.net

Authoritative answers can be found from:
apple.com.akadns.net
        origin = ns1-159.akam.net
        mail addr = hostmaster.akamai.com
        serial = 50
        refresh = 50 (50S)
        retry  = 50 (50S)
        expire = 50 (50S)
        minimum ttl = 50 (50S)
>
```

```
                        Terminal  File  Edit  Scrollback  Font  Window  Help
                                          ttyp1
[ferro:~] user% nslookup
Default Server:  sys1a.coretel.net
Address:  162.33.160.100

> set querytype=MX
> apple.com
Server:  sys1a.coretel.net
Address:  162.33.160.100

Non-authoritative answer:
apple.com       preference = 30, mail exchanger = mail-in.euro.apple.com
apple.com       preference = 10, mail exchanger = mail-in.apple.com

Authoritative answers can be found from:
apple.com       nameserver = nserver4.apple.com
apple.com       nameserver = nserver.asia.apple.com
apple.com       nameserver = nserver.euro.apple.com
apple.com       nameserver = nserver.apple.com
apple.com       nameserver = nserver2.apple.com
apple.com       nameserver = nserver3.apple.com
mail-in.apple.com       internet address = 17.254.0.58
mail-in.apple.com       internet address = 17.254.0.57
```

3 Type **nslookup** and press Return.

4 Type **set querytype=SOA** and press Return.

5 Type a domain name and press Return.

■ The screen displays the SOA record for the specified domain.

6 Type **set querytype=MX** and press Return.

7 Type a domain name and press Return.

■ The screen displays the MX records for the specified domain.

EXAMINE YOUR NETWORK CONNECTION

V iewing network connection information is especially helpful when you are troubleshooting connection problems. For example, you can check if your network connection is running or determine your netmask with the ifconfig command. You can examine your network connections, view the state of your network interfaces, determine what connections are established, and form an idea of how well your network connections are performing.

All networked Unix systems have at least two network connections. One is the normal connection associated with the network adaptor and used to communicate with other systems. The other is called a *loopback* and provides the means for a system to use network protocols while communicating with itself. The loopback address is associated with the same IP address on every Unix system. That address is 127.0.0.1. The normal or network IP address is different on every system and, if dynamically assigned, might also be different each time a system connects to the network.

Both network connections serve an important function and you can examine both with the ifconfig command. The ifconfig — interface configuration — command provides information on the network interfaces established on a system. This information includes what addresses are assigned to each interface and whether the network interface is operational. The ifconfig command also displays the subnet mask associated with your network connection. This information is critical to proper functioning on a network, both for proper functioning on the local network and the ability to communicate over the Internet.

Another informative command for examining your network connections is netstat. This command provides a listing of your routing table — a table used in directing network traffic — and details about current network connections as well as network statistics that provide insight about how well your network connection is working. This includes how busy your network interface is and what types of traffic your system is handling.

EXAMINE YOUR NETWORK CONNECTION

```
Terminal   File   Edit   Scrollback   Font   Window   Help
                              ttyp1
[ferro:screenshots] user% ifconfig
lo0: flags=8049<UP,LOOPBACK,RUNNING,MULTICAST> mtu 16384
        inet6 ::1 prefixlen 128
        inet6 fe80::1%lo0 prefixlen 64 scopeid 0x1
        inet 127.0.0.1 netmask 0xff000000
gif0: flags=8010<POINTOPOINT,MULTICAST> mtu 1280
stf0: flags=0<> mtu 1280
en0: flags=8863<UP,BROADCAST,SMART,RUNNING,SIMPLEX,MULTICAST> mtu 1500
        inet6 fe80::20a:27ff:fed8:53e6%en0 prefixlen 64 scopeid 0x4
        inet 10.0.0.3 netmask 0xff000000 broadcast 10.255.255.255
        ether 00:0a:27:d8:53:e6
        media: autoselect (100baseTX <half-duplex>) status: active
        supported media: none autoselect 10baseT/UTP <half-duplex> 10baseT/UTP
<half-duplex,hw-loopback> 10baseT/UTP <full-duplex> 10baseT/UTP <full-duplex,hw
-loopback> 100baseTX <half-duplex> 100baseTX <half-duplex,hw-loopback> 100baseT
X <full-duplex> 100baseTX <full-duplex,hw-loopback>
ppp0: flags=8051<UP,POINTOPOINT,RUNNING,MULTICAST> mtu 1500
        inet 162.33.107.34 --> 162.33.163.17 netmask 0xffff0000
[ferro:screenshots] user% []
```

USING IFCONFIG

Note: You must be connected to the Internet for this task.

1 Type **ifconfig** and press Return.

■ The loopback interface, dial-up IP address, and network interface addresses appear. Both interfaces are operational.

```
Terminal   File   Edit   Scrollback   Font   Window   Help
                              ttyp1
[ferro:~] user% netstat -rn
Routing tables

Internet:
Destination      Gateway           Flags   Refs    Use  Netif Expir
e
default          162.33.163.7      UGSc    3        21  ppp0
10               link#4            UCS     0         0  en0
10.0.0.3         127.0.0.1         UHS     0         9  lo0
127.0.0.1        127.0.0.1         UH      7      5016  lo0
162.33.163.7     162.33.116.237    UH      4         0  ppp0
169.254          link#4            UCS     0         0  en0

Internet6:
Destination                    Gateway                      Flags
  Netif Expire
                                                              UH
   lo0
fe80::%lo0/64                                                 Uc
   lo0
                               link#1                         UHL
   lo0
```

USING NETSTAT

1 Type **netstat** followed by a space.

2 Type **-rn** and press Return.

■ The screen displays a listing of your routing table with IP addresses.

Apply It

Unix systems, especially those that are servers, generally have many established connections at any point in time. At each end of a connection, a system is communicating via a port. A *port* is an address associated with a service requester on the client end and a service on the server end. Ports enable software such as Microsoft's Internet Explorer to communicate with a service such as Apache.

The netstat command allows you to view which systems are communicating and which ports they are using in the process.

Network connections are based on TCP. *TCP* is one of the primary protocols making up TCP/IP and the one that almost all network tools use. Network connections run through a series of states starting from the initial connection request and ending with its closure. Ports on servers listen for requests. When a client request arrives, the client and server exchange information and a connection is established. You can view established connections using a netstat command.

Information provided by the netstat -a command includes the names or addresses of the systems at both ends of each connection as well as the port or service address that is being used. Viewing netstat output can help you determine how many connections your system is supporting and how well it is performing under the load.

TYPE THIS:		RESULT:
`[ferro:~] netstat -a	grep ESTABLISHED`	▷	The screen displays a list of established connections.

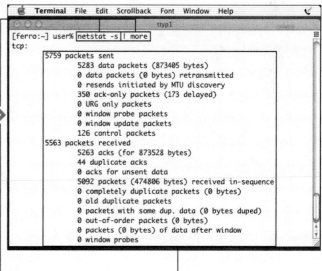

3 Type **netstat -a** followed by a space.

4 Type **| more** and press Return.

■ The screen displays a listing of your current network connections.

5 Type **netstat -s** followed by a space.

6 Type **| more** and press Return.

■ The screen displays a listing of your network statistics.

CHECK THAT ANOTHER COMPUTER IS REACHABLE

You can check whether a remote system is reachable using the `ping` command, and trace routes using `traceroute`. Whenever you have trouble making a connection to a system, you can test the connection using `ping` — a deceptively simple command that sends a small request in the form of a packet to the remote system, requesting a reply. The `ping` command was named after the sound that sonar makes when locating an object.

If the remote system is running and capable of replying, it responds to the request that `ping` generates, and you see the response on your screen. On Mac OS X systems, `ping` generates requests until you press Control + C. Then it displays a summary of the responses, including how many requests the remote system answered and how long each round trip took. This reply tells you whether you were able to reach the remote system and indicates the quality of the connection. If your system receives a reply for every request, you probably have a good connection.

Another useful command for testing network connections is `traceroute`. The `traceroute` command attempts to time the connection between your system and each successive router in the route between you and the target host. The result is a list of each hop, along with reports on how long it took to reach each system. This timing information can be used to interpret the quality of the connection.

Both `ping` and `traceroute` rely on a protocol called the *Internet Control Message Protocol (ICMP)* that is sometimes blocked on routers. Because of this blocking, you might get inaccurate results if you `ping` or run `traceroute` on a system. The results may suggest that the system is unreachable, but you may be able to reach it with a `telnet` or `ssh` command.

CHECK THAT ANOTHER COMPUTER IS REACHABLE

```
 Terminal   File   Edit   Scrollback   Font   Window   Help

                              ttyp1
[ferro:screenshots] user% ping www.apple.com
PING www.apple.com.akadns.net (17.112.152.32): 56 data bytes
64 bytes from 17.112.152.32: icmp_seq=0 ttl=48 time=185.225 ms
64 bytes from 17.112.152.32: icmp_seq=1 ttl=48 time=191.329 ms
64 bytes from 17.112.152.32: icmp_seq=2 ttl=48 time=185.518 ms
64 bytes from 17.112.152.32: icmp_seq=3 ttl=48 time=177.493 ms
64 bytes from 17.112.152.32: icmp_seq=4 ttl=48 time=175.085 ms
64 bytes from 17.112.152.32: icmp_seq=5 ttl=48 time=176.68 ms
64 bytes from 17.112.152.32: icmp_seq=6 ttl=48 time=178.282 ms
64 bytes from 17.112.152.32: icmp_seq=7 ttl=48 time=174.883 ms
64 bytes from 17.112.152.32: icmp_seq=8 ttl=48 time=179.485 ms
64 bytes from 17.112.152.32: icmp_seq=9 ttl=48 time=176.087 ms
^C
--- www.apple.com.akadns.net ping statistics ---
10 packets transmitted, 10 packets received, 0% packet loss
round-trip min/avg/max = 174.883/180.006/191.329 ms
[ferro:screenshots] user%
```

```
 Terminal   File   Edit   Scrollback   Font   Window   Help

                              ttyp1
[ferro:screenshots] user% ping www.microsoft.com
PING www.microsoft.akadns.net (207.46.249.27): 56 data bytes
^C
--- www.microsoft.akadns.net ping statistics ---
10 packets transmitted, 0 packets received, 100% packet loss
[ferro:screenshots] user%
```

Note: You must be connected to the Internet for this task.

1 Type **ping** followed by a space.

2 Type the domain name of a remote system and press Return.

3 Press Control + C after waiting 10 seconds or more.

■ The `ping` command displays a summary of its responses.

■ No packets were lost or unanswered.

4 Type **ping** followed by a space.

5 Type **www.microsoft.com** and press Return.

6 Press Control + C after waiting 10 seconds or more.

■ The `ping` command displays a summary of its responses.

■ If no replies were received, the ICMP protocol is probably being blocked.

Extra

You can often make your troubleshooting easier by reducing the complexity of your commands. Like many networking commands, `ping` relies on the services of DNS to resolve domain names into IP addresses. If you are having trouble reaching your DNS server, your `ping` and `traceroute` commands will be affected. To rule out name resolution when you are troubleshooting a network connection, use `ping` and `traceroute` with an IP address instead of a domain name. Of course, this only works if you know the IP addresses for the systems you want to reach.

Similarly, commands such as `netstat` usually run faster if they are not required to look up IP addresses and translate port addresses into names. You can turn off lookups by adding `n` to the argument list.

TYPE THIS:

```
ping 192.74.137.5
```

⌄

RESULT:

```
PING 192.74.137.5 (192.74.137.5): 56 data bytes
64 bytes from 192.74.137.5: icmp_seq=0 ttl=240 time=157.03 ms
64 bytes from 192.74.137.5: icmp_seq=1 ttl=240 time=166.589 ms

^C
--- 192.74.137.5 ping statistics ---
2 packets transmitted, 2 packets received, 0% packet loss
round-trip min/avg/max = 131.532/157.241/191.94 ms
```

TYPE THIS:

```
netstat -an | grep ESTABLISHED
```

⌄

RESULT:

```
[ferro:screenshots] user% netstat -a | grep ESTABLISHED
tcp4       0      0  east-18-34.dynam.49218 fajita.toad.
net.http   ESTABLISHED
```

 Terminal File Edit Scrollback Font Window Help

```
ttyp1
[ferro:screenshots] user% traceroute 162.33.163.17
traceroute to 162.33.163.17 (162.33.163.17), 30 hops max, 40 byte packets
 1  geese.coretel.net (162.33.163.17)  116.287 ms  113.714 ms  106.78 ms
[ferro:screenshots] user% []
```

 Terminal File Edit Scrollback Font Window Help

```
ttyp1
[ferro:screenshots] user% traceroute www.apple.com
traceroute to www.apple.com.akadns.net (17.112.152.32), 30 hops max, 40 byte pa
ckets
 1  geese.coretel.net (162.33.163.17)  115.781 ms   99.487 ms  118.174 ms
 2  162.33.163.1 (162.33.163.1)  103.565 ms   98.942 ms  101.54 ms
 3  hsrp-dmvptp.colo.coretel.net (162.33.163.103)  104.714 ms  106.687 ms  103.
346 ms
 4  7505-dmvptp.colo.coretel.net (162.33.163.102)  100.405 ms  101.796 ms  101.
757 ms
 5  12.119.70.97 (12.119.70.97)  131.474 ms  107.583 ms  107.94 ms
 6  gbr5-p59.wswdc.ip.att.net (12.123.194.66)  111.968 ms  106.495 ms  109.289
ms
 7  gbr3-p100.wswdc.ip.att.net (12.122.5.194)  108.253 ms  104.758 ms  106.499
ms
 8  gbr3-p40.sl9mo.ip.att.net (12.122.2.82)  172.125 ms  118.393 ms  124.247 ms
 9  gbr3-p20.sffca.ip.att.net (12.122.2.74)  164.742 ms  160.726 ms  165.341 ms
10  gbr1-p50.sffca.ip.att.net (12.122.1.162)  169.76 ms  162.623 ms  161.464 ms
11  gar1-p360.sffca.ip.att.net (12.123.13.57)  164.633 ms  257.139 ms  159.378
ms
[]
```

7 Type **traceroute** followed by a space.

8 Type the domain name of a system on the same network as your computer, or the IP address of your default gateway.

■ **Traceroute** responds with a header line and a single route timing line.

9 Type **traceroute** followed by a space.

10 Type the domain name of a remote system and press Return.

■ **Traceroute** returns lines of data describing the route taken to reach the remote system.

■ An asterisk in place of a time means that the response did not come back in time to be counted.

LOG ON TO ANOTHER COMPUTER

You can take advantage of accounts and applications on other systems. You can log on to a remote system using telnet or rlogin. Unix systems, such as Mac OS X, provide several ways for you to log on to other systems. The most established of these is a tool called telnet that has been available longer than the Internet. Telnet establishes a terminal-like connection to another system. If the remote system has telnet services enabled, it asks you for a username and password and logs you on.

Most telnet servers give you the option of logging on with the username you are using on your local system, but you are free to enter a different username at the prompt. You end a telnet session by logging out. For most systems, you can press Control + D or type the command logoff to exit.

Another tool for logging on to remote systems is rlogin. This tool is much like telnet, but less common. You are likely to find it only on Unix systems, and even then, it may be disabled. The rlogin command requires that you log on with the same username that you are using on the local system unless you add the -1 newname argument to the end of the command.

To use any of these tools, you must have an account on a remote system. If you do not have a shell account on another system, however, you can try telnet or rlogin by logging on to your Mac OS X system. The logon will only work if you have enabled remote access. See the section "Enable Remote Access to Your Computer" later in this chapter.

LOG ON TO ANOTHER COMPUTER

```
[ferro:screenshots] user% telnet achilles.tcsnet.net
Trying 205.244.232.4...
Connected to achilles.tcsnet.net.
Escape character is '^]'.

SunOS 5.8

login: user
Password:
Last login: Sun Dec 29 19:39:52 from core-east-5-26.
bash-2.03$ []
```

```
bash-2.03$ who am i
user      pts/9        Jan  2 11:15   (east-18-34.dynamic-dialup.coretel.net)
bash-2.03$ []
```

USING TELNET

Note: You must be connected to the Internet for this task.

1 In the Terminal window, type **telnet** followed by a space.

2 Type the domain name of a system on which you have a shell account.

*Note: Type **telnet localhost** if you do not have a remote system account.*

3 Type your username and password at the prompts.

4 Type **who am i** and press Return if the remote system is a Unix host.

■ The screen displays your logon on the list of logged on users.

Apply It

You can use `telnet` to test connections to other systems by supplying a port number in addition to the system name on the command line. If you want to check how many messages are in your inbox on a system that supports POP3, you can connect to the port that services the POP3 server and ask for this information using `telnet`. You can also use `telnet` to determine whether a mail server is responding. POP3 is a simple protocol used to download e-mail from the mail server.

TYPE THIS:

```
[ferro:~] telnet <servername> 110
```

Use the name of a server from which you receive e-mail using POP3. After the system responds, enter the following lines, replacing the text in brackets with your account information:

```
user <your username>
pass <your password>
stat
quit
```

RESULT:

After the `stat` command, the system displays a number telling you how many messages are in your inbox.

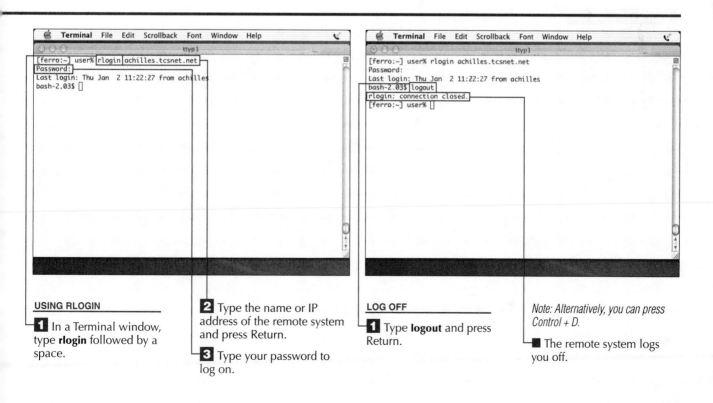

USING RLOGIN

1 In a Terminal window, type **rlogin** followed by a space.

2 Type the name or IP address of the remote system and press Return.

3 Type your password to log on.

LOG OFF

1 Type **logout** and press Return.

Note: Alternatively, you can press Control + D.

■ The remote system logs you off.

TRANSFER FILES

You can often obtain needed files and applications from other systems. You can move files between your system and others using `ftp`. Approximately as old as `telnet`, the `ftp` command has been enabling Unix users to upload and download files for a couple of decades. The protocol, or language, of `ftp` is fairly simple, although some `ftp` servers have implemented a wide range of commands.

In its simplest form, `ftp` allows you to log on to a system, upload files using the `put` command, download files using the `get` command, and move around the directory structure on the remote system. You can transfer data in binary mode or ASCII mode. ASCII mode is designed for text files, and `ftp` translates line endings if you are transferring text files between Unix and DOS systems. Binary mode is designed for software, image files, and other types of files that use non-printable characters that might otherwise interfere with the transfer.

One popular form of `ftp` is called *anonymous ftp*. When using `anonymous ftp`, you type the word **anonymous** as if it were your username and your e-mail address (or sometimes any string of characters) as your password. `Anonymous ftp` allows people who do not have accounts on a system to upload or download files. For example, if you set up a drop box for your customers to upload error logs so you can analyze problems they are having with software you sold them, you might chose anonymous ftp. Many companies, such as Apple, that provide documentation and software tools to their customers do so using `anonymous ftp`.

You should `cd` into the directory in which you want downloaded files stored before you start your ftp session. Like `telnet`, `ftp` is not enabled as a service on Mac OS X when you first install the operating system.

TRANSFER FILES

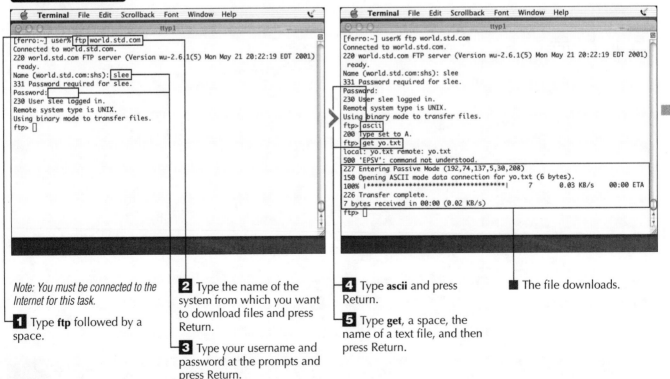

Note: You must be connected to the Internet for this task.

1 Type **ftp** followed by a space.

2 Type the name of the system from which you want to download files and press Return.

3 Type your username and password at the prompts and press Return.

4 Type **ascii** and press Return.

5 Type **get**, a space, the name of a text file, and then press Return.

■ The file downloads.

Extra

You will have an easier time figuring out what went wrong in a file transfer if you know what to look for. Files that you download incorrectly will have problems. Binary files that you transfer as if they are text files are likely to be corrupt and probably unusable. If you attempt to display or otherwise use the files, the system will display an error message.

Text files that you download as binary are likely to be fine if you download them from another Unix system. However, a text file that you download in binary mode from a Windows system is likely to have an extra character at the end of every line. This character represents the carriage return that Unix systems do not use. It displays as ^M when you open these files with an editor.

Example:
```
Making Better Use of Ping^M
^M
Long one of the system administrator's favorite tools for^M
troubleshooting network-related problems, ping is used^M
```

You can remove these unwanted characters using the Unix tr command.

Example:
```
[ferro:~] cat textfile | tr -d "\015" > textfile$$
[ferro:~] mv textfile$$ textfile
```

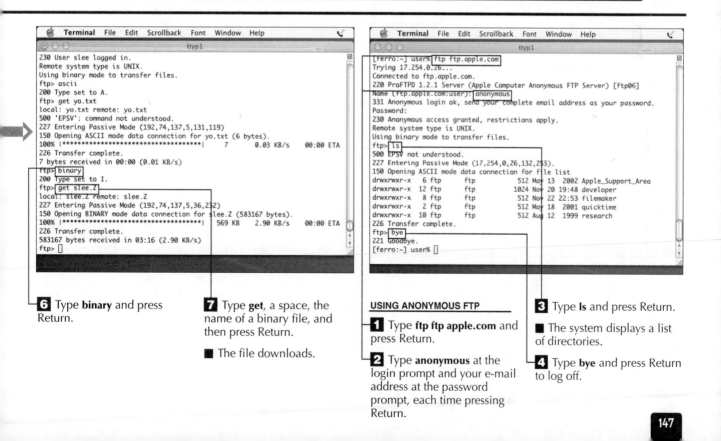

```
 🍎  Terminal   File   Edit   Scrollback   Font   Window   Help            ✎
 ○ ○ ○                              ttyp1
230 User slee logged in.
Remote system type is UNIX.
Using binary mode to transfer files.
ftp> ascii
200 Type set to A.
ftp> get yo.txt
local: yo.txt remote: yo.txt
500 'EPSV': command not understood.
227 Entering Passive Mode (192,74,137,5,131,119)
150 Opening ASCII mode data connection for yo.txt (6 bytes).
100% |***************************|     7     0.03 KB/s    00:00 ETA
226 Transfer complete.
7 bytes received in 00:00 (0.01 KB/s)
ftp> binary
200 Type set to I.
ftp> get slee.Z
local: slee.Z remote: slee.Z
227 Entering Passive Mode (192,74,137,5,36,232)
150 Opening BINARY mode data connection for slee.Z (583167 bytes).
100% |***************************|   569 KB   2.90 KB/s    00:00 ETA
226 Transfer complete.
583167 bytes received in 03:16 (2.90 KB/s)
ftp> □
```

```
 🍎  Terminal   File   Edit   Scrollback   Font   Window   Help            ✎
 ○ ○ ○                              ttyp1
[ferro:~] user% ftp ftp.apple.com
Trying 17.254.0.26...
Connected to ftp.apple.com.
220 ProFTPD 1.2.1 Server (Apple Computer Anonymous FTP Server) [ftp06]
Name (ftp.apple.com:user): anonymous
331 Anonymous login ok, send your complete email address as your password.
Password:
230 Anonymous access granted, restrictions apply.
Remote system type is UNIX.
Using binary mode to transfer files.
ftp> ls
500 EPSV not understood.
227 Entering Passive Mode (17,254,0,26,132,253).
150 Opening ASCII mode data connection for file list
drwxrwxr-x   6 ftp      ftp       512 May 13  2002 Apple_Support_Area
drwxrwxr-x  12 ftp      ftp      1024 Nov 20 19:48 developer
drwxrwxr-x   8 ftp      ftp       512 Nov 22 22:53 filemaker
drwxrwxr-x   2 ftp      ftp       512 May 18  2001 quicktime
drwxrwxr-x  10 ftp      ftp       512 Aug 12  1999 research
226 Transfer complete.
ftp> bye
221 Goodbye.
[ferro:~] user% □
```

6 Type **binary** and press Return.

7 Type **get**, a space, the name of a binary file, and then press Return.

■ The file downloads.

USING ANONYMOUS FTP

1 Type **ftp ftp apple.com** and press Return.

2 Type **anonymous** at the login prompt and your e-mail address at the password prompt, each time pressing Return.

3 Type **ls** and press Return.

■ The system displays a list of directories.

4 Type **bye** and press Return to log off.

ACCESS ANOTHER COMPUTER SECURELY

You can log on to a remote system more securely than with telnet by using ssh. The telnet, rlogin, and ftp commands have a long-recognized vulnerability. Each of these commands transmits usernames and passwords in clear text. Anyone situated along the network path between you and the system you are logging on to and capable of "sniffing" packets — capturing network traffic intended for another system — could capture your logon information and use your account. For this reason, secure tools have been created that provide remote logon access and file transfer without exposing username and password information. These tools use a process known as *encryption* to make the network traffic between client and server indecipherable.

To use ssh in place of telnet or rlogin, you need to have access to an ssh command or a tool that uses ssh, and the server that you want to connect to must have an

ssh server such as sshd. For some ssh connections, you will log on with username/password pairs. For others, you may be provided with a digital certificate. If your username is not the same on both systems, you must use the -l option.

From a user's point of view, using ssh in place of telnet or rlogin makes little difference. The process and the result are nearly the same, especially if the user logs on with a username and password. The encryption and decryption securing the transferred information is completely transparent. When digital certificates are installed on the client and server end of a connection, the process of logging on may be simplified even further. However, the logon only works on systems that have had the certificates installed.

Similarly, you can use sftp in place of ftp to securely transfer files. When you use sftp, the files you download are encrypted during the download.

ACCESS ANOTHER COMPUTER SECURELY

LOG ON WITH SSH

Note: You must be connected to the Internet for these tasks.

1 Type **ssh** followed by a space.

2 Type the name of a server for which you have an account and that has an **ssh** server running, and press Return.

3 Type your password at the prompts.

■ You are logged on to the server.

LOG ON WHEN YOUR USERNAMES DO NOT MATCH

1 Type **ssh -l** followed by a space.

2 Type your username for the remote system followed by a space.

3 Type the name of the remote system and press Return.

4 Type your password at the prompt and press Return.

■ You are logged on to the server.

Apply It

If you need a file that is on a remote system and your are limited to using secure connections, you can still download files, but you must use sftp instead of ftp. When you use sftp, your download files are encrypted between the remote server and your system, making it safer to download sensitive files. You can download a file using sftp in the way just described or by entering a one-line command in a Terminal window. Type the line shown below, replacing the portions of the command in brackets with your data.

Example:
```
[ferro:~] user% sftp user@remote.system.net:
/home/user/myfile.txt
Connecting to remote.system.net...
user@remote.system.net's password:
Fetching /home/user/myfile.txt to myfile.txt
```

Terminal — ttyp1
```
[ferro:~] user% sftp ferro@achilles.tcsnet.net
Connecting to achilles.tcsnet.net...
ferro@achilles.tcsnet.net's password:
sftp> 
```

Terminal — ttyp1
```
[ferro:~] user% sftp ferro@achilles.tcsnet.net
Connecting to achilles.tcsnet.net...
ferro@achilles.tcsnet.net's password:
sftp> ls
drwxr-xr-x    2 ferro    other         512 Jan  2 11:52 .
drwxr-xr-x  213 root     other        4096 Jan  2 11:51 ..
-r--r--r--    1 ferro    staff      206662 Jan  2 11:52 instructions.txt
-rw-------    1 ferro    staff          55 Jan  2 11:52 .bash_history
sftp> get instructions.txt
Fetching /world/home/ferro/instructions.txt to instructions.txt
sftp> bye
```

TRANSFER FILES SECURELY

1 Type **sftp** followed by a space.

2 Type your username followed by @.

3 Type the name of the remote system and press Return.

4 Type your password at the prompt.

■ You are logged on with sftp.

5 Type **ls** and press Return to display a list of the files in the remote account.

6 Type **get** followed by a space.

7 Type the name of a text file and press Return to download the file.

8 Type **bye** to exit.

DOWNLOAD WEB FILES

You can download files with very little effort by using the curl command. Although the most obvious way to download a Web page is to type or copy the URL in your browser's Address block and use the Save As feature, this is not necessarily the easiest or most efficient method. Mac OS X includes a command line tool called curl — copy URL — for downloading Web pages. Curl works with a number of protocols, including HTTP, HTTPS, FTP, GOPHER, DICT, TELNET, LDAP, and FILE.

Not only does curl allow you to download Web pages on the command line, but it also allows you to download files using curl commands in a script. In fact, you can download and install files in a completely unmanned fashion. The syntax of the curl command is flexible enough to allow you to access multiple pages or multiple sites with a single command.

To use curl, you type **curl** followed by any of the options that you want to specify and the URL string. A command such as curl -O http://www.sandrich.com/index.html copies the specified file from the specified site to your current directory using the same filename. Without the -O, the curl command downloads the file to your screen and presents you with lines of HTML.

Curl allows you to copy more than Web pages. You can also use it to download binary files, including image files and software. In fact, the command is so efficient that Unix tools designed to locate and download applications from the Internet often use curl to do the downloading. You can specify multiple URLs or portions of URLs by enclosing the strings you want to match within braces. The string www.{a,b,c}.com, for example refers to the three systems — www.a.com, www.b.com, and www.c.com.

DOWNLOAD WEB FILES

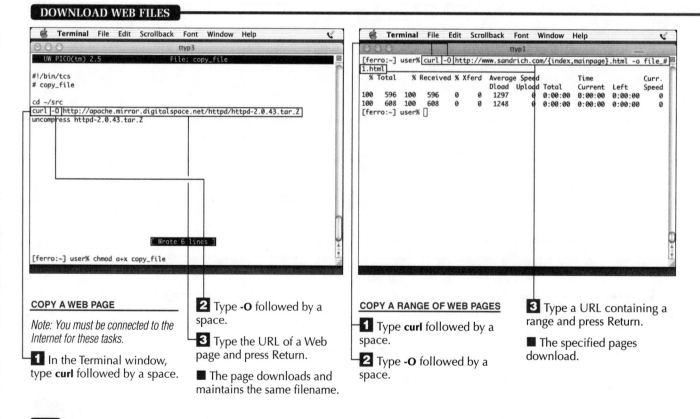

COPY A WEB PAGE

Note: You must be connected to the Internet for these tasks.

1 In the Terminal window, type **curl** followed by a space.

2 Type **-O** followed by a space.

3 Type the URL of a Web page and press Return.

■ The page downloads and maintains the same filename.

COPY A RANGE OF WEB PAGES

1 Type **curl** followed by a space.

2 Type **-O** followed by a space.

3 Type a URL containing a range and press Return.

■ The specified pages download.

Apply It

Curl can post to Web sites as well as download files of various kinds. Posting commands include the name of the script to be executed along with the parameters that you would enter in the online form. You need to know quite a bit about a form to successfully post to it. The example below assumes that the parameters `birthyear` and `vote` are being collected by the online form. It also assumes that the data is processed when a button is pressed and that the value of the press equals OK.

A post command in `curl` might look like the following:

```
curl -d "birthyear=1985&vote=1&press=OK" www.site.com/vote.cgi
```

This type of command can be used in a script to automate posting. To learn more about `curl` and how you can use it in scripts, you can read the man page or download a tutorial available online.

TYPE THIS:

```
[ferro:~] curl -O http://curl.planetmirror.com/
docs/httpscripting.html
```

RESULTS:

The httpscripting.html tutorial downloads.

DOWNLOAD A BINARY FILE

1 Type **curl** followed by a space.

2 Type **-O** followed by a space.

3 Type the URL of a Web page containing a compressed tar file and press Return.

Note: On a dial-up connection, this may take awhile to download.

■ The specified binary file downloads.

CREATE A SCRIPT FOR DOWNLOADING WEB PAGES WITH CURL

1 Start the Pico editor to create a file named copy_url.

2 Type **#!/bin/tcsh** and press Return twice.

3 Type **echo –n "URL> "** and press Return, then type **set URL = $<** and press Return twice.

4 Type **cd ~/src; curl –O http://$URL**.

5 Save your file, and exit Pico.

ENABLE REMOTE ACCESS TO YOUR COMPUTER

Y ou can allow others to log on to your computer or make it possible for you to log on to your Mac OS X system from another system. While Mac OS X systems make it possible for you to log on to remote systems, browse Web sites, and download files, they do not allow others to log on to your system or access files on your system. If you want to allow this type of access, you have to enable it by modifying your system's configuration.

There are two basic ways to provide a network service on your Mac OS X system. You can start the service — for example, start up a Web server — by typing the name of the server process on the command line. These services are designed to run in the background and continue running until you shut your system down or kill them. See Chapter 7 for

more information). Alternatively, you can configure the service to start whenever a request arrives. In this latter case, another process listens for requests on behalf of the service and starts it as needed. The decision as to which method to use depends on the particular service. Web servers, such as Apache's httpd, are better run all of the time. This provides better Web performance. Services such as ftp and telnet that are used only now and then are better run on an as-needed basis. You configure as-needed access through the /etc/inetd.conf file.

To modify system configuration information in Mac OS X, you need to be a privileged user. The sudo command, which allows you to run a command as root, works well for this purpose if you are allowed access.

ENABLE REMOTE ACCESS TO YOUR COMPUTER

1 Type **sudo vi /etc/inetd.conf** and press Return.

2 Type your password if prompted.

3 Type **/#ftp** and press Return.

■ Your cursor is positioned at the beginning of the line detailing the **ftp** service.

Extra

Files responsible for the configuration of a Unix system, Mac OS X included, are always set up so that only the root is able to make changes. This is important to system security because it ensures that only trusted users can modify the configuration of a system. As a system manager, you have two choices when you need to change a configuration file. You can switch users to the root account with the su command; su – sets you up as root with root's environment. Alternatively, you can use the sudo command to run the command that only root can run otherwise.

Whenever you use the sudo command, you are prompted to enter your password to ensure that you are the user entrusted with sudo privileges and not someone who has just walked up to your unattended Terminal window. If you enter another command shortly afterwards, you do not have to enter your password again. The sudo command includes a timer that allows you to work for five minutes before asking for your password again.

You must be set up as a system administrator or listed in the /etc/sudoers file to use sudo.

TYPE THIS:

```
[ferro:~] sudo date
[ferro:~] sudo date
```

RESULT:

On the first call to sudo, the system asks you to enter your password. On the second call, it does not.

```
  Terminal   File   Edit   Scrollback   Font   Window   Help
  ttyp1
#
# Internet server configuration database
#
#       @(#)inetd.conf   5.4 (Berkeley) 6/30/90
#
# Items with double hashes in front (##) are not yet implemented in the O
S.
#
#finger stream  tcp    nowait  nobody  /usr/libexec/tcpd        f
ingerd -s
ftp     stream  tcp    nowait  root    /usr/libexec/tcpd        f
tpd -l
#login  stream  tcp    nowait  root    /usr/libexec/tcpd        r
logind
#nntp   stream  tcp    nowait  usenet  /usr/libexec/tcpd        n
ntpd
#ntalk  dgram   udp    wait    root    /usr/libexec/tcpd        n
talkd
#shell  stream  tcp    nowait  root    /usr/libexec/tcpd        r
shd
telnet  stream  tcp    nowait  root    /usr/libexec/tcpd        t
:wq
```

```
  Terminal   File   Edit   Scrollback   Font   Window   Help
  ttyp1
#
#finger stream  tcp    nowait  nobody  /usr/libexec/tcpd        f
ingerd -s
ftp     stream  tcp    nowait  root    /usr/libexec/tcpd        f
tpd -l
#login  stream  tcp    nowait  root    /usr/libexec/tcpd        r
logind
#nntp   stream  tcp    nowait  usenet  /usr/libexec/tcpd        n
ntpd
#ntalk  dgram   udp    wait    root    /usr/libexec/tcpd        n
talkd
#shell  stream  tcp    nowait  root    /usr/libexec/tcpd        r
shd
telnet  stream  tcp    nowait  root    /usr/libexec/tcpd        t
/etc/inetd.conf: 57 lines, 2542 characters.
[ferro:~] user% ps -aux | grep inetd
root    318   0.0  0.1    1308    132   ??  Ss    6:27AM   0:00.01 inetd
[ferro:~] user% sudo kill -HUP 318
[ferro:~] user% ftp localhost
Connected to localhost.
220 localhost FTP server (lukemftpd 1.1) ready.
Name (localhost:shs): []
```

4 Type **x** to remove the # character below your cursor.

5 Type **:wq** and press Return.

6 Type **ps -aux | grep inetd** and press Return.

7 Type **sudo kill -HUP** followed by the process ID for inetd and press Return.

■ The inetd process reads the /etc/inetd.conf file, enabling the ftp server.

8 Type **ftp localhost** and press Return.

■ The ftp service that you just enabled responds to your request.

INTRODUCTION TO SYSTEM ADMINISTRATION

You can effectively administer a Mac OS X system by learning some basic commands. Unix administration is a complex job, but Mac OS X provides many tools for making the job manageable.

SYSTEM ADMINISTRATOR

The basic responsibilities of any Unix system administrator are to keep the system running smoothly and to ensure that important data and configuration files are preserved. To administer a Mac OS X system, you need to understand the fundamentals of file systems, know how to set up user accounts, recognize when the system is having problems, and be prepared to manage applications and disk space.

System administrators routinely back up the systems they manage. This allows them to restore files if the system crashes or if someone mistakenly deletes the wrong files from their account. System administrators also manage accounts for other users. They establish an account for each user and ensure that the user can use the tools and applications they need.

Users in large companies can often rely on help from a user support team. If you are using Mac OS X at home or in your small business, you are probably responsible for managing the system yourself; in effect, you are your own system administrator.

ACCESS PRIVILEGES

Critical to the role of a system administrator is the concept of privilege. In order to install applications and modify configuration files, you need to have access to the *root* or *superuser* account or to be a privileged user. A normal user on a Unix system can only work on files in their home directory.

The root user has virtually unrestricted access to the system. As a result, the root user can modify files belonging to any user, modify any configuration file, and shut the system down or reboot it from the command line.

While the privileges assigned to the root user are most significant when a Mac OS X system is managed by one person and used by many, use of the root account is important even on systems where root and user are one and the same person.

MANAGE MAC OS X

Mac OS X is not only different from Mac OS 9 and earlier versions of Mac OS, it is also different from other versions of Unix. For example, the root user on a Mac OS X system is disabled by default. This means that you cannot simply adopt the root identity and run commands that you are not allowed to run as a normal user. Instead, you need to either preface these commands with the word sudo, or you need to activate the root account.

You also need to know the basic file system layout — where the system stores files — and you must also know whether you should pay attention to the files you find in the /etc directory — the normal configuration directory on Unix systems.

The table below contains a list of some of the most important Mac OS X commands for system administrators.

COMMAND	MOST COMMON USE	COMMAND	MOST COMMON USE
apropos	Find related commands.	man	Present the manual page for a system command.
chown	Change the owner and, optionally, the group of a file.	mount	Attach a file system to the system.
compress	Compress a file.	netstat	Look at routing tables, network connections, or network statistics.
crontab -e	Edit a cron file.	newfs	Create a new file system.
crontab -1	List cron jobs.	nidump	Display network information from NetInfo.
df	Display free and used disk space.	nireport	Print tables from NetInfo.
du	Display disk space usage.	nslookup	Look up DNS information.
dump	Dump a file system to a backup device or a file.	passwd	Change the password for a user.
fastboot	Reboot the system without a disk check.	ping	Test the connection to a system by asking for a reply.
fdisk	Examine or change DOS partitioning information.	ps	Display information on running processes.
file	Determine the type of a file.	reboot	Shut down and reboot the system.
find	Find files using particular criteria.	shutdown	Shut down a system gracefully.
fsck	Check the integrity of a file system.	shutdown -r now	Shut down and reboot a system immediately.
gunzip	Unzip a file zipped with gzip.	strings	Display the strings in a binary file.
gzip	Compress a file.	tar	Create a file archive or read from one.
halt	Shut down a system immediately.	top	Display statistics on the most demanding processes.
ifconfig	Display or change network interface information.	touch	Update the last changed date on a file or create an empty file.
kill	Send a signal to a process, possibly terminating it.	umount	Unmount a file system which is currently mounted.
ln	Create a symbolic or hard link to a file.	uncompress	Uncompress a file compressed with the compress command.
lpq	Display a printer queue.		

SHUT DOWN AND RESTART THE COMPUTER

You can shut down or restart a Mac OS X system from the command line instead of the Aqua interface if you have access privilege. This is useful if you are not sitting at the system keyboard. The command to shut down Mac OS X is shutdown. Although it is not the only way to shut the system down, it is the safest. Using the shutdown command allows you to send warning messages to users still logged onto the system that you are shutting down the system. This gives them time to finish up what they are doing and log off.

You can specify the time at which the system shuts down by entering a time in the yymmddhhmm format, or you can enter a number, such as +15, to specify that the system shuts down in 15 minutes.

You can also specify a warning message that appears to users. You can tell users that, although the system will be shutting down, it will be available again at a specified time. For example, the command shutdown +15 "ferro must be shut down for emergency service, please log off" allows your users to finish work they are doing, while letting them know that the system may be down for quite a while.

The halt and reboot commands do not provide users with a grace period to complete their work, but terminate running processes before the shutdown. Both commands have options that change the way they run. For example, with a -q argument, both of these commands shut down without terminating processes first.

SHUT DOWN AND RESTART THE COMPUTER

```
 Terminal   File   Edit   Scrollback   Font   Window   Help
                              ttyp1
[ferro:~] user% sudo shutdown +5 "the system must be shut down"
Password:
Shutdown at Tue May 27 09:05:05 2003.
shutdown: [pid 657]
[ferro:~] user%

*** System shutdown message from shs@ferro.local. ***

System going down in 5 minutes


the system must be shut down


[]
```

```
 Terminal   File   Edit   Scrollback   Font   Window   Help
                              ttyp1
[ferro:~] user% sudo reboot
Password:
```

SHUT THE SYSTEM DOWN

1 Type **sudo** followed by a space.

2 Type **shutdown** followed by space.

3 Type **+5 "the system must be shut down"** and press Return.

4 If a prompt appears, type your password, and press Return.

■ The system displays a warning and shuts down after five minutes.

RESTART THE SYSTEM

1 Type **sudo** followed by a space.

2 Type **reboot** and press Return.

3 Type your password at the prompt, and press Return.

■ The system restarts immediately.

Extra

If you enable the `root` account, you can shut down or restart the system without using the `sudo` command. When you do not have the `root` account enabled, you need the `sudo` command to give you the authority of root while you execute the `shutdown` command. The same is true of the `reboot` and `halt` commands. Though the `shutdown`, `reboot`, and `halt` commands may appear simple, there is a lot that happens during the shutting down or booting of a system.

You can simplify the process of restarting or halting a system by using the `fastboot` or `fasthalt` commands. These commands save time in the boot and halt processes, respectively, by skipping the process of checking your disks for integrity. Though these commands may save you time, you should use the more comprehensive `shutdown` and `halt` commands as they help ensure that your file systems remain intact.

If you look at /rc.boot and /etc/rc files, you can get an idea about the processes that run when a system boots. The scripts in these files manage a large part of the boot process.

```
 Terminal   File   Edit   Scrollback   Font   Window   Help

                              ttyp1
[ferro:~] user% sudo halt
Password:
```

```
 Terminal   File   Edit   Scrollback   Font   Window   Help

                              ttyp1
[ferro:~] user% sudo shutdown +5 "system going down for maintenance"
Shutdown at Tue May 27 09:14:28 2003.


*** System shutdown message from shs@ferro.local. ***

System going down in 5 minutes



system going down for maintenance



shutdown: [pid 708]
[ferro:~] user% ps -aux | grep shut
root    708   0.0  0.1    1432    140 std  S<    9:09AM   0:00.00 shutdown
[ferro:~] user% sudo kill 708
[ferro:~] user%
```

HALT THE SYSTEM

1 Type **sudo** followed by a space.

2 Type **halt** and press Return.

3 If a prompt appears, type your password, and press Return.

■ The system halts immediately.

STOP A SHUTDOWN

1 Type **sudo shutdown +5 "system going down for maintenance"** and press Return.

2 If a prompt appears, type your password, and press Return.

3 Type **ps -aux | grep shut** and press Return.

4 Type **sudo kill** followed by the process ID of the shutdown process, then press Return.

5 If a prompt appears, type your password, and press Return.

■ The shutdown aborts.

157

CREATE A NEW USER

You can easily add a new user to your Mac OS X system by using the Accounts tool found in System Preferences, or from the command line in a Terminal window. When you add a new user to your system using the Accounts tool, you must fill out a form with information describing the new user. You need to assign a username and a password. If you want, you can supply a password hint to help the user when they cannot remember the password. You can also incorporate an image into the logon page.

When you use the command line method to add new users, you can create a file containing the information describing the new users, or you can build a script containing a series of commands that add the new users to the system. Current account information may or may not appear in the /etc/passwd file on your system. Mac OS X does not use the information in the /etc/passwd file but uses similar information stored in a database called NetInfo.

You can use the `nidump` command to list the password information that your system uses. Similarly, you can load new information into the NetInfo databases using the `niload` command. The `niutil` command allows you to read and write NetInfo data. For example, using the `niutil` command, you can add each portion of a user record to the database using a separate command, or modify a portion of a user record.

CREATE A NEW USER

```
 Terminal  File  Edit  Scrollback  Font  Window  Help
                          ttyp1
[ferro:~] user% nidump passwd .
nobody:*:-2:-2::0:0:Unprivileged User:/dev/null:/dev/null
root:zH3/rHp8bxG4E:0:0::0:0:System Administrator:/var/root:/bin/tcsh
daemon:*:1:1::0:0:System Services:/var/root:/dev/null
unknown:*:99:99::0:0:Unknown User:/dev/null:/dev/null
www:*:70:70::0:0:World Wide Web Server:/Library/WebServer:/dev/null
shs:Op3gXxxoJzTWI:501:20::0:0:Sandra Henry-Stocker:/Users/shs:/bin/tcsh
mysql:*:74:74::0:0:MySQL Server:/dev/null:/dev/null
sshd:*:75:75::0:0:sshd Privilege separation:/var/empty:/dev/null
smmsp:*:25:25::0:0:Sendmail User:/private/etc/mail:/dev/null
user:cJv0UtGSAlcac:502:20::0:0:Man T. User:/Users/user:/bin/tcsh
eastocker:HX/ObG45KIo5Q:503:20::0:0:Eric A. Stocker:/Users/eastocker:/bin
/tcsh
amaranthe:ouyOB0zjOWrfg:504:20::0:0:Amaranthe Stocker:/Users/amaranthe:/b
in/tcsh
kbartlett::500:20::0:0:Kynn Bartlett:/Users/kbartlett:/bin/tcsh
anna::505:20::0:0:Anna Easley Roberts:/Users/anna:/bin/tcsh
zoe:OOMCzCHng/Fqk:511:20::0:0:Zoe Chloe Doe:/Users/zoe:/bin/tcsh
postfix:*:23456:23456::0:0:Mail:/tmp:/usr/bin/false
[ferro:~] user% nidump passwd . > passwd.txt
[ferro:~] user%
```

```
 Terminal  File  Edit  Scrollback  Font  Window  Help
                          ttyp1
[ferro:~] user% vi passwd.txt
```

1 Type **nidump passwd .** and press Return.

■ A copy of your current user information appears.

2 Type **nidump passwd . > passwd.txt** and press Return.

■ A copy of your current user information is placed into a text file.

3 Type **vi passwd.txt** and press Return.

■ The text editor opens with a copy of the current user information.

Extra

If you add users frequently or manage a system remotely, you can build a script to reduce typing and make the process more efficient. The script below contains `niutil` commands that prompt for each piece of information it needs to create a new user, $user.

Example:
```sh
#!/bin/sh
# add a user

echo -n "username: "   ; read user
echo -n "full name: "  ; read fname
echo -n "shell: "      ; read shell
uhome=/Users/$user

niutil -create .  /users/$user
niutil -createprop    . /users/$user passwd
niutil -createprop    . /users/$user uid $uid
niutil -createprop    . /users/$user gid $gid
niutil -createprop    . /users/$user realname $fullname
niutil -createprop    . /users/$user shell $shell
niutil -createprop    . /users/$user home $homedir
niutil -createprop    . /users/$user _shadow_passwd ""

mkdir $uhome
chmod 755 $uhome
chown $user $uhome

echo "password: "
passwd $user
```

4 Press Shift + G, and then press Return.

5 Press O, and then type **sbob::512:20:Spong Bob:/Users/sbob/bin/tcsh**, ensuring no other user is assigned UID 512.

6 Save your file, and exit vi.

7 Type **sudo niload passwd . < passwd.txtPassword:** and press Return.

8 If a prompt appears, type your password, and press Return.

9 Type **nidump passwd .** and press Return.

■ Your changes are loaded into NetInfo.

■ The new password information appears, confirming your changes.

ENABLE THE ROOT USER ACCOUNT

You can enable the root user account, which allows you to switch user to root — or to log on as root — in addition to exercising root authority using the sudo command that allows you to run commands as root if you are an administrator. The root account on a Unix system is the only account that can perform any action; you should use it sparingly as the system is not protected from any action that this user takes. While normal users cannot overwrite files that do not belong to them, root can overwrite any file on the system, regardless of who owns it and how important it is to the proper running of the system. To use the sudo command, you type **sudo** followed by the command you want to run as root.

There are times when logging on as root or switching user to root simplifies the work that you have to do, but you must always be careful when you do so. Use of root privilege allows you to modify system configuration files, store files in directories that are owned by root, shut down or reboot the system, and add or remove user accounts.

The root account is disabled by default in the root account information stored in your NetInfo database. This means that you cannot log on as root, nor can you use the su command to switch users. You can enable it in one of two ways. The first is to use the NetInfo Manager. To do this, you need to authenticate yourself by entering your password, after which you can initiate the change in the root account by selecting an option to enable the root account. The second method is to change the root password from the command line.

ENABLE THE ROOT USER ACCOUNT

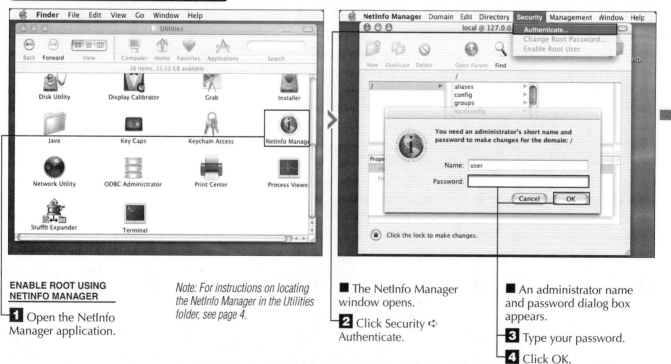

ENABLE ROOT USING NETINFO MANAGER

1 Open the NetInfo Manager application.

Note: For instructions on locating the NetInfo Manager in the Utilities folder, see page 4.

■ The NetInfo Manager window opens.

2 Click Security ➪ Authenticate.

■ An administrator name and password dialog box appears.

3 Type your password.

4 Click OK.

Apply It

After you enable the root account, you can log on as root or switch user to root. The su command allows you to adopt the identity of another user if you know their password; if you are root, you do not need the password. Entering su - invokes the environment of the new user in addition to assuming their username. This command leaves you positioned in the home directory of the user, with the path of the user being active, and the aliases of the user defined. You can use the su command to assume the identity of any user but, without an argument, it defaults to root.

TYPE THIS:

```
[ferro:~] user% su
Password:
[ferro:~] # pwd
```

RESULT:

```
/Users/user
```

TYPE THIS:

```
[ferro:~] user% su -
Password:
[ferro:~] root# pwd
```

RESULT:

```
/private/var/root
```

NetInfo Manager Domain Edit Directory **Security** Management Window Help

Deauthenticate
Change Root Password...
Enable Root User

local @ 127.0.0.

Alert

You must re-authenticate to make additional changes.

[OK]

Property	Value(s)
master	localhost/local
trusted_networks	<no value>

Click the lock to prevent further changes.

Terminal File Edit Scrollback Font Window Help

ttyp1

```
[ferro:~] user% sudo passwd root
Password:
Changing password for root.
New password:
Retype new password:
[ferro:~] user% 
```

5 Click Security ➪ Enable Root User.

■ An Alert message box appears informing you that you must re-authenticate to make additional changes.

6 Click OK.

■ The root user password is changed, enabling the account.

ENABLE ROOT ON THE COMMAND LINE

1 In a Terminal window, type **sudo passwd root** and press Return.

2 Type your password at the prompt.

3 Type the new password for root at the prompt.

4 Retype the new password at the prompt.

■ The root user password is changed, enabling the account.

EXECUTE COMMANDS AS ROOT

Y ou can run arbitrary commands as root by using the sudo command regardless of whether you decide to enable the root account on your Mac OS X system. In order to use the sudo command, you must be a user with system management privilege. If you have this privilege, you can make use of root privilege when you need it by inserting the word sudo in front of any command that you require root permission to execute.

You do not need root privilege to work on your own files, and you should not use root privilege when you do not need it because the system has no protection against the actions of this all-powerful user.

The sudo command uses a configuration file that includes a list of the users or user groups allowed to run commands as root. While this configuration file permits a precise level of

control over privileges, the default setup gives privileged users the ability to run any command as root. Privileged users are given privilege when they first establish their accounts. However, this privilege derives from their membership in the admin group.

The sudo command prompts you to enter your password every five minutes. This process of re-authenticating the user helps to ensure that the user running the command is really the privileged user.

You can use the nidump command to display a list of users allowed to use the sudo command. The default sudo setup places no restrictions on the commands that privileged users can run and is not a mechanism for limiting privilege.

EXECUTE COMMANDS AS ROOT

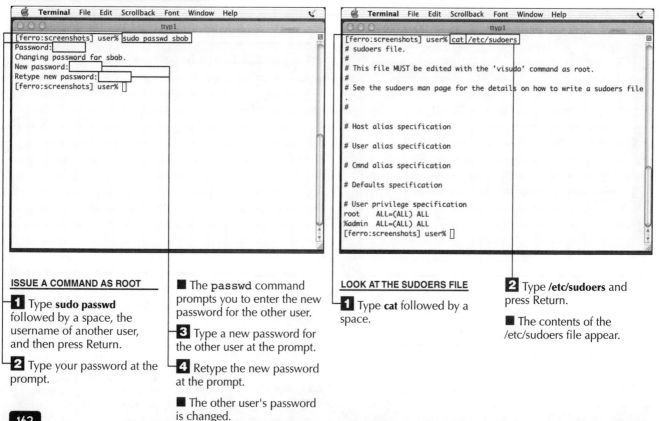

ISSUE A COMMAND AS ROOT

1 Type **sudo passwd** followed by a space, the username of another user, and then press Return.

2 Type your password at the prompt.

■ The **passwd** command prompts you to enter the new password for the other user.

3 Type a new password for the other user at the prompt.

4 Retype the new password at the prompt.

■ The other user's password is changed.

LOOK AT THE SUDOERS FILE

1 Type **cat** followed by a space.

2 Type **/etc/sudoers** and press Return.

■ The contents of the /etc/sudoers file appear.

Extra

The `sudo` command allows you to give limited root privilege to trusted users. For example, you can allow a junior administrator to set up accounts for new users or to cancel print jobs. By configuring a limited set of commands in the /etc/sudoers file for certain users, a system administrator can delegate certain system privileges while not giving out access to the root account. To use `sudo` in this way, you need to create a list of commands that one or more users can run as root, and then restrict them to the list of commands. Type **sudo visudo** and add system and usernames to reflect users on your system.

Example:
```
kynn,sandra,eric      ferro=/sbin/dump,/sbin/restore
kynn                  ferro=/sbin/shutdown
```

These lines allow the first group of users to use the `dump` and `restore` commands and the second to shut down the system.

```
  Terminal  File  Edit  Scrollback  Font  Window  Help
                              ttyp1
[ferro:screenshots] user% nidump group .
nobody:*:-2:
nogroup:*:-1:
wheel:*:0:shs
daemon:*:1:root
kmem:*:2:root
sys:*:3:root
tty:*:4:root
operator:*:5:root
mail:*:6:
bin:*:7:
staff:*:20:root
guest:*:31:root
utmp:*:45:
uucp:*:66:
dialer:*:68:
network:*:69:
www:*:70:
admin:*:80:root,shs,user
unknown:*:99:
mysql:*:74:
sshd:*:75:
```

```
  Terminal  File  Edit  Scrollback  Font  Window  Help
                              ttyp1
[ferro:~] user% su -
Password:
[ferro:~] root# whoami
root
[ferro:~] root# who am i
user     ttyp2    May 27 12:09  (localhost)
[ferro:~] root# []
```

LIST PRIVILEGED USERS

■1 Type **nidump group** followed by a space.

■2 Type **.** and press Return.

■ A list of the group file appears, including a listing of the members of the admin group.

SWITCH USER TO ROOT

■1 Type **su -** and press Return.

■2 Type the password for root at the prompt, and press Return.

■3 Type **whoami** and press Return.

■4 Type **who am i** and press Return.

■ You are now running as root.

Note: The system remembers your original logon.

BACK UP YOUR FILES

You can safeguard your work and protect your system by backing up your files. Maintaining a set of backups is always a good idea. Mac OS X cannot prevent a user from removing a file or a set of files that they may still need. There are, however, quite a few tools that you can use to back up your files.

Some Unix commands such as cp and ditto allow you to make copies of files. Many long-time Unix users make a habit of copying important files before editing the originals, in case they need to restore them and start over again.

Other Unix commands allow you to create archives of important files. This is a great way to save a copy of all the files associated with the project in a single file. The tar command works well for this purpose.

Most Unix systems use the dump command for regular system backups, although you may need to dump to a remote tape drive to use this command. The dump command can back up a complete file system or select only those files that have changed since the last backup. This latter method of backing up is called an *incremental backup*.

While dump is a good Unix command, the Mac OS X version can only back up an entire file system, fully or incrementally, and only works with Unix file systems (UFS). If your Mac OS X installation is an upgrade from Mac OS 9 or earlier, your file systems may all be HFS+. If this is the case, you might consider downloading the hfspax software available from www.homepage.mac.com/howardoakley. This software works well with data and resource forks and provides a command-line interface.

BACK UP YOUR FILES

```
[ferro:~] user% cp myfile myfile$$
[ferro:~] user%
```

```
[ferro:~] user% tar cvf "/Volumes/Zip 100/project_X.tar" project_X
project_X
project_X/.DS_Store
project_X/12-16-02_ping.txt
project_X/adding_user.txt
project_X/adduser
project_X/after
project_X/b4
project_X/backup
project_X/Chap07.txt
project_X/Chap08.txt
project_X/Chap10.txt
project_X/Chap11.txt
project_X/commands
project_X/Copy_Commands.html
project_X/curl
project_X/EnabingRoot
project_X/enable_access
project_X/files
project_X/MacOSX_top10.hml
project_X/myfile.txt
project_X/osxguide2_11mq.pdf
```

BACK UP A FILE WITH CP

1 Type **cp** followed by a space.

2 Type the name of a file, followed by a space.

3 Type the name of the file followed by **$$**, and then press Return.

■ A copy of your file is created with a process ID appended to the end.

BACK UP FILES WITH TAR

1 Type **tar cvf** followed by a space.

2 Type " followed by a filename.

3 Type " followed by a space.

4 Type the name of a directory, and press Return.

*Note: You can also type the name of a set of files, such as ***.txt**.*

■ The system adds the specified files to the new archive, updating you on-screen as it works.

Extra

To initiate a restoration from a dump, use the `restore -ivf` command followed by the name of your backup device or dump file. Use `cd` to move between directories, followed by the name of a file to select it for restoration, and extract when you are ready to begin restoring the files.

On Mac OS X systems, the `dump` command can only back up an entire file system. Because you are probably working with a single partition, it requires a large-capacity device to create a backup. The `dump` command can write to the tape drive on a remote system if you configure the remote system to allow this.

You can use the `restore` command to restore files from the backup that you create with the `dump` command. The `restore` command can restore an entire file system, although you usually only need to restore a single file or set of files from your backup. In this case, you can use the interactive mode of the `restore` command to navigate within the backed-up files. You can then select those files that you want to restore and initiate their restoration. The restored files appear in a subdirectory of the directory where you run the `restore` command.

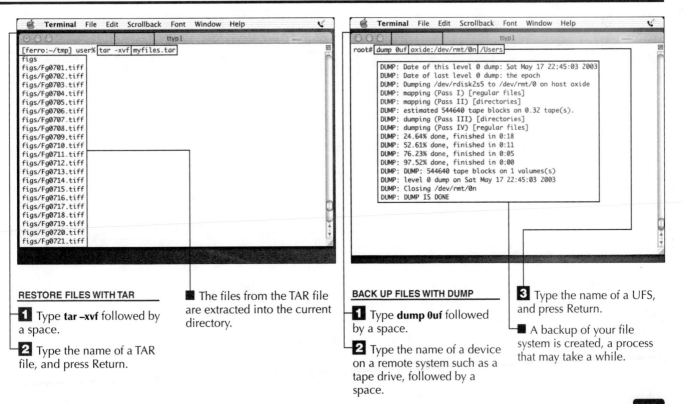

RESTORE FILES WITH TAR

1 Type **tar –xvf** followed by a space.

2 Type the name of a TAR file, and press Return.

■ The files from the TAR file are extracted into the current directory.

BACK UP FILES WITH DUMP

1 Type **dump 0uf** followed by a space.

2 Type the name of a device on a remote system such as a tape drive, followed by a space.

3 Type the name of a UFS, and press Return.

■ A backup of your file system is created, a process that may take a while.

CHANGE FILE OWNERSHIP

You can change ownership of a file so that you or someone else can modify the contents of the file. The chown command reassigns ownership of a file to a new user. This command can only be run by root or by a privileged user with the sudo command. The syntax of the chown command is chown newuser filename, but you can also change both the owner and the group associated with a file if you specify both at once. To do this, you enter the username of the new user and the group name separated by a colon. A command like chown horace:devt myapp.java, for example, changes the owner to horace and the group to devt for the file myapp.java.

Like many commands, you can use chown to work on an entire directory if you add an argument to run the command recursively. A chown command that starts with chown -R is run against all the files in the directory name that you supply.

A similar command is chgrp. The chgrp command changes the group associated with a file or set of files. If you need to share a set of files with a group of other users, you can add these users to the group associated with the file or change the group for the file. In general, changing the group for the file is easier.

The chgrp command has a similar syntax to chown. If you type chgrp devt myapp.java, then anyone in the development team obtains group access to the file. If members of the group can write to the file, this allows anyone in that group to modify the file. Like chown, chgrp can be run recursively with the -R option.

CHANGE FILE OWNERSHIP

```
  Terminal  File  Edit  Scrollback  Font  Window  Help
                          ttyp1
[ferro:~] user% sudo chown shs myfile
Password:
[ferro:~] user% ls -l myfile
-rw-r--r--  1 shs  staff  42414 May 17 21:17 myfile
[ferro:~] user% []
```

```
  Terminal  File  Edit  Scrollback  Font  Window  Help
                          ttyp1
[ferro:~] user% sudo chgrp guest myfile
Password:
[ferro:~] user% ls -l myfile
-rw-r--r--  1 shs  guest  42414 May 17 21:17 myfile
[ferro:~] user% []
```

CHANGE THE OWNERSHIP OF A FILE

1 Type **sudo chown** followed by a space.

2 Type the username of a user on your system followed by a space.

3 Type the name of a file, and press Return.

4 Type **ls -l** followed by a space, then the name of the file, and press Return.

■ The file now has a new owner.

CHANGE THE GROUP OF A FILE

1 Type **sudo chgrp** followed by a space.

2 Type the name of a group on your system followed by a space.

3 Type the name of a file, and press Return.

4 Type **ls -l** followed by a space, the name of the file, and then press Return.

■ The file now has a new group.

Apply It

When you change the group and ownership of a file, you do not affect the contents of the file in any way. Information about a file, referred to as metadata, is stored in a separate location from the file itself. You affect this metadata when you change ownership or the permissions associated with a file. Metadata is stored in a file system structure known as an *inode*. You see metadata every time you list file information using the `ls -l` command. You can list files with the numbers of the inodes that are associated with these files by using the `-i` option instead. It is sometimes useful to know which inodes are being used. For example, two files in the same file system with the same inode refer to the same content.

TYPE THIS:

```
[ferro:~] user % ls -i *
```

RESULT:

139742 AnnaRoof.JPG	140953 NoLaneBridge.JPG
143416 AnnaSky.JPG	140093 OldBarn.JPG
141835 AugSky1.JPG	140095 OldBarn2.JPG

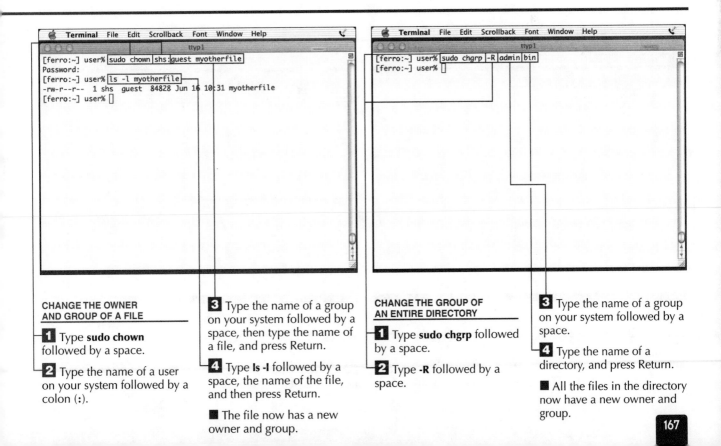

CHANGE THE OWNER AND GROUP OF A FILE

1 Type **sudo chown** followed by a space.

2 Type the name of a user on your system followed by a colon (:).

3 Type the name of a group on your system followed by a space, then type the name of a file, and press Return.

4 Type **ls -l** followed by a space, the name of the file, and then press Return.

■ The file now has a new owner and group.

CHANGE THE GROUP OF AN ENTIRE DIRECTORY

1 Type **sudo chgrp** followed by a space.

2 Type **-R** followed by a space.

3 Type the name of a group on your system followed by a space.

4 Type the name of a directory, and press Return.

■ All the files in the directory now have a new owner and group.

CREATE SYMBOLIC LINKS

You can simplify the navigation of your file system by creating symbolic links. A *symbolic link* is a special file that acts as a pointer or shortcut to another file or directory at another location in the system.

By creating a symbolic link to a directory with a long or difficult pathname, you can move to the directory by typing **cd** followed by the name of the link you create. If you want to create a shortcut for moving into or listing the contents of the directory /Applications/Utilities, you can type the command **ln -s /Applications/Utilities util**. The full pathname specifies where you want your link to point, while the final argument specifies what you want to call your link. The −s argument tells the ln command that you want to create a symbolic link.

After you type this command and press Return, you can type commands such as ls utils or cd utils. If you only specify the file or directory that you want to point to when you type the ln -s command, the link receives the same name as the original file.

If you share a set of files with other users, and those files are not stored in your home directories, you can use symbolic links to simplify the sharing process and better organize the shared files. If you do not include the −s argument, you create a hard link instead of a symbolic one. A hard link is a special copy of a file, in that it is a reference to the original file. Though it looks like a file that is completely independent of the original, it is the original file with a new file system reference; any changes to the original file are reflected in the link.

CREATE SYMBOLIC LINKS

Terminal	File	Edit	Scrollback	Font	Window	Help

ttyp1

```
[ferro:~] user% ln -s /etc/syslog.conf
[ferro:~] user%
```

Terminal	File	Edit	Scrollback	Font	Window	Help

ttyp1

```
[ferro:~] user% ls -l syslog.conf
lrwxr-xr-x  1 user  staff  16 May 17 22:49 syslog.conf -> /etc/syslog.conf
[ferro:~] user%
```

CREATE A SYMBOLIC LINK

1 Type **ln -s** followed by a space.

2 Type the full pathname of a text file, and press Return.

■ A symbolic link is created which points to the file.

3 Type **ls -l** followed by space.

4 Type the name of your new symbolic link, and press Return.

■ A long listing of your symbolic link appears.

■ The l in the first column indicates that this file is a symbolic link.

Apply It

You can use hard links to make files easier to access or to give them additional names. Hard links offer a particular advantage over copies of files, unlike copies, hard links require no additional disk space. The contents of the file are stored in only one place on the system, regardless of how many hard links you create.

If you and another user maintain personal copies of a file, the contents of those files can easily become out of synch. However, if you use a hard link, you can both keep a hard link file in your home directory, with the assurance that any changes that either of you makes are reflected in both hard link files.

You create hard links with the `ln` command. For example, the command `ln java myapp` allows you to refer to java as myapp.

Hard links are similar to symbolic links, except that hard links point to the contents of a file, while symbolic links point to the name of a file. When two files use the same inode, you know they are hard links.

TYPE THIS:

```
[ferro:~] ls -l /bin/csh
[ferro:~] ls -l /bin/tcsh
```

⌄

RESULT:

```
167100 /bin/csh
167100 /bin/tcsh
```

```
 Terminal   File   Edit   Scrollback   Font   Window   Help
                              ttyp1
[ferro:~] user% less syslog.conf
*.err;kern.*;auth.notice;authpriv,remoteauth.none;mail.crit          /
dev/console
*.notice;*.info;authpriv,remoteauth,ftp.none;kern.debug;mail.crit    /
var/log/system.log

# Send messages normally sent to the console also to the serial port.
# To stop messages from being sent out the serial port, comment out this
line.
#*.err;kern.*;auth.notice;authpriv,remoteauth.none;mail.crit         /
dev/tty.serial

# The authpriv log file should be restricted access; these
# messages shouldn't go to terminals or publically-readable
# files.
authpriv.*;remoteauth.crit                    /var/log/secure.l
og

lpr.info                                      /var/log/lpr.log
mail.*                                        /var/log/mail.log
ftp.*                                         /var/log/ftp.log
netinfo.err                                   /var/log/netinfo.
```

```
 Terminal   File   Edit   Scrollback   Font   Window   Help
                              ttyp1
[ferro:~] user% ln myfile mylink
[ferro:~] user% ls -l myfile mylink
-rwxr-xr-x  2 shs  guest  233 May 17 21:21 myfile
-rwxr-xr-x  2 shs  guest  233 May 17 21:21 mylink
[ferro:~] user% []
```

5 Type **less** followed by a space.

6 Type the name of your symbolic link, and press Return.

■ The contents of the original file appear, showing that your symbolic link connects to the original file.

1 Type **ln** followed by a space.

2 Type the name of a text file in your directory followed by a space.

3 Type a new filename, and press Return.

4 Type **ls -l** followed by a space, the names of the two files separated by a space, and then press Return.

■ The files appear identical except for their names.

CHECK DISK USAGE

You can use the `df` and `du` commands to determine how much space is available on your disks and how much space is used, respectively. The `df` command tells you how much disk space is allocated, used, and available. When you use the `df` command with a `-k` argument, disk space appears in kilobytes instead of 512-byte blocks.

One of the columns that appears in the `df` output is Capacity. This column shows you how much room in that file system is already used as a percentage of the overall space available. Most Unix system administrators try to keep file systems at less than 90 percent of capacity simply because they perform better when there is adequate free space.

You can use the `du` command to determine how much space a particular directory uses. This command can help you track down files that consume a lot of space in a file

system that is running out of space. For example, if you `cd` into a particular directory and use the command `du -sk * | sort -n`, you receive a list of the contents of that directory sorted in size order. This is very helpful if you want to know where most of the disk space is being consumed.

You can use the `df -k` command periodically to see how much space remains on your disk. When a file system approaches full capacity, the responsiveness of the system decreases, although any file system that is less than 90 percent full is not a reason for concern. At the same time, any file system that jumps in size by 10 percent in a short amount of time may do so again. The rate at which a file system is growing suggests how soon you will run out of space.

CHECK DISK USAGE

```
         Terminal   File   Edit   Scrollback   Font   Window   Help
                                    ttyp1
[ferro:~] user% df
Filesystem            512-blocks       Used    Avail Capacity  Mounted on
/dev/disk0s5            53545168   20079136 32954032    37%     /
devfs                        180        180        0   100%     /dev
fdesc                          2          2        0   100%     /dev
<volfs>                     1024       1024        0   100%     /.vol
automount -fstab [323]         0          0        0   100%     /Network/Servers
automount -static [323]        0          0        0   100%     /automount
[ferro:~] user% []
```

DISPLAY DISK FREE SPACE IN BLOCKS

1 Type **df** and press Return.

■ The system displays your file system usage in blocks.

```
         Terminal   File   Edit   Scrollback   Font   Window   Help
                                    ttyp1
[ferro:~] user% df -k
Filesystem            1K-blocks        Used    Avail Capacity  Mounted on
/dev/disk0s5            26772584   10039680 16476904    37%     /
devfs                         90         90        0   100%     /dev
fdesc                          1          1        0   100%     /dev
<volfs>                      512        512        0   100%     /.vol
automount -fstab [323]         0          0        0   100%     /Network/Servers
automount -static [323]        0          0        0   100%     /automount
[ferro:~] user% []
```

DISPLAY DISK FREE SPACE IN KILOBYTES

1 Type **df -k** and press Return.

■ The system displays your file system usage in kilobytes.

Apply It

The df command can also report on the number of inodes allocated and used on your file systems. While this may not be an issue on your system, it is possible for a file system to run out of inodes just as it is possible for a file system to run out of disk space. In either case, you cannot create new files until you solve the disk space or the inode issue. When you first create a file system, the system also creates a generous allocation of inodes. When you type the command **df -i**, the system displays the number of inodes used as iused and the number available as ifree. Unless the ifree value is extremely small, you are unlikely to have any problems. The ratio of inodes to disk space is usually set so that running out of inodes is nearly impossible.

TYPE THIS:

```
[ferro:~] df -i
```

RESULT:

Filesystem	512-blocks	Used	Avail	Capacity	iused	ifree	%iused	Mounted on
/dev/disk0s	53545168	17462872	35570296	32%	2246857	4446287	33%	/
devfs	201	201	0	100%	644	0	100%	/dev
fdesc	2	2	0	100%	4	253	1%	/dev
<volfs>	1024	1024	0	100%	0	0	100%	/.vol

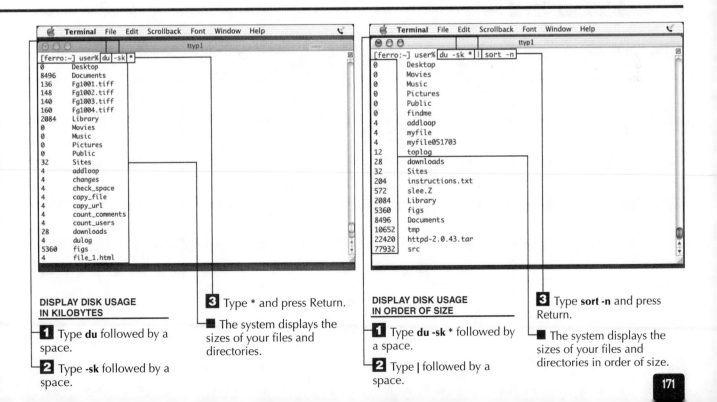

DISPLAY DISK USAGE IN KILOBYTES

1 Type **du** followed by a space.

2 Type **-sk** followed by a space.

3 Type ***** and press Return.

■ The system displays the sizes of your files and directories.

DISPLAY DISK USAGE IN ORDER OF SIZE

1 Type **du -sk *** followed by a space.

2 Type **|** followed by a space.

3 Type **sort -n** and press Return.

■ The system displays the sizes of your files and directories in order of size.

MANAGE THE PRINT QUEUE

You can use the `lpq` command to examine your print queue and cancel print requests. This command also lists print jobs that are waiting in the queue. As the printer handles each print request, the job disappears from the queue and the next job in line starts printing. The `cancel` command cancels a selected print job, removing it from the queue and leaving the remaining jobs to be printed.

You have numerous reasons to examine a print queue and to cancel jobs. For example, if you are waiting a long time for a printout, you can check the queue to see what other jobs are printing or should be printing. If the printer has been out of paper for a while, you can view where your print job is in the queue, and decide whether to cancel the job.

Some users request a printout of a document several times in a row before checking to see if the reason that it does not print is because there is no paper. When this happens, it is a good idea to cancel all but one of these print jobs. Other users may print a document in the wrong format and end up printing a pile of paper that they cannot use. Canceling these jobs can save you both time and paper.

To submit a print job from the command line, you can use the `lpr` command followed by the name of the file you want to print. Applications, such as Photoshop, also submit print jobs and these also appear in your print queue. You can view all of the pending print jobs using `lpq`, whether the print requests are generated by applications or the `lpr` command and regardless of who submitted each print request.

MANAGE THE PRINT QUEUE

```
[ferro:~] user% lpr myfile
[ferro:~] user% 
```

```
[ferro:~] user% lpr myfile
[ferro:~] user% lpq
DESKJET_930C is ready and printing
Rank    Owner   Job     File(s)                    Total Size
active  user    32      myfile                     1024 bytes
[ferro:~] user% 
```

EXAMINE THE PRINT QUEUE

1 Type **lpr** followed by a space.

2 Type the name of a text file, and press Return.

■ The file queues for printing.

3 Type **lpq** and press Return.

■ The print queue displays.

Apply It

If you need to cancel all of the jobs in a print queue, you can use the `cancel` command with a `-s` argument. This command option saves you the time of canceling jobs individually.

The Print Center is a useful tool for monitoring and controlling your printer; it allows you to: determine the status of a printer; restart the printer; view the jobs that are waiting to print; and determine whether the printer is active. If the `lpq` command indicates that your printer is not ready, you can set it back to operational status using the Print Center. To do this, double-click the name of the printer that the `lpq` command tells you is inactive, and activate it again. The Print Center is located in the /Applications/Utilities folder.

TYPE THIS:

```
[ferro:~] user% lpq
```

RESULT:

```
DESKJET_930C is ready and printing
Rank    Owner   Job   File(s)        Total Size
active  user    3     Chap11.txt     36864 bytes
1st     user    4     oldhouse.jpg   919552 bytes
```

Each job in the queue has a rank, an owner, and a job number. To cancel a job in the queue, use the command `cancel` followed by a space and the job number.

CANCEL A PRINT JOB

1 Type **lpq** and press Return.

■ The print queue displays.

2 Type **cancel** followed by a space.

3 Type a job number from one of the print jobs in the list, and press Return.

■ The print job is cancelled.

CHECK ON THE PRINTER STATUS

1 Type **lpc** followed by a space.

2 Type **status** and press Return.

■ The status of the printer displays.

INSPECT SYSTEM LOGS

Y ou can learn a lot about system operations and problems by inspecting your system logs for error messages and various anomalies. System logs, stored in /var/log, record the activities of many system services such as e-mail and printing. You will find these files to be valuable as they can be an important source of information when system problems arise.

The most important messages about your current logon sessions appear in a log file called console.log. You can view these messages using the Console tool, available in /Applications/Utilities. The scrollable window allows you to read the messages that accumulate after you log on. These messages include authentication failures and mounting problems.

A system daemon called syslog maintains most system log files. Like numerous other daemons, the syslog daemon, syslogd, has a configuration file that it reads when it starts

up. This configuration file tells syslogd where to write each type of log message. By using the services of syslogd, other services do not have to do their own logging. The syslog configuration file, /etc/syslogd.conf, provides you with an opportunity to change where logs are written or to deactivate certain types of logging. To modify the logging operations of syslogd, you can modify the configuration file for syslogd and instruct the daemon to check the file for changes. Do not edit the default /etc/syslogd.conf file unless you want to separate particular messages or stop collecting them altogether.

If you keep the Console tool open while you work, you can see these messages display as the daemon generates them. This is a good troubleshooting technique as it informs you of problems immediately and reminds you to check your log files.

INSPECT SYSTEM LOGS

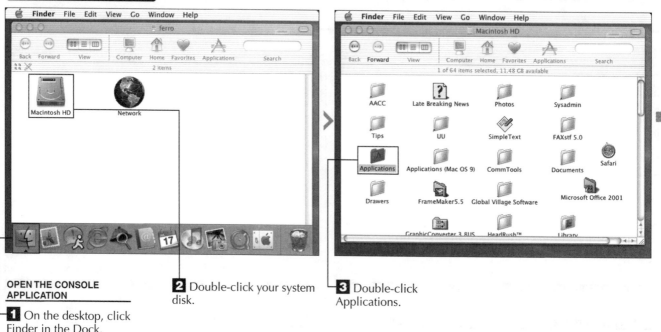

OPEN THE CONSOLE APPLICATION

1 On the desktop, click Finder in the Dock.

2 Double-click your system disk.

3 Double-click Applications.

Extra

The log file that gathers the most information on most Mac OS X systems is *system.log.* The system writes many routine messages to this file, and the *system.log* file is routinely rotated. Older *system.log* files are renamed system.log.0, system.log.1, and so on, and are compressed with gunzip to save space. At any point, you may have a number of these files available to you to help you track down a problem. Any log file may have thousands of records — far too many for you to read the file from top to bottom. Using commands like grep and awk to extract some of this data can make the job of reviewing log data much easier. You might consider writing scripts that check for certain types of errors in your log files and report the findings to you. You can check the /etc/syslog.conf file to see where particular types of messages are written.

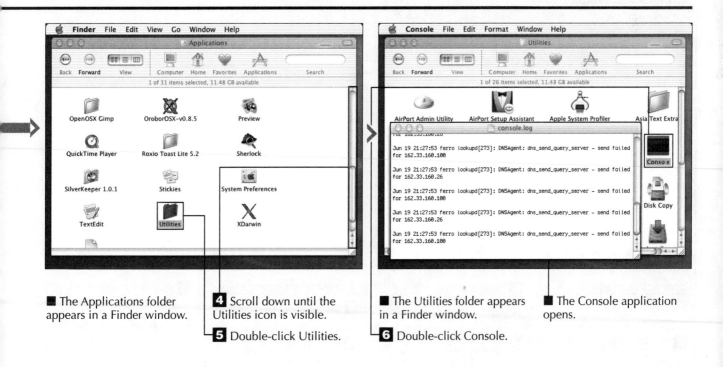

■ The Applications folder appears in a Finder window.

4 Scroll down until the Utilities icon is visible.

5 Double-click Utilities.

■ The Utilities folder appears in a Finder window.

6 Double-click Console.

■ The Console application opens.

COMPRESS LARGE FILES

You can greatly reduce the size of a file by compressing it — down to a sixth or less of its original size when you use a good compression tool. Compression is a good solution for managing your disk space while not sacrificing files that you may need later on.

For most files, gzip is one of the best compression tools available. It is both quick and effective, reducing files down to a fraction of their original size. It is also available on many systems, allowing you to move your compressed files to another system, confident that you can unzip them. To compress a file, you can type **gzip** followed by the name of the file. The gzip command creates a new file with the extension .gz appended to the end of the filename. For example, when you compress the /var/log/system.log.0 file, the resultant file is called system.log.0.gz. Unlike Windows, Unix does not care how many extensions a file has.

The other command that you can use to compress a file is called compress. The compress command compresses a file using a different algorithm than gzip. It also uses a different file extension. Files compressed with the compress command take on the extension .Z.

The gzip and gunzip tools are members of the GNU tools that many Unix systems use whether they are included in the distribution or added later. These commands are included in the standard distribution of Mac OS X.

Both the gzip and the compress commands use the filenames to determine whether a file is already compressed. It is possible to compress a file again after renaming it, but the subsequent gain is small, and the likelihood of confusion high.

COMPRESS LARGE FILES

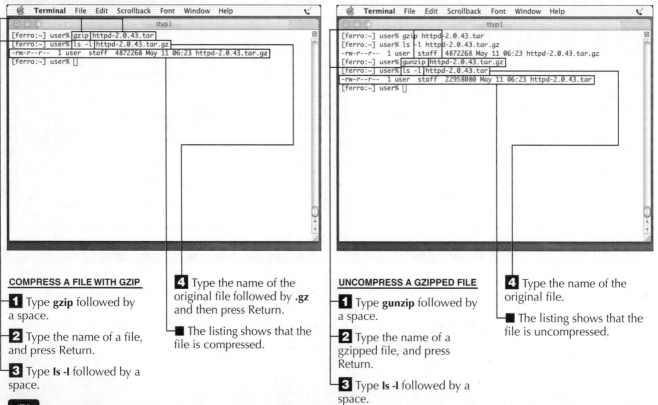

COMPRESS A FILE WITH GZIP

1 Type **gzip** followed by a space.

2 Type the name of a file, and press Return.

3 Type **ls -l** followed by a space.

4 Type the name of the original file followed by **.gz** and then press Return.

■ The listing shows that the file is compressed.

UNCOMPRESS A GZIPPED FILE

1 Type **gunzip** followed by a space.

2 Type the name of a gzipped file, and press Return.

3 Type **ls -l** followed by a space.

4 Type the name of the original file.

■ The listing shows that the file is uncompressed.

Extra

Most software that you download from FTP sites is compressed to reduce both the storage space requirements on the server and the time required to download the file. You can determine the type of compression used by looking at the file extensions. Files that end in .Z have been compressed with the `compress` command, while those that end in .gz have been compressed with `gzip`. You may also see file endings such as .zip, .tar.Z, and .tgz.

FILE EXTENSION	DESCRIPTION	BENEFIT
ZIP	Files ending in .zip are ZIP files.	Many systems have `zip` and `unzip` commands and can both create and extract from these files.
TAR	Files ending in .tar are tape archive or TAR files.	These files are not compressed but contain a number of files that you can individually or collectively extract with the `tar -xf` command.
TARZ/TGZ	Files ending in .tar.Z or .tgz are TAR files that have also been compressed with the `compress` command.	To extract the contents of one of these files, you must first uncompress it. This leaves you with a TAR file. You then use the `tar -xf` command to extract the contents.

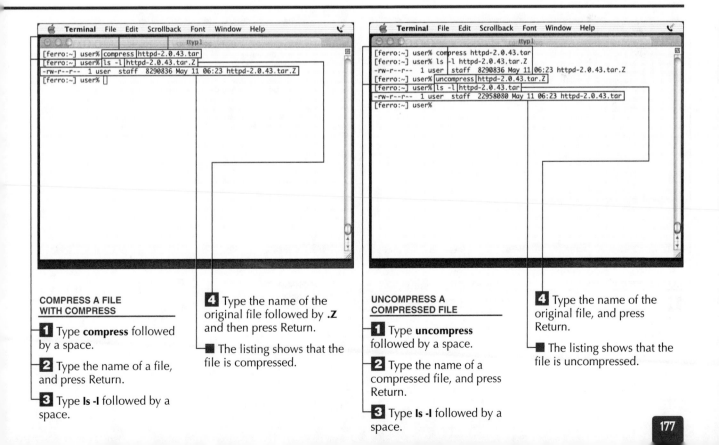

COMPRESS A FILE WITH COMPRESS

1 Type **compress** followed by a space.

2 Type the name of a file, and press Return.

3 Type **ls -l** followed by a space.

4 Type the name of the original file followed by **.Z** and then press Return.

■ The listing shows that the file is compressed.

UNCOMPRESS A COMPRESSED FILE

1 Type **uncompress** followed by a space.

2 Type the name of a compressed file, and press Return.

3 Type **ls -l** followed by a space.

4 Type the name of the original file, and press Return.

■ The listing shows that the file is uncompressed.

USING NETINFO

You can explore and modify the contents of your NetInfo database. NetInfo is a service that replaces the simply formatted text files that were once used exclusively in Unix to store information about systems, users, and so on. The early Unix systems stored all user information in the /etc/passwd file, and information about the local system and other systems in /etc/hosts. Along with some additional files, also stored in /etc, the records in these files determined who could log on and what services the system could support.

In the past, new lines were added to the /etc/passwd file as new user logons were created. New hosts were added to the /etc/hosts file so that the systems could communicate. Today, we use network information and lookup services such as NetInfo, NIS, and LDAP on many systems to replace the simple text files.

NetInfo is a lookup service or database that contains many types of system information. In fact, if you look for your

account in the /etc/passwd file, you are not likely to find it. The system does not use these files; it uses NetInfo. Therefore, learning to browse the NetInfo information base and make changes is essential for understanding and monitoring your system.

The most important NetInfo commands are nidump, niload, and niutil. The nidump command displays the NetInfo contents. The command nidump passwd . displays the passwd entries that were stored in the /etc/passwd file on older Unix systems.

You can use the niload command to load new contents into NetInfo, and the niutil command for various read and write processes. NetInfo refers to the types of information that it contains as formats. There are also nifind, nigrep, and nireport commands. Read about these by entering a man command; for example, man nigrep.

USING NETINFO

```
[ferro:~] user% nidump
usage: nidump [-r] [-T timeout] {directory | format} [-t] domain
known formats:
        aliases
        bootptab
        bootparams
        ethers
        exports
        fstab
        group
        hosts
        networks
        passwd
        printcap
        protocols
        resolv.conf
        rpc
        services
        mountmaps
[ferro:~] user%
```

```
[ferro:~] user% nidump passwd .
nobody:*:-2:-2::0:0:Unprivileged User:/dev/null:/dev/null
root:zH3/rHp8bxG4E:0:0::0:0:System Administrator:/var/root:/bin/tcsh
daemon:*:1:1::0:0:System Services:/var/root:/dev/null
unknown:*:99:99::0:0:Unknown User:/dev/null:/dev/null
www:*:70:70::0:0:World Wide Web Server:/Library/WebServer:/dev/null
shs:hDC5kOnN6kurA:501:20::0:0:Sandra Henry-Stocker:/Users/shs:/bin/tcsh
mysql:*:74:74::0:0:MySQL Server:/dev/null:/dev/null
sshd:*:75:75::0:0:sshd Privilege separation:/var/empty:/dev/null
smmsp:*:25:25::0:0:Sendmail User:/private/etc/mail:/dev/null
user:cJvOUtGSAlcac:502:20::0:0:Man T. User:/Users/user:/bin/tcsh
eastocker:HX/ObG45KIo5Q:503:20::0:0:Eric A. Stocker:/Users/eastocker:/bin/tcsh
amaranthe:ouyOB0zjOWrfg:504:20::0:0:Amaranthe Stocker:/Users/amaranthe:/bin/tcsh
kbartlett::500:20::0:0:Kynn Bartlett:/Users/kbartlett:/bin/tcsh
anna::505:20::0:0:Anna Easley Roberts:/Users/anna:/bin/tcsh
zoe:OOMCzCHng/Fqk:511:20::0:0:Zoe Doe:/Users/zoe:/bin/tcsh
[ferro:~] user%
```

LIST NETINFO FORMATS

1 Type **nidump** and press Return.

■ The nidump command displays a usage statement along with a list of the formats that it can dump for you.

DUMP INFORMATION FROM NETINFO

1 Type **nidump** followed by a space.

2 Type the name of a format followed by a space.

3 Type . and press Return.

■ The contents of that format are displayed.

Extra

While the `nidump` and `niload` commands are relatively straightforward, the `niutil` command has a number of options, each of which is like a separate command. These options include `-create`, `-destroy`, `-createprop`, `-appendprop`, `-mergeprop`, `-insertval`, `-destroyprop`, `-destroyval`, `-renameprop`, `-read`, and `-list`.

Although NetInfo works well, you should consider making your changes with a carefully written and well-tested script, and not attempt to enter all of the necessary `netutil` commands manually. Read the man pages for `niload`, `nidump`, and `netutil` to learn more about how you can use these commands.

NetInfo uses terminology that is different from that of the system. For example, not only does NetInfo maintain formats in place of files, but it also has directories in place of records and properties in place of fields. If you use the `niutil` command to create a new user record, you can use the `niutil -create` command, which creates a new directory. You can then set the values associated with the full name of the user, their Home directory, and so on, by using the `niutil -createprop` command.

```
  Terminal   File   Edit   Scrollback   Font   Window   Help
                              ttyp1
[ferro:~] user% nidump passwd . > passwd.txt
[ferro:~] user% sudo niutil -destroy . /users/zoe
[ferro:~] user%
```

```
  Terminal   File   Edit   Scrollback   Font   Window   Help
                              ttyp1
[ferro:~] user% sudo niload passwd . < passwd.txt
[ferro:~] user%
```

BACK UP NETINFO INFORMATION IN A FILE

1 Type **nidump** followed by a space.

2 Type the name of a format followed by a space.

3 Type . followed by a space.

4 Type > followed by a space, a filename, and then press Return.

■ The `nidump` command dumps the contents of that format into your file.

5 Type **sudo niutil –destroy . /users/zoe** and press Return.

■ The user zoe is removed from NetInfo.

RELOAD NETINFO FROM YOUR FILE

1 Type **sudo niload** followed by a space.

2 Type the name of a format followed by a space.

3 Type . followed by a space, and then < followed by a space.

4 Type the name of the file into which you dumped the contents of the format, and press Return.

■ The system reloads the dumped data back into NetInfo, including the account information for zoe.

INSTALL DEVELOPER TOOLS

You can load a variety of software development tools onto your Mac OS X system. The Developer Tools CD that ships with the OS contains a complete set of development tools. This includes a number of standard programming languages, utilities, and libraries along with software management tools and debuggers. There are compilers that allow you to turn your source code into programs your system can run from scratch, debuggers — special tools that help you to locate errors in your code, and tools to help you analyze performance.

You can load all of the tools available on the Developer Tools CD at once, or you can open the Packages folder and select any of six individual packages that you want to install. These are BSDSDK, DevDocumentation, DevExamples, DevPBW0, DevSDK, and DevTools.

During the installation of the developer tools, the installer goes through a number of phases, including an optimization phase in which the installer attempts to improve the overall performance of your system. Do not be alarmed if your system slows down during this part of the installation process; this is not uncommon. The installation process may take longer than you think it should. Be patient and allow it to complete.

To make your system easier to manage, you should install the developer tools on the same disk as your Mac OS X installation, if possible. You can load the developer tools from the CD in roughly half an hour. If you are operating on a local area network, you can make the developer tools available on one system and install them on other systems over the network.

The README.html file is a good starting point to help you find the documentation that you need to get started. You can keep your developer tools current by periodically looking for updates at www.apple.com.

INSTALL DEVELOPER TOOLS

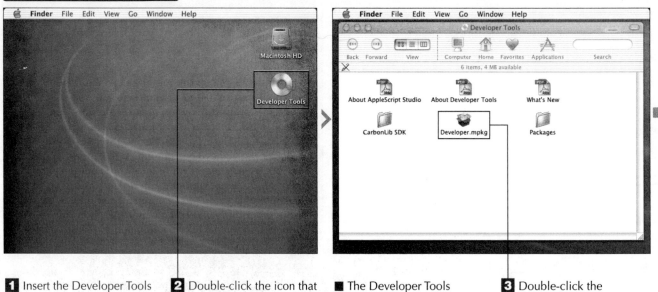

1 Insert the Developer Tools CD-ROM into your drive.

■ The tools CD icon appears on your screen.

2 Double-click the icon that appears on your desktop

■ The Developer Tools window opens.

3 Double-click the Developer.mpkg icon.

Extra The developer tools include the gcc 3.1 compiler. This GNU C compiler compiles code written in C, C++, Objective-C, and Objective-C++. Developers on other Unix systems — Linux, Solaris, FreeBSD, and others, use this same compiler extensively. In fact, gcc is used to compile Mac OS X. This particular version of the compiler has been enhanced to compile faster, and produce more efficient executables.

If you load the entire contents of the Developer Tools CD, you will also install Project Builder, Interface Builder, AppleScript Studio, New BSD SDK, gdb debugger, Thread Viewer, and Sampler along with the associated documentation. Project Builder is Apple's integrated developer environment and assists with development tasks from editing and searching through building and debugging.

If you are a seasoned developer, you will appreciate all the tools that are packaged in this tool kit. If you are a new developer, you will probably appreciate all the documentation and sample code that will help you get off to a productive start. Many other features of Mac OS X, such as fine-grained multithreading, make this operating system an extremely versatile development environment.

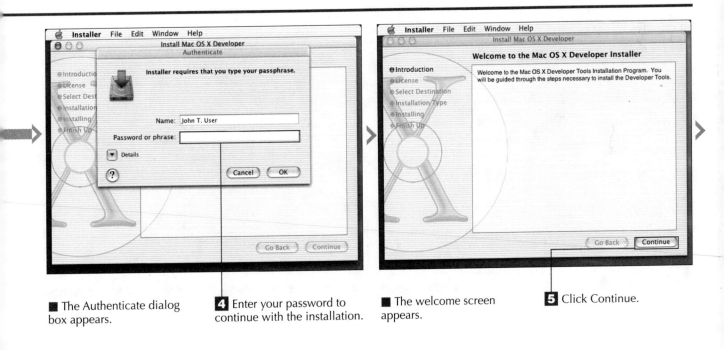

■ The Authenticate dialog box appears.

4 Enter your password to continue with the installation.

■ The welcome screen appears.

5 Click Continue.

INSTALL DEVELOPER TOOLS (CONTINUED)

After you have loaded the Developer Tools on your system, you may notice that a new directory has been added to your system — /Developer. This directory contains the sample code and documentation that is provided with the software. The subdirectories inside /Developer are set so that anyone on the system can read their contents.

In the Applications directory, you can find many useful tools to help with your development projects. Among these, you find PackageMaker — a tool to help you package your software for easy installation. You can also find Interface Builder — a graphical interface editor for Cocoa and Carbon applications and MallocDebug — to measure an application's use of dynamic memory. The Java Browser can make it easier to analyze and view your Java code. More than 20 tools are available.

The Documentation directory contains documentation on many aspects of development. To get started with the Java development documentation, for example, you can open

Developer/Documentation/Java/java.html with a browser or by double-clicking the file. This page provides links to essential information on using Java on Mac OS X, including information about the Java 2 API, WebObjects, and so on.

Before viewing the Java 2 API reference for the first time, type **sudo /Developer/Documentation/Java/scripts/ unjarJavaDocumentation.sh** in a Terminal window. This command extracts Java API documentation from a Java archive file — a jar file — so that you can read it. There is also a PDF file entitled Java Development on Mac OS X that introduces you to Java development on your Mac OS X system, including Basic Java, double-clickable applications, and how to use Project Builder. QuickTime for Java provides cross-platform APIs to allow you to build multimedia components, such as streaming audio and video, for both Macintosh and Windows systems.

INSTALL DEVELOPER TOOLS (CONTINUED)

■ The Software License Agreement appears.

6 Read the license agreement and click Continue.

7 Click Agree.

Extra

You can begin your browsing of the developer documentation by opening /Developer/Documentation in your Finder. The README file, README.html, provides a gentle introduction to the thousands of pages of documentation that you find on the system from tutorials and conceptual overviews to detailed release notes.

ProjectBuilder allows you to move smoothly from looking at your code to viewing documentation. By holding down the option button and double-clicking on the particular API element, the tool takes you swiftly to the proper document or provides you with a list of relevant choices.

The developer tools are installed with a large collection of pages to help you learn about various commands. These pages should have been installed during the installation of the developer tools. You need to have /usr/share/man on your MANPATH to view the pages. You can add this directory to your path by typing **setenv MANPATH $MANPATH":"/usr/share/man** or by adding to the path defined in your .tcshrc file. The latter method is a better choice as it adds this to your path every time you log on.

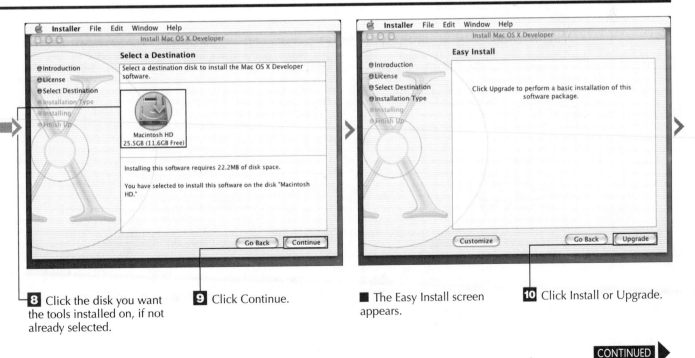

8 Click the disk you want the tools installed on, if not already selected.

9 Click Continue.

■ The Easy Install screen appears.

10 Click Install or Upgrade.

CONTINUED ▶

INSTALL DEVELOPER TOOLS (CONTINUED)

While many of the tools on the developers CD are intended for Java development, there is also a large set of tools to help you build applications in other languages. The version of gcc that is included is a compiler for C, C++, and Objective-C applications. The cpp-precomp and cpp tools are preprocessors. The first works with C and Objective-C. The latter works with C++.

The `as` command is the system assembler. *gdb* is a debugger from the GNU Foundation that is well known in the industry. The developer tools provide a debugging guide as well as a quick reference to get you started.

`ld` is the static link editor. It combines object files into binary files such as those that make up applications and shared libraries.

`dyld` is the dynamic link editor for Mac OS X. This tool is used by applications that load libraries as needed, rather than incorporating them as is the case when libraries are linked statically.

`libtool` creates both dynamic and status libraries and is used by gcc as needed.

The developer tools also provide CVS, a tool for maintaining source code that also comes from the GNU Foundation. CVS allows you to maintain multiple versions of an application and to create any particular version as needed. CVS also allows multiple developers to work on the same code without the danger of overwriting each other's changes. Code is checked in and checked out so that only one individual can change a module at a time. You can determine differences between multiple versions of the same code and merge code as needed to facilitate incorporating changes from more than one individual.

INSTALL DEVELOPER TOOLS (CONTINUED)

■ The system prepares to load the new software.

■ The system continues loading the new software.

Extra

The release notes provided with the developer tools help you to understand what has changed in a tool since the last release. If you are new to development on Mac OS X, the release notes may not mean a lot to you today, but you may find them important after you have spent considerable time developing software and are ready to upgrade to a newer release of the developer tools. In this case, reading the release notes is a great idea as it tells you what to watch out for as you begin to work with the newer software.

For an unusual introduction to Java programming, double-click /Developer/Examples/Java/Sound/Sound. After clicking Start, you can read the README.txt file and begin to learn how this sample application was created. The application loops, so you may want to hit the Stop button after several times.

You can find two of the Aqua dots, DotBlue.tif and DotGray.tif, in the Developers directory. These TIFF images look like the dots in the upper-left hand corner of your Terminal window.

Sample Applescript programs are available to help with your scripting efforts.

The installation software optimizes performance.

■ Installation is complete.

12 Click Close.

FIND UNIX APPLICATIONS ON THE WEB

You can download software in one of two forms: as precompiled binaries that you can run after a quick installation process, or as source code that you must compile before you can run it. The easiest way to obtain new tools for your Mac OS X system is to find precompiled binaries. While many sources of precompiled binaries exist on the Web, you can only use those that are built specifically to run on Mac OS X.

The advantages of starting with source code are first, that you can study the source code and determine exactly how a tool works, and second, that you can modify the code for your own purposes.

As you might expect, one of the best sources of precompiled tools for Mac OS X is Apple Computer. In fact, to facilitate your access to their software tools, Apple has included the Get Mac OS X Software option in the Apple drop-down menu on your desktop, which takes your browser to their comprehensive download site.

When you download a software tool from the Apple site, the Download Manager appears, allowing you to monitor the progress of your downloads. At this point, you can close your browser window. The software continues downloading, although you must remember not to shut down your network connection if you are on a dial-up line.

There are several sites that provide Mac OS X precompiled binaries. For example, you can obtain a precompiled binary for Fink, a sophisticated software package manager for Mac OS X, from www.fink.sourceforge.net. Other useful tools include Mozilla from www.mozilla.org, PHP from www.entropy.ch/software/macosx/php, and XFree86 from www.apple.com/downloads. OpenOffice, an office suite that rivals Microsoft Office, may be officially released by the time you read these words.

FIND UNIX APPLICATIONS FROM THE WEB

1 Click Apple OS X ⇨ Get Mac OS X Software.

■ Your browser opens and takes you to the Mac OS X Downloads site.

2 Locate the software you want to download.

3 Command-click the download link for the software you select.

Extra

There are literally thousands of programs that you can download and install to increase the usefulness and versatility of your Mac OS X system; some of these programs may prove to be essential add-ons to your system, while you may install others simply because they are interesting or fun. The most beneficial programs are those that either complement the tools that you already have, or do a much better job than the tools delivered with the OS.

For example, Mac OS X does not include a spell checker. If you intend to do a lot of writing on your Mac system, installing ispell provides you with a versatile spell-checking system. Another tool, aspell, purports to be a more intelligent spell checker, but requires some additional configuration.

Programs that need to generate character-based displays in a terminal-independent manner require a copy of libtermcap, another program that is not included in the standard Mac OS X installation. You can find libtermcap at www.gnu.org.

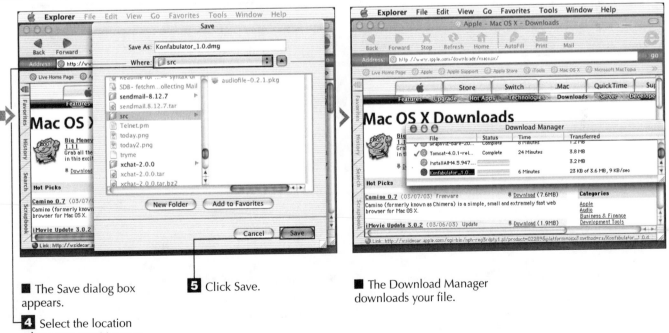

■ The Save dialog box appears.

4 Select the location where you want to save the downloaded file.

5 Click Save.

■ The Download Manager downloads your file.

USING OPEN SOURCE SOFTWARE

You can download, install, and use open source software to great advantage. Open source software is free, and is developed and tested by some of the most dedicated people in the industry. The intention of open source licensing is to encourage collaboration and innovation while shifting the focus of control from large companies to end-users.

The Open Source movement is dedicated to quality and fair practice. The basic idea behind open source is that, with the potential to have hundreds of people improving and testing code, the software development cycle is shortened and the quality of the software improves. In addition, no individual or company can leverage that development toward goals that are against the interests of the overall population of users.

Now roughly twenty years old, the Open Source movement is finally achieving a presence in the commercial world. As a result, companies like Red Hat can achieve financial success even though they are selling software that is essentially free. Commercial success and open source software are not incompatible with each other. In fact, Mac OS X is itself built on an open source foundation, a core operating system known as Darwin.

Although the development of Linux has been very important to the Open Source movement, open source development has also brought us tools that are critical to the Internet such as BIND, sendmail, and Apache.

A sizable portion of open source software falls under the GNU public licensing (GPL) agreement that states that any software incorporating GPL-based software must itself be licensed as GPL software. Not all open source, however, falls under this licensing agreement, so you need to know how source code is licensed to know how you can use it. While open source code is available for anyone to use, the original developers may retain some intellectual property rights.

USING OPEN SOURCE SOFTWARE

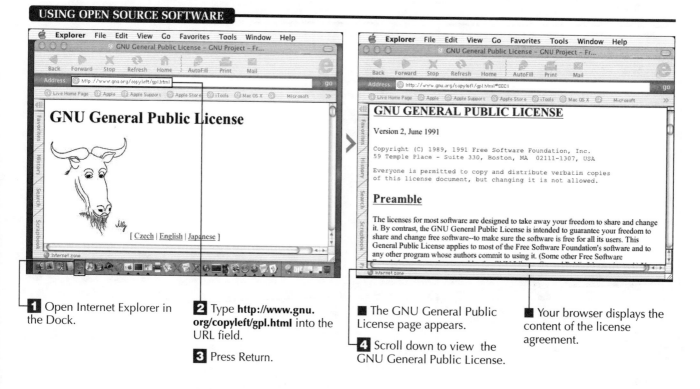

1 Open Internet Explorer in the Dock.

2 Type **http://www.gnu.org/copyleft/gpl.html** into the URL field.

3 Press Return.

■ The GNU General Public License page appears.

4 Scroll down to view the GNU General Public License.

■ Your browser displays the content of the license agreement.

FIND OPEN SOURCE SOFTWARE

You can find plenty of open source software on the Web and even participate in open source development if it interests you. The best sites for open source software are those that are dedicated only to open source. These sites include www.freshmeat.org and www.sourceforge.net. You can also find useful links and a lot of additional information about open source software by visiting www.opensource.org.

You can also look for source code on the original development sites of software applications. For example, you can go to www.apache.org to download the latest or earlier versions of the Apache server. You can get sendmail from www.sendmail.com, and you can get GNU tools from www.gnu.org.

If you intend to use open source software for your business or projects, the issue of open source certification can become very important to you. Open source certification,

performed by Open Source Initiative (OSI), assures you that the source code that you are using meets all the requirements that qualify it as open source.

The process of compiling an application from source code can range from straightforward to extremely difficult. Fortunately, most popular tools have the development bugs removed from them a long time before you obtain a copy of the source code. These include bugs in the compilation process as well as bugs in the code. If you are wary of code with bugs, you should avoid any code that is described as Beta. Beta is a word for code that has not been fully tested.

A useful tool that you can download first is Fink. Fink is an open source tool for managing software installation and can save you a tremendous amount of time in finding, downloading, and installing other software.

FIND OPEN SOURCE SOFTWARE

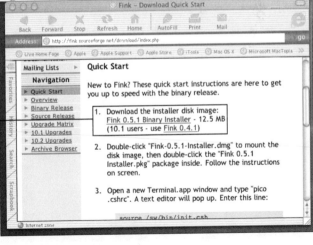

1 Type **http://fink.sourceforge.net/download/index.php** into a browser.

■ The Web page for downloading Fink appears.

2 Scroll down the page to the link for downloading Fink.

INSTALL APPLICATION PACKAGES

You can install an application package on Mac OS X quite easily. This is because a package is a specially formatted application file that is designed for easy installation. To let you know that a file is prepared for easy installation on your system, the Finder uses an icon that looks like an opened parcel.

To install an application package, you can simply double-click the icon for the package in the Finder. This initiates a process that walks you through each step in the installation. You are asked to enter your password to authenticate yourself as a privileged user, to accept the license agreement, and to select the disk for the installation. You can monitor the progress of the installation by watching the progress bar. When the installation is complete, a message appears informing you that the installation was successful. You install all software packages in this manner.

Mac OS X also includes an install command, which you can use to move binary files into a chosen location from where you want to run them. You can specifically avoid overwriting earlier versions of the software if you use a -b option with the install command. With a -o option, you can specify who owns the application when it moves into the target directory. Similarly, a -g option allows you to specify the group. You can use a -d option to create missing directories. With a -m option, you can override the default mode of the file, restricting access as needed.

While downloading and installing software is relatively easy, managing it can be much more challenging. Mac OS X does not place restrictions on where you install software, so you should maintain and enforce a convention to prevent your system from becoming disorganized.

INSTALL APPLICATION PACKAGES

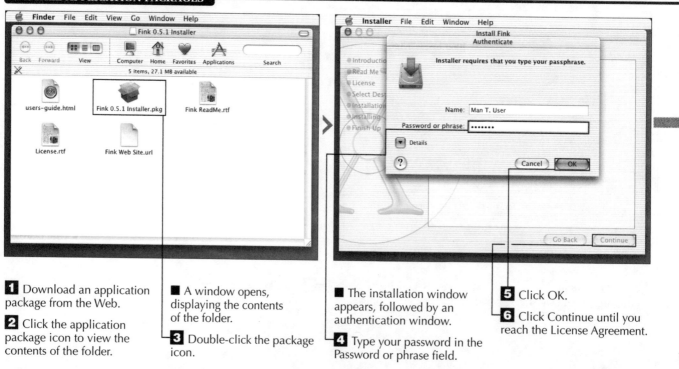

1 Download an application package from the Web.

2 Click the application package icon to view the contents of the folder.

■ A window opens, displaying the contents of the folder.

3 Double-click the package icon.

■ The installation window appears, followed by an authentication window.

4 Type your password in the Password or phrase field.

5 Click OK.

6 Click Continue until you reach the License Agreement.

Extra

When you install software in many different locations on your hard drive, it can become difficult to keep track of both where you have installed your software and what software you have installed. This situation is exacerbated when you frequently download new tools and utilities.

While you can manually organize your software, you have another option for making the software easier to find and use: You can update your search path to include all directories into which you install software.

You can update your search path by editing your shell configuration file. If you are using the default shell in Mac OS X, tcsh, your shell configuration file is defined in the .tcshrc file in the root of your Home directory. The system reads this file every time you log on, as well as every time you open a new shell or a new Terminal window.

To update your path in tcsh, edit your .tcshrc file by adding the line, `setenv PATH $PATH":"/usr/local/bin:/sw/bin"`, where the specified paths match the locations of your new software. Each system user needs to make this change in order to find software without knowing the software locations.

7 Scroll down to read the agreement.

8 Click Continue.

■ The Select a Destination screen appears.

9 Click the appropriate device to select a hard drive for your installation.

10 Click Continue.

■ The installation proceeds and installs the software on your disk.

INSTALL TAR ARCHIVES

You can install software from a tape archive, or TAR file, by using the `tar` command with a `-x` argument. The `-x` argument instructs the command to extract from a specified file. You also use the `tar` command to create these archives, for example, in preparing applications for distribution. Many Unix users employ the `tar` command to prepare archives of important personal files. You must add a `-f` argument, making the command `tar -xf`, to indicate that you are including the TAR file in the command, and a `-v` argument, making the command `tar -xvf`, if you want to list the files as you extract them.

To ensure that the TAR file is intact, it is always a good idea to examine the contents of the TAR file before you extract from it. If you downloaded a TAR file without using binary mode, you may end up with a file that is corrupt. Checking the contents also tells you where the software installs when you extract it. Most TAR files install in the directory that you are in when you issue the `tar` command.

You can use the `tar -tvf` command to examine the contents of a TAR file. For example, to extract from a file called drawfigs.tar, you can type **tar -tvf drawfigs.tar**. If the filenames that appear start with a /, the `tar` command attempts to extract the file with the path shown, starting at /. Otherwise, TAR extracts the commands into your current directory.

The command for extracting files from an archive named drawfigs.tar is `tar -xvf drawfigs.tar`. The `-v` argument of the `tar` command stands for verbose. When you use this option, the `tar` command displays each filename as it extracts the file.

INSTALL TAR ARCHIVES

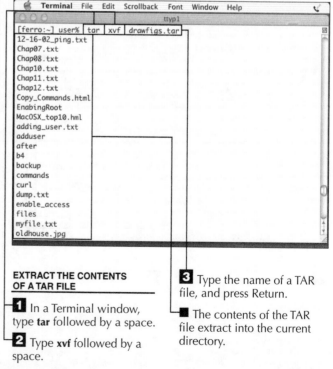

LIST THE CONTENTS OF A TAR FILE

1 In a Terminal window, type **tar** followed by a space.

2 Type **tvf** followed by a space.

3 Type the name of a TAR file, and press Return.

■ The contents of the TAR file appear.

EXTRACT THE CONTENTS OF A TAR FILE

1 In a Terminal window, type **tar** followed by a space.

2 Type **xvf** followed by a space.

3 Type the name of a TAR file, and press Return.

■ The contents of the TAR file extract into the current directory.

Extra

You can use the `tar` command to extract a single file or directory from an archive instead of the entire contents. For example, you may want to first read the license agreement or README file before proceeding to extract the remaining contents from the archive.

To extract a single file from a TAR file, add the name of that file to the end of the `tar` command. The command `tar -xvf drawfigs.tar README` extracts only the README file. If you are extracting a file from a directory inside the TAR file, be careful to type the directory name and filename exactly as they appear in the file listing produced by the `tar -tvf` command. For example, if the file you want to extract appears as tmpls/template1.tmpl, type the command **tar xvf drawfigs.tar tmpls/template1.tmpl**.

If you want to change some part of the pathname for the extracted files while you are extracting them, you can use the `-s` option. For example, if want to change the tmpls directory to orig_tmpls during the extraction, you can type **tar -s /tmpls/orig_tmpls/ -xvf drawfigs.tar**.

Terminal File Edit Scrollback Font Window Help

ttyp1

```
[ferro:~] user% gunzip httpd-2.0.43.tar.gz
[ferro:~] user% ls -l httpd-2.0.43.tar
-rw-r--r--  1 user staff  22958080 May  7 02:24 httpd-2.0.43.tar
```

Terminal File Edit Scrollback Font Window Help

ttyp1

```
[ferro:~] user% uncompress httpd-2.0.43.tar.Z
[ferro:~] user% ls -l httpd-2.0.43.tar
-rw-r--r--  1 user staff  22958080 May  7 02:24 httpd-2.0.43.tar
[ferro:~ user%
```

EXTRACT FROM A GUNZIPPED TAR FILE

1 In a Terminal window, type **gunzip** followed by a space.

2 Type the name of a gunzipped TAR file, and press Return.

■ The TAR file is uncompressed.

UNCOMPRESS A COMPRESSED TAR FILE

1 In a Terminal window, type **uncompress** followed by a space.

2 Type the name of a compressed TAR file, and press Return.

■ The TAR file is uncompressed.

COMPILE A PROGRAM WITH MAKE

You can compile software from source code with a utility called make, a tool favored by many users of open source software. make is not itself a compiler, but a tool that manages compilation. With the Mac OS X system, make calls gcc, the GNU C compiler, to compile the source code.

While the process of compiling your own applications might seem tedious at first, some developments have arisen that have made source code compiling much more efficient. For one, the process of going from source code to executable has become significantly standardized; if you can remember this sequence of steps — configure, make, make install, and make clean — you can build and install most software that you find. For another, you can often avoid the manual process of compiling by using a tool such as Fink.

One reason why make is efficient is because it does not recompile a program when the existing program is newer

than the source code; after all, this indicates that no changes have been made to the code since it was last compiled. Large applications containing many source files recompile much faster than they first compiled because only the updated source files are recompiled. You can also run make without a Makefile to compile a program with a single source file.

Source code prepared specifically for Mac OS X may already include a Makefile. Generic source code requires an additional step that evaluates the configuration of your system and creates an appropriate Makefile.

The make install step uses instructions in the Makefile to install the application into the directory from which you want it to run. The make clean step removes object files, which are intermediate files in the compilation of a complex application.

COMPILE A PROGRAM WITH MAKE

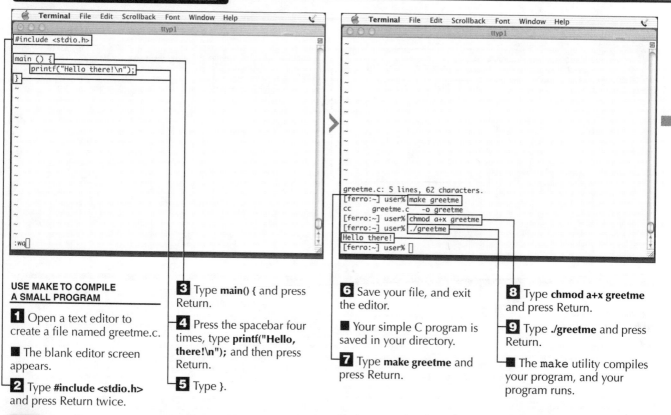

**USE MAKE TO COMPILE
A SMALL PROGRAM**

1 Open a text editor to create a file named greetme.c.

■ The blank editor screen appears.

2 Type **#include <stdio.h>** and press Return twice.

3 Type **main() {** and press Return.

4 Press the spacebar four times, type **printf("Hello, there!\n");** and then press Return.

5 Type **}**.

6 Save your file, and exit the editor.

■ Your simple C program is saved in your directory.

7 Type **make greetme** and press Return.

8 Type **chmod a+x greetme** and press Return.

9 Type **./greetme** and press Return.

■ The make utility compiles your program, and your program runs.

Extra

When you compile Apache from the compressed TAR file that you download from www.apache.org, there are several steps you must follow. First, you must uncompress the file, and extract the contents. You must then run the `configure` command to prepare your Makefile, execute the `make` command to read the Makefile, and call gcc to compile each piece of code and create your executables. After this, you run `make install` to place the new binaries and associated configuration files in the directories from which you want to run them, and then run `make clean` to remove intermediate files. While that process involves a number of steps, these steps become second nature after you build several applications this way.

It is always a good idea to read the included README or INSTALL files before you begin the compilation process. These files often contain instructions that make building the application easier. For example, you may run through all the steps of the building process for Apache without realizing that adding a prefix specification such as `—prefix=/sw/apache` to your `configure` command tells Apache to install as /sw/apache/httpd and to look for configuration files in /sw/apache/conf.

```
 Terminal  File  Edit  Scrollback  Font  Window  Help
                          ttyp1
[ferro:~] user% make greetme
make: `greetme' is up to date.
[ferro:~] user%
```

```
 Terminal  File  Edit  Scrollback  Font  Window  Help
                          ttyp1
[ferro:~] user% make greetme
make: `greetme' is up to date.
[ferro:~] user% touch greetme.c
[ferro:~] user% make greetme
cc     greetme.c    -o greetme
[ferro:~] user%
```

10 Type **make greetme** and press Return.

■ The make process tells you there is nothing to be done because the source file has not changed.

11 Type **touch greetme.c** to give your source file a newer timestamp than the compiled file.

12 Type **make greetme** and press Return.

■ The make process compiles your code again.

■ The **make** utility compiles your software.

COMPILE APACHE

You can compile and install a new version of Apache from source code. New versions are available from time to time from www.apache.org. Installing a new version may give you additional features, better security, or improved performance.

You compile Apache with the standard set of steps for compiling open source software. You generally start with a gzipped TAR file freshly downloaded from apache.org. You then need to unzip that file with gunzip, and untar the resulting file with `tar xvf`. After your untar operation is complete, you have a directory containing all of the files needed for configuring and compiling the new version of Apache.

After moving into the new Apache source directory with the `cd` command, you run the configure script that is included with the distribution. This step takes several minutes to

complete. During this stage of preparing for compilation, information about your system is being collected and analyzed and a Makefile is being prepared that guides the compilation process on your Mac OS X system. Keep in mind that the Apache distribution was built so that it would compile on many different types of systems. Therefore, this configuration step is critical to the compilation on any particular operating system.

After the configuration operation is complete, you can begin the actual compilation using the `make` command. The `make` command starts by reading the Makefile that the configuration process created and using it to drive the compilation process. Unlike the use of `make` with a simple C source code file, this `make` process compiles many different programs and builds a small number of programs, in particular the httpd process that represents the Web server you have just built.

COMPILE APACHE

```
 Terminal  File  Edit  Scrollback  Font  Window  Help
                         ttyp1
[ferro:~] user% gunzip httpd-2.0.43.tar.gz
[ferro:~] user% tar xf httpd-2.0.43.tar
[ferro:~] user% cd httpd-2.0.43
[ferro:~/httpd-2.0.43] user% []
```

```
 Terminal  File  Edit  Scrollback  Font  Window  Help
                         ttyp1
[ferro:~/httpd-2.0.43] user% ./configure --prefix=/sw
checking for chosen layout... Apache
checking for working mkdir -p... yes
checking build system type... powerpc-apple-darwin6.3
checking host system type... powerpc-apple-darwin6.3
checking target system type... powerpc-apple-darwin6.3

Configuring Apache Portable Runtime library ...

checking for APR... reconfig
configuring package in srclib/apr now
checking build system type... powerpc-apple-darwin6.3
checking host system type... powerpc-apple-darwin6.3
checking target system type... powerpc-apple-darwin6.3
Configuring APR library
Platform: powerpc-apple-darwin6.3
checking for working mkdir -p... yes
APR Version: 0.9.2
checking for chosen layout... apr
checking for gcc... gcc
checking for C compiler default output... a.out
checking whether the C compiler works... yes
```

1 Type **gunzip** followed by the name of your downloaded Apache source file, for example **httpd-2.0.43.tar.gz**, and press Return.

■ Your downloaded file is unzipped.

2 Type **tar xf** followed by the name of your Apache TAR file, for example **httpd-2.0.43.tar**, and press Return.

3 Type **cd** followed by the name of your new source directory, for example **httpd-2.0.43**, and press Return.

4 Type **./configure --prefix=** followed by the name of the directory in which you want your new Apache server installed, for example **/sw**, and press Return.

■ Your Apache Makefile is created.

Extra

After compiling and installing Apache, you have to start the server. Along with the files that you just installed is a script named apachectl. This script starts, restarts, and stops the Apache server. If you installed Apache in /sw/apache, through the `-prefix=/sw` configure option, you can find apachectl in /sw/apache/bin/apachectl. To start Apache, you then type **/sw/apache/bin/apachectl start**.

The configuration and installation process described on these pages is probably the most standard process for installing Apache. Without the `-prefix` argument provided with the `configure` command, Apache compiles to run from the default directory. The remainder of the process as described uses only default values.

To learn about the many different options that you can use to build a customized Apache server, use the command `./configure -help`.

While your new Apache server is ready to run, it uses the default `DocumentRoot` — the directory in which your Web pages will install — and serves only the set of pages that the installation process installs. Refer to Chapter 14 for information on configuring your Apache server and populating your new Web site.

```
[ferro:~/httpd-2.0.43] user% make
Making all in srclib
Making all in apr
Making all in strings
/bin/sh /Users/user/httpd-2.0.43/srclib/apr/libtool --silent --mode=compi
le gcc -g -O2   -DHAVE_CONFIG_H -DDARWIN -DSIGPROCMASK_SETS_THREAD_MASK -
no-cpp-precomp   -I../include -I../include/arch/unix  -c apr_cpystrn.c &&
 touch apr_cpystrn.lo
/bin/sh /Users/user/httpd-2.0.43/srclib/apr/libtool --silent --mode=compi
le gcc -g -O2   -DHAVE_CONFIG_H -DDARWIN -DSIGPROCMASK_SETS_THREAD_MASK -
no-cpp-precomp   -I../include -I../include/arch/unix  -c apr_snprintf.c &
& touch apr_snprintf.lo
/bin/sh /Users/user/httpd-2.0.43/srclib/apr/libtool --silent --mode=compi
le gcc -g -O2   -DHAVE_CONFIG_H -DDARWIN -DSIGPROCMASK_SETS_THREAD_MASK -
no-cpp-precomp   -I../include -I../include/arch/unix  -c apr_strnatcmp.c
&& touch apr_strnatcmp.lo
/bin/sh /Users/user/httpd-2.0.43/srclib/apr/libtool --silent --mode=compi
le gcc -g -O2   -DHAVE_CONFIG_H -DDARWIN -DSIGPROCMASK_SETS_THREAD_MASK -
no-cpp-precomp   -I../include -I../include/arch/unix  -c apr_strings.c &&
 touch apr_strings.lo
/bin/sh /Users/user/httpd-2.0.43/srclib/apr/libtool --silent --mode=compi
le gcc -g -O2   -DHAVE_CONFIG_H -DDARWIN -DSIGPROCMASK_SETS_THREAD_MASK -
```

```
[ferro:~/httpd-2.0.43] user% make install
Making install in srclib
Making all in strings
Making all in passwd
Making all in tables
Making all in file_io/unix
Making all in network_io/unix
Making all in threadproc/unix
Making all in misc/unix
Making all in locks/unix
Making all in time/unix
Making all in mmap/unix
Making all in shmem/unix
Making all in user/unix
Making all in memory/unix
Making all in atomic/unix
Making all in poll/unix
Making all in support/unix
Making all in dso/unix
if [ ! -d /sw/include ]; then  /Users/user/httpd-2.0.43/srclib/apr/build/
x: 24 lines, 615 characters.
[ferro:~/httpd-2.0.43] user% clear
```

5 Type **make** and press Return.

■ Compilation begins.

6 Type **make install** and press Return.

■ Your new Apache server will be installed in the directory you specified.

MANAGE SOFTWARE INSTALLATION WITH FINK

You can manage the installation of software on your system using a software package management utility known as Fink. Fink is a versatile tool that allows you to download, extract, configure, compile, install, update, and remove software to and from your system, often with no more input from you than a single command. Fink works with software that is configured as a package. A package is a special format that contains binary files along with source code and patches that you may need to facilitate installation and subsequent management of the installed software.

Fink maintains a database that allows it to locate software packages. It downloads the packages using curl and then proceeds to install your new software while giving you progress updates on-screen.

Fink is intuitive to software dependencies, and so does not install a software package if you have not installed prerequisite software. It also does not remove software if other packages on your system require it.

Fink is not included in Mac OS X, but you can download it from www.sourceforge.net. You can visit www.fink.sourceforge.net/download to find links and instructions on how to obtain a copy.

Fink is a port of a tool called the Advanced Package Tool or APT from Debian. Fink allows you to install a package from source code or from binary files, depending on what is available. Binary package files come in a format known as dpkg and have a .deb extension.

After you install Fink on your system, it is easy to use. The command `fink list` displays a list of available software packages. Those that are installed on your system appear with a lowercase i in the leftmost column. To install an application, you can use the `fink install` command followed by the name of the package you want to install.

MANAGE SOFTWARE INSTALLATION WITH FINK

■ Fink displays a list of packages.

3 Type **fink** followed by a space.

4 Type **install** followed by a space.

5 Type the name of a package, and press Return.

■ Fink downloads the package you select.

Extra

To operate well, Fink needs to work with the most recent data possible. If you install Fink and fail to update the inventory of available software, your installation of Fink gradually becomes out of date and unable to recognize new releases of packages.

To update the list and descriptions of packages that Fink uses to find and install software, use the command `fink selfupdate`. To update all of the packages that you have already installed, type **fink update-all**.

You can also use dselect to install software. This tool comes from the Debian Linux community and provides a text-based interface. The dselect tool guides you through the process of choosing the access method you want to use, updating the list of available packages, requesting the packages you want to install, configuring packages which are not yet configured, and removing unwanted software. The tool opens with the following menu.

Example:

```
Debian `dselect' package handling frontend.

0.  [A]ccess     Choose the access method to use.
1.  [U]pdate     Update list of available packages, if possible.
2.  [S]elect     Request which packages you want on your system.
3.  [I]nstall    Install and upgrade wanted packages.
4.  [C]onfig     Configure any packages that are unconfigured.
5.  [R]emove     Remove unwanted software.
6.  [Q]uit       Quit dselect.
```

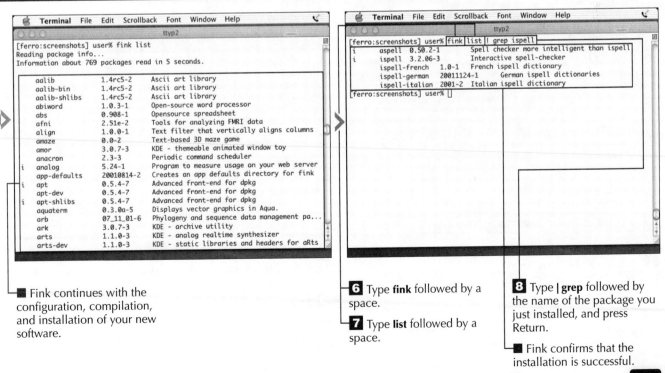

■ Fink continues with the configuration, compilation, and installation of your new software.

6 Type **fink** followed by a space.

7 Type **list** followed by a space.

8 Type **| grep** followed by the name of the package you just installed, and press Return.

■ Fink confirms that the installation is successful.

MANAGE FINK WITH FINKCOMMANDER

You can download software using FinkCommander, a graphical interface that works with Fink. FinkCommander provides a GUI front end to the Fink software package management tool. Using this front end, you can select the software that you want to install and initiate the installation by picking the software from a list of available packages. Fink provides a variety of information on each of the available packages.

While using Fink, you can pick and choose which of the information columns you want to see by selecting or deselecting them from the View menu. Latest is the most recent available version. Installed is the version that is currently installed on your system. Binary is the most recent binary version. Stable is the most recent stable version. Unstable is the most recent unstable version. Status is the status of your installation — current or outdated. Category is the software category, such as base, crypto, database, or

game. Description is a description of the tool. Maintainer is the name of the person who maintains the tool.

You can also filter the list by selecting a column, such as Name, from the menu in the toolbar. When you select a column, you can then type in your selection text in the field to the right. For example, you can list the available games by selecting Category in the menu and typing games into the text field. You can sort by any column by clicking the top of that column.

When you download software, you can watch the progress of your download in the bottom window of the screen. FinkCommander even allows you to provide positive or negative feedback to the maintainer of a package by selecting the green for positive or red for negative stamp icons in the menu bar.

MANAGE FINK WITH FINKCOMMANDER

1 Click the FinkCommander icon to launch the utility.

2 Select Name from the drop-down menu.

3 Type **spell** in the text field.

■ The list updates to show only items with the word spell in their names.

4 Click aspell to select it.

■ A binary format is not available.

■ A stable source code version is available.

Extra

As with Fink, FinkCommander configures, compiles, and installs your software when you select Install from the Source menu. The bottom left corner of the FinkCommander window displays a message describing each phase of the installation. The message Done appears when the installation process is complete. At this point, the Status column for the newly installed tool contains the word current, telling you that you now have the current release of that tool.

While the main purpose of FinkCommander is to make installing software easier, it also provides a convenient way for you to take an inventory of the software on your system. It provides a list of each package that is installed along with their version numbers, and the current or outdated status indicator tells you whether to install a newer version of a tool.

You can also use FinkCommander to remove software. The Remove option appears under each of the Source and Binary menus.

While the software installs, you can continue to peruse the list of available tools. This does not interfere with the installation process. You can select FinkCommander Help from the Help menu to better understand how to take full advantage of this utility.

5 Click Source ⇨ Install.

■ The software begins to download.

6 Select Category from the drop-down menu.

7 Type **games** in the text field.

■ A list of downloadable games appears.

INSTALL LIBRARIES

You can install system libraries for your personal use or for use by software applications. While Mac OS X is an extremely versatile operating system, there are numerous libraries that you can download to increase the functionality of your system. Tools that you download and install often need some of these libraries.

You install libraries in much the same manner as other software except that libraries are usually single binary files. When you place these files in the correct locations on your system, other software can use them by making calls to various routines. For example, if you install a library that contains routines for displaying graphics in the PNG format, you do not have to build these routines into your own code. Instead, you can use the library routines in your code and compile your software to dynamically load the libraries when you need them.

System libraries are stored in /usr/lib. By convention, most third-party libraries reside in /usr/local/lib. You should be careful to install these libraries in the appropriate directories so that the applications that need them can find them.

When you install libraries on your Mac OS X system, acquaint yourself with an environment variable called DYLD_LIBRARY_PATH. This variable is essential in helping your executables to locate the libraries they need. If all of your libraries are not installed in /usr/lib, you must add the list of directories in which libraries are stored to the DYLD_LIBRARY_PATH variable of every user. You must assign this variable a colon-separated list of all directories containing libraries. For tcsh users, you can insert a command, such as setenv DYLD_LIBRARY_PATH /usr/local/lib:/sw/lib , to add these two directories to the locations where the dynamic linker

searches for libraries. You can read the man page for DYLD to learn more about how the dynamic linker uses DYLD_LIBRARY_PATH as a search path for libraries.

You can download many libraries by launching the FinkCommander utility, selecting Category from the menu in the toolbar, and typing libs in the text field; FinkCommander displays a list of libraries that it can install for you.

When you install software through the traditional configure-make-make install process, you may have an opportunity to install libraries as well. This is because, although the basic make-install process may install binaries in /sw/bin or /usr/local/bin, it may fail to install necessary libraries. Read the README and INSTALL files to determine if there is an optional make install-lib step that takes care of this.

The table on the next page provides descriptions for a variety of libraries that you can install on your Mac OS X system. While incomplete, this list contains many of the most useful libraries that you are likely to find. Like other applications, libraries undergo changes as developers build and test new versions.

Just as there are many locations from which you can download open source software, there are many places where you can find useful libraries. You can find references to any library you need by using a search engine such as Google.

USEFUL LIBRARIES

The list below contains libraries that you may want to install on your Mac OS X system. These libraries are especially useful if you plan to develop software.

LIBRARY	DESCRIPTION	LIBRARY	DESCRIPTION
db3	Berkeley DB embedded database	libghttp	HTTP client library
db4	Berkeley DB embedded database	libiconv	Character set conversion library
dlcompat	Dynamic loading compatibility library	libiodbc	ODBC libraries
dtdparser	Java DTD Parser	libjpeg	JPEG image format handling library
expat	C library for parsing XML	libmpeg	GIMP MPEG library
fnlib	Font rendering library for X11	libpoll	System V poll(2) Emulation Library
freetype	TrueType font rendering library, version 1	libtiff	TIFF image format library
freetype2	TrueType font rendering library, version 2	libungif	GIF image format handling library, LZW-free version
gc	General-purpose garbage collection library	libunicode	Low-level Unicode processing library
gd	Graphics generation library	libwww	General-purpose Web API written in C for Unix and Windows
gdbm	GNU dbm	libxml	XML parsing library
giflib	GIF image format handling library, LZW-enabled version	libxml++	C++ interface to the libxml2 XML parsing library
glib	Low-level library that supports GTK+ and GNOME	libxml2	XML parsing library, version 2
gmp	GNU multiple precision arithmetic library	libxpg4	Locale-enabling preload library
gnomelibs	GNOME libraries	netpbm	Graphics manipulation programs and libraries
gnujaxp	Basic XML processing in Java	pcre	Perl Compatible Regular Expressions library
gtk	GTK+, the GIMP widget toolkit used by GNOME	pdflib	A library for generating PDFs
imlib	General image-handling library	pil	The Python Imaging Library; adds image-processing capabilities to Python
libdnet	Networking library	readline	Terminal input library
libdv	Software decoder for DV format video	libghttp	HTTP client library
libfame	Fast Assembly MPEG Encoding library		

INSTALL THE LYNX BROWSER

Y ou can install the Lynx Web browser on your Mac OS X system. Lynx is a text-based Web browser that is useful for troubleshooting Web connections and accessing files and information from the Web, especially when you are limited to a text-only environment, such as a telnet or ssh connection. Lynx does not install with the Mac OS X distribution, but you can download it using Fink or FinkCommander.

While Lynx does not fill your screen with dancing frogs and pop-up ads, the simplicity of this tool gives you a definite advantage because it is fast. While Lynx recognizes graphics and links, it displays only the text equivalents. For example, in place of a link, you see [Link Name] or [Image Name], as in [company_logo.gif].

You can use Lynx to browse the Web as you would Internet Explorer and Netscape Navigator. To start Lynx, you can type **lynx** followed by the URL that you want to visit.

You can click links, even though they appear as text, to move around within the site. You can use the arrow keys on your keyboard, the spacebar, or a number of single-letter commands. The third line from the bottom of the Lynx screen gives you suggestions as to what you may want to do next. For example, you may see a message such as press space for next page. To move forward in the document, you can press the spacebar, and to move backward you can type the letter **b**. As a text-only browser, Lynx seems strange at first, but you may find it a handy, and sometimes indispensable, tool. The name Lynx is a homonym for links.

INSTALL THE LYNX BROWSER

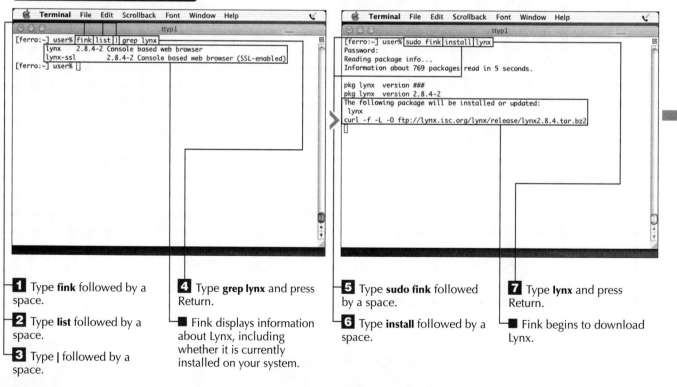

1 Type **fink** followed by a space.

2 Type **list** followed by a space.

3 Type **|** followed by a space.

4 Type **grep lynx** and press Return.

■ Fink displays information about Lynx, including whether it is currently installed on your system.

5 Type **sudo fink** followed by a space.

6 Type **install** followed by a space.

7 Type **lynx** and press Return.

■ Fink begins to download Lynx.

Extra

You can set numerous options to define how Lynx works for you. The best way to learn about these options is to consult the Lynx User Guide. To do this, type **lynx localhost** to start Lynx. Your local home page displays. Then type **h** and press Return. This command activates the Lynx online help, and positions your active link on the Lynx User Guide. When you press Return, the User Guide displays. You can use your arrow keys to move around within the User Guide. When you are done, you can use the Left Arrow key to move to your home page, or type the letter **q** to quit Lynx altogether.

You can use Lynx to perform basic troubleshooting of Web sites. If you have trouble connecting to a Web site using a traditional browser, you can use Lynx to quickly determine whether the site is working. Because Lynx omits graphics and takes very few resources to run, you can test and display your sites in very little time. If you are responsible for a Web site, you can use Lynx to check whether your site is up and working.

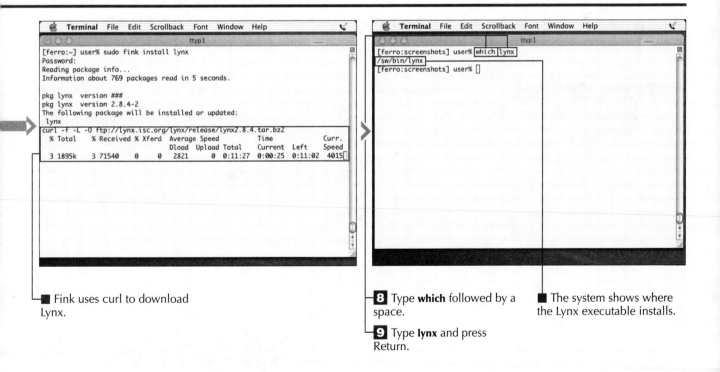

■ Fink uses curl to download Lynx.

8 Type **which** followed by a space.

9 Type **lynx** and press Return.

■ The system shows where the Lynx executable installs.

BROWSE THE WEB WITH LYNX

You can browse the Web with Lynx. At first, Lynx may appear to be a browser of limited capability, but as you become familiar with Lynx, you find how useful it is to quickly retrieve information from the Web; in less time than it normally takes you to start Internet Explorer, Lynx has your entire Web site on your screen.

You can follow links, search for text, and download pages in a similar manner to using a normal browser. The difference is that, instead of clicking links that hide under images or display as underlined text, you move around with simple keystrokes. The currently active link appears highlighted. For example, the colors reverse so you see white letters on a black background if the rest of your screen is black on white.

With Lynx you can use single-letter commands to navigate the Web. For occasional browsing, you only need a few basic navigational commands, but if you want to learn the more advanced browsing capabilities of Lynx, you can use the Lynx help facility to learn what each of these one-letter commands means. To access the information on these commands, you can type **lynx -help | less** on the command line. You can also get help on using Lynx by typing the letter **h** after you have started Lynx. You can then open the Lynx User's Guide by pressing Enter or you can press your down-arrow key and then press Enter, to bring up a listing of the keystroke commands.

If you find yourself stuck at any point or change your mind while waiting for a sluggish site to respond, you can type **z** to stop the current request. This command acts just like clicking the Stop button in Internet Explorer.

BROWSE THE WEB WITH LYNX

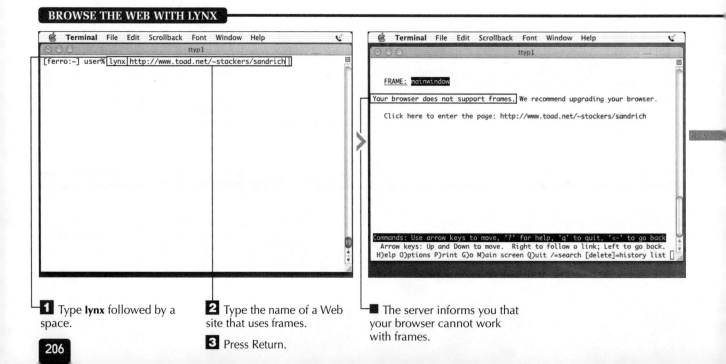

1 Type **lynx** followed by a space.

2 Type the name of a Web site that uses frames.

3 Press Return.

■ The server informs you that your browser cannot work with frames.

Extra

Lynx highlights links on a Web site to make it easier for you to find them. When you first see a screen, the link nearest to the top of the page is highlighted. You can use the arrow keys to follow or move between links.

The down-arrow key takes you to the next link on the page, and the up-arrow key takes you to the previous link. The left-arrow key allows you to follow a link backwards to the previous page; this is similar to the Back button on a normal browser. The right-arrow key follows the current link, taking you to the next page. The spacebar loads the next page.

KEY LYNX COMMANDS	DESCRIPTION
?	Display a list of commands
a	Add the current link to bookmarks
d	Download the current link
g	Go to a specified URL
l	Show an index of documents
k	Show a list of single key commands and what they do
m	Return to main screen
o	Set your options
p	Print
q	Quit
/	Search for a string in the current document
n	Go to the next search string

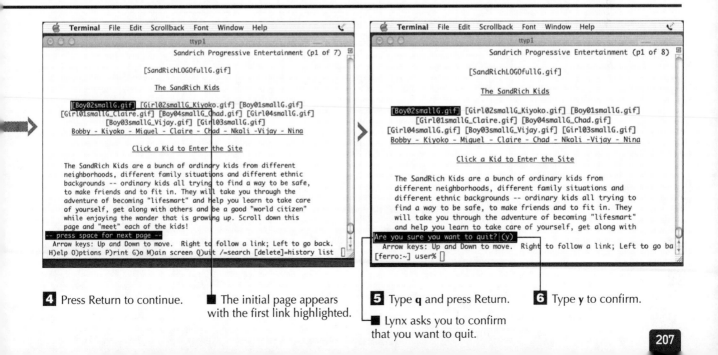

4 Press Return to continue.

■ The initial page appears with the first link highlighted.

5 Type **q** and press Return.

■ Lynx asks you to confirm that you want to quit.

6 Type **y** to confirm.

INSTALL WGET

You can install Wget, an automatic Web-site retriever. Wget is a handy tool for downloading a Web site in order to back it up for safekeeping, or to move it to another host. The best feature of Wget is that you do not have to download your Web pages one at a time; the recursive nature of the tool allows you to download an entire site with a single command.

You can download Wget using Fink. When you type the command **fink list | grep wget**, Fink tells you that the package is available and that it is not yet installed on your system. The current release of Wget is 1.8.2-1. To start the download using Fink, you can type the command **fink install wget**. Fink then runs the `curl` command to download the Wget installation file. Fink manages the uncompression, extraction, and installation of the Wget files onto your system.

Because Fink installs software into the /sw directory, Wget installs as /sw/bin/wget. After you complete the installation, you can type **which wget** and have this pathname returned to you. If not, you must update your search path to include /sw/bin by editing the .tcshrc file in your Home directory.

Fink installs man pages in /sw/share/man. If you type **man wget** and get the response no manual entry for wget, you can add this directory to your MANPATH by adding setenv MANPATH /sw/share/man to your .tcshrc file.

To make the changes to your search path and your MANPATH permanent, you should update these paths as they are defined in your .tcshrc file. Keeping these paths up to date with the applications you have installed will save you a lot of trouble in the end.

INSTALL WGET

```
        Terminal  File  Edit  Scrollback  Font  Window  Help
                                    ttyp1
[ferro:~] user% fink list | grep wget
       wget    1.8.2-1 Automatic web site retreiver
       wget-ssl        1.8.2-1 Automatic web site retreiver, with SSL support
[ferro:~] user%
```

```
        Terminal  File  Edit  Scrollback  Font  Window  Help
                                    ttyp1
[ferro:~] user% sudo fink install wget
Password:
Reading package info...
Information about 769 packages read in 5 seconds.

pkg wget  version ###
pkg wget  version 1.8.2-1
The following package will be installed or updated:
 wget
curl -f -L -O ftp://ftp.gnu.org/gnu/wget/wget-1.8.2.tar.gz
```

1 Type **fink list** followed by a space.

2 Type **| grep wget** and press Return.

■ Fink displays the information it has on Wget.

3 Type **sudo fink install wget** and press Return.

■ Fink immediately starts the download of Wget.

DOWNLOAD WEB SITES WITH WGET

Y ou can download an individual Web page or an entire Web site with Wget. Wget is an extremely fast command-line tool that retrieves files from Web sites using HTTP and FTP. You can download an entire site by typing a single line of text.

Wget works well even on slow and troublesome connections, and if you are using a slow dial-up line, you can start the download and let it run. In all likelihood, it will run to completion with no monitoring or other attention. Wget can run in the background, making it an ideal tool to back up a Web site.

To start a download, all you have to do is type **wget** followed by a URL. For example, the command `wget http://www.dragonflyditch.com` downloads the Dragonfly Ditch Web page; you will see this default document in your browser if you type the same URL.

If you use the recursive option, you can download all of the Web pages and image files from the site. It is a good idea to download sites only if you know how many files you are downloading and how large they are. Downloads from a very large site could consume all of your free disk space. Wget creates a subdirectory by the same name as the URL from which you are downloading, so that if you download from multiple sites, Wget drops the files from each site into separate directories to avoid confusion.

The Wget tool includes many options, such as setting a username and password for access, limiting the depth of your retrieval, and determining whether Wget overwrites downloaded files. You can read the Wget man page to learn more about this tool.

DOWNLOAD WEB SITES WITH WGET

DOWNLOAD A PAGE

1 Type **wget** followed by a space.

2 Type a URL, and press Return.

■ Wget downloads the page.

DOWNLOAD A SITE RECURSIVELY

1 Type **wget** followed by a space.

2 Type **-r** followed by a space.

3 Type a URL, and press Return.

■ Wget downloads the entire site.

INSTALL AN IRC CLIENT

You can install an Internet Relay Chat (IRC) client on Mac OS X. IRC, or chat, clients allow you to participate in interactive dialog with other people on the Internet. Unlike e-mail dialog in which days may elapse between when you send a message and when the recipient reads the message, chat dialog is immediate. You chat with people who are active chat clients themselves.

Chat tools, such as AOL Instant Messenger (AIM), are based on the IRC protocol. IRC relays your message between chat servers. If you do not have iChat on your Mac OS X system or if you want to upgrade your chat client, you can use the Get Mac OS X Software option on your Apple menu to access the download site for Apple binaries. From there, you can scroll down and find the AOL Instant Messenger

application. By right-clicking the download link, you can select the Download Link to Disk option and then click Save to download the BIN file. When you double-click this file, it installs the AOL Instant Messenger software.

Whatever chat client you decide to install, you probably want to keep it in the Dock so that you can start it up by clicking the icon. Before you can use any chat client, however, you need to register a screen name. If you are a .Mac subscriber, you can use your .Mac screen name. If you are already an AOL Instant Messenger user, you can use that screen name. Otherwise, you need to register a new screen name so that you can chat and so that other people can find you.

INSTALL AN IRC CLIENT

1 In your Web Browser, go to www.apple.com/downloads/macosx.

2 Type **AOL** into the search box.

■ The Mac OS X Downloads: Search Results page appears.

3 Click the Email Chat - AOL Instant Messenger link.

Extra

Other IRC clients are available for Mac OS X and offer various features that you may prefer to those of AIM. The site www.irchelp.org is a good place to get information on other chat clients; in particular, the www.irchelp.org/irchelp/mac/ page provides information on other chat clients and links to the sites where you can find these tools.

Ircle from www.ircle.com is one of the most popular chat clients for the Mac OS community. You can download the Carbon version of this tool for your Mac OS X system.

You can also download an IRC client using Fink or FinkCommander. To determine what clients are available through FinkCommander, type **chat** into the text field and select Name and then Description. This should provide you with information on chat tools, such as xchat, that you can download or install with FinkCommander.

■ The AOL Instant Messenger page appears.

4 Scroll to find the download link.

5 Click the Download link.

■ The Download Manager downloads your file.

CHATTING ON IRC

You can chat with a person when you know their screen name. A screen name enables you to find someone on IRC and determine whether the person is online. When you know the screen name of another user, you can add the user to your buddy list, thereby making it easier for you to open a chat session with the friend.

When you first open iChat, your buddy list appears and you can determine which of your buddies are available to chat. You can add buddies to this list by using the Add a Buddy option from your Buddies menu. When you select this option, a form appears that you fill out with information on the new buddy. This information includes the full name and screen name of the buddy. You can also use this form to keep track of the e-mail address of your buddy.

After you select a buddy, you can invite that buddy to chat with you by right-clicking the buddy from your buddy list and clicking Invite to Chat.

Because you may not always be in the mood to chat, you can alter your status to control whether others can initiate a chat session with you. When you start iChat, you are listed as Available. You can change this status to Away, or you can even create a custom status to tell your buddies when you are too busy to chat.

When you engage a buddy in chat, you can exchange dialog in a chat window. For example, if you start a chat with someone from your buddy list or select New Chat with Person from the File menu, a dialog window then opens in which your dialog with the other person appears with proper annotation so that you can easily see what each of you is typing.

CHATTING ON IRC

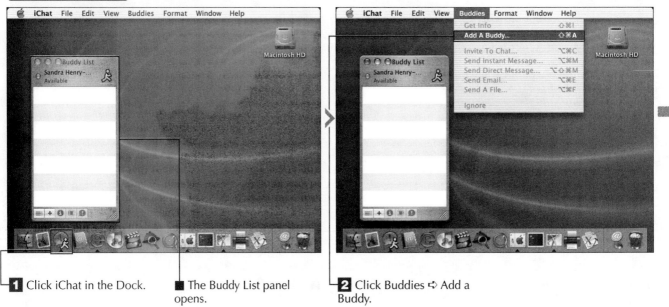

1 Click iChat in the Dock.

■ The Buddy List panel opens.

2 Click Buddies ➪ Add a Buddy.

Extra

If you like working on the Unix command line, you can download and install a command line IRC tool called ircII from www.irchelp.org/irchelp/ircii. You download a TARGZ file from this site, which you can compile and install.

After installation, when you type **ircii**, your Terminal window splits into two sections. You then use commands such as /server and /join to connect to a chat server and join in a discussion. You can use the /help command to learn some basic commands, and the /quit command to exit the program.

While IRC clients such as iChat provide the means for you to chat with people around the globe, there are other tools that you can use in UNIX to communicate with other users. One of these tools is called talk. Talk allows you to enter a chat-like session with other users on the same system. You can read the man page for more information.

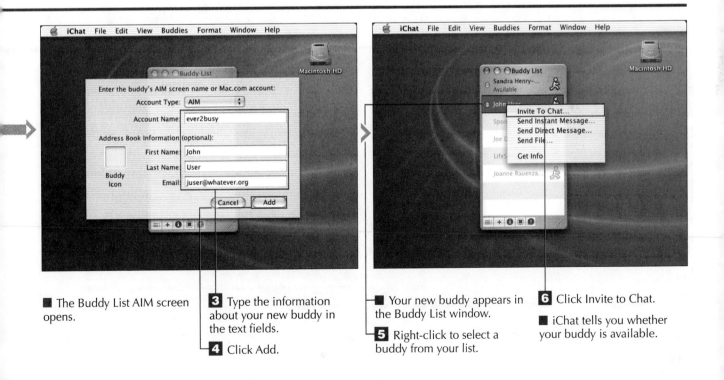

■ The Buddy List AIM screen opens.

3 Type the information about your new buddy in the text fields.

4 Click Add.

■ Your new buddy appears in the Buddy List window.

5 Right-click to select a buddy from your list.

6 Click Invite to Chat.

■ iChat tells you whether your buddy is available.

CONFIGURE SENDMAIL

You can configure sendmail on your Mac OS X system. Sendmail is a mail server; it can listen for e-mail requests from other systems. Sendmail configuration is one of the most difficult tasks in Unix administration. The software itself is complicated and its initial deployment on Mac OS X brings along some additional problems that must be resolved. However, with a little care and some insight, you may get off easily and end up with a mail server that behaves properly.

Some of the difficulties related to sendmail on Mac OS X are due to a conflict between the way that Mac OS X and sendmail deal with directory permissions. Where sendmail wants to be sure that directories it uses can only be modified by root, Mac OS X is far more lenient about directory permissions in order to support privileged users who want to do things like dragging files into root-owned directories. If you try to start sendmail using the default configuration, sendmail will balk at world writable directories and not start.

The easiest way to resolve the conflict between sendmail's cautious character and the lenient directory permissions of Mac OS X is to modify the DontBlameSendmail setting in sendmail's configuration file. This name refers to the fact that the developers of sendmail do not want you blaming the software if you reduce its level of security. Modifying the setting will, however, allow sendmail to start and will not reduce your system security.

Sendmail's configuration file is stored in /etc/mail and is called sendmail.cf. You should always use care in editing this file as the lines in this file are difficult to understand and easy to mistype. However, it is not especially difficult to generate a new sendmail configuration file and the tools you need to do so are already on your system.

CONFIGURE SENDMAIL

```
 Terminal  File  Edit  Scrollback  Font  Window  Help
000                          ttyp1
[ferro:~] user% sudo vi /etc/mail/sendmail.cf
```

```
 Terminal  File  Edit  Scrollback  Font  Window  Help
000                          ttyp1
#
# Copyright (c) 1998-2001 Sendmail, Inc. and its suppliers.
#       All rights reserved.
# Copyright (c) 1983, 1995 Eric P. Allman.  All rights reserved.
# Copyright (c) 1988, 1993
#       The Regents of the University of California.  All rights reserved
.
#
# By using this file, you agree to the terms and conditions set
# forth in the LICENSE file which can be found at the top level of
# the sendmail distribution.
#
#

#####################################################################
#####################################################################
#####
#####           SENDMAIL CONFIGURATION FILE
#####
#####
#####################################################################
/DontBlame
```

EDIT SENDMAIL.CF

1 Type **sudo vi /etc/mail/sendmail.cf**.

2 Press Return.

■ The editor opens your file.

3 Type **/DontBlame** and press Return.

Extra

To ensure that sendmail does not read its configuration file from NetInfo, you may need to type the following commands found in the /etc/mail/README file:

```
niutil -create . /locations/sendmail
niutil -createprop . /locations/sendmail
sendmail.cf /etc/mail/sendmail.cf
```

These commands tell sendmail, whenever it tries to look at NetInfo, to look instead at /etc/mail/sendmail.cf.

If you encounter errors that indicate you cannot write temp files, you must open permissions on the /var/spool/mqueue and /var/spool/clientmqueue directories. You can do this with the command chmod 777 /var/spool/*mqueue. These directories are used to temporarily store the details and content of e-mail messages before the messages are delivered.

If you have trouble starting or running sendmail, you can check your /var/log/system.log file for messages that may pertain to the problem. If you see an error message that the file /etc/mail/access.db does not exist, you can create this file from /etc/aliases with the command makemap hash /etc/mail/access.db < /etc/aliases. The /etc/aliases file contains lines such as test: user where test is an alias and user is a real username.

```
      Terminal   File   Edit   Scrollback   Font   Window   Help
                                   ttyp1
##### $Id: proto.m4,v 1.1.1.4 2002/03/12 17:59:50 zarzycki Exp $  #####

# level 10 config file format
V10/Berkeley

# override file safeties - setting this option compromises system securit
y,
# addressing the actual file configuration problem is preferred
# need to set this before any file actions are encountered in the cf file
#O DontBlameSendmail=safe

# default LDAP map specification
# need to set this now before any LDAP maps are defined
#O LDAPDefaultSpec=-h localhost

#################
#   local info   #
#################

# my LDAP cluster
:s/#O DontBlameSendmail=safe/O DontBlameSendmail=GroupWritableDirPathSafe
/
```

■ Your cursor moves to the line you need to edit.

4 Type **:s/#O DontBlame Sendmail=safe/O DontBlame Sendmail=GroupWritableDir PathSafe/** and press Return.

```
      Terminal   File   Edit   Scrollback   Font   Window   Help
                                   ttyp1
##### $Id: proto.m4,v 1.1.1.4 2002/03/12 17:59:50 zarzycki Exp $  #####

# level 10 config file format
V10/Berkeley

# override file safeties - setting this option compromises system securit
y,
# addressing the actual file configuration problem is preferred
# need to set this before any file actions are encountered in the cf file
O DontBlameSendmail=GroupWritableDirPathSafe

# default LDAP map specification
# need to set this now before any LDAP maps are defined
#O LDAPDefaultSpec=-h localhost

#################
#   local info   #
#################

# my LDAP cluster
:wq
```

■ Your edits appear.

5 Save your file and exit vi by typing **:wq** and pressing Return.

CONTINUED ▶

CONFIGURE SENDMAIL (CONTINUED)

To modify DontBlameSendmail, you would do one of two things. For one, you would edit the sendmail.cf file and then try starting sendmail again. The line `#O DontBlameSendmail=safe` will have to be changed to `O DontBlameSendmail=GroupWritableDirPathSafe`. Another way is to generate an entirely new configuration file. While this may sound like it would be a lot more work, the file that you need to edit to generate a new configuration file is far more approachable than sendmail.cf. In addition, while you are at it, you can also add some other useful options to your configuration.

To start the process of creating a brand new configuration file, you will make a copy of the default mail configuration file. To find this file, you will move into the /usr/share/ sendmail/conf/cf directory. The default file is called generic-darwin.mc. Your copy should be called yourdomain. mc, though you can replace yourdomain with your domain name if you have one. The basic idea is to preserve the original file for safekeeping.

You then want to edit this file. The lines of interest are all lumped together at the bottom. After the first line starting with the word define, you should add a line that reads `define('confDONT_BLAME_SENDMAIL','GroupWrit ableDirPathSafe')`. Then, save file.

The next thing you need to do is run `m4` to use the specifications that you just edited into a new configuration file. That command would look like this: `m4 ../m4/cf.m4 yourdomain.mc > /tmp/sendmail.cf`. That leaves your new configuration file in /tmp. You then back up your current configuration file and install your new configuration file in its place. You then start sendmail.

To ensure that sendmail starts up every time your system is booted, you need to modify /etc/hostconfig. This file plays a critical role in starting services. You will change `MAILSERVER=-NO-` to `MAILSERVER=-YES-`.

CONFIGURE SENDMAIL (CONTINUED)

GENERATE NEW SENDMAIL.CF FILE

1 Type **cd /usr/share/ sendmail/conf/cf** and press Return.

2 Type **sudo cp generic-darwin.mc yourdomain.mc** and press Return.

■ A copy of the generic file is created.

3 Type **vi yourdomain.mc** and press Return.

■ vi opens your new file.

4 Type **/^define** and press Return.

Extra

You can test sendmail by typing the words in blue in the following interaction.

Example:
```
[ferro:~] user% telnet localhost 25
Trying 127.0.0.1...
Connected to localhost.
Escape character is '^]'.
220 ferro.local ESMTP Sendmail 8.12.2/8.10.2; Tue, 24 Jun 2003 19:46:36 -0400 (EDT)
hello whatever.org
250 ferro.local Hello localhost [127.0.0.1], pleased to meet you
MAIL FROM: rustydog@whatever.org
250 2.1.0 rustydog@whatever.org... Sender ok
RCPT TO: user
250 2.1.5 user... Recipient ok
DATA
354 Enter mail, end with "." on a line by itself
this is a message
.
250 2.0.0 h5ONkaCw000883 Message accepted for delivery
quit
221 2.0.0 ferro.local closing connection
Connection closed by foreign host.
```

```
# See the files in /usr/share/sendmail/conf for more information on how t
o
# generate a new one with the features and values you want. The file READ
ME
# in that directory has instructions.
###

VERSIONID(`$Id: generic-darwin.mc,v 1.3 2002/04/12 18:41:47 bbraun Exp $'
)
OSTYPE(darwin)dnl
DOMAIN(generic)dnl
undefine(`ALIAS_FILE')
define(`PROCMAIL_MAILER_PATH',`/usr/bin/procmail')
define(`confDONT_BLAME_SENDMAIL',`GroupWritableDirPathSafe')
FEATURE(`smrsh',`/usr/libexec/smrsh')
FEATURE(local_procmail)
FEATURE(`virtusertable',`hash -o /etc/mail/virtusertable')dnl
FEATURE(`genericstable', `hash -o /etc/mail/genericstable')dnl
FEATURE(`mailertable',`hash -o /etc/mail/mailertable')dnl
FEATURE(`access_db')dnl
MAILER(smtp)
:wq
```

```
#
# By using this file, you agree to the terms and conditions set
# forth in the LICENSE file which can be found at the top level of
# the sendmail distribution.
#
#

divert(0)dnl

###
# This file provides a very generic configuration for sendmail.
#
# To customize your configuration, you probably don't want to edit this f
yourdomain.mc: 39 lines, 1322 characters.
[ferro:~] user% m4 ../m4/cf.m4 yourdomain.mc > /tmp/sendmail.cf
[ferro:~] user% sudo mv /etc/mail/sendmail.cf /etc/mail/sendmail.cf.`date
+%y%m%d`
Password:
[ferro:~] user% sudo mv /tmp/sendmail.cf /etc/mail/sendmail.cf
[ferro:~] user% sudo sendmail -bd -q15m
[ferro:~] user%
```

■ Your cursor is positioned at the first line starting with the word define.

5 Type the letter **o**.

■ A new line opens up.

6 Type **define(`confDONT_BLAME_SENDMAIL',`GroupWritableDirPathSafe')** and press Esc to exit input mode.

7 Type **:wq** and press Return to save your file and exit vi.

8 Type **m4 ../m4/cf.m4 yourdomain.mc > /tmp/sendmail.cf** and press Return.

9 Type **sudo mv /etc/mail/sendmail.cf /etc/mail/sendmail.cf.`date +%y%m%d`** and press Return.

10 Type **sudo mv /tmp/sendmail.cf /etc/mail/sendmail.cf** and press Return.

11 Type **sudo s -bd -q15m.**

SEND E-MAIL FROM UNIX

You can create and send messages from the command line in Mac OS X, as you can with most UNIX systems. You do not need to open up a mail client. The easiest and fastest way to do this is by using the `echo` command to create a message and then piping the message to the `mail` command. For example, you can type the following message on the command line to create a message with the subject line lunch and add it to the inbox of user shs.

```
echo Please do not forget we have a lunch
date today | mail -s "lunch" shs
```

If you want to send a longer message, you can run the `mail` command — for example, `mail shs` — and then type your subject line and message. When you are finished typing your message, you enter a period (.) on a line by itself, and the system sends the message.

Your recipient can read your message in a variety of ways. If they are a command line user like you, they may opt to use the `mail` command by typing **mail** on a line by itself. A list of messages appears, and they can read them one at a time or delete them without reading them. If they want to respond, they can do that, too. The `mail` command includes the arguments `r` for reply and `d` for delete. To read a message, the user simply presses Return or, in the case of multiple e-mails, selects the message number and presses Return. If your system is set up with a mail client, such as pine or elm, you may prefer to open your mailbox using one of these tools.

SEND E-MAIL FROM UNIX

```
  Terminal   File   Edit   Scrollback   Font   Window   Help
                              ttyp1
[ferro:mail] user% echo "Can you read this?" | mail -s "test" user
[ferro:mail] user% []
```

```
  Terminal   File   Edit   Scrollback   Font   Window   Help
                              ttyp1
[ferro:~] user% echo "Can you read this?" | mail -s "test" user
[ferro:~] user% mail user
Subject: today's meeting
I will be arriving late to the meeting this afternoon.  Please tell
jokes until I get there.  I need everyone to be in a good mood.

Thanks --

s.
.
EOT
[ferro:~] user% []
```

2 Type **| mail -s "test"** followed by a space.

3 Type your username, and press Return.

4 Type **mail** followed by a space and the name of a user, and press Return.

5 Type a subject line at the prompt, and press Return.

6 Type your message, and press Return.

7 Type a dot (.) on a line by itself, and press Return.

■ The mail system delivers your message.

read
ce.

ndmail

217

Extra

While the `mail` command is useful, most UNIX users today prefer to use more versatile tools for sending and receiving e-mail. The simple `mail` command, after all, cannot properly display e-mail that arrives in HTML format or allow you to fetch and use attachments. The `mail` command was created before HTML and attachments were used in e-mails.

Even so, the `mail` command continues to provide a service. For example, simple e-mail messages sent from the command line can help you to determine whether a mail server is working.

Mail files, typically thought of as inboxes, are stored in `/var/mail`. Each user on the system with pending mail will have a single file in this directory. The inbox for user would be `/var/mail/user`.

The `mail` command is also very helpful for use within scripts. For example, if you write a script to routinely check disk space, you may want the script to send the results of the disk check to you via e-mail. You can use a line of code such as `df -k | mail -s "disk usage" user@mydomain.org` in a script that runs once a day through cron to remind yourself to look at your disk space.

```
  Terminal  File  Edit  Scrollback  Font  Window  Help

                        ttyp1
[ferro:~] user% mail
Mail version 8.1 6/6/93.  Type ? for help.
"/var/mail/user": 2 messages 2 new
>N  1 shs                 Wed Jun 25 07:17  13/359    "test"
 N  2 shs                 Wed Jun 25 07:17  18/498    "today's meetin"
& []
```

```
  Terminal  File  Edit  Scrollback  Font  Window  Help

                        ttyp1
>N  1 shs                 Wed Jun 25 07:17  13/359    "test"
 N  2 shs                 Wed Jun 25 07:17  18/498    "today's meetin"
&
Message 1:
From shs  Wed Jun 25 07:17:56 2003
Date: Wed, 25 Jun 2003 07:13:18 -0400 (EDT)
From: Sandra Henry-Stocker <shs>
To: user
Subject: test

Can you read this?

& 2
Message 2:
From shs  Wed Jun 25 07:17:57 2003
Date: Wed, 25 Jun 2003 07:15:27 -0400 (EDT)
From: Sandra Henry-Stocker <shs>
To: user
Subject: today's meeting

I will be arriving late to the meeting this afternoon.  Please tell
jokes until I get there.  I need everyone to be in a good mood.
```

READ A MESSAGE

1 Type **mail** and press Return.

■ The mail system presents you with a list of waiting messages.

2 Press Return and read the first message.

3 Type the number **2** and press Return to read the next message.

■ The mail system displays your messages. Typing **q** will exit mail.

LOOK AT YOUR MAIL FILE

You can examine your Unix inbox without using commands, such as mail or mail clients like Mac OS X's Mail, by locating and displaying your mail file in your file system. Any time your mail setup does not appear to be working properly, knowing where and how to examine this file will help you determine whether mail is arriving as it should.

To view your e-mail inbox, you should move into the /var/mail directory. This folder will contain a mail file for each user on your system who has mail in his or her inbox. Even if you have 300 individual messages, your inbox will consist of a single file. Each message in this file will begin with a From line that includes the sender and the time and date that the message arrived. For example, the line From gumby@example.org Mon Feb 17 15:30:02 2003

will indicate the start of the message you received from Gumby on that date. Each message in your inbox will begin with a line that has this form. No other lines in your inbox will begin with the word From followed by a space. These lines allow mail clients to determine where each message starts. The message header lines that begin with tags such as Date:, From:, To:, and Subject: come next and are followed by the text of the message that was sent to you. The end of each message is only indicated by the beginning of another message or the end of the file.

If you send a message to yourself on the command line, using a command such as echo testing | mail user, you should see the size of your inbox increase, the timestamp on the file to change, and the content of this message added to the bottom of your mail file.

LOOK AT YOUR MAIL FILE

1 Type **cd /var/mail** and press Return.

2 Type **ls –l** and press Return.

■ A listing of mail files on your system displays.

3 Type **more** followed by the name of your mail file, such as **user**, and press Return.

■ The top of your mail file displays.

FETCH E-MAIL FROM OTHER SERVERS

Y ou can fetch e-mail from remote servers using the fetchmail tool. Fetchmail is a retrieval and forwarding tool that supports all of the important protocols for retrieving mail from an e-mail server. These include the most popular protocols — POP3 and IMAP — as well as a number of others: POP2, RPOP, APOP, KPOP, ETRN, and ODMR.

Like many tools, fetchmail uses a configuration file, .fetchmailrc, to store information about your accounts. You can add lines like the following to your .fetchmailrc file:

```
poll mail.mailserver.org protocol POP3 user
nici password worx4me is noh
```

In this example, nici is the username for the remote account, while noh is the local user. The server you check for downloadable e-mail is called mail.mailserver.org. As you can see, the password appears in clear text. For this reason, you must set permissions on the .fetchmailrc file so

that only the individual user can read this file. In fact, fetchmail warns you if the permissions on the file are not set to 710. This means that the owner has read, write, and execute permission, while the group has only execute permission, and no one else can access the file.

Storing the password in the file saves you from having to enter it each time you use fetchmail. This also allows fetchmail to automatically run through cron for daily or more frequent downloads.

Your system must be running sendmail for fetchmail to work properly. Fetchmail works by transferring the mail to the smtp port on your local system. If you are not using sendmail, you can change your .fetchmailrc file to use procmail instead by making it look like this:

```
poll mail.mailserver.org protocol POP3 user
nici password worx4me mda "/usr/bin/procmail
-d noh"
```

FETCH E-MAIL FROM OTHER SERVERS

USE FETCHMAIL ON THE COMMAND LINE

1 Type **fetchmail -v** followed by a space.

2 Type **--keep -a** followed by a space

3 Type **>> /var/log/fetchmail 2>&1** and press Return.

■ Fetchmail downloads your mail from the remote server.

RUN FETCHMAIL THROUGH CRON

1 Type **crontab -e** and press Return.

■ Your crontab file opens.

2 Type **11 23 * * * /sw/bin/fetchmail -a >> /var/log/fetchmail 2>&1** in your crontab file.

■ Your crontab file updates, and fetchmail runs every night at 11:11 P.M.

INSTALL PINE

Pine is a text-based e-mail program that has been in use on UNIX systems for many years. You can install pine on your Mac OS X system using Fink or FinkCommander. Otherwise, you can download pine from www.Washington.edu/pine/getpine. You can then uncompress and untar the installation file as is described in Chapter 12.

To create the pine application, you can type **build osx**. This command takes the place of the normal make command and builds a pine binary for your Mac OS X system. When the build process is finished, you have a directory containing the pine binary along with a series of other programs that you can copy to other locations on your system. You can refer to the README file for directions that may pertain to your installation.

The first time you run pine, it creates a configuration file in your Home directory called .pinerc. This file allows you to modify a number of configuration parameters, such as how your name appears in messages that you send. Like most UNIX configuration files, the .pinerc file contains numerous comments; any line starting with a # symbol is a comment.

To make pine easy to use, you should ensure that it is on your search path. This allows you to start pine by typing **pine** on the command line. You can verify that pine is on your search path by typing **which pine**. This command returns the full path to the pine executable.

Some of the other tools that are compiled along with pine are useful if your system is to act as a mail server. The imapd, ipop2d, and ipop3d tools are servers that allow mail clients to download e-mail. These tools support the IMAP, POP2, and POP3 protocols, respectively.

INSTALL PINE

```
 Terminal   File   Edit   Scrollback   Font   Window   Help
000                         ttyp1
[ferro:~] user% sudo fink install pine
Reading package info...
Information about 769 packages read in 5 seconds.

pkg pine   version ###
pkg pine   version 4.44-2
The following package will be installed or updated:
 pine
curl -f -L -O ftp://ftp.cac.washington.edu/pine/pine4.44.tar.gz
curl: (19) pine4.44.tar.gz: No such file or directory.
### execution of curl failed, exit code 19
Downloading the file "pine4.44.tar.gz" failed.

(1)  Give up
(2)  Retry the same mirror
(3)  Retry another mirror

How do you want to proceed? [2] []
```

```
 Terminal   File   Edit   Scrollback   Font   Window   Help
000                         ttyp1
[ferro:~/src] user% tar xvf pine*
./pine4.52/
./pine4.52/CPYRIGHT
./pine4.52/README
./pine4.52/build
./pine4.52/build.cmd
./pine4.52/buildcyg
./pine4.52/contrib/
./pine4.52/contrib/ports/
./pine4.52/contrib/ports/vms/
./pine4.52/contrib/ports/vms/readme.vms
./pine4.52/contrib/ports/vms/vmsbuild.com
./pine4.52/contrib/ports/vms/vms_link.opt
./pine4.52/contrib/ports/vms/vms_multinet_link.opt
./pine4.52/contrib/ports/vms/vms_netlib_link.opt
./pine4.52/contrib/ports/vms/vmsbuild_cclient.com
./pine4.52/contrib/ports/vms/readme.1st
./pine4.52/contrib/ports/aos/
./pine4.52/contrib/ports/aos/README
./pine4.52/contrib/ports/aos/aos.diff
./pine4.52/contrib/ports/sequent_ptx_4.4.6
./pine4.52/contrib/carmel/
./pine4.52/contrib/carmel/pine/
./pine4.52/contrib/carmel/pine/makefile.ult.patch
```

INSTALL PINE WITH FINK

1 Type **sudo fink install pine** and press Return.

■ A warning may appear saying Fink failed to locate the software.

INSTALL PINE FROM A TAR FILE

1 Type **tar xvf** followed by a space.

2 Type the name of your TAR file or **pine*** and press Return.

■ This command extracts the contents of your TAR file.

Extra

You can start pine with a new .pinerc file two ways. You can remove your current file by typing **rm .pinerc** in your home directory. When you start pine the next time, it will greet you as if you had never used the program, setting up a brand new .pinerc file for you in the process. Alternately, you can type the command **pine –conf > .pinerc** in your home directory. This pipes the output of the `pine -conf` command, which generates the settings in a default .pinerc file to the file you specify.

Pine, by default, stores diagnostic information in files called .pine-debug1, .pine-debug2 and so on. These files might prove to be of some interest to you, but they are of no value. The easiest way to turn off this feature is to add the line **alias pine "pine –d 0".** to your .tcshrc file that sets the debug level or pine to 0. The next time you log on or type **source .tcshrc**, the .pine-debug files will no longer be created. Remember that you have to type **ls –a** to list files that begin with a period.

```
🍎 Terminal  File  Edit  Scrollback  Font  Window  Help

                            ttyp1
[ferro:pine4.52] user% ./build osx
make args are CC=cc  osx

Including LDAP functionality
  File /System/Library/OpenSSL/certs/factory.pem is missing
  This might indicate that CA certs did not get properly
  installed.  If you get certificate validation failures
  in Pine, this might be the reason for them.

Including SSL functionality
Making c-client library, imapd, and ipopd
eval make CC=cc SSLTYPE=nopwd SPECIALS=SSLDIR=/System/Library/OpenSSL osx
make sslnopwd
make[1]: `sslnopwd' is up to date.
Applying an process to sources...
tools/an "ln -s" src/c-client c-client
tools/an "ln -s" src/ansilib c-client
tools/an "ln -s" src/charset c-client
tools/an "ln -s" src/osdep/unix c-client
tools/an "ln -s" src/mtest mtest
tools/an "ln -s" src/ipopd ipopd
tools/an "ln -s" src/imapd imapd
tools/an "ln -s" src/mailutil mailutil
tools/an "ln -s" src/mlock mlock
```

```
🍎 Terminal  File  Edit  Scrollback  Font  Window  Help

                            ttyp1
PINE 4.52   GREETING TEXT                                    No Messages

              <<<This message will appear only once>>>

          Welcome to Pine ... a Program for Internet News and Email

We hope you will explore Pine's many capabilities. From the Main Menu,
select Setup/Config to see many of the options available to you. Also
note that all screens have context-sensitive help text available.

SPECIAL REQUEST: This software is made available world-wide as a public
service of the University of Washington in Seattle. In order to justify
continuing development, it is helpful to have an idea of how many people
are using Pine. Are you willing to be counted as a Pine user? Pressing
Return will send an anonymous (meaning, your real email address will not
be revealed) message to the Pine development team at the University of
Washington for purposes of tallying.

              Pine is a trademark of the University of Washington.


                        [ALL of greeting text]
? Help          E Exit this greeting          PrevPage   Print
                Ret [Be Counted!]             Spc NextPage
```

3 Type **cd** and the name of your new directory, and press Return.

4 Type **./build osx** and press Return.

■ This command builds the pine software for Mac OS X.

5 Type **bin/pine** and press Return.

■ The pine welcome page appears.

READ E-MAIL WITH PINE

You can read your e-mail with pine. Using pine is not difficult after you get used to the pine commands and how pine organizes your e-mail. To start pine, you can type **pine** on the command line. When in pine, you can access your inbox, read and delete messages, and compose and send e-mail.

The first screen of data that you see when you start pine is an upper-level menu that allows you to ask for help, compose a message, view a message in your current folder, list your folders, update your address book, or quit pine. You can access each of these options by typing a single command, such as C to compose a message. This screen is called the main menu. The default choice in the main menu is to list your folders; if you simply press Return, pine lists your folders.

You can then open your inbox or another folder. The up- and down-arrow keys move you between messages. You can display a message by pressing Return. To return to the message index, you can type the letter **i**. You can mark a message for deletion by typing the letter **d** when that message is highlighted. This means that pine deletes the message when you quit the program. If you change your mind, you can un-delete the message by moving back to it and typing the letter **u**.

While these one-letter commands may seem cryptic at first, pine provides a list of the most common commands at the bottom of the screen. You can return to the main menu by pressing the < key one or more times. You can get help at the main menu by pressing the ? key. To quit pine, you can type **q**.

READ E-MAIL WITH PINE

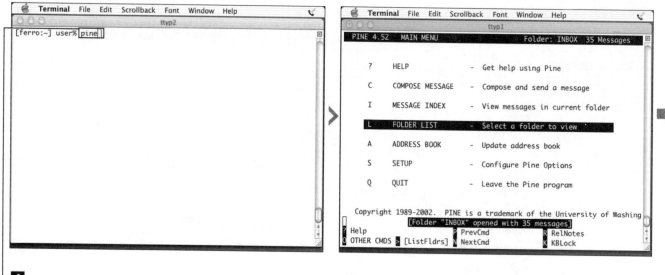

1 Type **pine** and press Return.

■ Pine opens, displaying the main menu.

2 Press Return twice.

Extra

To reply to a message using pine, you can type **r** when you select the message in the message list or when you view the message. Pine addresses your reply to the sender of the original message and asks you whether you want to include the original message in your reply.

You can change your pine options by editing your .pinerc file or by selecting SETUP from the main menu. If you elect to use SETUP, another list appears. Selecting C brings you to a long list of configuration options over several screens. Although these options are numerous, if you are like most pine users, you will stay with the default settings.

To move a message to a different folder, you can type **s** when pine displays the message list or the message itself. Pine then asks you to type in the name of the folder where you want to place the message. It defaults to the saved-messages folder.

```
 Terminal  File  Edit  Scrollback  Font  Window  Help
                            ttyp1
 PINE 4.52   MESSAGE INDEX          Folder: INBOX  Message 12 of 35 NEW

    1 May 21 Sandra Henry-Sto   (328) saying hello
    2 May 21 Sandra Henry-Sto   (362) lunch
  N 3 May 28 Sandra Henry-Sto   (304)
  N 4 May 28 Sandra Henry-Sto   (304)
  N 5 May 28 Sandra Henry-Sto   (304)
  N 6 May 28 slee@achilles.tc   (368)
  N 7 Jan 16 Pharmacy          (1689) amazing youth regained
  N 8 Jan 16 Pharmacy          (1689) amazing youth regained
  N 9 Jan 18 Drugstore         (3575) Viagra,Phentermine,Xenical
  N 10 Jan 16 brtsbiornyjxi@ms  (1862) Look at F.H.W.! 082-3
  N 11 Jan 16 sites3977@yahoo.  (2386) Goodbye to debt.
  N 12 Jan 16 maxusmedia@msn.c  (3444) Lose 32 pounds by February
  N 13 Jan 16 yisbkolp@netscap  (1779) *| Dont miss out!! *
  N 14 Jan 18 nitezephyr@msn.c  (1341) Mortgage Aprroved... get the home
  N 15 Jan 17 Donald24sgxn@cs.  (3218) INC 500 Company seeks leaders!! T
  N 16 Jan 16 ncdki@hotmail.co  (2138) hey
  N 17 Jan 15 Kathyrn           (2911) Time in a bottle

? Help        < FldrList  P PrevMsg  - PrevPage D Delete   R Reply
O OTHER CMDS  > [ViewMsg] N NextMsg  Spc NextPage U Undelete F Forward
```

```
 Terminal  File  Edit  Scrollback  Font  Window  Help
                            ttyp1
 PINE 4.52   MESSAGE TEXT       Folder: INBOX  Message 12 of 35 23% NEW

Date: Thu, 16 Jan 2003 18:17:45 -1000
From: maxusmedia@msn.com
To: ftp@tcsnet.net
Subject: Lose 32 pounds by February

  [ The following text is in the "iso-8859-1" character set. ]
  [ Your display is set for the "US-ASCII" character set.  ]
  [ Some characters may be displayed incorrectly. ]

Hi !

If you're like me, you've tried EVERYTHING to lose
weight.  I know how you feel - the special diets,
miracle pills, and fancy exercise equipment never helped
me lose a pound either.  It seemed like the harder I tried,
the bigger I got, until I heard about a product called
Power Diet Plus.

? Help        - MsgIndex  P PrevMsg  - PrevPage D Delete   R Reply
O OTHER CMDS  > ViewAttch N NextMsg  Spc NextPage U Undelete F Forward
```

■ A list of messages appears in your inbox.

■ You can press the up- and down-arrow keys to move between messages.

3 Highlight the message you want to read and press Return.

■ The selected message appears.

SEND E-MAIL WITH PINE

You can compose and send e-mail with pine. To compose a message in pine, you can type **c** while in the main menu. This moves you into a simple text-editor in which pine pre-inserts message parts such as the To and Subject tags. You can move around in this form by using arrow keys, inserting your recipient and your message text.

As you type your message, the form area dedicated to the message text grows larger to accommodate your message. To insert a text file into your message, you can press Ctrl + R. Pine then asks you to enter the name of the file that you want to insert into your message. You must supply the name of the text file, including the pathname if it is not located in your Home directory.

Pine allows you to add carbon copy (cc) recipients to your messages and to include attachments. To add an attachment, you can type the name of the file, along with the pathname if it is in a subdirectory, in the Attchmnt line. Pine attaches the file to the message when you send it. You can add additional attachments by pressing Ctrl + J.

To change the format of your message to a rich header, you can press Control + R. This adds some additional fields to your message header, such as Bcc and Newsgrps. If you have defined a signature, the contents of your signature file appear at the bottom of your message text.

When you are ready to send your message, you can press Control + X. Pine asks if you want to send your message. If you type **s**, pine sends the message. The Control + X command and other options appear along the bottom of your screen.

SEND E-MAIL WITH PINE

1 Type **pine** and press Return.

■ Pine opens, displaying the main menu.

2 Press C.

Extra

Messages that you move to other folders are stored in files in your mail directory. For example, if your username is sbob and your home directory is /Users/sbob, your mail folders are stored in /Users/sbob/mail. Each file within this directory represents one of your mail folders, and pine stores it as a standard UNIX mail file. Messages begin with the string `From`, followed by the e-mail address of the sender, and a date/time stamp.

If you copy a mail file to your mail directory or remove one, pine accomodates and lists the new set of folders. This shows that Pine does not maintain any internal representation of your mail folders. It simply looks at the files in your mail directory and displays them to you as a series of individual messages.

To add a signature to the messages you send with pine, you can create a .signature file in your Home directory. Pine reads the contents of this file and appends your signature to the bottom of every message that you compose. You can create a signature file using any text editor or on the command line.

Example:
```
echo "————-" > .signature
echo "Fred T. User,  Minstrel" >> .signature
```

```
 Terminal  File  Edit  Scrollback  Font  Window  Help
                              ttyp1
  PINE 4.52    COMPOSE MESSAGE          Folder: INBOX  40 Messages

To      : slee@world.std.com
Cc      :
Attchmnt:
Subject : Today's Meeting
----- Message Text -----
I am going to be late to this afternoon's meeting, but I will bring
slides and donuts.  Please tell jokes until I get there.  I need for
everyone to be in a really good mood.

pj.

--------------------
never on time




^G Get Help  ^X Send      ^R Read File ^Y Prev Pg  ^K Cut Text  ^O Postpone
^C Cancel    ^J Justify   ^W Where is  ^V Next Pg  ^U UnCut Text^T To Spell
```

```
 Terminal  File  Edit  Scrollback  Font  Window  Help
                              ttyp1
  PINE 4.52    COMPOSE MESSAGE          Folder: INBOX  40 Messages

To      : slee@world.std.com
Cc      :
Attchmnt:
Subject : Today's Meeting
----- Message Text -----
I am going to be late to this afternoon's meeting, but I will bring
slides and donuts.  Please tell jokes until I get there.  I need for
everyone to be in a really good mood.

pj.

--------------------
never on time



Send message?
? Help       Y [Yes]
^C Cancel    N No
```

■ Pine opens the Compose Message form.

3 Type an e-mail address in the To field, and press Return.

4 Type a subject for your e-mail.

5 Type your message.

■ Pine adjusts the form to accommodate your text.

6 Press Control + X to send your message.

■ Pine asks for confirmation before sending your message to the specified recipient.

7 Press Y to send your message, or N to cancel your message.

■ Your message is sent.

INTRODUCTION TO APACHE

A pache is the most popular Web server on the Internet today. Accounting for roughly 60 percent of Web servers and probably 80 percent of the available Web-server books, Apache is one of the open source products that has become a part of the foundation of the Internet. It is well used, well understood, and well implemented.

HOW WEB SERVERS WORK

The purpose of the Apache Web server is to listen for requests from Web browsers and serve up the pages requested. Like any important Internet service, Apache runs on a dedicated port. This port is dedicated not to Apache, but to the HTTP protocol that Apache and browsers use to communicate with each other.

After you install and run a Web service, curious visitors can type your URL into their Web browsers and peruse what your site has to offer. Whenever a visitor types an address such as www.dragonflyditch.com into a Web browser, the address is first passed on to a DNS server for translation into an IP address. Then, a request is made to port 80 on the remote system. This request is essentially GET / — a request for the home page or default document on your site.

When a Web server receives such a request, it looks at certain configuration variables to determine which page it should send back to the client. For Apache servers, that page is usually called index.html, though with the prevalence of Java and other tools on the Web, it may just as likely be mainpage.jsp. If the home page is a static HTML file, the server transfers it to the client immediately. Many other types of pages are created only after the request arrives on the server, with information read from cookies on the computer of the client or from a database on the server. This information allows customized pages to be created for each user. In any case, when the page is ready, it is sent to the client. This all happens in a matter of seconds even when the server is halfway around the world.

FREE AND CONFIGURABLE

Apache is popular largely because it is free to any user, although this is not the only reason. Apache is also extensible through a collection of modules and can be customized for an intended use. You can add or remove modules at build time, so the resulting binary contains only the features that you need. Apache also supports all of the features that anyone might expect in a Web server. Configuring Apache for name-based virtual servers, where multiple sites all run on the same machine while appearing to be independent, is easy in Apache. Configuring security and tuning the server for expected traffic are also simple processes.

FITTING INTO THE INTERNET

Web servers depend on the Domain Name System (DNS) to function, just like other Internet services. When you type a URL such as **http://www. dragonflyditch.com**, you are simultaneously specifying a number of things. By typing http, you are designating that HTTP is the protocol – the limited language that describes communications between client and server — used to communicate with the server. This is the primary protocol used by the Web, but not the only one. By typing www.dragonflyditch.com, you are identifying a particular server and relying on the services of DNS to translate this textual name into an IP address so that the DNS can use the IP of the address to locate and communicate with that server. By typing nothing more, you are indicating that you want to communicate with the server running on the default port for Web servers, port 80, and you are saying that you want the home page or default document for the site.

APACHE CONFIGURATION

The configuration on the server end determines which directory on the server contains the documents and files available for viewing. For Apache, this directory is called the document root. On a properly configured Web server, visitors cannot view or download files outside of this directory.

The configuration on the server end also determines which file the server transfers to you when you type **www.dragonflyditch.com** in the URL field. Whenever you enter a URL that does not contain a filename, Apache looks through a list of default documents for one that matches a document in the requested directory. If the default documents list contains index.html and login.jsp, and the document root contains neither of these files, Apache returns to you one of two things: an error code or a directory listing. The choice depends on whether directory browsing is enabled.

BEHIND THE SCENES

While a `GET /` request may at first appear to be a very modest service request, retrieval of the home page for most Web sites results in a number of requests as each frame and each image contained in the file is subsequently requested. Until your browser obtains all the parts of a page from the server, the Web page is incomplete.

While the earliest Web servers delivered static Web pages to their clients, Web servers today often produce custom pages. For example, they may offer forms for you to fill out whose contents are posted, or sent to the server for additional processing, or they may call on encryption services to hide sensitive data from prying eyes as the data transfers to the server for processing.

While the protocol that the Web uses to move files and data back and forth is itself fairly simple, with only a handful of commands such as `GET` and `POST`, the communications between client and server often include a lot of additional information. Much of this is contained in the headers that you send with your simple requests. Through the use of these headers, clients and servers can compare notes on what each of them is capable of doing. For example, a Web server does not send you a file in a format that your browser cannot display. When multiple sites are supported on a system, and differentiated only by their names — such as the difference between dragonflyditch.com and idyllmtn.com — the server knows which site you are requesting because the site name is included in the headers.

START APACHE

You can start your Apache server after you install the software. The Apache installation includes a script that facilitates starting and shutting down the service. When Apache is not running, you can start it by typing **apachectl start**. The Apache bin directory must be on your search path for this command to work without a pathname. You will probably find Apache installed in /sw/apache, or usr/local/apache, and the script is bin/apachectl, but you can determine if it is on your search path by typing **which apachectl**. If you are using the Apache server that ships with Mac OS X, look in /usr/sbin.

When Apache starts, you can examine the processes running on your system; you can expect to see several processes named httpd. In a normal configuration, one of these processes is started by root, while another five to eight are started by a user called nobody. Nobody is a special user with no particular privileges on a Unix system. By running Apache processes as nobody, you ensure that a hacker

cannot commandeer these processes, and that these processes do not offer up files that only a privileged user should access.

By starting up multiple servers, Apache can handle considerable traffic. While all connection requests from clients arrive at the same port, Apache turns over each request to one of the idle httpd processes. When all of the processes are occupied, Apache can start others. The ratio of busy to idle processes depends on specifications in the Apache configuration file. The number of processes grows and shrinks in such a way that the server is always prepared for additional traffic, but not so over-prepared that the overhead is excessive.

When you install Apache, it is generally configured to start automatically when the server boots. However, if you change the Apache configuration file and want the changes to take effect immediately, you must restart the server with the `apachectl restart` command.

START APACHE

```
[ferro:~] user% sudo /sw/apache/bin/apachectl start
[ferro:~] user%
```

```
[ferro:~] user% ps -ax | grep http
4954  ??  Ss    0:00.07 /sw/apache/sbin/httpd
4955  ??  S     0:00.00 /sw/apache/sbin/httpd
4956  ??  S     0:00.00 /sw/apache/sbin/httpd
4957  ??  S     0:00.00 /sw/apache/sbin/httpd
4958  ??  S     0:00.01 /sw/apache/sbin/httpd
4959  ??  S     0:00.00 /sw/apache/sbin/httpd
5001 std  R+    0:00.00 grep http
[ferro:~] user%
```

1 Type **sudo /sw/apache/bin/apachectl** followed by a space.

2 Type **start** and press Return.

3 If a prompt appears, type your password, and press Return.

■ Apache starts running.

4 Type **ps -ax** followed by a space.

5 Type **| grep http** and press Return.

■ A list of the Apache processes appears.

230

STOP APACHE

You can stop your Apache server at any time. To stop Apache, you can use the `apachectl` script with a `stop` argument. This stops all of the Apache processes. Both the `stop` and `start` commands are arguments to the script that you supply to Apache to control the operation. This script can also respond to `restart` and `status` arguments. The `restart` command shuts down and restarts Apache, while the `status` command tells you whether or not Apache is running.

When you stop Apache, you terminate the server process. The server is no longer listening on the port assigned to HTTP, and clients who continue requesting service receive a message indicating that their browser has encountered a DNS error, or that it cannot find the server. This indicates that the client is not finding a responsive process on the HTTP port.

Before you attempt to stop Apache, you may first want to confirm that it is running. You can do this in one of two ways. You can use the `apachectl` script with a `status` argument; however, this technique only works if you also have lynx installed. You can also run the command `ps -aux | grep httpd` to view the processes that are running. If you run this command, you must be careful not to mistake your `grep` command for an Apache process.

You can also determine whether the HTTP port is listening for client requests. If Apache is not running, no processes should be listening for connections on port 80. You can perform this test with the `netstat` command. The command `netstat -a | grep http` returns a LISTEN message when Apache is running. The output looks like this:

```
tcp46  0     0      *.http *.*   LISTEN
```

STOP APACHE

STOP THE APACHE SERVER

1 Type **sudo /sw/apache/bin/apachectl** followed by a space.

2 Type **stop** and press Return.

3 If there is a prompt, type your password, and press Return.

■ Your Apache processes stop.

CHECK FOR LISTENS ON THE HTTP PORT

1 Type **netstat** followed by a space.

2 Type **-a** followed by a space.

3 Type **| grep http** and press Return.

■ No LISTENs are reported for the HTTP port.

CONFIGURE APACHE

Y ou can configure Apache to run according to your specifications. Configuration parameters for Apache reside in a single configuration file, and you can make configuration changes by editing this file. This configuration file is called httpd.conf, and it contains a great deal of explanatory text and examples to simplify the process of configuring your server. In fact, if you want to set up a Web site very quickly, you can simply install your custom Web pages in the default document directory and start Apache with the `apachectl start` command.

The default location for Web pages is the htdocs directory in your Apache directory — for example, /sw/apache/htdocs. When you install Apache, the installer puts a small set of files into this directory to act as a placeholder for your intended content. If you start Apache and visit your Web site without doing anything else, you see these documents. The logs directory stores log files that contain records reflecting each page that transfers from your site, including information on the client such as when they visit and from what system. The configuration directory, containing your all-important httpd.conf file, is called conf — for example, /sw/apache/conf.

APACHE DIRECTIVES

Configuration commands in Apache are called *directives*. The basic form of a directive is the name of the directive followed by the value that Apache assigns, such as `User nobody`. Each directive controls some aspect of how your Web server runs. While there are several hundred possible directives, you are not likely to make many changes in your default configuration file. If you are curious, you can access a complete list of Apache directives by visiting www.apache.org. The set of available directives depends, in part, on the version of Apache that you are running.

The most critical directives are `DocumentRoot` and `DocumentIndex`. The `DocumentRoot` directive tells your Apache server where to go to retrieve pages when requests arrive from clients. The `DocumentIndex` directive is a list of files that tells your server what files to look for when a client does not include a filename in

their request. If you do not set these two variables correctly, your Web server does not work as you intend.

The ServerRoot is the directory in which the configuration and log file directories reside. If your Apache ServerRoot is /sw/apache, your configuration files reside in /sw/apache/conf, and your log files in /sw/apache/logs. In fact, your Apache binary is likely to reside there as well, in /sw/apache/bin.

Although there are many other critical directives, most, if not all of these, default to very reasonable and secure settings. There are two forms of Apache directives: *simple directives* and *block directives*. Simple directives set a value for a specific setting, such as the port the server runs on. Block directives group other directives into a set, such as the settings you want to apply to a virtual Web server.

BUILT-IN APACHE SERVER

Mac OS X ships with a built-in Apache server that you can configure and run without having to download and compile it from source code files. To start the server, you can click System Preferences ⇨ Sharing. When the Sharing panel appears, you can select Personal Web Sharing, and then click Start. If you open a Web browser and type http://127.0.0.1 in the URL field, a test page appears.

The built-in Apache server is identified on your system as /usr/sbin/httpd. If you type /usr/sbin/httpd –V, a list appears which contains information about the settings

that Apache uses, including the location of your default configuration file. The location of this file appears in a line that reads –D SERVER_CONFIG_FILE="/etc/httpd/httpd.conf".

You can use the command `grep ^LoadModule /etc/httpd/httpd.conf` to list any modules that are enabled. For example, cgi_module appears in the output of the `grep` command, indicating that CGIs are enabled. It is a good practice to store CGIs that you develop in the /Library/WebServer/CGI-Executables directory.

BUILT-IN APACHE SERVER

To enable PHP, you can remove the initial # symbol from the following lines in your httpd.conf file: # LoadModule php4_module; # AddModule mod_php4.c; # AddType application/x-httpd-php .php; and # AddType application/x-httpd-php-source .phps. **You must then stop and restart Apache. After restarting, you can create the PHP test file and save it as /Library/WebServer/test.php. To confirm that PHP is working, you can type http://127.0.01/test.php into the URL field of your browser; if PHP is working, a table appears containing information about PHP.**

PHP Test File

```
<html>
    <body>
        <? phpinfo()?>
    </body>
</html>
```

The built-in Apache server also initializes personal Web sites for your users. For example, the personal Web site for the user Smith, is defined in the file /Users/smith/Sites/index.html. You can find the access and error logs for the built-in Apache server in the /var/log/httpd file.

APACHE DIRECTIVES

The directives in the table below are some of the most critical in setting up your Web site in the way that you want it to work. Most, if not all, of these reside in your httpd.conf file, though some appear in comment lines.

OPTION	DESCRIPTION
Options	Specifies options, such as whether directory browsing is enabled
<Directory *name*> and </Directory>	Block directive for handling a specific directory
DirectoryIndex	Lists default documents, like index.html
DocumentRoot	Specifies directory where Web pages reside
ErrorLog	Specifies log directory relative to ServerRoot
HostnameLookups	Specifies whether reverse lookups should be performed
KeepAlive	Determines whether sessions endure beyond the first request
Listen	Specifies port that server listens on, usually port 80
LogFormat	Defines content for the access log file
LogLevel	Determines what level errors should be logged
MaxClients	Sets a limit on the number of simultaneous connections
ScriptAlias	Connects a virtual name such as /cgi-bin/ with an actually directory
ServerAdmin	Provides e-mail address of Web site admin
ServerRoot	Identifies directory containing your Web pages
StartServers	Determines how many server processes run when the server starts
StartThreads	Determines how many threads a single process may support
Timeout	Limits time that an inactive session is maintained
User nobody	Specifies userid under which Web processes run
UserDir	Identifies directory name that is used for personal Web sites
<VirtualHost pattern> ... </VirtualHost>	Block directive for virtual hosts

SET UP YOUR DOCUMENT DIRECTORY

Y ou can build a simple site using a single directory, or organize your Web pages using a series of directories. The document directory or document root that you set up for your Apache server holds all the files that are part of your site. These files can all reside in the directory that you assign to the DocumentRoot directive, or you can, instead, divide your files into a series of directories to make them easier to organize. For example, if you use a lot of image files, you may want to keep these in a separate images directory apart from your HTML files. Most people find that it is distracting to have hundreds of files in a single directory.

The single point of entry for most visitors to your site is the page that you set up as your default document, assigned to the DirectoryIndex directive in your configuration file. Called index.html by default, this is the document that your Web server sends to visitors whenever they type your URL into their browsers.

If your default document contains references to other files, such as image files, the links in your document must correspond to the directory structure that you create. For example, if you refer to an image called mylogo.gif that resides in the images directory within your document directory, you must refer to this file as images/mylogo.gif.

Your default document, index.html, not only has relevance to your document root, but it also plays a role in every directory that you create. Any time a visitor types in a URL ending in a directory name, your Web server attempts to send back a default document from that directory. If it does not find one, it returns a directory listing or an error, depending on whether you have disabled directory browsing.

SET UP YOUR DOCUMENT DIRECTORY

DISPLAY CONTENTS OF YOUR DOCUMENT DIRECTORY

1 Type **cd** followed by a space.

2 Type the name of your document directory, and press Return.

3 Type **ls –l** and press Return.

■ The contents of your document directory appear.

CREATE A DIRECTORY FOR YOUR IMAGE FILES

1 Type **sudo mkdir** followed by a space.

2 Type **images** and press Return.

3 If there is a prompt, type your password, and press Return.

■ The system creates a directory for your image files.

CREATE A SIMPLE WEB SITE

You can create a simple Web site in less than an hour. After you install Apache on your system, you can create a Web site by using a text editor to enter text and a few formatting commands, and by copying image files as you need them.

Static Web pages contain special formatting commands in a language called HTML, along with the text or content of your pages. For example, if you create a Web site that you want to call My Life Story in 50 Words or Less, you can enter your title and your text and then proceed to insert the commands necessary to display the content as you want it to appear.

If you type multiple paragraphs into your Web document without HTML formatting, the text that appears in a browser looks like a single long paragraph. To break this text into separate paragraphs, you must insert an HTML tag, <p>, in between your paragraphs.

Web pages must have the extension .html or .htm, and must start with a tag, <html>, that identifies the content as HTML. Most formatting commands in HTML have both an opening and a closing tag. For example, you start a Web page by typing the opening tag **<html>** and end it by typing the closing tag **</html>**. All closing tags in HTML follow the convention of starting with a forward slash (/).

The simplest Web page, therefore, starts with <html>, contains text, and <p> markers to indicate paragraph breaks, and ends with </html>. A document as simple as this can constitute a Web site. There is no requirement that you insert images or links that point to other sites, or other pages in your own Web site.

CREATE A SIMPLE WEB SITE

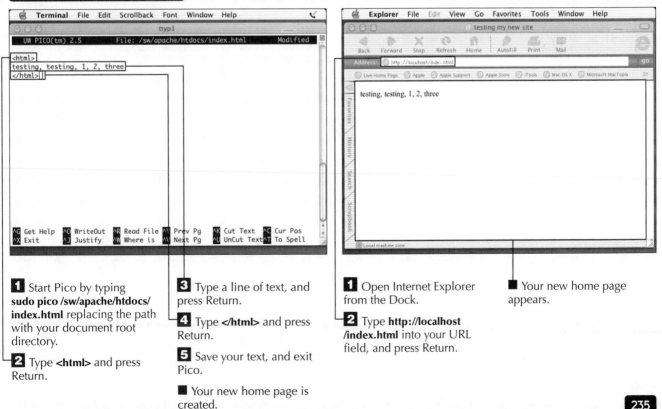

1 Start Pico by typing **sudo pico /sw/apache/htdocs/index.html** replacing the path with your document root directory.

2 Type **<html>** and press Return.

3 Type a line of text, and press Return.

4 Type **</html>** and press Return.

5 Save your text, and exit Pico.

■ Your new home page is created.

1 Open Internet Explorer from the Dock.

2 Type **http://localhost/index.html** into your URL field, and press Return.

■ Your new home page appears.

235

INTRODUCTION TO HTML

You can create Web pages using the most basic HTML markup code. While you can use the HTML language to create extremely complex and extensive Web pages, you can also create attractive and functional pages by inserting a few simple HTML tags into your documents. These tags allow you to change the font of selected text, making it bold or turning it into a heading that stands out. They allow you to insert images, build tables, and insert links to other pages on your site or to other Web sites. You can also mark selected text as preformatted so that Apache does not wrap the text lines together.

Most HTML tags come in pairs. That is, there is an open tag as well as a close tag. For example, if you want to underline a phrase in your document, you indicate the text you want to underline by inserting <ul> where the underlining should start, and </ul> where it should end.

In some cases, you do not require tag pairs to format the text you want to change, but it is considered good form to use them. For example, if you mark the beginning of a paragraph by inserting <p>, you should also mark the end of the paragraph with </p>. Similarly, list items should begin with <li> and end with </li>.

To insert an image into your Web page, you can use the <img src=url> command. In the simplest form, this command provides the location of an image file that you want to display within your Web page. However, you can also specify additional commands to control the size and placing of the image.

To add a link to another page or Web site, you can insert a command such as <a href="http://www.idyllmtn.com">click here</a>.

INTRODUCTION TO HTML

ADD AN IMAGE TO YOUR WEB PAGE

1 Type **sudo pico /sw/apache/htdocs/index.html** and press Return.

■ Pico opens with your current Web page.

2 Position your cursor at the end of a line of text, and press Return.

3 Type **<p>** and press Return.

4 Type another line of text, and press Return.

Extra

The most fundamental HTML tags should enable you to construct a basic Web page.

TAG(S)	DESCRIPTION
`<html>` and `</html>`	Start and end of HTML formatting
`<head>` and `</head>`	Start and end of header
`<title>` and `</title>`	Start and end of title, often displayed in browser title bar
`<body>` and `</body>`	Start and end of body
`<p>` and `</p>`	Start and end of a paragraph
` `	Insertion of a line break
`<a>` and `</a>`	Start and end of a link definition
`<h?>` and `</h?>`	Start and end of a heading, where ? is a number between 1 and 9
`<li>` and `</li>`	Start and end of an individual item in a list
`<img src="?">`	Image insertion, where ? is the location and name of an image
`<table>` and `</table>`	Start and end of a table
`<tr>` and `</tr>`	Start and end of a row in a table
`<td>` and `</td>`	Start and end of a cell in a table
`<th>` and `</th>`	Start and end of a column header

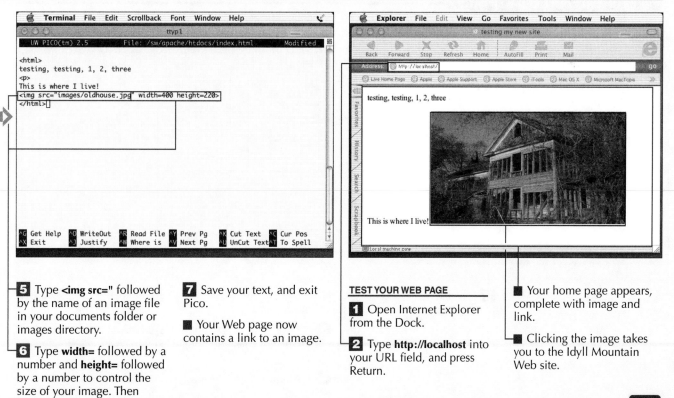

5 Type **<img src="** followed by the name of an image file in your documents folder or images directory.

6 Type **width=** followed by a number and **height=** followed by a number to control the size of your image. Then type **">** and press Return.

7 Save your text, and exit Pico.

■ Your Web page now contains a link to an image.

TEST YOUR WEB PAGE

1 Open Internet Explorer from the Dock.

2 Type **http://localhost** into your URL field, and press Return.

■ Your home page appears, complete with image and link.

■ Clicking the image takes you to the Idyll Mountain Web site.

CREATE A STRUCTURED WEB PAGE

You can create a structured Web page by inserting HTML tags in the proper sequence. While you can build a very simple Web page with almost no formatting commands, you can add to the functionality of your Web page by creating some additional structure.

One simple but important rule that you must keep in mind is that when you use tag pairs, such as <b> and </b>, you should use them in conjunction with other tag pairs — such as <li> and </li> — in such a way that one set of tags fully encapsulates the other. For example, to create a list item that is in bold, you should type **<li><b>Last one to leave must turn off the coffee pot!</b></li>**. While this rule is not strictly enforced for all tags, it is generally a good rule to follow.

A well-formed Web page has an overall structure that identifies the major portions of the page and follows this order of encapsulation: The outermost tags are <html> and </html>. Within these tags, you may have a section that starts with <head>, ends with </head>, and contains your title between <title> and </title> tags. Following the head, you may have a body that starts with <body> and ends with </body>. You then insert your paragraphs and links within the body section. The major sections of a Web page therefore follow a pattern as follows: <html>, <head>, <title>, </title>, </head>, <body>, </body>, and </html>. In between these major tags that provide the overall structure to your Web page, you insert the title, headings, links, and text that define the content as well as the look of your Web page.

CREATE A STRUCTURED WEB PAGE

1 Type **sudo pico** followed by a space.

2 Type the name of your home page, and press Return.

■ Pico opens and displays your home page.

3 Position your cursor at the end of the first line, and press Return.

4 Type **<head>** and press Return.

5 Type **<title>testing my new site</title>** and press Return.

6 Type **</head>** and press Return.

■ The text that you type between the title tags appears at the top of browser windows.

Extra

The structure of an HTML table follows a pattern that resembles the structure of an HTML document. That is, it begins with an opening `<table>` tag and ends with a closing `</table>` tag. Between these two tags, your browser identifies rows between `<tr>` and `</tr>` and cells between `<td>` and `</td>`. The tags `<th>` and `</th>` are used for column headings.

Example:
```
<table>
   <tr>
      <th>Item</th>
      <th>Price</th>
   </tr>
   <tr>
      <td>pizza</td>
      <td>$11</td>
   </tr>
   <tr>
      <td>salad</td>
      <td>$4.50</td>
   </tr>

</table>
```

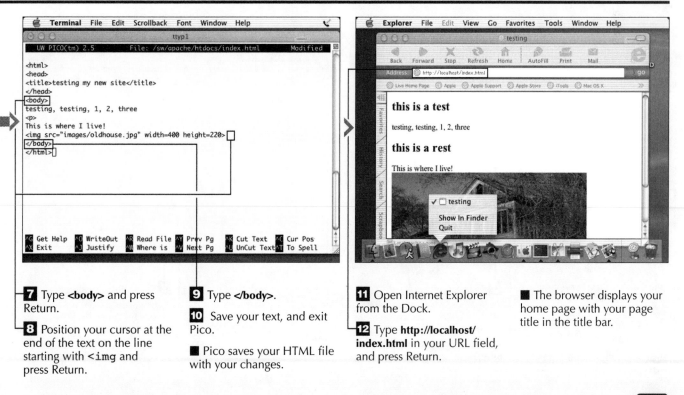

7 Type **<body>** and press Return.

8 Position your cursor at the end of the text on the line starting with **<img** and press Return.

9 Type **</body>**.

10 Save your text, and exit Pico.

■ Pico saves your HTML file with your changes.

11 Open Internet Explorer from the Dock.

12 Type **http://localhost/index.html** in your URL field, and press Return.

■ The browser displays your home page with your page title in the title bar.

ADD SIMPLE STYLES TO YOUR WEB SITE

You can add simple styles to give your Web pages a more interesting and uniform look. The Cascading Style Sheets (CSS) model allows you to define styles within or independent of your Web pages, and to apply these styles to your Web pages in conjunction with HTML formatting.

A style is simply a rule that associates display properties — such as bold and blue — with a particular HTML tag. The simplest way to define an internal style is to insert the style definition into your document. For example, to specify that a single heading is to be both bold and blue, you can type:

<h2 style="color: blue; font-style=bold">From Birth Until Now</h2>.

This style only applies to the text between the <h2> and </h2> tags.

To force all of your <h2> level headings to be bold and blue, you can type the command **h2{font-weight: bold; color: blue;}** within the head of your document.

You can also define in one centralized file, or external style sheet, the formatting and layout for multiple Web pages. This approach allows you to apply consistent styles without having to recreate them in every page. In addition, if you need to make a change in the overall style of your Web site, you only need to change one file.

To create a separate style sheet, you must create a file that contains the style definitions that you want to use. You identify this file with the extension .css. A CSS file contains style definitions such as the following:

```
h1{font-weight: bold; color: black;}
h2{font-weight: bold; color: blue;}
```

You can then use a link or an @import command to use your cascading style sheet in your Web pages.

ADD SIMPLE STYLES TO YOUR WEB SITE

USE AN INTERNAL STYLE SHEET

1 Type **sudo pico** followed by the name of an existing Web page, press Return.

2 Press Return and type **<style type="text/css">**, and press Return again.

3 Type **<!** and press Return, then type **/* H2 headings are bold and blue */** and press Return again. Then type **h2{font-weight: bold; color: blue;}** and press Return.

4 Type **-->** and press Return, then type **</style>**.

5 Save your text, and exit Pico.

6 Open Internet Explorer from the Dock.

7 Type **file://localhost/mystory.html** in your URL field, and press Return.

■ The browser displays your home page with the first heading in a bold, blue font.

Extra

When you use an external style sheet, it is far easier to maintain a collection of pages in the same format. To use the `link` command with an external style sheet called styles.css, you can enter similiar text after the opening HTML tag in each Web page:

Example:
```
<head>
<title>life story</title>
<link rel=stylesheet type="text/css"
    href="styles.css">
</head>
```

To access the same external style sheet using the `@import` command, you can enter text similar to the following:

Example:
```
<head>
<title>life story</title>
<style>
   <!--
      @import url(styles.css);
   -->
</style>
</head>
```

While using an internal style sheet may seem to be the easiest approach, you must define the style in every document you create, and you save little time and effort if you only use the style once. You place an internal style sheet in the head section of a document.

Example:
```
<head>
<title>My life story in 50 words or
less</title>

<style type="text/css">
   <!--
   /* H2 headings are bold and blue */
   h2{font-weight: bold; color: blue;}
   -->
</style>

</head>
```

USE AN EXTERNAL STYLE SHEET

1 Type **echo "h1{font-weight: bold; color: black;}" > styles.css** and press Return.

2 Type **echo "h2{font-weight: bold; color: blue;}" >> styles.css** and press Return.

3 Type **sudo mv styles.css /sw/apache/htdocs** and press Return.

4 Enter your password if prompted.

5 Start Pico using sudo to edit an existing Web page.

6 Press Return and type **<link rel=stylesheet type="text/css"** and press Return again.

7 Press the Spacebar four times, then type **href="styles.css">**.

8 Save your text, and exit Pico.

■ Your document now uses styles that you defined in your styles.css file.

INSTALL CGI SCRIPTS

You can install Common Gateway Interface, or CGI, scripts to make your Web site interactive. CGIs enable your Web pages to exchange information with other programs running on your system. Many CGI programs collect information from visitors to your Web site, usually through a form, and pass that information to a program that processes the data. Other CGI programs simply collect data and display it.

You can find many CGI programs on the Web and install them on your system. These programs can include counters that increment each time a new client visits your site, and forms that allow your visitors to sign a guest book.

To use CGIs on your Web site, you must enable them in your httpd.conf file, and you must store them in the proper directory. CGIs normally reside in the cgi-bin directory, most likely /sw/apache/cgi-bin on your system.

You must set CGI programs to be executable before you can run them from your Web site. This means that they must have execute permission enabled so that anyone can execute them. You can add Execute permission using the `chmod a+x` command.

Programmers usually write CGIs in Perl, because Perl is one of the most versatile and popular programming languages. You can, however, write CGIs using many different languages.

There are many Web sites from which you can download pre-existing CGI scripts. You can also create your own CGI scripts; there are many books and Web sites that can teach you what you need to know to code in Perl and to build effective CGIs. An excellent book is *Perl: Your visual blueprint for building Perl scripts,* by Paul Whitehead, Wiley Publishing. You can also find a Web tutorial at www.cgi101.com/class/.

INSTALL CGI SCRIPTS

1 Type **grep** followed by a space.

2 Type **^ScriptAlias** followed by a space.

3 Type **/sw/apache/conf/httpd.conf** and press Return.

■ The output should display a line showing you where CGI scripts should reside.

4 Type **sudo pico /sw/apache/cgi-bin/mycgi.pl** and press Return.

5 Type **#!/usr/bin/perl –w** and press Return twice.

6 Type **use CGI qw(:standard);** and press Return, then type **print header;** and press Return again.

7 Type **print start_html("this is a CGI");** and press Return, then type **$greet="Thanks for visiting";** and press Return twice.

8 Type **print h1("$greet");** and press Return, type **print hr;** and press Return twice, and then type **print end_html;**

Extra

To make use of the Perl CGI module, add the command line `use CGI`. In the following CGI example, this command is included with standard options.

Example:
```
#!/usr/bin/perl -w

use CGI qw(:standard);
print header;
print start_html("this is a CGI");
$greet="Thanks for visiting";
print h1("$greet");
print hr;
print end_html;
```

Most of the print lines in this simple CGI script are actually calls to the CGI module. When you type **print header**, for example, a routine in the module composes a proper HTML header. When you type **print h1** and include a text message or a string variable inside parentheses, another module composes HTML code for a level-1 HTML heading.

9 Save your file, and exit Pico.

■ Pico saves your CGI.

10 Type **sudo chmod a+x /sw/apache/cgi-bin/mycgi.pl** and press Return.

11 If a prompt appears, type your password.

12 Open Internet Explorer in the Dock.

13 Type **http://localhost/cgi-bin/mycgi2.pl** into the URL field, and press Return.

■ Your new CGI runs and displays the output.

INSTALL APACHE MODULES

Y ou can download and install additional Apache modules to expand the capabilities of your Apache server. While the default Apache installation sets up a very adequate and responsive Web server, the default set of modules that are included may not meet all of your needs. You can obtain a list of the modules that your installation of Apache already supports by typing **httpd –l**.

To upgrade your Apache server to include additional modules, you must download the new modules. If your Apache installation includes the mod_so module, you can install additional modules without having to recompile Apache. This is normal with recent installations of Apache. The mod_so module provides Apache with support for dynamic shared objects (DSO). This means that you can use an external module without changing Apache itself — that is, without having to recompile. DSO modules load when Apache starts up.

After you compile a module into a DSO, you can use the LoadModule command that is part of the mod_so module in your httpd.conf file. This causes the module to load when you start or restart Apache. The exact line that you enter depends on the module that you are installing. The instructions that you obtain with the module, often found in a file called README or INSTALL, tell you which line to enter.

To build a module into your Apache binary, you need to download the module, install the files into the modules directory for your Apache distribution, and recompile. Again, the exact process depends on the module that you are installing. Read the README and INSTALL files for Apache and the module that you are installing.

Fortunately, the Apache Web site offers a list of modules along with a description of each one. This information helps you to find a module that can add the functionality that you require.

INSTALL APACHE MODULES

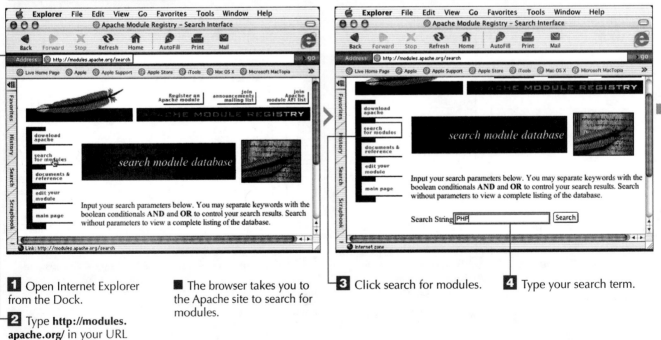

1 Open Internet Explorer from the Dock.

2 Type **http://modules. apache.org/** in your URL field, and press Return.

■ The browser takes you to the Apache site to search for modules.

3 Click search for modules.

4 Type your search term.

Extra

Most, if not all, Apache modules arrive as gzipped TAR files. This means that you must use the `gunzip` and `tar -xf` commands to extract your source files. You must then type **cd** into the target directory and look for a README or INSTALL file, which should contain detailed instructions for installing the module.

To install a module using DSO, you follow directions similar to these:

Example:
```
$ ./configure —with-apxs
$ make
$ make install
```

Most Apache modules contain fairly detailed instructions that tell you the commands you must type to install your new module.

If you install modules using the dynamic method, you must confirm that your Apache daemon supports mod_so; to do this, type the command **httpd –l** and look for mod_so in the output. If you prefer the static method, whereby the new module is built into your apache binary, or if your Apache daemon does not support DSO, you must first compile the new module, then follow instructions to move the compiled files into your Apache source tree, and then recompile Apache.

5 Scroll through the list of modules containing your search string.

6 Click the module you want to download.

■ The download page appears.

7 Click the link provided to download your module.

WRITE PHP APPLICATIONS

You can develop PHP applications for use in your Web site. PHP is a relatively new language that integrates easily with the Apache Web server. When you can code in PHP, you can dramatically reduce the time that it takes for you to develop Web applications. In order to use PHP, your Apache binary must support it.

To understand the similarities between PHP and HTML, you have only to look at some sample code. For example, to print a variable on a Web page, PHP mimics the style of HTML commands while using special tags that only belong to PHP:

```
<html>
  <head><title>Latest Counts</title></head>
  <body><?php echo $grp1cnt<br>; ?></body>
</html>
```

PHP files do not need to be executable, and the output appears indistinguishable from HTML.

You must always enclose PHP scripts between two PHP tags. The tag pairs can be in one of several forms, such as `<?` and `?>` or `<?php` and `php?>`, although some programmers use `<?php` and `?>`.

PHP uses many commands, including printing, looping, `if` commands, arrays, and forms, but if you are already familiar with HTML, you should grasp the fundamentals of PHP quite easily.

PHP is a server-side scripting language. This means that the interpreter has to be installed and configured on the server before it can be used. No special client-side setup is required. The language combines features from Perl, Java, and C, so most people who have programmed in any of these languages will feel at home with PHP.

All text to be written to the screen must be enclosed in double-quotes and almost all commands will end in a semicolon. Pages containing PHP commands should be saved with the extension .php.

WRITE PHP APPLICATIONS

TEST PHP

1 Type **sudo pico** followed by a space.

2 Type **/sw/apache/htdocs /testme.php** and press Return.

3 Type **<html>** and press Return, then type **<title>testing</title>** and press Return again.

4 Type **<body>** and press Return, then type **<?php phpinfo(); ?>** and press Return again.

5 Type **</body>** and press Return, then type **</html>**.

6 Save your text, and exit Pico.

246

Extra

You can mix PHP and HTML easily in a single file. When you do so, you enclose each of your PHP statements in a pair of PHP tags, as in the sample below:

Example:
```
<?php $season="summer"; ?>
We are now accepting reservations for our
<?php print $season season; ?>
Call 1-800-FUN-VACS today.
```

This code segment assigns a value to $season and then uses this value to customize the content of the remainder of the display. In a similar manner to Perl, PHP allows you to create simple data types, like $season, and arrays in which you can use both a variable name and an index, such as $season[1].

Basic comparison operators include all those listed in the table below.

OPERATOR	DESCRIPTION
==	Equal
!=	Not equal
=	Assignment
*	Multiplication
/	Division
+	Addition
-	Subtraction
.	Concatenation
&&	Logical AND
||	Logical OR

PHP Version 4.3.0

System	Darwin ferro.local. 6.3 Darwin Kernel Version 6.3: Sat Dec 14 03:11:25 PST 200(root:xnu/xnu-344.23.obj~4/RELEASE_PPC Power Macintosh
Build Date	May 22 2003 10:31:16
Configure Command	'./configure'
Server API	Apache
Virtual Directory Support	disabled
Configuration File (php.ini) Path	/usr/local/lib/php.ini

```
<? php
$times=11;
$x=0;
while ($x < $times) {
    echo "Hello, World";
    ++$x;
}
?>
```
[Wrote 8 lines]
[ferro:~/project_X] user%

7 Open Internet Explorer in the Dock.

8 Type **http://localhost/testme.php** in your URL field, and press Return.

■ The browser displays a page of information about PHP if your PHP installation is active.

CREATE A PHP

1 Start Pico to create a file name hello.php.

2 Type **<? php** and press Return, type **$times=11;** and press Return again, and then type **$x=0;** and press Return twice.

3 Type **while ($x < $times) {** and press Return, type **echo "Hello, World";** and press Return again, and then type **++$x;** and press Return.

4 Type **}** and press Return, then type **?>**.

5 Save your file.

ANALYZE WEB TRAFFIC

You can analyze your Web traffic using a tool called Analog. Analog is a free, open source program that you can use to analyze Web traffic based on records stored in your log files. Analog can produce as many as 32 different reports. For example, it can provide you with charts that highlight heavy traffic times — for instance, times of the day or days of the week. It can also show you which of your files visitors access most frequently, which files are not found, or where visitors are coming from when they follow links to your Web site.

Analog has a configuration file, called analog.cfg. Fink installs this file into the /sw/etc/analog directory. Like most configuration files, analog.cfg is full of helpful comments, and has a number of configuration options. The most important of these options is the line that identifies where

you store your Web log files. If you store your Web logs in /sw/apache/logs, you must change the line that starts with LOGFILE to read LOGFILE /sw/apache/logs/access_log. If you do not have the correct log file location, Analog cannot analyze your Web traffic.

Analog analyzes Web traffic by individual file requests, as this is the manner in which your system records Web traffic in your log files. Traffic can be reported hourly, daily, weekly, or monthly by turning report options on and off. For example, to turn monthly reports off, you can add MONTHLY OFF to your configuration file. To turn weekly reports on, you can add WEEKLY ON. To produce one of the many types of reports available from Analog, you can scan a list of the available reports and insert commands such as REFERRER ON in your configuration file.

ANALYZE WEB TRAFFIC

```
[ferro:screenshots] user% fink list | grep analog
i    analog   5.24-1  Program to measure usage on your web server
     arts     1.1.0-3 KDE - analog realtime synthesizer
[ferro:screenshots] user% []
```

```
 UW PICO(tm) 2.5          File: /sw/etc/analog/analog.cfg          Modified

# Lines starting with # are comments.
#
# There is a much more extensive configuration file in examples/big.cfg
#
# If you need a LOGFORMAT command (most people don't -- try it without first$
# it must go here, above the LOGFILE commands.
# LOGFILE logfile.log
# LOGFILE /old/logs/access_log.*
LOGFILE /sw/apache/logs/access_log
OUTPUT HTML
OUTFILE /sw/apache/htdocs/analog0.html
PNGIMAGES ON
MONTHLY OFF
# Default location on Mac OS X --cp
#
DNS READ
# DNS lookups turned off to avoid an apparent bug in Mac OS X. --cp

^G Get Help  ^O WriteOut  ^R Read File ^Y Prev Pg  ^K Cut Text  ^C Cur Pos
^X Exit      ^J Justify   ^W Where is  ^V Next Pg  ^U UnCut Tex ^T To Spell
```

CHECK IF ANALOG IS INSTALLED

■1 Type **fink list |** followed by a space.

■2 Type **grep analog** and press Return.

■ Fink tells you whether you have installed analog.

■ A lowercase letter i in the leftmost column indicates that Fink is installed.

CONFIGURE ANALOG

■1 Start Pico with sudo to edit /sw/etc/analog/analog.cfg.

■2 Change the LOGFILE line to include the pathname of your access_log, and press Return.

■3 Type **OUTPUT HTML** and press Return.

■4 Type **OUTFILE /sw/apache/ htdocs/analog0.html** and press Return.

Extra

Until you start to use the reports that Analog produces, you may not know which reports are the most useful to you in analyzing your log files. In addition, your requirements may change over time. The following table describes some of the reports available to you. To include any of these reports in your Analog output, insert the keyword, then the word ON, into your analog.cfg file.

REPORT	DESCRIPTION
MONTHLY	One line for each month
WEEKLY	One line for each week
DAILYREP	One line for each day
HOURLYREP	One line for each hour of the day
GENERAL	A general summary
REQUEST	Files that are requested
FAILURE	Files that are not found
REFERRER	Where visitors come from using links
FAILREF	Sites from which visitors follow broken links
SEARCHWORD	Phrases and words visitors use to find your site
STATUS	Count of each type of success and failure

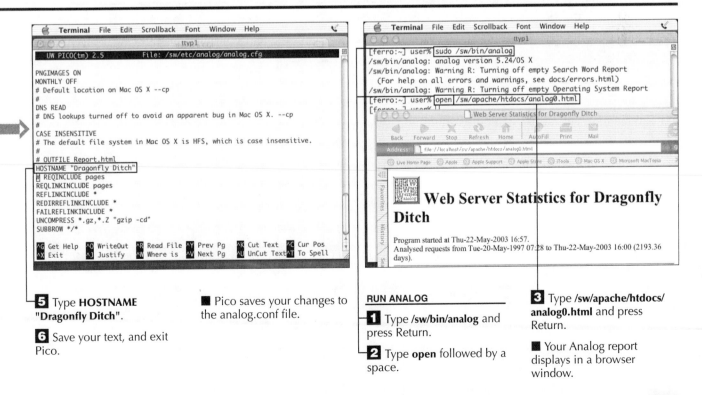

5 Type **HOSTNAME "Dragonfly Ditch"**.

6 Save your text, and exit Pico.

■ Pico saves your changes to the analog.conf file.

RUN ANALOG

1 Type **/sw/bin/analog** and press Return.

2 Type **open** followed by a space.

3 Type **/sw/apache/htdocs/analog0.html** and press Return.

■ Your Analog report displays in a browser window.

WRITE A SIMPLE PERL SCRIPT

You can use Perl to write a simple script that does not require compiling. Perl is an interpreted language. However, Perl looks like a compiled language in a number of ways. For example, each statement in Perl ends in a semicolon, and a $ symbol precedes variable names, even when you first declare them and assign them a value. More importantly, Perl allows you to build subroutines, pass variables, and return values like most compiled languages. Perl also has sophisticated array handling.

However, the feature that most distinguishes Perl from other languages is the versatile use of regular expressions. If your only experience with regular expressions comes from working in one of the Unix shells, you may be amazed at the versatility of the Perl language. For example, you can use regular expressions in Perl to do fuzzy matching. With fuzzy matching, instead of asking whether one number is greater than another, or looking for a number in a string, you can ask if a line of text contains an e-mail address or a date/time stamp by describing these items as patterns.

Although the use of regular expressions can make Perl code difficult to interpret at first, when you become more familiar with each of the symbols, you can begin to appreciate the succinct form of the language.

The elements of a Perl pattern are referred to as metacharacters. For example, \s represents a single whitespace character – a blank or a tab — and \S represents any non-whitespace character. You can also amend these patterns to match some or none or a string of any size. Where \d represents a digit, \d+ represents any number of digits and \d* represents any number of digits, but will also match no digits at all.

WRITE A SIMPLE PERL SCRIPT

1 Type **pico** followed by a space.

2 Type **sam.pl** and press Return.

■ A blank Pico screen appears.

3 Type **print** followed by a space.

4 Type **"Hello, World -- ";** and press Return.

Extra

As with most Unix scripting languages and configuration files, you create a comment in Perl by placing a # symbol at the beginning of the line. You can place a comment on a line by itself or append it to the end of a line of code. Either of these forms is correct:

Example:
```
# say hello

print "Hello, World - ";       # say hello
```

When you create a complex script, you should include some comments that explain what your script is doing, but avoid superfluous comments that may annoy someone who reads your code. In Perl, comments are often used to explain complex regular expressions.

The "\n" shown in the screens below indicates a newline character. If this character were omitted from our print statement, the script would print the output without moving to the new line, and the next system prompt would be on the same line. You usually include newline characters in the print statements along with text that you want to print. For example, you can type the line **print "Hello, World\n";** in a Perl script to print the message and move to the next line.

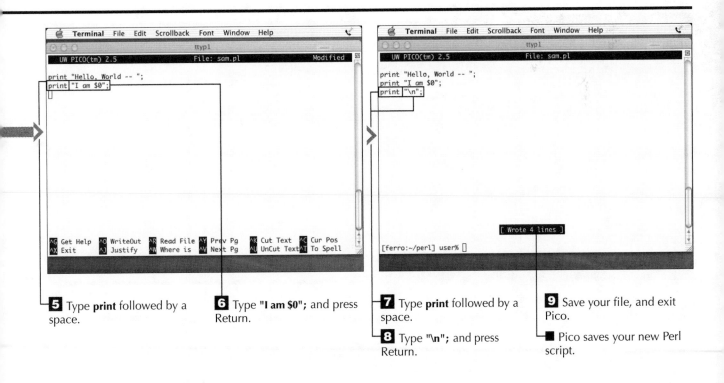

5 Type **print** followed by a space.

6 Type **"I am $0";** and press Return.

7 Type **print** followed by a space.

8 Type **"\n";** and press Return.

9 Save your file, and exit Pico.

■ Pico saves your new Perl script.

RUN A PERL SCRIPT

You can run a Perl script by using it as an argument to the Perl interpreter, or by making it executable. After you create a Perl script, you can instruct Perl to interpret and execute the script, for example, by typing **perl myscript.pl**. This is the simplest way to run a script, but not the most convenient. Most users prefer to run scripts as though they are new commands, and without having to know anything about the language in which they are written. Thus, they may not want to type **perl** before the name of the script.

For the convenience of users, and to avoid errors that may generate if they type the name of the script on a line by itself, you can insert a line at the top of the script that identifies your file to the shell as a Perl script, and you can make the script executable. You refer to this line as the

shebang line, and the syntax for this line is # ! followed by the name of the interpreter. For a Perl script, you can type **#!/usr/bin/perl**.

If you make your Perl script executable without the shebang line, the system cannot determine what tool to use to run the script, and it attempts to run the commands using your shell. This action generates a number of errors, as tcsh does not include a print command. If you mistype your shebang line, your system cannot find the interpreter and issues an error such as "not found: myscript.pl".

You can force yourself to use rules that are more restrictive in your Perl coding by adding use strict; to the top of your scripts. While adding this to your scripts may generate warning messages, these messages may help you avoid many potential errors in your code.

RUN A PERL SCRIPT

1 Type **perl** followed by a space.

2 Type **sam.pl** and press Return.

■ Perl runs your script.

3 Type **chmod a+x** followed by a space.

4 Type **sam.pl** and press Return.

5 Type **./sam.pl** and press Return.

■ The shell cannot run your print command.

6 Type **pico sam.pl** and press Return.

Extra

You can use the command line option -w on the shebang line — by typing **#!/usr/bin/perl -w** — to instruct Perl to issue warnings regarding your syntax. For example, if you define a variable, such as `$counter`, and then never use it, Perl warns you that this variable appears only once in your code. By doing this, Perl is telling you that you have made a mistake or, at least, strayed from your original intent in writing the script.

Perl warnings are very useful when you are first learning the language, as they can help you to spot problems that prevent your script from running, or represent poor scripting style.

The shebang line tells the shell which language you used to write the script and, consequently, what tool the shell can use to run the commands. For the script to run, the shebang line must contain the full path to the Perl interpreter. This is the case whether or not the Perl binary is on your search path. Also, this line must be the first line in the script and must start with #!.

```
#!/usr/bin/perl
print "Hello, World -- ";
print "I am $0";
print "\n";
```

```
[ Wrote 5 lines ]

[ferro:~/perl] user%
```

```
[ferro:~/perl] user% ./sam.pl
Hello, World -- I am ./sam.pl
[ferro:~/perl] user%
```

■ Pico opens with your file.

7 Type the line **#!/usr/bin/perl** at the top of your script, and press Return.

8 Save your file, and exit Pico.

■ Pico saves your modified script.

9 Type **./sam.pl** and press Return.

■ Perl runs your script.

MANIPULATE TEXT WITH PERL

You can use the ability of Perl to recognize patterns to help you manipulate text. If you are able to describe a pattern that you are looking for in a stream of text, then you can represent it as a Perl regular expression with which you can easily extract and manipulate it.

For example, if you are looking for dates that look like 05/01/03, you can tell Perl that you want strings that match the pattern \d{2}\/\d{2}\/\d{2}. While this expression may look complicated, a quick breakdown makes it easier to understand. The string \d matches a digit, and when changed to \d{2}, it matches a two-digit number. The date above includes three of these strings. The two extra forward slashes in the search pattern indicate that the strings you are searching for contain slashes. Because slashes are a part of the Perl syntax, you must precede any slashes that you

include as characters you want to match with an escape character. The escape character tells Perl to take the following character literally and not to interpret it as part of the Perl syntax. Thus, \/ represents / in your search pattern.

Perl has many special character sequences, such as \d, to help you to locate and manipulate text. Users refer to these character sequences as metacharacters or escape sequences. Many metacharacters have both a positive and negative form. For example, while \d represents a digit, \D represents a non-digit — any character that is not a digit. While \s+ represents any amount of whitespace, \S+ represents any string of characters that does not contain any whitespace. The biggest challenge to most Perl beginners is to remember what each of the metacharacters represents.

MANIPULATE TEXT WITH PERL

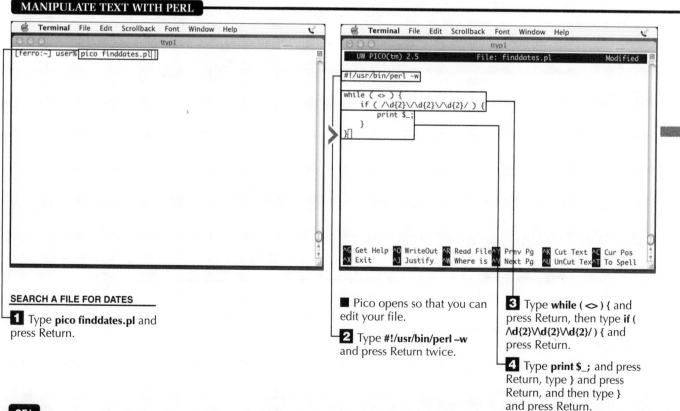

SEARCH A FILE FOR DATES

1 Type **pico finddates.pl** and press Return.

■ Pico opens so that you can edit your file.

2 Type **#!/usr/bin/perl –w** and press Return twice.

3 Type **while (<>) {** and press Return, then type **if (/\d{2}\/\d{2}\/\d{2}/) {** and press Return.

4 Type **print $_;** and press Return, type **}** and press Return, and then type **}** and press Return.

Extra

Perl recognizes many different metacharacters, allowing you to closely describe text that you are looking for and to manipulate it. The table below shows some of the most common metacharacters and what they represent. You can use the + and * qualifiers with any of the metacharacters.

METACHARACTER	MATCHES	METACHARACTER	MATCHES
\d	A digit.	\s+	Any amount of whitespace.
\d+	One or more digits.	\S*	Some whitespace or no whitespace.
\d*	Zero or more digits.		
\D	A non-digit.	\t	A tab.
\e	The escape character.	\u	An uppercase character.
\f	A form feed.	\w	A word character — a letter, digit, or underscore.
\l	A lowercase letter.		
\n	A newline.	\W	A non-word character.
\r	A carriage return.	\0?	An octal character.
\s	A whitespace character.	\x?	A hexadecimal character.

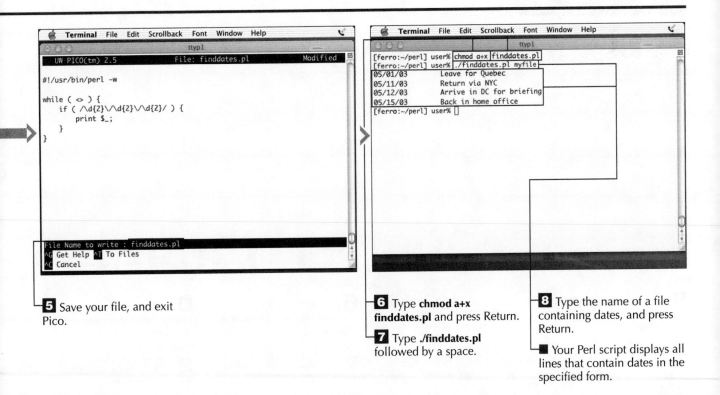

5 Save your file, and exit Pico.

6 Type **chmod a+x finddates.pl** and press Return.

7 Type **./finddates.pl** followed by a space.

8 Type the name of a file containing dates, and press Return.

■ Your Perl script displays all lines that contain dates in the specified form.

READ THE COMMAND LINE

You can build Perl scripts that read data from the command line. Like other scripting languages, Perl allows you to prompt the user to enter information. Perl does this by issuing a `print` statement containing the prompt and then reading the answer from standard input. For example, you can include a prompt in the script with the line `print "Enter your favorite number> ";` and then collect the answer with `$favnum=<STDIN>;`. When the script runs, Perl prompts you for the number and stores it in `$favnum`.

You can also place your prompt-and-read statement into a loop. A `while` statement continues looping until the specified conditions are met. A `foreach` loop is good to use if you want to collect a specific number of answers from the user. For example, you can enter the following commands:

```
$tothrs=0;
foreach day ( Mon,Tue,Wed,Thu,Fri ) {
    print "hours worked on $day> ";
    $hrs = <STDIN>;
    $tothrs = $tothrs + $hrs;
}
print "You only worked $tothrs hours!";
```

This script prompts the user to enter the number of hours that they work each weekday, and computes a total. However, this script generates an error message if the user enters anything other than a number, because the addition fails. You can insert a `while` statement inside the `foreach` statement to repeat the prompt until the user enters a number.

1 Type **pico favnum.pl** and press Return.

2 Type **#!/usr/bin/perl –w** and press Return twice, then type **print "Enter your favorite number> ";** and press Return.

3 Type **$favnum = <STDIN>;** and press Return.

4 Type **print "What a coincidence! $favnum is my favorite number too.\n";** and press Return.

5 Type **print "Maybe we should go out.\n";**.

Extra

There are times when you do not want to use data exactly as a user enters it. For example, when you tell the user that their favorite number just happens to be your favorite number, too, as in the `favnum.pl` script, your message displays on two lines instead of three. This unintended line break results when Perl reads the input line, including the linefeed, and retains the linefeed. As a result, when the output displays to the user, the linefeed is still present in the `$favnum` variable.

You can remove these unwanted linefeeds by using the `chomp` command. The `chomp` command simply removes the linefeed from the end of the line. The format for the `chomp` command is `chomp($variable)`. Thus, you can add the line `chomp($favnum);` to the script immediately after the line that reads the response from the user. When the `chomp` command removes the linefeed, the output changes to reflect this.

BEFORE:

```
What a coincidence! 111
 is my favorite number too.
Maybe we should go out.
```

AFTER:

```
What a coincidence!
111 is my favorite
number too.

Maybe we should go
out.
```

```
 UW PICO(tm) 2.5              File: favnum.pl

#!/usr/bin/perl -w

print "Enter your favorite number> ";
$favnum = <STDIN>;
print "What a coincidence!  $favnum is my favorite number too.\n";
print "Maybe we should go out.\n";

File Name to write : favnum.pl
^G Get Help ^T To Files
^C Cancel
```

```
print "What a coincidence!  $favnum is my favorite number too.\n";
print "Maybe we should go out.\n";

                    [ Wrote 6 lines ]
[ferro:~] user% chmod a+x favnum.pl
[ferro:~] user% ./favnum.pl
Enter your favorite number> 111
What a coincidence!  111
 is my favorite number too.
Maybe we should go out.
[ferro:~] user%
```

6 Save your script, and exit Pico.

7 Type **chmod a+x** followed by a space.

8 Type **favnum.pl** and press Return.

9 Type **./favnum.pl** and press Return.

■ The script runs, asking you for your favorite number.

257

READ FILES WITH PERL

You can read any number of files from within a Perl script. There are also a number of ways to read files in Perl, the most straightforward being to use the open command with the name of the file as an argument. For example, to open the file myfile.txt, you can use the command open(INFILE, "myfile.txt");. This command opens the file and associates it with the file handle INFILE. You can also assign the name of the file to a variable using a command such as $myfile="/Users/user/ myfile.txt"; and then open the file with an open command such as open(INFILE, $myfile);. If you assign the filename at the beginning of the script, your script is easier to modify later.

You can also open a file explicitly for reading by using a < symbol within your open command. For example, you can use the command open(INFILE, "<myfile.txt");. This

is good practice if you want to ensure that the files that you read are preserved, as it opens the file only for reading, and disallows any write operations.

Just as the < symbol indicates that a command is opening a file for reading, the > symbol indicates that a command is opening a file for writing. Using the > symbol indicates that a command is opening a file for appending. In other words, you write from the end of the file, preserving the current contents of the file.

To be sure that your scripts do not malfunction when input files do not exist or are unreadable, you can add an or die clause to your open command. The command open(INFILE, "<myfile.txt") or die "Cannot open myfile.txt for reading"; displays the cautionary message if the input file is unreadable, and exits the script.

READ FILES WITH PERL

1 Type **pico read1** and press Return.

2 Type **#!/usr/bin/perl –w** and press Return twice.

3 Type **open(INFILE, "<myfile.txt");**, replacing myfile.txt with the name of your file, and press Return twice.

4 Type **while (<INFILE>) {** and press Return.

5 Press the Spacebar four times, type **print $_;** and press Return, and then type **}**.

Extra

Another way to read files in Perl is to use backticks. For example, if you want to read the contents of a file into an array, you can use a command such as @lines=`cat myfile.txt`;. This command runs the cat command, collects the output, and stores each line in that output as an element in the array @lines. While this operation is as simple as the more formal open commands, it also involves more overhead — especially for very large files — as it stores the data it reads into memory. When the operation reads a file one record at a time, it stores one record at a time.

Backticks are a good way to get information from your system. For example, if your script needs to use the current date, you can assign the date to a variable using a line such as $date=`date +%m%d%y`;. This command stores a date of the form 05/01/03 to the $date variable. You can then use this variable to name output files or to add records with a date stamp to a file you are creating. For example, you can open an output file with a command such as open(OUTFILE, ">myfile.$date");.

```
#!/usr/bin/perl -w

open(INFILE,"<myfile.txt");

while (<INFILE>) {
    print $_;
}
```

File: read1 — UW PICO(tm) 2.5

File Name to write : read1

6 Save your script, and exit Pico.

```
[ Wrote 7 lines ]

[ferro:~] user% chmod a+x read1
[ferro:~] user% ./read1
Here is the schedule:

05/01/03        Leave for Quebec
                take photos and manuscript
                drop the cat at the sitter's on the way
05/11/03        Return via NYC
                stop for meeting in Upper West Side offices
                lunch with Candice and Madeleine
05/12/03        Arrive in DC for briefing
05/15/03        Back in home office
                send notes to hok@company.com
[ferro:~] user%
```

7 Type **chmod a+x** followed by a space.

8 Type **read1** and press Return.

9 Type **./read1** and press Return.

■ Your script runs, displaying each line in the file to your screen.

WRITE FILES WITH PERL

You can write files with Perl as easily as you can read files with Perl. In fact, the command for opening a file for writing is almost the same as that for opening a file for reading. The command `open(OUTFILE, ">myfile.out")` or die "Cannot open myfile.out for writing"; attempts to open the specified file for writing and exits the script if this cannot be done. Changing the > symbol to the >> symbol appends any subsequent output to the file instead of overwriting it.

After a file is open for writing, you can use the `print` command to write to it. While a command such as `print "Maybe we should go out\n";` prints to the screen, the same line with an additional argument — `print OUTFILE "Maybe we should go out\n";` — writes the line to the output file.

If you write text that does not contain linefeeds, you will not have separate lines in your output file. The print operation does not add linefeeds whether it is writing to the screen or to a file.

When you are finished writing to a file or reading from a file, you can close the file. The `close` command is very similar to the `open` command except that you only need to use the file handle, and you do not need to specify the filename. For example, if you want to close the file associated with the file handle `OUTFILE`, you type the command **close OUTFILE;** and the file closes and is no longer available for reading.

If you are creating a temporary file and you want to remove it when you finish with it, you can use the `unlink` command in place of the `close` command. The `unlink` command removes the file from the file system.

USE A WHILE LOOP

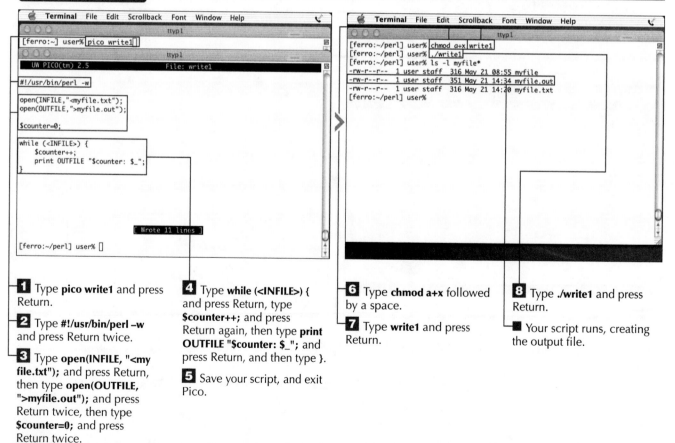

1️⃣ Type **pico write1** and press Return.

2️⃣ Type **#!/usr/bin/perl –w** and press Return twice.

3️⃣ Type **open(INFILE, "<my file.txt");** and press Return, then type **open(OUTFILE, ">myfile.out");** and press Return twice, then type **$counter=0;** and press Return twice.

4️⃣ Type **while (<INFILE>) {** and press Return, type **$counter++;** and press Return again, then type **print OUTFILE "$counter: $_";** and press Return, and then type }.

5️⃣ Save your script, and exit Pico.

6️⃣ Type **chmod a+x** followed by a space.

7️⃣ Type **write1** and press Return.

8️⃣ Type **./write1** and press Return.

■ Your script runs, creating the output file.

Extra

One of the advantages of using Perl over other scripting languages is that it allows you to read and write any number of files at the same time. For each file that you want to use, you type an `open` command, specify the filename, indicate whether you are opening the file for reading, writing, appending, or both reading and writing, assign a file handle, and write records to the file. When you are done, you type a `close` or an `unlink` command.

For readability, your file handles should be meaningful. If you use a temporary file, calling it TMP or TMP1 makes it clear to anyone reading your code that you do not intend to preserve the file. If you use temporary files, you must always remember to unlink them when you are done; otherwise, your script may not run the next time you try to use it because it may not be able to open a file that already exists. In addition, scripts that leave unnecessary files behind when they finish running create clutter in your file system. Giving temporary files random names, such as myfile$$, reduces conflict over filenames.

USE A FOREACH LOOP

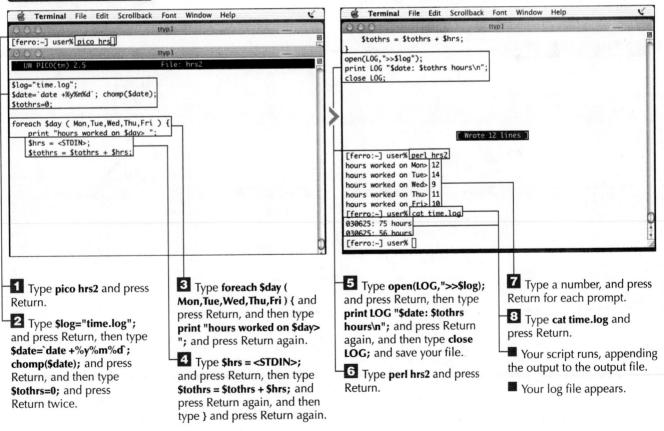

■ Type **pico hrs2** and press Return.

② Type **$log="time.log";** and press Return, then type **$date=`date +%y%m%d`; chomp($date);** and press Return, and then type **$tothrs=0;** and press Return twice.

③ Type **foreach $day (Mon,Tue,Wed,Thu,Fri) {** and press Return, and then type **print "hours worked on $day> ";** and press Return again.

④ Type **$hrs = <STDIN>;** and press Return, then type **$tothrs = $tothrs + $hrs;** and press Return again, and then type **}** and press Return again.

⑤ Type **open(LOG,">>$log);** and press Return, then type **print LOG "$date: $tothrs hours\n";** and press Return again, and then type **close LOG;** and save your file.

⑥ Type **perl hrs2** and press Return.

⑦ Type a number, and press Return for each prompt.

⑧ Type **cat time.log** and press Return.

■ Your script runs, appending the output to the output file.

■ Your log file appears.

INSTALL PERL MODULES

Perl modules are collections of reusable code that can make your Perl programs more powerful and easier to maintain by downloading and installing Perl modules. Perl modules are meant to be used in other programs using statements such as use Net::Telnet; that make these procedures accessible in your own Perl scripts. Perl modules are well designed and well documented and can save you a lot of programming effort.

The best place to begin your search for a Perl module that meets your needs is search.cpan.org. When you go to this site, you can enter a name into the search field if you know the name of the module that you want or you can search by category.

In the process of downloading your module, you should take advantage of the online documentation available for your module. This documentation will provide instructions

and examples of how the module can be used. After you click on the link that takes you to the page describing the module you want, you can scroll down the page to find a description of the module along with information on usage, debugging, parameters, and more.

There are many Perl libraries and modules already installed on your system. You can list the installed modules with the command find/System/LibraryPerl -name "*.pm" -print. This directory even includes a module for making the process of downloading other Perl modules from CPAN even easier. You can look at CPAM.pm or read about this on the CPAN Web site to find out more.

INSTALL PERL MODULES

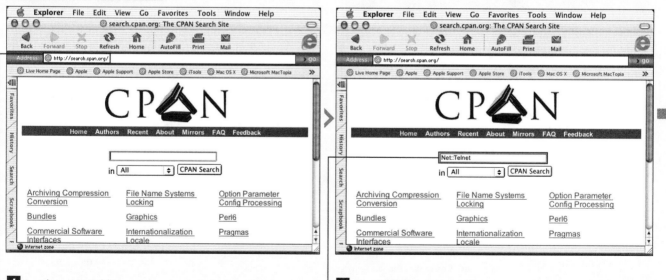

1 In a browser Address window, enter **search.cpan.org** and press Return.

2 Enter the name of a Perl module, such as **Net::Telnet**, in the search window and click CPAN Search.

Extra

Before you can use a Perl module in your script, you must load it with the use command. The command use diagnostics; loads the module diagnostics.pm from your /System/Library/Perl directory. The command use Net::Telnet; loads /System/Library/Perl/Net/Telnet.pm.

You can also build your own Perl modules. If you develop Perl code that may be used in many scripts or by many users, you may want to turn the reusable code into a module and install it into the /System/Library/Perl directory.

You must use the package command to create Perl modules, and you must organize them as subroutines, and name them with the file extension .pm. Construction of a module also requires the use of commands to export items that you create in the module. For more information about creating Perl modules, you can consult *Perl: Your visual blueprint for building Perl scripts*, by Paul Whitehead.

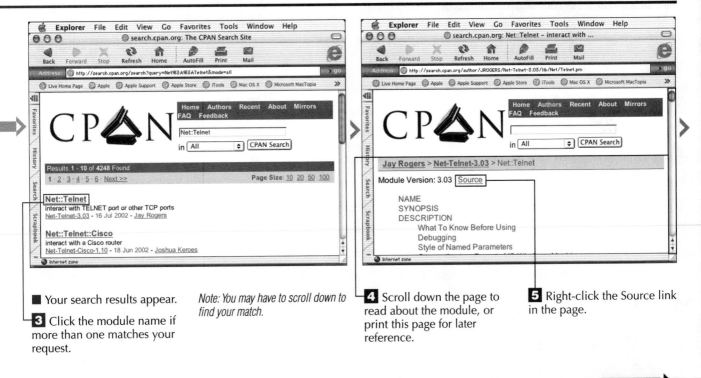

■ Your search results appear.

3 Click the module name if more than one matches your request.

Note: You may have to scroll down to find your match.

4 Scroll down the page to read about the module, or print this page for later reference.

5 Right-click the Source link in the page.

CONTINUED ▶

INSTALL PERL MODULES (CONTINUED)

You can install Perl modules to increase your productivity as a Perl programmer. There are many Perl modules that you can download and install to increase the sophistication of your Perl scripts. Each Perl module contains a number of routines that are relevant to a particular type of processing. For example, the CGI module reduces the code that you must produce to create CGI scripts. Most modules are free, and you can modify them, if needed, to suit your application. Modules are contributed by their authors who consider them useful enough to be generally valuable. If you are now or become a proficient Perl programmer, you might consider contributing modules that you develop to the Perl community.

You may sometime acquire a Perl modules in the form of a gzipped TAR file. When this is the case, the process of installing looks much like the process of compiling open

source software from the same kind of file. However, because Perl is not compiled, the make step will not result in a compilation. The steps for installing a Perl module packaged as a tar.gz file are as follows:

```
gzip <module-name.tar.gz>
tar xf <module-name.tar>
cd <module-name>
perl Makefile.PL
make
make test
make install
```

Some Perl modules will require other modules to be installed before they can be used. When a module that you are trying to install has a prerequisite, you will get a message when you type the perl Makefile.PL command.

INSTALL PERL MODULES (CONTINUED)

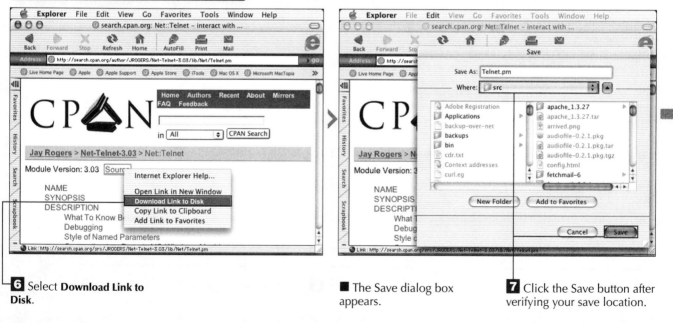

6 Select **Download Link to Disk**.

■ The Save dialog box appears.

7 Click the Save button after verifying your save location.

Extra

A *pragma* is a special Perl module that comes with your installation of Perl. If you have tried the `use strict;` command, you have already used one of these special modules. You can learn more about the pragmas that are included in your release of Perl with the command `man perlmodlib`.

Perl has a search path that it uses to look for modules. You can view this by issuing the `perl -e 'print "@INC"'` command as shown here.

If you are interested in the format and other technical details of how Perl modules are organized, the Perl mod man page will provide you with many insights. In a Terminal window, type **man perlmod** and press Return.

TYPE THIS:

```
[ferro:~] user% perl -e
'print "@INC"'
```

RESULT:

```
/System/Library/Perl/darwin
/System/Library/Perl
/Library/Perl/darwin
/Library/Perl /Library/Perl
/Network/Library/Perl/darwin
/Network/Library/Perl
/Network/Library/Perl
.[ferro:~] user%
```

■ The download manager downloads your module.

8 In a Terminal window, type **sudo cp Telnet.pm /System/Library/Perl/Net** or copy your Perl module to the proper location in /System/Library/Perl using the name of the module to determine if the library belongs in a directory.

9 Press Return.

10 Enter your password if prompted.

WRITE A CGI SCRIPT

You can write a CGI script to create a Web page that interacts with your visitors. While the term CGI identifies a class of script that allows Web pages to interact with the system on which the script is running, most scripts are written in Perl. This is because the versatility of Perl makes it a good language to use on the Web. The basic function of a CGI script is to perform a process and then to prepare the output in HTML format so that it can display in a Web page.

To use the CGI module that installs on your system, you can use the Perl command use CGI;. This command loads the CGI module into your script. For most CGI scripts, you amend this command by specifying that you want to use the most command functions. The altered use command then becomes use CGI qw(:standard);. This allows you to access HTML, form generation, and CGI functions.

The CGI module uses functions to generate HTML code. These include header and start_html — functions that create the HTML header — and tags such as <html> and <body>, which you need to format an HTML page.

Other functions include h1, hr, and end_html. As you see, these commands resemble HTML codes. A command such as print h1("My Life in 50 Words or Less"); takes the place of a print command containing the beginning and ending tags for heading level 1 text.

You can use CGI scripts to build pages that contain dynamic text, because you can use Perl commands to gather information from the system or vary the contents of the page in other ways. You can also build CGI scripts that create a form allowing the user to enter text, and then process that text.

WRITE A CGI SCRIPT

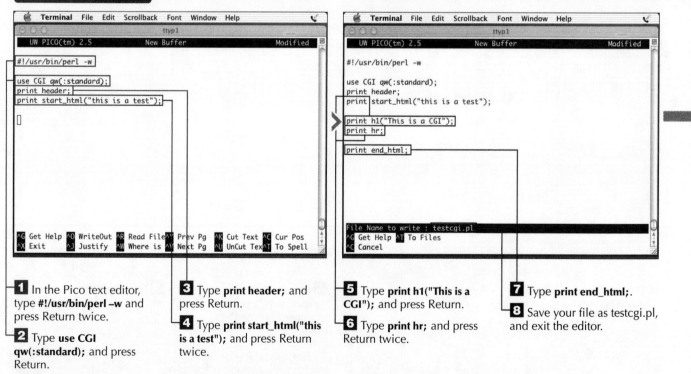

1 In the Pico text editor, type **#!/usr/bin/perl –w** and press Return twice.

2 Type **use CGI qw(:standard);** and press Return.

3 Type **print header;** and press Return.

4 Type **print start_html("this is a test");** and press Return twice.

5 Type **print h1("This is a CGI");** and press Return.

6 Type **print hr;** and press Return twice.

7 Type **print end_html;**.

8 Save your file as testcgi.pl, and exit the editor.

To create a Web form with CGI, you can use commands that create form elements such as text fields. While you can create these elements without the assistance of the CGI module, the CGI commands simplify the work considerably. For example, to create a text field into which a user types information, you can use a command such as `print textfield('comment','Enter your comment',70,80);`. This command creates a text field, displays the phrase "Enter your comment" in the text field, and sizes the field to 70 text characters. You can add a submit button with a command such as `print submit("submit comment");`. What happens next depends on the remainder of your code. When you run this script, it submits the comments to a process called process_comments.pl.

Example:
```
#/usr/bin/perl
use CGI qw(:standard);
print header;
print start_html;
print h1("We want your comments");
print start_form(get,'process_comments.pl');
print textfield('comment','Enter your comment here',70,80);
print end_html;
```

```
use CGI qw(:standard);
print header;
print start_html("this is a test");

print h1("This is a CGI");
print hr;

print end_html;
```

[Wrote 11 lines]

```
[ferro:~] user% chmod a+x testcgi.pl
[ferro:~] user% sudo cp testcgi.pl /sw/apache/cgi-bin
Password:
[ferro:~] user%
```

This is a CGI

9 Type **chmod a+x testcgi.pl** and press Return.

10 Type **sudo cp testcgi.pl /sw/apache/cgi-bin** and press Return, replacing /sw/apache/cgi-bin with the correct path to your cgi-bin directory if different.

11 Enter your password if prompted.

12 In the URL field of a browser, enter **http://localhost /cgi-bin/testcgi.pl** and press Return.

■ The CGI runs, creating a Web page containing system information.

INTRODUCTION TO THE X WINDOW SYSTEM

Y ou can install and use the X Window System to enhance the capabilities of your Mac OS X system. The X Window system is a windowing system that facilitates the sharing of windows on a network. For example, you can run an application on one system and send the display of that application to another system.

In addition, if you install X Windows on your Mac OS X system, you can take advantage of numerous tools that were specifically built to work on the system. X is a windowing system that works through the cooperation of separate components. The native windowing system on Mac OS X is called Aqua.

FULL SCREEN VERSUS ROOTLESS

The X Window System, often referred to simply as X Windows or X, can be run in one of two modes. The first is *full-screen* mode. In full-screen mode, the X window server takes over your desktop, replacing Aqua.

The second is called *rootless* mode. In rootless mode, the X windows live side by side with your Aqua tools rather than taking over the screen.

WHICH X IS WHICH?

There are several versions of X Windows that you can run on Mac OS X. *XDarwin* is a port of the XFree86 software and is free. You can also get an *X11* implementation from Apple that is also based on XFree86 and is a relative newcomer to the X scene. There is a commercial X

Window System implementation called *XTools* available from Tenon. All X servers perform the same function and support the X protocol. Given the significant efforts, installing an X server on your Mac OS X system should not be difficult.

SERVERS AND CLIENTS

In the world of X Windows, the terms server and client take on new meanings. The *X server* is your display — the screen in front of you that you can think of as serving you windows — and the environment in which your X applications run. The *X client* is any application that produces output for the server to display. Another important player in the world of X Windows is the *window manager*. A window manager, such as *twm* or *Enlightenment*, adds a layer of control to your desktop and stylistic elements to your windows. Desktops attempt to provide a more complete interface to the

system and generally provide a suite of integrated tools and applications.

Many Unix desktop environments support X Windows natively. This is true, for example, of the common desktop environment (CDE) run on Solaris, and GNOME and KDE on Linux systems. Aqua does not provide support for X Windows without add-on software such as XFree86 any more than Microsoft Windows does. For these systems, you may acquire and install X server software separately.

DESKTOPS

While you will probably install only one version of X Windows on your system, the choice of which window manager and *desktop* to use is up to you. Two of the more popular desktops are *GNOME* and *KDE*, both of which are popular with the Linux community and increasingly available for Mac OS X users. The *XonX* project, which refers to X Windows on Mac OS X, is a good source of information and software.

You also have a choice of what clients to run on your server. The xterm client is a terminal tool much like the Terminal application on your Mac OS X Aqua desktop, except that xterm runs on an Xserver. Similarly, xclock is an X Windows clock. While these tools are fairly basic and part of every X Windows implementation, they do not define the limits of what an installation of X Windows can do for you. Many powerful applications, such as OpenOffice, an office automation tool much like Microsoft Office, and the Gimp, a sophisticated image-editing tool, are available to you free if you first install X Windows.

HISTORY OF X WINDOWS

The X Windows System was originally developed at MIT with support from DEC. It was originally meant to provide a distributed hardware-independent user interface for the Athena project. The software reached version 11, sometimes referred to as X11, before a general interest had developed. Control of X11 has since been taken over by the X Consortium which now maintains the standard.

DISPLAY AND THE XHOSTS COMMAND

When using X Windows, your display has an address that is associated with the environment variable DISPLAY. If you print the value of this variable by typing **echo $DISPLAY** in a Terminal window while running an X server, you will notice that the value will be set to 0:0.0 or simply 0.0. While this address may seem to have no significance, it actually refers to the first screen associated with the first X server on your system. The address of your display from the perspective of another system on your network would be `ferro:0.0` if your hostname were ferro.

When you are generating a display on one system and sending it to another, you need to do two things:

1) Set your DISPLAY variable on the system where the client is running; this is the system generating the display.

2) Run the `xhost` command on the X server to give permission to the remote system to write to your screen.

The `xhost` command can be run in such a way that it only adds the specific client or so that it allows any system to write to its display. It is generally more secure to restrict access to your screen but this, of course, depends on your situation with respect to the security of the network to which you are connected.

To send the output from an X client system to the X server running on ferro, you would type **setenv DISPLAY ferro:0.0** on the client system and **xhost + on ferro** to allow any system to update your display. Enter a specific hostname instead of the plus sign (+) if you want to restrict this access.

GET X SOFTWARE FOR MAC OS X

F ree software for running X Windows is available on the Web. While downloading and installing this software takes a lot of time, the process is straightforward and you are unlikely to have any problems with the basic installation of X Windows.

Before you begin to download X Windows, you should determine which release is the latest. As of this writing, XFree86 is available in version 4.2.1.1 and the instructions in this chapter detail how to download the proper files and install this release on your Mac OS X system. If a newer release is available, you should install it instead. The process of obtaining the files and installing the software is not likely to change, but the exact names of the files will reflect the newer release.

To begin the process of installing XFree86 for your Mac OS X system, enter the URL http://sourceforge.net/projects/ xonx in your browser.

When you scroll down the page, you will find a section that provides information on the latest file releases. This will provide you with the current release information you need. When you click the View ALL Project Files link, you will see a list of the current files. The largest file in this list, the SIT file, will be the major release of XFree86. You will need to install this release before the ZIP files, which update the major release with patch files. When there are two or more for the same sub-release, as there are with 4.2.0.1, you will only need to install one of these files. You will install each of the patch releases in order. That is, you will install the oldest sub-release first. After installing the major release and each of the sub-releases, you will have 4.2.1.1 of XFree86 installed on your system.

GET X SOFTWARE FOR MAC OS X

1 In your browser window, type **http://sourceforge. net/projects/xonx** and press Return.

■ The Project: XonX: Summary page appears.

2 Scroll down the page until you find information on the latest file releases.

3 Click View ALL Project Files.

Extra

When downloading software such as XFree86 to your system for subsequent installation, it is good practice to store all of your downloaded files in a single directory. While file systems like that which Unix uses are meant to help keep your personal files and application software organized, it is easy to allow your file holdings to become disorganized and difficult to clean up sufficiently after the fact.

Some files, like the XFree86 XInstall_10.1.sit file are large and will take a long time to download on a dial-up connection. If you are installing this software on a personal system and using a dial-up line, you may want to consider starting late at night and checking in the morning to see if the download completed properly. The ZIP files needed to bring this release up to the current release are relatively small and do not take long to download.

The sourceforge.org site is a good site to bookmark. This site is one of the major places for learning about and obtaining open source software.

■ A list of project files appears.

4 Right-click XInstall_10.1.sit.

5 Click Download Link to Disk.

■ The Save dialog box appears.

6 Click the drop-down menu to select the location where you want to save the file.

7 Click Save.

■ The file saves to the location you chose in step 6.

CONTINUED

GET X SOFTWARE FOR MAC OS X (CONTINUED)

I f someone says the word "windows" in the context of computers, most people today immediately think of Microsoft Windows, but the original windowing systems predate Microsoft's products by many years. XFree86 is a direct descendant of the X11 Window System — the first windowing system used on Unix. X Windows was developed in the 1980s, originating as part of the Athena project at MIT and intended to provide a hardware-independent windowing environment. Today, X Windows runs on many types of systems and under many different names. Hummingbird's Exceed is an X Windows server for Intel-based systems. The CDE desktop environment used on Solaris and other Unix desktops is an X Windows environment. XFree86 is an implementation of X Windows that has more than 12 years of development behind it.

By the late 1980s, the X Consortium had taken control of X Windows development. With powerful members like Sun, Hewlett-Packard, AT&T, DEC, and IBM, the consortium

provided X Windows with a legitimacy that furthered its importance in the commercial world. At the same time, the XFree86 Project continued development of X for the open source community. The Open Group formed X.org in 1999 to continue fostering the development of X.

Today, XFree86 is one of the most critical of the open source projects. It provides X windowing support to a large portion of the open source Unix systems and ships with most Linux distributions. Currently in Release 4.2.1.1 and available for the latest Mac OS X release, XFree86 is a solid implementation of X Windows and one that will continue to develop along with the open source community.

The name XFree86 was first used in 1992, replacing the name X386 used in the preceding year of development.

GET X SOFTWARE FOR MAC OS X (CONTINUED)

8 Right-click the XFree86-4.2.0.1-10.2.zip file.

9 Click Download Link to Disk.

■ The Save dialog box appears.

10 Click the drop-down menu to select the location where you want to save the file.

11 Click Save.

■ The files save to the location you chose in step 10.

Extra

Getting XFree86 on CD-ROM

If the procedure for downloading XFree86 seems overly complex or time-consuming, you can obtain XFree86 on CD-ROM. For a modest fee, the same version of XFree86 that you can download from the Web is available on CD. Purchasing the CD will save you the trouble of downloading the proper set of files from the Web. Visit www.xdarwin.org for information on purchasing the CD and for other information on the XDarwin project.

XDarwin is the name of the X server for Mac OS X that is included in the XFree86 distribution. XonX is a SourceForge project used by XFree86 for Darwin developers to share code.

You can get all of the XFree86 source code from www.xfree86.org.

After your XFree86 software is installed, you start it by double-clicking the XDarwin icon. You will probably find that keeping XDarwin in the Dock is the most convenient way to use the software.

12 Right-click the XFree-86-4.2.1.1.zip file.

13 Click Download Link to Disk.

■ The Save dialog box appears.

14 Click the drop-down menu to select the location where you want to save the file.

15 Click Save.

■ The files save to the location you chose in step 14.

INSTALL AN X SERVER

You can install an X server on your Mac OS X system. After X Windows is installed, you can then run many applications built to run in X Windows.

To install XDarwin, the port of XFree86 to Mac OS X, you will need to download a series of files or procure an installation CD. As of this writing, you will need to install XFree86 4.2.0 followed by two patch releases — 4.2.0.1 and 4.2.1.1 — to get a trouble-free installation for Mac OS X 10.2. This gives you a basic X environment. You will probably then want to quickly move beyond the default window manager, twm, to one that provides a more attractive and useful desktop.

One of the simplest ways to install Xfree86 is to acquire the 4.2.0 release in the form of a SIT file from sourceforge.net. The URL sourceforge.net/projects/xonx where "xonx"

means X Windows on Mac OS X is the place to start. The XFree86 4.2.0 file is roughly 56 Mbytes in size, so be prepared for a long download time if you are using a dial-up connection. Check the XonX site for updates. Any X server that is more than six months old is likely to have new patches available or have moved to a new release.

After this file is downloaded, you can double-click the SIT file to install the initial X Windows server and then install each of your patch files in release order. The patch files are available as ZIP files. You can install these updates, or patches, by double-clicking the icons.

If you are working on a dial-up Internet connection, you might prefer to install XFree86 from a CD-ROM. You can acquire CDs at minimal cost from sites such as www.gnu-darwin.org.

INSTALL AN X SERVER

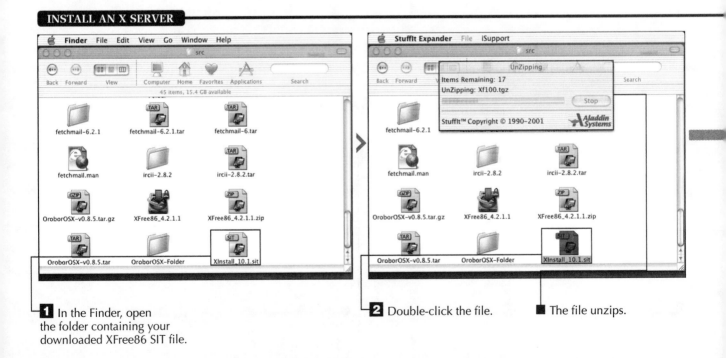

1 In the Finder, open the folder containing your downloaded XFree86 SIT file.

2 Double-click the file.

■ The file unzips.

Extra

While the procedure described below installs basic X Windows, keep in mind that the version of XFree86 that you should install will change as time passes. Consult the XonX site and amend the filenames and your procedure according to the information available on this site.

You can also install an X server using Apple's Get MacOS X Software... link from your Apple menu. Apple's X server is called X11 for Mac OS and, at this writing, is a Public Beta release. Apple's implementation of X Windows is also based on XFree86.

Files used in X Windows include .Xdefaults, which sets default preferences for windows services, and .xinitrc, which establishes your initial screen setup. A typical .xinitrc file might start several windows on your display. These will often include the more typical X clients, such as xterm — a terminal emulator; xlock — a simple analog clock; and xeyes — a pair of eyeballs that follow your cursor around the screen.

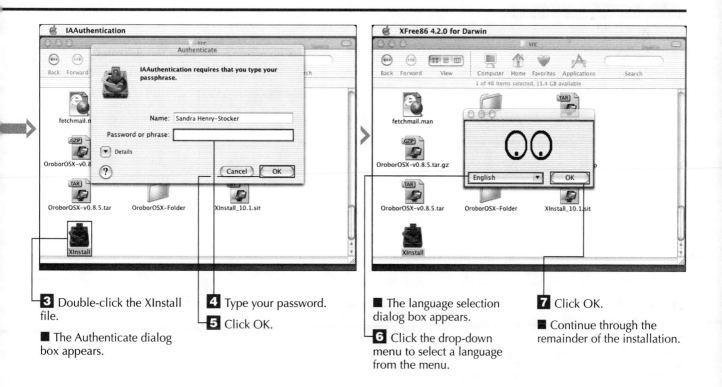

3 Double-click the XInstall file.

■ The Authenticate dialog box appears.

4 Type your password.

5 Click OK.

■ The language selection dialog box appears.

6 Click the drop-down menu to select a language from the menu.

7 Click OK.

■ Continue through the remainder of the installation.

INSTALL XFREE86 UPGRADES

You can install XFree86 upgrades to bring your XFree86 installation up to the current release from the base release. Upgrades will usually bring bug fixes and performance improvements and are generally worth the time that it takes to install them. Because the ZIP files containing the modified files are generally small, the process of downloading and installing them takes little time and little effort.

The upgrade installations complete the installation and assume that the two upgrade files have been downloaded as described in the "Get X Software for Mac OS X" section. While one specific upgrade is being installed in this section, this process is repeated for both of the upgrades downloaded in the previous section and for other upgrades that you may need to install in the future.

XFree86 upgrades are distributed as ZIP files. The easiest way to install one of these files is to double-click the icon in the Finder. This will unzip the file and create an install file. When you double-click the install file, your upgrade installation will begin.

As with most installations of this type, you will be required to authenticate yourself so that the system can verify that you are an administrator on the system and have the authority to install applications.

The process will then run through a couple of additional steps. You will have to select the disk on which the software is to be installed. You should select your Mac OS X system disk to simplify administration. Click Next to proceed with the installation and click Install before the software starts to load onto your drive. The installation can be restarted if needed. Whenever you install more than one upgrade, be sure to install them in the order in which they were created.

INSTALL XFREE86 UPGRADES

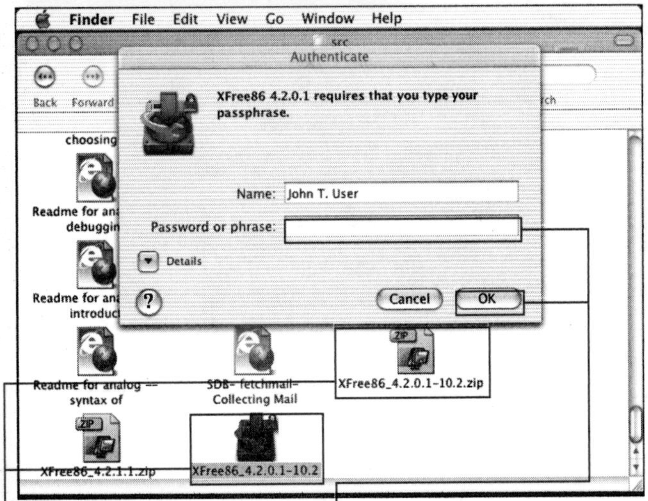

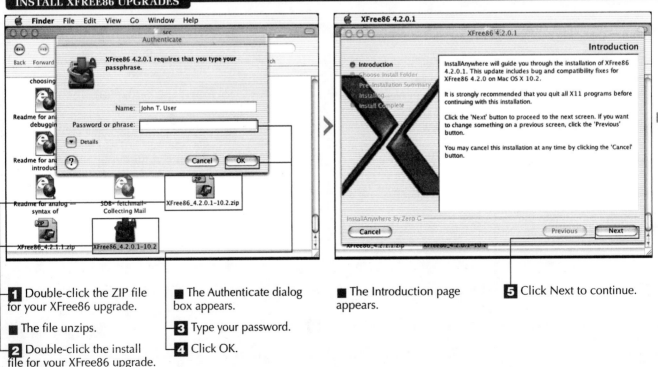

1 Double-click the ZIP file for your XFree86 upgrade.

■ The file unzips.

2 Double-click the install file for your XFree86 upgrade.

■ The Authenticate dialog box appears.

3 Type your password.

4 Click OK.

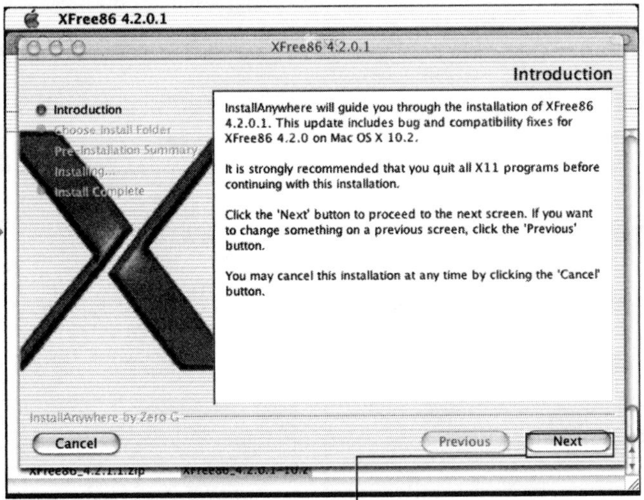

■ The Introduction page appears.

5 Click Next to continue.

Extra

After XFree86 is installed on your system and you have verified that it works properly, you can remove the ZIP and install files for the upgrades along with the SIT file for the major release. If you do not need the space, keeping these files available in case a re-install is needed is probably a good idea. There is little reason to keep these files after you install and verify a new major release, like XFree86 4.3.

While XFree86 is an extremely useful tool and enables you to run many applications previously not available on Mac OS X, the look and feel of your X environment depends on the window manager that you decide to use. For most X users, installing XFree86 is just the beginning of setting up a versatile X Windows environment.

If you need help with XDarwin, you can take advantage of the discussion forum on the www.xdarwin.org site. You can also look for in-depth information on technical issues at the SourceForge/projects/XonX site. The XonX site provides a public discussion forum as well as several mailing lists that are devoted to such topics as porting Unix software to Mac OS X.

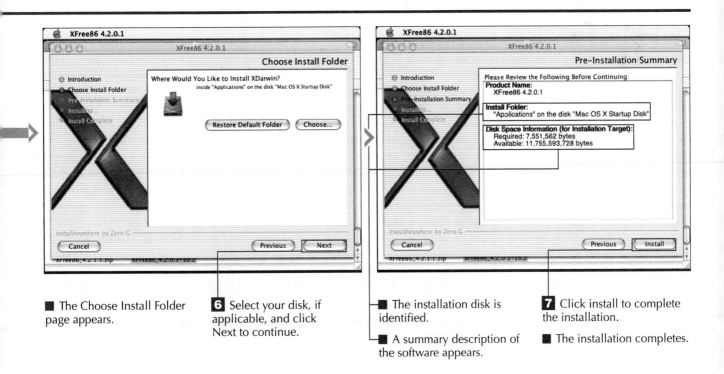

■ The Choose Install Folder page appears.

6 Select your disk, if applicable, and click Next to continue.

■ The installation disk is identified.

■ A summary description of the software appears.

7 Click install to complete the installation.

■ The installation completes.

START XFREE86 IN ROOTLESS MODE

You can start up your X Windows server in rootless mode. This allows you to run X applications side-by-side with Mac OS X applications.

Each time you start XDarwin, the system will ask whether you want to run in full-screen or rootless mode. If you will always be running in one mode or the other, you can select your mode and click the check box so that the application stops asking you this question. Both modes have their advantages, however.

To start in rootless mode, click the Rootless button after double-clicking the icon for your XFree86 application or after starting it from the Dock. The X Windows that launch when you do this depend on the contents of your system's .xinitrc file or on your personal .xinitrc file if you have one. For example, the following lines from an .xinitrc file would start up several xterm windows and a clock:

```
xclock -geometry 50x50-1+1 &
xterm -geometry 80x50+0+0 &
xterm -geometry 80x20+400-0 &
exec xterm -geometry 80x66+0+0 -name login
```

You will notice these windows when you start your X session. The numbers associated with the xterm command define the number of columns, the number of rows, and the screen location. For example, the first xterm defined in the lines above will have 80 columns and 50 rows; 80 columns wide is equivalent to the width of 80 mono-spaced characters side-by-side. Its upper-left corner will be placed in the upper-left corner of the screen.

The most convenient way to start X Windows is to elect to keep it in the Dock after you first bring it up. You can then customize the windows that start by making a copy of the system-wide .xinitrc file and installing that copy as .xinitrc in your home directory.

When you first install XFree86, you will be using the default window manager. It is called *twm* and, while it adds some window controls to your windows, it is a dull window manager.

START X86FREE IN ROOTLESS MODE

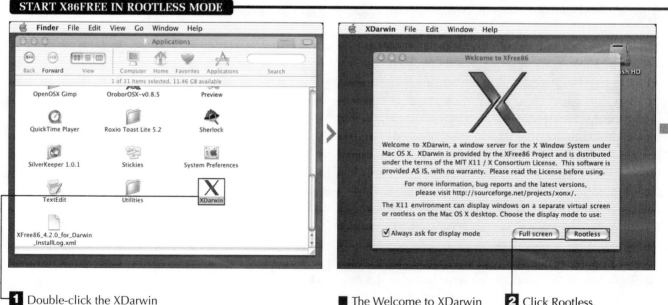

1 Double-click the XDarwin application icon.

■ The Welcome to XDarwin window appears.

2 Click Rootless.

Extra

You can update your search path to include X Windows tools. This will allow you to start X tools by entering their names without a full pathname. X tools will usually install in the directory /usr/X11R6/bin. By including this path in your PATH variable, you instruct your shell to look in that directory when you enter a simple name such as xeyes.

Your search path, defined in your .tcshrc file, will look something like this:

Example:
```
setenv PATH /usr/bin:/bin:/sbin:/
sw/bin:/usr/local/bin:/usr/X11R6/bin
```

You can change the colors used on a xterm window by modifying the parameters used in your .xinitrc file. The command "xterm -n xterm-blahblahblah -bg black -fg white -geometry 80x25+0+0 &", for example, generates a window named "xterm-blahblahblah" with a black background and white letters. The Terminal window would be 80 columns wide (standard width) and 25 lines long beginning in the upper-left corner of the screen.

■ X clients launch on your Aqua desktop, displaying three screens by default.

3 Type **xeyes** in an xterm window and press Return.

■ The xeyes tool opens on your desktop.

RUN THE GNOME DESKTOP

You can install the GNOME desktop on your Mac OS X system if you have first installed an X server such as XFree86.

GNOME is one of the most popular X Window System desktops. Developed for the Linux community, GNOME now runs on Solaris and Mac OS X systems as well. Because this porting effort is recent, installing Gnome can be a slow and somewhat problematic installation – especially on a slow dial-up connection. You can also acquire binaries on CD-ROM. The following sites provide information on X Windows for Mac OS X.

```
http://sourceforge.net/projects/xonx
http://www.xdarwin.org
```

After GNOME is installed on your system, you can use it as your X Windows desktop. To use GNOME, you should edit your .xinitrc file and add the line `exec gnome-session` to the bottom of the file. Be sure to comment out the line that starts the default window manager, twm. The bottom of your .xinitrc file, after editing, might look like this:

```
gnome-wm &
exec gnome-session
```

The next time you start X Windows after making these changes, your desktop will start running with GNOME. As with XFree86 out of the box, you can run GNOME in rootless or full-screen mode. When you run rootless, your X Windows will take on the appearance of GNOME windows, using the GNOME window dressings. The rest of your windows will retain their Aqua look. You will be able to start additional X tools from your xterm windows. For example, you can start the xeyes tool by typing **/usr/X11R6/bin/xeyes** in an xterm window and pressing Return.

When you start GNOME in full screen mode, as is generally the case, GNOME will take over your desktop. All vestiges of your Aqua tools and menus will disappear from view. GNOME menus will be available on your desktop for starting any of a number of X applications.

RUN THE GNOME DESKTOP

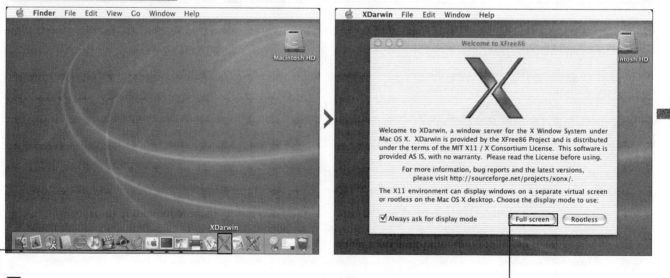

1 Click XDarwin in the Dock.

■ The XDarwin welcome screen appears.

2 Click Full screen.

Extra

Many of the applications available through the GNOME desktop are traditional X tools such as `xterm`, a terminal emulator, and `xcalc`, a simple calculator. Other applications, such as `xv` and the GIMP are quite sophisticated tools for manipulating images.

GNOME supports the concept of virtual desktops. The small object in the bottom left hand corner of the screen represents each of four virtual desktops. You can move from one desktop to the next by clicking any of the four rectangles. The upper left rectangle represents your default screen. If you do not like working with a cluttered desktop, you can start different applications on each of the four virtual desktops and move from one to the other as needed.

To exit the GNOME desktop, click Desktop ⇨ Log Out.

You can also start other X applications, those not included in the GNOME menus but installed on your system, by typing their names in an xterm window.

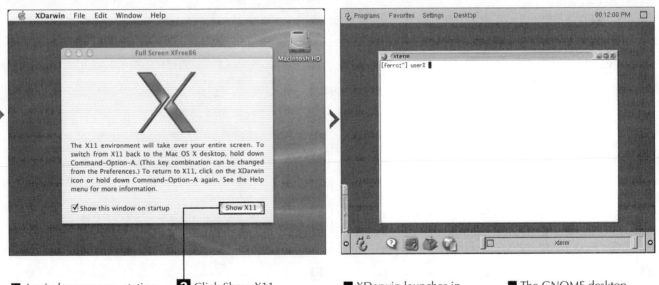

■ A window appears, stating that full-screen mode will take over your screen, and telling you how to return to the Mac OS X desktop.

3 Click Show X11.

■ XDarwin launches in full-screen mode.

■ The GNOME desktop appears.

EXPLORE GNOME APPLICATIONS

You can take advantage of an impressive collection of useful tools and applications when you run the GNOME desktop.

The GNOME desktop includes a number of utilities and applications that are built into the desktop. That is, you can start up these tools by selecting them from the menus available to you on your GNOME desktop. Some of these tools are simple applications that can make your system a little nicer to use. Others will make a tremendous difference in what you are able to accomplish on your system.

The GNOME Programs menu contains a number of sub-menus, each with a variety of tools. The Applications menu includes tools such as emacs — a highly configurable editor, and *Gnumeric* — a spreadsheet program. The Utilities menu provides access to a simple calculator, a color browser, and other tools. The graphics menu provides access to *GNOME Ghostview*, a tool for viewing PostScript files; the GIMP, an

image editing program; and *xv*, a program for viewing and modifying image files. Each of these tools can be an extremely useful addition to your desktop.

The look of your GNOME desktop will vary quite a bit depending on the window manager that you decide to use. Several are available to you and others can be obtained. Enlightenment and Window Maker are used in screenshots in this book. These two window managers have extremely different appearances, but will, of course, run the same applications. The third choice, twm, is also available. To alter your window manager, click Settings ➪ Desktop ➪ Window Manager. When you change your window manager, you will have an opportunity to save your new settings.

Xterm windows are similar in character and to Terminal windows; therefore, you should be able to use these windows in the same manner that you would use the Terminal application when you are running in Aqua.

EXPLORE GNOME APPLICATIONS

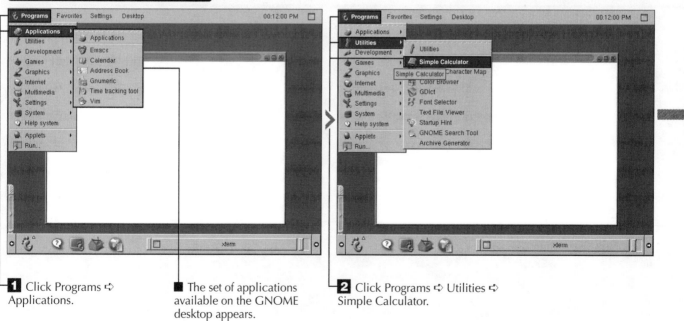

1 Click Programs ➪ Applications.

■ The set of applications available on the GNOME desktop appears.

2 Click Programs ➪ Utilities ➪ Simple Calculator.

Extra

If your GNOME desktop opens without the panels at the top and bottom of the screen, type **panel –no-xshm** in an xterm window.

Clicking the globe in the bottom panel will open Mozilla, the Web browser. With this tool, you can browse the Web the same as you would using Internet Explorer or Safari on your Mac OS X desktop.

You can make the bottom panel slide over to the edge of your screen by clicking either end where the small arrow is displayed.

The Window Maker window manager gives your GNOME desktop an entirely different look and feel. If you selected this desktop by clicking Settings ⇨ Desktop ⇨ Window Manager, your desktop will change character. You can start up additional virtual desktops or workspaces by right-clicking in the background and clicking Workspaces ⇨ New. You will then be able to navigate between these workspaces by clicking the backward and forward buttons on the icon in the upper-left corner of your screen.

Within each workspace, you can then start different tools as if you had a number of work surfaces for working on different projects.

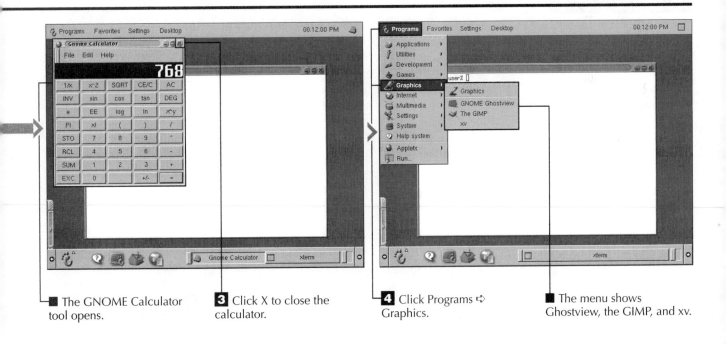

■ The GNOME Calculator tool opens.

3 Click X to close the calculator.

4 Click Programs ⇨ Graphics.

■ The menu shows Ghostview, the GIMP, and xv.

INSTALL OROBOROSX

You can install the OroborOSX desktop to take advantage of X tools on your Aqua desktop. OroborOSX allows you to run X applications while maintaining the look and feel of your normal Mac OS X desktop.

The OroborOSX window manager actually provides several graphical themes. One of these mimics the look of your Aqua desktop and gives your Mac OS X and your X applications a seamless appearance. OroborOSX also provides a drop-down menu of applications that can be launched from your desktop when you are running OroborOSX. This menu appears at the top of your OroborOSX screen and is titled Launch. One of these tools is the GIMP, the impressive open source image-editing tool that rivals the capabilities of PhotoShop.

Installing OroborOSX is a smooth process after XFree86 has been installed. The OroborOSX application can be retrieved from any of several places – http://oroborosx.sourceforge. net/download.html and both binary and source distributions

are available. This section outlines the process of installing the binary file, which is downloaded as a gzipped TAR file. When you double-click this file, you will walk through the installation process. OroborOSX will be installed in a matter of minutes and will be ready for use.

You might want to keep OroborOSX in the Dock to facilitate its use. You will then be able to start X applications by first clicking on OroborOSX in the Dock and then starting your X application through the Launch menu or by entering the pathnames for the binaries in an xterm window. When you launch OrorborOSX, it will in turn launch XDarwin.

OroborOSX is a good choice for anyone who wants to work in their normal Mac OS X desktop while adding some applications that only run in X Windows. Installation is trouble-free and extremely quick.

INSTALL OROBOROSX

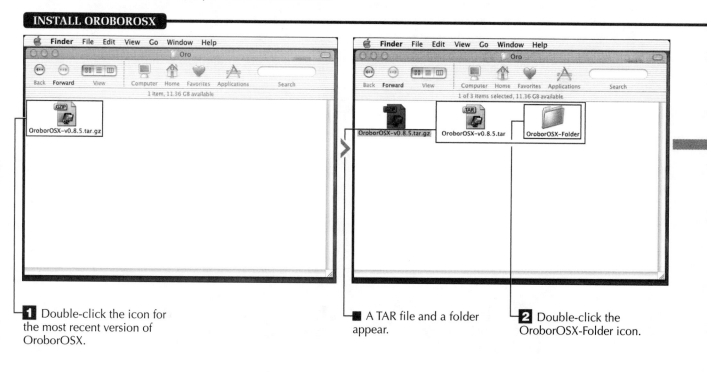

1 Double-click the icon for the most recent version of OroborOSX.

■ A TAR file and a folder appear.

2 Double-click the OroborOSX-Folder icon.

Extra

After OroborOSX is started, you can keep it in the Dock to make it easier to start when you want to use it again. Because OroborOSX works so well with your Mac OS X desktop, you may sometimes forget that you are running X Windows simultaneously with your Mac desktop.

If you would like your inactive windows to appear dimmed, you can accomplish this by clicking Options ➪ Dim Inactive Windows.

OroborOSX does not make use of your .xinitrc file. However, you can get it to read and execute the commands in this file if you click Launch ➪ xinitrc.

When you are running OroborOSX, all of the windows that you have open will be listed at the bottom of your Windows menu. To move from one to the next, you can click the window of your choice as you would normally do, or you can choose the window that you want to make active by clicking Windows and the name of the window that you want to make active.

OroborOSX is an Aqua-like window manager based on a window manager named Oroborus.

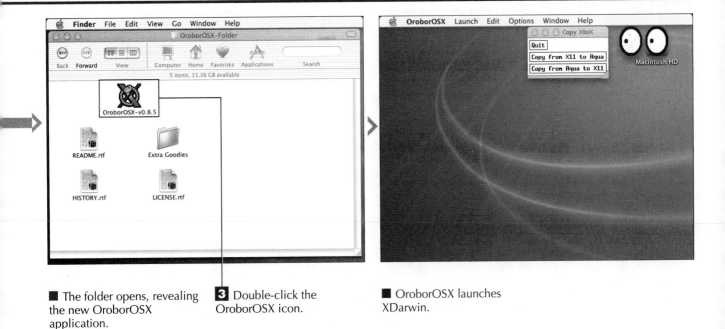

■ The folder opens, revealing the new OroborOSX application.

3 Double-click the OroborOSX icon.

■ OroborOSX launches XDarwin.

VIEW IMAGES WITH XV

Y ou can use xv, an interactive image manipulation program for X Windows, to display, crop, stretch, and dither images of many different types. To start xv, type xv in an xterm window. If you are using GNOME, you will find the program in the Graphics menu. A colorful fish-out-of-the-water banner will greet you. Near the bottom of the page, you will see the message Press <right> mouse button for menu. To view the control panel for xv, press Control + click.

To load an image, click the Load button. This will open a file browse window that allows you to select the image that you want to load. The image will load on your screen after you

click OK. You can use the options under the Image Size button to control the size of the image on your screen. The algorithms included in the Algorithms menu include a number of image manipulation routines that you can apply to the image. These include blur, sharpen, edge detect, emboss, oil painting, and copy and clear that rotate the image with and without blanking out the corners, pixelize, spread, and despeckle. For dabblers, there is also an Undo All option that reverses any changes you have made, bringing you back to the original image. xv operates on GIF, JPEG, TIFF, PBM, PGM, XPM, X11 Bitmap, Sun rasterfile, Targa, RLE, RGB, BMP, PCX, FITS, and PM image files. It can also generate postscript.

VIEW IMAGES WITH XV

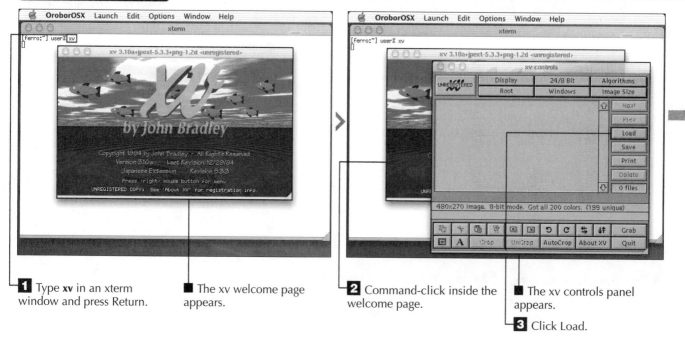

1 Type **xv** in an xterm window and press Return.

■ The xv welcome page appears.

2 Command-click inside the welcome page.

■ The xv controls panel appears.

3 Click Load.

Extra

The program can be downloaded from www.trilon.com/xv/downloads.html in source form and is included in binary format in the Darwin Collection: Free Software for Darwin OS and Mac OS X CD set for those who don't want to compile their own code. The program is available in binary form on the trilon site, but not for Mac OS X. Manuals are available in PostScript, PDF, and HTML format.

You can close the xv controls panel any time you like. To get it back again, press ⌘ + click in the displayed image.

After you have modified an image, you can save it using the Save button. The Format menu in the upper-right corner allows you to select the format for your saved image and, depending on the image type you select, asks if you want to use compression.

You can load a number of images and flip through them using the Next and Prev buttons.

You can crop an image by first selecting the area you want to retain using your left mouse button and then pressing Crop in the xv controls.

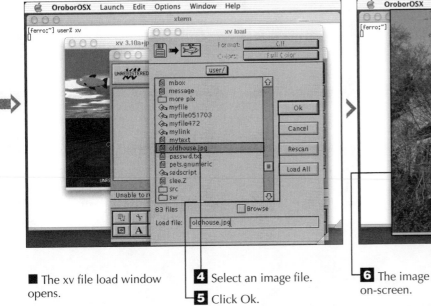

■ The xv file load window opens.

4 Select an image file.

5 Click Ok.

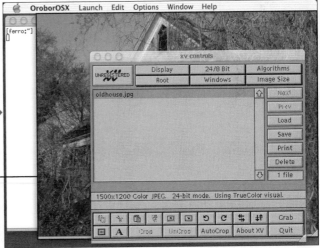

6 The image file displays on-screen.

EDIT IMAGES WITH GIMP

You can use the GIMP to manipulate photo quality images. The GIMP, which stands for GNU Image Manipulation Program, is a freely distributed software tool that allows you to retouch photos and compose interesting images using a massive set of features. The tool is available from www.gimp.org/download.html and is often loaded when you install an X desktop, such as GNOME. GIMP is also included on the CD that accompanies this book.

In an X windowing environment such as OroborOSX or GNOME, you can launch the GIMP through a menu. To launch the GIMP in OroborOSX, you click Launch ➪ MacGimp.

Unlike most of the tools that you will use in X Windows, the GIMP opens a number of windows on your desktop. The toolbox provides the main controls by offering a grid of icons, each of which represents a different function, such as selecting a portion of the image, zooming in or out, and painting on top of the image with brush strokes.

The toolbox also contains the File menu that provides for opening and saving images. It also allows you to modify preferences, such as the default image size and resolution, that apply each time you use GIMP. The toolbox is like a toolbar that lies along the top of most applications. Because it is a separate window, you can open and close it as needed.

For serious image work, you will probably find layers essential. The best way to think of layers is to picture your image as composed of a number of transparencies, each which contributes a portion of the overall image, and yourself as looking through all of them at once. As you work with your images, the layers that you create will display in the Layers, Channels & Paths window that opened when you first started the GIMP. The active layer will always appear highlighted.

EDIT IMAGES WITH GIMP

1 Click Launch ➪ MacGimp in OroborOSX.

■ The GIMP window appears on your screen.

2 Click File ➪ Open from the GIMP menu.

Extra

You can delete a layer by pressing and holding down the right mouse button in the Layers, Channels & Paths window and sliding down to Delete Layer. The ability to delete a layer is one of the best reasons to work with layers in the first place. They allow you to easily remove elements that you add to an image if they do not look as you had intended.

If you have many layers, you can switch between them, determining which layer you are editing at any point in time, by selecting the layer in the Layers, Channels & Paths window. When you are completely satisfied with the overall image that you have created, you can collapse your image into a single layer. After performing this step, you cannot manipulate layers separately.

To save an image, press ⌘ + click within the image window and click File ➪ Save As from the pop-up menu. If you want to save an image in the original format, you can leave the option for Determine File Type by Extension as is and type in your new filename. GIMP's format is called XCF.

If your image has layers, you will have to collapse the layers using the Layers ➪ Flatten Image option or export the image to save it in a format that does not support image layers. You can preserve the layers by using GIMP's xcf format.

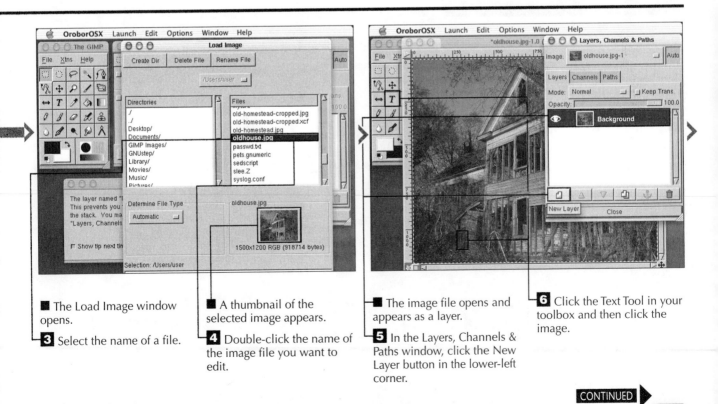

■ The Load Image window opens.

3 Select the name of a file.

■ A thumbnail of the selected image appears.

4 Double-click the name of the image file you want to edit.

■ The image file opens and appears as a layer.

5 In the Layers, Channels & Paths window, click the New Layer button in the lower-left corner.

6 Click the Text Tool in your toolbox and then click the image.

CONTINUED ▶

EDIT IMAGES WITH GIMP (CONTINUED)

You can apply many transformations to your images by pressing ⌘ + click within an image and selecting from the menu. For example, if you click Filters ⇨ Glass Effects ⇨ Apply Lens, your image will appear distorted as if you were looking through a (convex) lens. The filter effects also include edge detection, *colorification* options, and various other distortions that you can apply to get the effect that you want. Unless you are a full time graphics professional, it is likely that you will never use most of the tools available in the GIMP. Experimenting with the various options, on the other hand, is bound to be good entertainment on some otherwise uneventful day and is probably the only way to fully understand what this tool can do for you.

There is also an option to revert to the original image. This is available through File ⇨ Revert. This is useful if you apply a transformation and do not like the way it looks. Many

people who use GIMP make a habit of preserving their original images and saving their modified images using different names so that they can always start over.

To crop an image, select the crop tool from the toolbox. The icon resembles a craft knife. Then left-click within the image window. When you click twice, you should notice two sets of corners appear like the diagonal corners of a box that move independently. The space between these corners, or elbows, defines the portion of the image that will remain after you click the Crop button.

While you might find quite a bit of information on using the GIMP on the Web — because this is a very popular tool — using the tool is the best way to unveil all of the manipulations that are possible and which of them is going to work best with your own graphical style.

EDIT IMAGES WITH GIMP (CONTINUED)

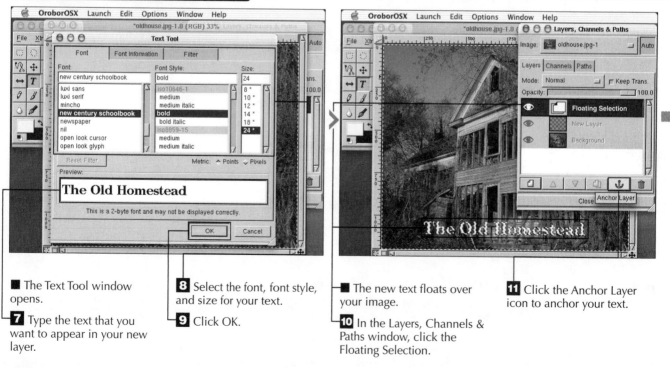

■ The Text Tool window opens.

7 Type the text that you want to appear in your new layer.

8 Select the font, font style, and size for your text.

9 Click OK.

■ The new text floats over your image.

10 In the Layers, Channels & Paths window, click the Floating Selection.

11 Click the Anchor Layer icon to anchor your text.

Extra

The 5 x 5 element toolbox allows you to easily access the tools available for use within the GIMP. Pausing your cursor over any of the icons will cause a brief description to appear.

The magnifying glass tool allows you to quickly zoom in on an image so that you can see more detail and have a finer degree of control over your work. To zoom back out, double-click the magnifying glass and click Zoom out in the Tool Options. Then click the image again. The effect of the magnifying glass will then cause you to zoom out. You can toggle between zooming in and zooming out as needed.

If you want to draw on top of an image, you can use the pencil tool. The Tool Options window for this tool allows you to modify the opacity of your pencil stroke and to select a color for your pencil strokes.

The icon in the middle of the toolbox that looks like an eyedropper allows you to pick colors from your image. This allows you to work with colors that match the colors in your image instead of trying to match the colors by selecting them from a palette.

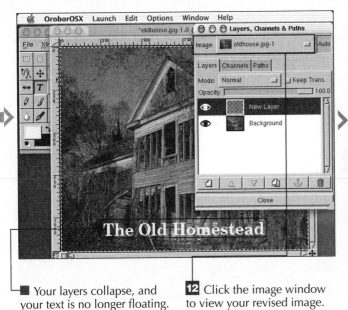

■ Your layers collapse, and your text is no longer floating.

12 Click the image window to view your revised image.

■ Your image appears full-screen with the text anchored in place.

WORD PROCESSING WITH ABIWORD

You can display and edit Word documents with AbiWord. AbiWord is an intuitive word processing application with the same basic features as Microsoft Word. You start AbiWord when you are running an X Windows server by typing **abiword** in an xterm window. The tool will open up on your screen, allowing you to begin entering the text of your document. You can also open a pre-existing Word file.

You use the AbiWord program in the same way as you would use other GUI word processors such as MS Word or Corel Word Perfect. If you trained on older, keyboard-oriented word processing systems, you must get used to clicking on icons to make things happen. For example, formatting a page for right or left justification of text requires an easy click near the upper-right corner of the screen where pictograms display your choices.

Other icons may be less obvious but clicking on any of them will usually bring up a menu with a logical suite of choices. For instance, if you want to save your work, you click File in the top menu bar and see a menu with Save and Save As choices along with open and print options. Moving your cursor over the diskette icon causes the description to appear — Save the document. If you select the diskette with a pencil pointing at it instead, you can rename the document.

To concentrate on writing, you can easily remove most of the clutter of your AbiWord menus by clicking on View and then checking the Full screen box; only the menu at the top of the screen will then remain along with your text. You can manipulate tabs and margins with menus, or adjust their bars and pointers along the edges of the screen, as though you were using a real typewriter.

As with any program, the fastest way to do something may be revealed only after some experimentation with different menus and patterns of keystrokes that suit your style of typing. If you are an experienced wordsmith, you can use these tricks intuitively in AbiWord and save a bundle of money by not purchasing expensive commercial products.

WORD PROCESSING WITH ABIWORD

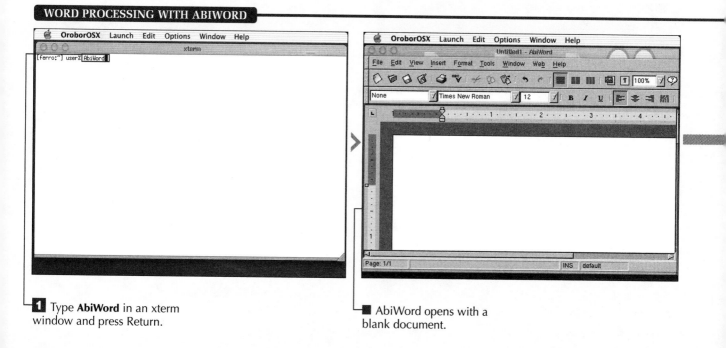

1 Type **AbiWord** in an xterm window and press Return.

■ AbiWord opens with a blank document.

Extra

If you are writing a newsletter or other publication, you can choose one, two, or three columns to suit the style of your publication.

You can find documentation for AbiWord, including an overview and a tutorial, at www.abisource.com/help. If you have any questions about quirks in the program, contact the authors at AbiSource.com. As with other open source products, news about problems experienced can be sent upstream to the community and tips and tricks can be downloaded from other users via discussion groups or FAQ pages.

AbiWord enables you to import images into your document by using the icon that looks like a landscape snapshot. It is probably wise to begin a document with this step and then write around the image.

You can open Microsoft Word files, identified by their .doc file extensions, directly in AbiWord and then edit and save the files in the Rich Text Format.

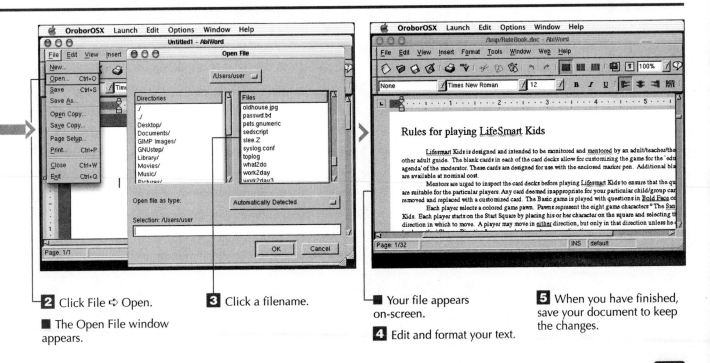

2 Click File ▷ Open.

■ The Open File window appears.

3 Click a filename.

■ Your file appears on-screen.

4 Edit and format your text.

5 When you have finished, save your document to keep the changes.

CREATE SPREADSHEETS IN GNUMERIC

You can use Gnumeric for simple calculations to complex numerical analysis. Gnumeric is a free spreadsheet released under the GNU General Public License. It has all the features that you would expect in a quality spreadsheet application, including a built-in manual, support for graphs, an extensive range of functions, cell formatting, and printing. It also has a powerful set of import and export filters that allow it to work with Excel, Lotus 1-2-3, Sylk and other spreadsheet formats. Graphic support, however, requires that you also have Guppi installed.

To start Gnumeric, you can type **Gnumeric** in an xterm window. The tool will open with an empty spreadsheet. Entering data is as simple as clicking in a cell and typing text or a number. To enter a formula, you start by typing = and then you enter the formula, such as cos(100) or sum(A2:A20)

where A2:A20 defines a range of cells. If you are not used to spreadsheets, you will have to get accustomed to this nomenclature. The columns in a spreadsheet are labeled A, B, C, and so on while the rows are numbered 1, 2, 3, and so on. A2 is the cell defined by the second row in the first column.

You can also select data by holding down your left mouse button and sliding over it. This often simplifies the process. Gnumeric, like most modern spreadsheets, will allow you to copy and paste a formula, adjusting the cell addresses in the process. If you sum A2:A20 and then copy your formula from A21 to B21, the new formula will sum B2:B20. If you are familiar with any spreadsheet application, you will probably be perfectly at home using Gnumeric.

CREATE SPREADSHEETS IN GNUMERIC

1 Type **gnumeric** in an xterm window and press Return.

■ Gnumeric opens with a blank spreadsheet.

2 Type **=sqrt(64)** in a cell and press Return.

■ The answer appears in your cell, and the formula displays in the toolbar field.

Extra

You can turn a number in a cell into a percentage simply by clicking the percentage sign in the toolbar after clicking on the particular cell. This speeds up the process of modifying the format of your numbers, but uses the default format with two decimal points. Similarly, you can convert a number to display in monetary format by clicking the symbol that looks like a stack of dollar bills.

You can use the green and red arrow keys near the upper-right corner of the spreadsheet to sort a series of cells in alphabetic or reverse alphabetic order. Simply select the cells that you want to sort and click the arrow representing the sort order of your choice.

The undo operation is available both as Edit ⇨ Undo and through use of the curved arrow in the toolbar. Anytime you make a mistake, you can quickly reverse your most recent operation.

You can add arrows and other annotations to your spreadsheet by selecting these tools from your toolbar.

Icons in the toolbar allow you to change the justification of data in cells to right, left, or center justified.

Click Help ⇨ Gnumeric Manual to open a very handy user's guide.

3 Type some numbers in several cells in the same column.

4 Type =**sum(** in the cell below.

5 Select the numbers in the cells with your mouse.

6 Type) and press Return.

■ The spreadsheet calculates your total.

VIEW OFFICE DOCUMENTS WITH OPEN OFFICE

Y ou can use Open Office to create documents, spreadsheets, illustrations, and presentations. You can also open documents that were created by other applications, such as Microsoft Office. Open Office is a suite of office applications that includes a word processor, spreadsheet, drawing program, presentation package, data source editor, HTML editor, formula editor, and macro and scripting language. Each tool is a professional and full-featured office automation tool that has years of development behind it from talented volunteers from around the world. Completely free, Open Office is based on code from StarOffice and 15 years of development by Sun Microsystems. It runs on Sparc systems as well as Windows and Linux and, as of this writing, is in the final stages of development for Mac OS X.

To use Open Office, you need to first install X Windows. The word processor that is included in the Open Office suite is called Writer. You can use it to read, write, and

modify Microsoft Word documents. Open Office comes with spell check, clip art, and many of the same formatting features that you would expect in other professional word processing applications.

When you start Open Office from the Dock or by double-clicking on its icon in the Finder, the tool opens with Writer. From this application, you start the other applications as well. For example, File ➪ New ➪ Spreadsheet launches the spreadsheet application. Open Office will start XDarwin if it is not already running.

Most of the items in the toolbar along the top and down the left side of the Writer's window will look familiar to you if you have used Microsoft Word or another word processor. If you are unsure of the meaning of any of the icons, position and hold your cursor over them and a short description appears.

VIEW OFFICE DOCUMENTS WITH OPEN OFFICE

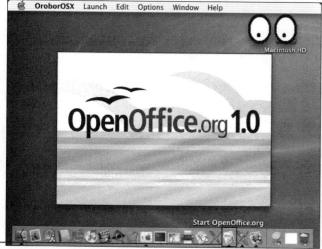

1 Click the Open Office icon in the Dock.

■ Writer opens with an empty document.

2 Click File ➪ Open.

Extra

To view nonprinting characters, click View ⇨ Nonprinting characters or press Control + F10. If you press Control + F10 several times in a row, you will notice how the nonprinting characters toggle on and off.

Depending on the type of document you are creating, autocorrection can be a blessing or an annoyance. Tools ⇨ AutoCorrect/AutoFormat . . . allows you to control the extent to which autoformatting and autocorrection are used in your documents.

You can save documents created in Writer in many formats, such as OpenOffice text or template, Word 6.0, 95, or 97/2000/XP, StarWriter, Rich Text Format, and HTML.

You can turn the spell checker on and off by clicking the symbol that contains the letters ABC with a wavy line underneath. You can choose to see your spelling mistakes as you type or spell check later.

You can insert tables by clicking Insert Table . . . or by clicking on the table icon near the top of the left window border.

You can easily number the lines in your document and have control over the frequency with which lines are numbered. For example, you can number every fifth or tenth line in a document. Line numbering is selected through Tools ⇨ Line Numbering.

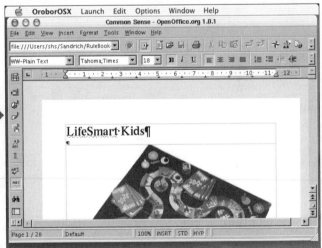

■ A file browser opens.

3 Select the document you want to open.

4 Click Open.

■ The document appears on-screen.

CREATE SPREADSHEETS WITH OPEN OFFICE

You can create spreadsheets using Open Office or import spreadsheets created by other popular spreadsheet applications. The spreadsheet that is included with Open Office is called Calc and, like Gnumeric, is likely to be familiar and, thus, easy to use if you have used any spreadsheet application. The labeling of the rows and columns and the symbols in the toolbars are generally self-explanatory and, if you pause over them with your cursor, a short description will appear to explain their functions.

To start Calc, click File ➪ New ➪ Spreadsheet from Writer. This will open an empty spreadsheet in another window on your screen.

Clicking the Help button will bring up a useful guide on how to use Calc along with a panel in which you can enter or browse search terms, look through the contents of the Open Office documentation or create and use bookmarks.

As with other spreadsheets, you can enter data or formulas in cells and can copy and paste these items to avoid having to enter the same data more than once.

Calc also includes graphing. If you select data and click the Insert Object icon, a short series of forms for creating a number of graphs, such as pie charts and scatter diagrams, will appear.

Insert ➪ Graphics lets you import images into your spreadsheets.

Like Gnumeric, Calc has one-click options for transforming the format of a cell to a percentage or monetary figure.

Edit ➪ Repeat:Attributes is a very useful function that allows you to repeat changes that you make in one cell to others. If you change one cell to bold and then use this function, the new cell or group of cells will also take on the changed attribute.

CREATE SPREADSHEETS WITH OPEN OFFICE

1 In the Writer window, click File ➪ New ➪ Spreadsheet.

■ Calc opens with a blank spreadsheet.

2 Enter some text and numbers into your spreadsheet.

3 Select your cells.

4 Click the Insert Object button.

Extra

Spreadsheets created in Calc can be stored in Open Office format or you can choose from other formats which include several versions of MicrosoftExcel, StarCalc, Data Interchange Format, dBASE, and SYLK.

You can also create HTML documents in Open Office by clicking File ⇨ New ⇨ HTML Document. This tool will allow you to enter text and will provide the HTML code. You can insert links and create tables using options from the Insert menu. While you work with the context of the page, the HTML code is being constructed for you.

You can create a slide presentation by clicking File ⇨ New ⇨ Presentation from Writer or from Calc. The presentation package is called Impress and is a multimedia presentation tool that includes clip art, animation, and high-quality drawing tools. When you start Impress, you will complete a series of forms in which you make selections for your presentation — such as whether to use wipes of some type as your slide show moves from one slide to the next. Impress simplifies preparation of a presentation and includes many features for creating a dynamic slide show.

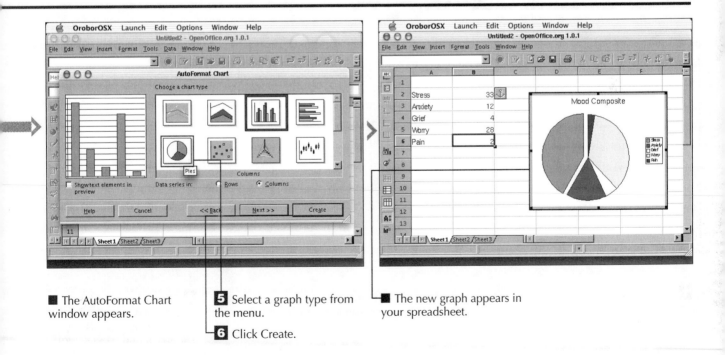

■ The AutoFormat Chart window appears.

5 Select a graph type from the menu.

6 Click Create.

■ The new graph appears in your spreadsheet.

DEVELOP C AND C++ APPLICATIONS

Y ou can develop applications in C and C++ on your Mac OS X system. Developing applications in C or related languages, such as C++, depends largely on your ability as a programmer, although the Mac OS X environment offers excellent support for your development efforts. The gcc compiler that accompanies the Mac OS X developer tools is the default compiler for C, C++, Objective-C, and Objective-C++.

Before you begin working in any of the programming languages available on Mac OS X, you should update your MANPATH to include /usr/share/man. This ensures that the man pages for the developer tools are available to you. If you type the line **setenv MANPATH /sw/share/man:/usr/local/man:/usr/share/man** into your .tcshrc file, these and other pages appear when you use the `man` command.

You should use the text editor to create your source code. Many developers prefer emacs because they can configure

them to properly indent source code. However, you should use the text editor that allows you to work most effectively.

After typing your source code, you can compile it using gcc, or you can use the `make` command, which manages the compilation process. The `make` command only compiles a program if the associated binary code is older than the source code. In other words, it only recompiles your program if you have changed the source code. If your application consists of multiple source files, you must create a Makefile to describe the relationship between those files. `make` calls gcc to compile C programs.

`make` works with many different programming languages, although it is most often used with C. In fact, `make` is not limited to compiling software. You can read the make man page to learn about this versatile command.

DEVELOP C AND C++ APPLICATIONS

1 Type **vi hello.c** and press Return.

2 Press I and type **#include <stdio.h>**, then press Return twice.

■ The `include` command adds the standard IO header file to your program.

3 Type **main () {** and press Return, then press the Tab key and type **printf("Hello, World\n");** and press Return again.

4 Type **}** and press Esc, then type **:wq**.

■ vi saves your source code.

Extra

Whenever you develop an application using multiple source files, you can build a Makefile to define the dependency relationships between files. If you have ever installed any applications from source code, you have probably used a Makefile to orchestrate the compilation process.

With a simple program like hello.c, a Makefile is unnecessary. However, when you are compiling tools such as fetchmail, the Makefile ensures that you compile all of the proper files and that you create the final executable fetchmail. You can also write Makefiles to include installation and cleanup instructions. This allows the user to use the `make install` and `make clean` commands to install an application and remove object files. When you use a Makefile, you do not need to type commands such as `make hello.c`. The `make` command uses the Makefile in your current directory. With the following Makefile, you only need to type **make** to compile hello.c. Be careful to use tabs after the : and before gcc.

Example:
```
hello: hello.o
  gcc hello.o -o hello
```

Makefiles allow you to control the compilation and installation processes. If someone else is installing your application, you can give the installer the source files and a Makefile, to ensure their installation is successful.

```
 Terminal  File  Edit  Scrollback  Font  Window  Help
 ○○○                    ttyp2
[ferro:~/project_X] user% make hello
cc    -c -o hello.o hello.c
gcc hello.o -o hello
[ferro:~/project_X] user% ▯
```

```
 Terminal  File  Edit  Scrollback  Font  Window  Help
 ○○○                    ttyp2
[ferro:~/project_X] user% make hello
cc    -c -o hello.o hello.c
gcc hello.o -o hello
[ferro:~/project_X] user% ./hello
Hello, World
[ferro:~/project_X] user% ▯
```

5 Type **make hello** and press Return.

■ Make calls gcc to compile your program.

6 Type **./hello** and press Return.

■ Your program runs.

DEVELOP JAVA APPLICATIONS

You can develop Java applications on your Mac OS X system. You run Java applications with the java interpreter, but you first compile them with a program called javac. Examination of the HelloWorld program below illustrates why you need a compiler to compile Java code into a special intermediate form called bytecode, and an interpreter to run the compiled code.

The following lines of code represent the HelloWorld program written in Java. The single print command is similar to the printf command in C. The second line defines the main method and is the entry point for every Java application. In Java, each method or function exists within a class or an object, where an object is an instance of a class. Thus, you must enclose this simple program for printing a single line of text within a class definition.

```
public class HelloWorld {
   public static void main(String[] args) {
      System.out.println("Hello, World!");
   }
}
```

You normally precede code like this with a line or two of comments. Java comments start with /* and end with */ and can span multiple lines. Single-line comments can start with // and need nothing else. Comments that start with /** are special comments, and a tool called javadoc — which is intended to provide automated code documentation — extracts the text from these comments. The javadoc command produces documentation for public classes.

To compile the HelloWorld.java program, use the javac command. The command javac HelloWorld.java reads your source code and produces a class file, HelloWorld.class. You can then run this program with the command java HelloWorld.

Java applications are often distributed as Java archive (JAR) files, and you can list the contents with the jar command.

DEVELOP JAVA APPLICATIONS

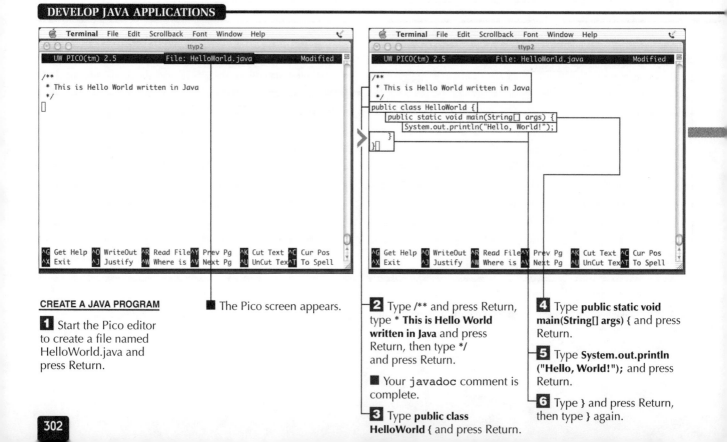

CREATE A JAVA PROGRAM

1 Start the Pico editor to create a file named HelloWorld.java and press Return.

■ The Pico screen appears.

2 Type /** and press Return, type * This is Hello World written in Java and press Return, then type */ and press Return.

■ Your javadoc comment is complete.

3 Type public class HelloWorld { and press Return.

4 Type public static void main(String[] args) { and press Return.

5 Type System.out.println ("Hello, World!"); and press Return.

6 Type } and press Return, then type } again.

Apply It

You can create a Java archive from your HelloWorld application with the `jar` command. Syntactically, the `jar` command is like the `tar` command. To create a JAR file, you can use the `jar cvf` command. To extract from a JAR file, you can use the `jar xvf` command. To list the contents of a JAR file, you can use the `jar tvf` command.

TYPE THIS:
```
[ferro:~] user%
jar cvf
HelloWorld.jar
HelloWorld.class

[ferro:~] user%
jar tvf
HelloWorld.jar
```

RESULT:
```
     0 Thu May 29
21:18:32 EDT 2003
META-INF/

    67 Thu May 29
21:18:32 EDT 2003
META-INF/MANIFEST.MF

   427 Thu May 29
20:57:50 EDT 2003
HelloWorld.class
```

You can create a Web page containing the javadoc comments from your HelloWorld application by using the `javadoc` command. Javadoc comments provide easy to access documentation for Java programs and are generally considered essential to proper Java programming. These comments are especially critical when multiple programmers work on the same project.

To view extracted javadoc comments, use the open command, as in `open HelloWorld.html`. This will open the javadoc Web page in a browser.

TYPE THIS:
```
[ferro:~] user%
javadoc
HelloWorld.java

[ferro:~] user%
ls -l
HelloWorld*
```

RESULT:
```
-rw-r—r—  1 user staff   427
May 29 20:57 HelloWorld.class

-rw-r—r—  1 user staff  6967
May 29 20:58 HelloWorld.html

-rw-r—r—  1 user staff   754
May 29 21:18 HelloWorld.jar

-rw-r—r—  1 user staff   181
May 29 20:57 HelloWorld.java
```

```
[ferro:~/project_X] user% javac HelloWorld.java
[ferro:~/project_X] user% java HelloWorld
Hello, World!
[ferro:~/project_X] user% []
```

```
[ferro:~/project_X] user% ls -l HelloWorld*
-rw-r--r--  1 user  staff  427 May 29 21:39 HelloWorld.class
-rw-r--r--  1 user  staff  181 May 29 20:57 HelloWorld.java
[ferro:~/project_X] user% []
```

7 Save your file and exit Pico.

8 Type **javac HelloWorld.java** and press Return.

■ Your program compiles.

9 Type **java HelloWorld** and press Return.

■ Your program runs.

10 Type **ls -l HelloWorld*** and press Return.

■ The system lists your source file and Java program.

DEVELOP PYTHON APPLICATIONS

Y ou can develop Python applications on your Mac OS X system. Python installs with the Mac OS X Developer Tools as /usr/bin/python. The command which python prints this path; if it does not, you must check your PATH variable and this location.

Python is an interpreted, interactive, object-oriented programming language. Unlike C programs which you compile, and Java programs which you run on top of a virtual machine, Python programs are more like Perl scripts. However, the object orientation of Python gives Python programs a distinctively different character.

Even if you are not already familiar with object-oriented programming, you can still write useful Python scripts. However, to make full use of the language, you must develop an understanding of object-oriented programming. In fact, many people consider languages such as Python to

be transitional languages, because they allow you to write programs while you are only beginning to grasp the concepts of object-oriented programming.

Languages like C and scripting languages like Perl are procedural languages. This means that portions of code are organized into functional elements called procedures or subroutines that you can use in the remainder of the code. Object-oriented languages work differently in that they define objects and then a set of operations that you can perform on these objects. You refer to these operations as methods.

Where Perl prints to a file using a command such as print LOG "$num records processed";, Python uses a command such as out_file.write("Testing, testing, 1, 2, three\nThat's all folks\n"). While, on the surface, these commands may not seem very different, the implementation and coding method are radically different, and you encounter these differences as you write your own methods.

DEVELOP PYTHON APPLICATIONS

CREATE HELLO WORLD PROGRAM IN PYTHON

1 Start Pico to create a file name HelloWorld.py.

2 Type **#!/usr/bin/python** and press Return.

3 Type **print "Hello, World!"** and press Return.

4 Save your script and exit Pico.

■ Pico saves your script.

5 Type **python HelloWorld.py** and press Return.

■ Your script runs.

6 Type **chmod a+x HelloWorld.py** and press Return.

7 Type **./HelloWorld.py** and press Return.

■ Your script runs again.

Extra

While a program as simple as HelloWorld does not display the object orientation of Python, creating and working with objects reveals some of the advantages of using objects. You can define objects and assign attributes to these objects quite easily in Python. To define a class, you can use the `class` command, such as `class Farm`. To define an instance of this class, you can use a statement like `my_farm = Farm ()`. You can then define the attributes of your farm with lines such as `my_farm.cows`.

Example:
```
#!/usr/bin/python
# simple program using objects and attributes

class Farm:
    pass

my_farm = Farm()
my_farm.acres = 45
my_farm.cows = 6
my_farm.crops = 2

print "My farm is ", my_farm.acres, "acres."
print "We have", my_farm.cows, "cows and"
if my_farm.crops:
    crop_text = "we grow " my_farm.crops
else:
    crop_text = "no"
print "crops."
```

```
    Terminal   File   Edit   Scrollback   Font   Window   Help
                            ttyp1
   UW PICO(tm) 2.5              File: write2file

#!/usr/bin/python

out_file = open("mytest","w")
out_file.write("Testing, testing, 1, 2, three\nThat's all\n")
out_file.close()




                        [ Wrote 5 lines ]

[ferro:~/bin] user% []
```

```
    Terminal   File   Edit   Scrollback   Font   Window   Help
                            ttyp1
[ferro:~/bin] user% chmod a+x write2file
[ferro:~/bin] user% ./write2file
[ferro:~/bin] user% cat mytest
Testing, testing, 1, 2, three
That's all
[ferro:~/bin] user% []
```

WRITE TO A FILE USING PYTHON

■ Start Pico to create a file name write2file.

2 Type **#!/usr/bin/python** and press Return twice, then type **out_file = open("mytest","w")** and press Return.

3 Type **out_file.write("Testing, testing, 1, 2, three\nThat's all\n")** and press Return.

4 Type **out_file.close()**.

5 Save your file, and exit Pico.

■ Pico saves your script.

6 Type **chmod a+x write2file** and press Return.

7 Type **./write2file** and press Return.

8 Type **cat mytest** and press Return.

■ Your script runs.

■ The system displays the file your script creates.

DEVELOP RUBY APPLICATIONS

You can quickly develop object-oriented applications in Ruby. Like Python, Ruby is an object-oriented scripting language that installs with the Mac OS X developer tools. In fact, there is considerable debate about which of the two is the better language.

The interpreter is /usr/bin/ruby, and the syntax is relatively easy to use and, like Perl, extensible. The language is similar to SmallTalk, a programming language that is object-oriented. For example, in Ruby, you can use the command `3.times { print "Hello, World!" }` to print "Hello, World!" three times in a row.

Because the language has many built-in types, you can accomplish a lot with just a few lines of code. Some of these types include match and replace commands that are similar to commands that you use in Perl. For example, the

command `string.gsub!(/this/, "that")` replaces *this* with *that*. If you do not find a built-in type that meets your needs, you can define your own using the `def` command.

Because Ruby is interpreted, you can run scripts by using them as arguments to the interpreter — such as `ruby HelloWorld.rb` — or by including the shebang line in your script and making the script executable. The command `ruby -v` tells you what version of Ruby you are using.

Print commands in Ruby look much like print commands in Perl or C, but do not require the use of a semicolon at the end of the line. New lines are represented with \n. While file extensions are not critical on Unix systems, Ruby scripts are generally given the file extension .rb to indicate that they are Ruby programs.

DEVELOP RUBY APPLICATIONS

CREATE HELLO WORLD IN RUBY

1 Start Pico to edit a file named HelloWorld.rb.

2 Type **#!/usr/bin/ruby** and press Return twice.

3 Type **print "Hello, World!"** and press Return.

4 Save your file, and exit Pico.

■ Pico saves your script.

5 Type **ruby ./HelloWorld.rb** and press Return.

6 Type **chmod a+x HelloWorld.rb** and press Return.

7 Type **./HelloWorld.rb** and press Return.

■ Your script runs.

Apply It

You can print a string in Ruby with or without a carriage return at the end, just as you can in Perl and Python. The syntax that each language uses is different, as shown in the comparison below.

PERL	RUBY	PYTHON
print "Hello World";	print "Hello World"	print "Hello World",
print "Hello World\n";	puts "Hello World"	print "Hello World"

You can iterate through a sequence of values in Ruby by defining an `iterate` method such as that shown below.

TYPE THIS:

```
def iterate(max)
    i = 0
    while i < max
        yield i
        i += 1
    end
end

iterate(5{|val| puts "#{val}: Hello World"}
```

RESULT:

```
0: Hello World
1: Hello World
2: Hello World
3: Hello World
4: Hello World
```

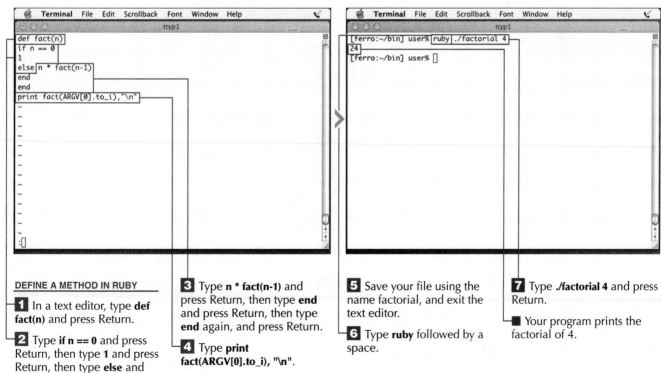

DEFINE A METHOD IN RUBY

1 In a text editor, type **def fact(n)** and press Return.

2 Type **if n == 0** and press Return, then type **1** and press Return, then type **else** and enter a space.

3 Type **n * fact(n-1)** and press Return, then type **end** and press Return, then type **end** again, and press Return.

4 Type **print fact(ARGV[0].to_i), "\n"**.

5 Save your file using the name factorial, and exit the text editor.

6 Type **ruby** followed by a space.

7 Type **./factorial 4** and press Return.

■ Your program prints the factorial of 4.

RUN A DATABASE ON MAC OS X

You can install and run a database on your Mac OS X system. In fact, you can choose between two free relational database packages — MySQL and PostgreSQL.

When you install PostgreSQL, you first download a gzipped TAR file and go through the steps of unzipping and untarring this file. You must read the INSTALL file that comes with the installation files before you run the `configure` command, as it contains many options that you can use to modify your installation. These options include the location where you want to install the software and whether you want to include readline support if you have already installed readline. You can then run the `configure` command with or without options, followed by the `make` command. The `make install` command installs the software on your system. By default, the software installs in the directory/usr/local/pgsql.

Installing the PostgreSQL software does not automatically enable you to start issuing SQL commands. You must follow a series of steps to create your database.

The first thing you must do is to add a special database user to your system. For PostgreSQL, this user is usually called postgres. Your database software runs under this account.

The next thing you must do is to log onto the postgres account and enter the `initdb` command to create a database. You must not use this command as root or with the `sudo` command.

If you install into the default location, your binaries — including initdb — go into this /usr/local/pgsql/bin directory. You must therefore add this directory to your path so that you can easily invoke any of the PostgreSQL commands.

After you run initdb from the postgres account, you can create tables, add data, and enter queries.

RUN A DATABASE ON MAC OS X

```
Terminal  File  Edit  Scrollback  Font  Window  Help
ttyp1
[ferro:~] user% gunzip postgresql-7.3.tar.gz
[ferro:~] user% tar xf postgresql-7.3.tar
[ferro:~] user% cd postgresql-7.3
[ferro:~] user%
```

```
Terminal  File  Edit  Scrollback  Font  Window  Help
ttyp1
[ferro:~] user% gunzip postgresql-7.3.tar.gz
[ferro:~] user% tar xf postgresql-7.3.tar
[ferro:~] user% cd postgresql-7.3
[ferro:~] user% ./configure --without-readline
checking build system type... powerpc-apple-darwin6.3
checking host system type... powerpc-apple-darwin6.3
checking which template to use... darwin
checking whether to build with 64-bit integer date/time support... no
checking whether to build with recode support... no
checking whether NLS is wanted... no
checking for default port number... 5432
checking for default soft limit on number of connections... 32
checking for gcc... gcc
checking for C compiler default output... a.out
checking whether the C compiler works... yes
checking whether we are cross compiling... no
checking for suffix of executables...
checking for suffix of object files... o
checking whether we are using the GNU C compiler... yes
checking whether gcc accepts -g... yes
configure: using CFLAGS=-g -O2
checking whether the C compiler still works... yes
```

1 Type **gunzip** followed by the name of your postgres install file, and press Return.

■ Your install file uncompresses.

2 Type **tar xf** followed by the name of your TAR file, and press Return.

■ Your TAR file is extracted.

3 Type **cd** followed by the name of your install directory, and press Return.

4 Type **./configure** if you have installed, or **./configure --without-readline** if you have not, and press Return.

■ Your software configures for compilation.

Extra

To allow other users to use your new database software, you must enable them from the postgres account. Otherwise, the users will get an error of this type: `psql: FATAL:  user "kbartlett" does not exist`. To enable a new user, use the `su` command to access the postgres account by typing **su - postgres**. Then connect to the database using the `psql testdb` command. After you establish the connection, add the user with a `create user username;` command, where you replace `username` with the username of the user you want to enable.

After connecting to PostgreSQL to create tables or run queries, you need to disconnect from the database. To do this, type **\q**. This command returns you to your normal system prompt.

To add the man pages for your new database software to your search list, append /usr/local/pgsql/man to your `MANPATH` environment variable. This path may contain a number of directories separated by colons. The following example adds all the man directories shown to your search path for man pages.

Example:
```
setenv MANPATH /sw/share/man:/usr/local/
man:/usr/share/man:/usr/local/pgsql/man
```

```
 Terminal  File  Edit  Scrollback  Font  Window  Help
                          ttyp1
ig_os.h
config.status: linking ./src/makefiles/Makefile.darwin to src/Makefile.po
rt
[ferro:~] user% make
make -C doc all
gzip -d -c man.tar.gz | /usr/bin/tar xf -
for file in man1/*.1; do \
  mv $file $file.bak && \
  sed -e 's/\\fR(l)/\\fR(7)/' $file.bak >$file && \
  rm -f $file.bak || exit; \
done
/bin/sh ../config/mkinstalldirs man7
mkdir man7
for file in manl/*.l; do \
  sed -e '/^\.TH/s/"l"/"7"/' \
              -e 's/\\fR(l)/\\fR(7)/' \
      $file >man7/`basename $file | sed 's/.l$/.7/'` || exit; \
done
make -C src all
make -C port all
make[2]: Nothing to be done for `all'.
make -C backend all
```

```
 Terminal  File  Edit  Scrollback  Font  Window  Help
                          ttyp1
[ferro:~] user% sudo make install
make -C doc install
gzip -d -c postgres.tar.gz | ( cd /usr/local/pgsql/doc/html && /usr/bin/t
ar xf - )
for file in man1/*.1 man7/*.7 ; do \
  /bin/sh ../config/install-sh -c -m 644 $file /usr/local/pgsql/man/$file
  || exit; \
done
```

5 Type **make** and press Return.

■ The software begins to compile.

6 Type **sudo make install** and press Return.

■ Your software compiles and installs.

CONTINUED ▶

RUN A DATABASE ON MAC OS X (CONTINUED)

While it might not be immediately obvious, a database is a form of server – a process that supplies information to clients. After a database is created with `createdb`, initiated with `initdb`, and populated with tables and data, the database is ready to start answering queries. Most databases run all the time whether or not anyone is using them.

When you start a `psql` session and connect to a database, you are acting as a client of the database. You can select data from tables by searching for certain values and by restricting what you want to see from these tables by columns as well.

PostgreSQL, like most modern databases, is a *relational* database. That term implies that all data are stored in a uniform manner – in tables. Unlike a hierarchical database, in which data elements have parent/child relationships, relational databases have no such relationships. Instead, data of all kinds is stored in tables and all records are accessed in the same manner.

The basic query command is select. When you issue a query that selects phone from contacts, phone is a column in a table named contacts. If you select phone from contacts where areacode is equal to 415, you are listing your contacts in San Francisco. In this case, you are asking to view one particular column from particular rows in your table of contacts.

While SQL, the standard language used for relational databases, is not exactly free-flowing English, it is still easy to use and understand. The command `select phone from contacts where areacode=415;` is about as close to flowing speech as computer syntax comes.

SQL also allows you insert data into tables with `insert`, remove data from tables with `delete`, modify data in tables with `update` and sort data with `order by`.

RUN A DATABASE ON MAC OS X (CONTINUED)

```
[ferro:~] user% sudo adduser
username: postgres
full name: postgres user
uid: 23456
shell: /bin/tcsh
password:
Changing password for postgres.
New password:
Retype new password:
```

```
[ferro:~] user% sudo mkdir /usr/local/pgsql/data
[ferro:~] user% sudo chown postgres /usr/local/pgsql/data
[ferro:~] user% su - postgres
Password:
su-2.05a$
```

7 Type **adduser** and press Return.

Note: To complete step 7, you must have already created an adduser script. If not, see Chapter 11.

8 Type **sudo mkdir /usr/local/pgsql/data** and press Return.

9 Type **sudo chown postgres /usr/local/pgsql/data**.

10 Type **su - postgres** and press Return, then type the postgres password at the prompt.

Extra

You can get help during your `psql` session by typing \?. When you enter this command, a list of slash commands, such as \l for creating a list of your databases, appears. You can use the \h command to get help on a particular command. For example, typing **\h select** describes the syntax and use of the select command.

To exit your psql session, type **\q**.

SQL syntax provided by the help function will display optional portions of a command inside square brackets. If you type **\h modify**, for example, you will notice that the word ONLY appears within square brackets – [ONLY]. This part of the command is, therefore, optional. Similarly, [WHERE condition] means that you can optionally specify a condition, such as where areacode=415.

```
su-2.05a$ /usr/local/pgsql/bin/initdb -D /usr/local/pgsql/data
The files belonging to this database system will be owned by user "postgr
es".
This user must also own the server process.

The database cluster will be initialized with locale C.

Fixing permissions on existing directory /usr/local/pgsql/data... ok
creating directory /usr/local/pgsql/data/base... ok
creating directory /usr/local/pgsql/data/global... ok
creating directory /usr/local/pgsql/data/pg_xlog... ok
creating directory /usr/local/pgsql/data/pg_clog... ok
creating template1 database in /usr/local/pgsql/data/base/1... ok
creating configuration files... ok
initializing pg_shadow... ok
enabling unlimited row size for system tables... ok
initializing pg_depend... ok
creating system views... ok
loading pg_description... ok
creating conversions... ok
setting privileges on built-in objects... ok
vacuuming database template1... ok
```

```
su-2.05a$ nohup /usr/local/pgsql/bin/postmaster -D /usr/local/pgsql/data
</dev/null >>server.log 2>&1 </dev/null &
[1] 8496
su-2.05a$ createdb testdb
CREATE DATABASE
su-2.05a$ psql testdb
Welcome to psql 7.3, the PostgreSQL interactive terminal.

Type:  \copyright for distribution terms
       \h for help with SQL commands
       \? for help on internal slash commands
       \g or terminate with semicolon to execute query
       \q to quit

testdb=#
```

11 Type **/usr/local/pgsql/bin/initdb -D /usr/local/pgsql/data** and press Return.

12 Type **nohup /usr/local/pgsql/bin/postmaster -D /usr/local/pgsql/data </dev/null >>server.log 2>&1 </dev/null &** and press Return.

■ Your database service starts.

13 Type **createdb testdb** and press Return.

■ Your database is created.

14 Type **psql testdb** and press Return.

■ You connect to the database.

WRITE SQL COMMANDS

You can issue SQL commands to your PostgreSQL database. To use all of the features of your database software, you need to learn a number of SQL commands. In particular, you need to learn how to create tables, insert and remove records from these tables, and run queries to extract information from these tables.

The command for creating a table is `create table tablename`. When you define a table, you need to specify the number of columns you want to add. For example, the SQL command for adding a book table to the database may look like this:

```
create table books (

    author          varchar(32),
    title           varchar(64),
    publisher       varchar(16),
    pubyear         int,
    ISBN            varchar(13)
    );
```

You define each column in the table as having a particular type. Most of these types are character fields of a specified length. After you define a table, you can add records to it. You can do this one record at a time, or you can bulk load a table from a flat text file. To add a single record, you can identify the table and the value you want to assign to each column in the new record. For example, you may say `insert into books values('Paul Whitehead and Eric Kramer','Your visual blueprint for building Perl scripts','Wiley Publishing',2000,'0-7645-3478-5');` paying particular attention to the semicolon at the end.

You can list the contents of the books table in its entirety with the command `select * from books;` or you can select some of the records by running a `select` command with a `where` clause. For example, to list the titles of the books in your table that were published in the year 2000, you can type **select title from books where pubyear = 2000;**.

WRITE SQL COMMANDS

1 Type **psql testdb** and press Return.

2 Type **create table pets (** and press Return.

3 Type **name varchar(12),** and press Return.

4 Type **type varchar(6),** and press Return.

5 Type **age int,** and press Return.

6 Type **fixed varchar(1)** and press Return.

7 Type **);** and press Return.

■ Your table is added to the database.

Extra

You can insert records into a PostgreSQL table by typing an `insert` command for each record, or you can create a text file containing the commands and load that file. To create a table and load it from a text file, you can type the `table create` command along with each of the `insert` commands into a file, such as pets.sql.

Example:
```
create table pets name varchar(12), type varchar(6), age int, fixed varchar(1));
insert into pets values('Amaranthe','cat',1,'y');
insert into pets values('Raven','dog',6,'y');
insert into pets values('Maize','cat',.5,'n');
```

You can enter the following to load the data into the database:

```
psql -d testdb -f /Users/user/pets.sql
```

To count the records in a table, you can use an SQL `count` command.

TYPE THIS:
```
select count(*) from pets;
```

RESULT:
```
count
--------
      3
```

```
 🍎  Terminal  File  Edit  Scrollback  Font  Window  Help
                           ttyp1
testdb=# insert into pets values('Amaranthe','cat',1,'y');
INSERT 16979 1
testdb=# insert into pets values('Raven','dog',6,'y');
INSERT 16980 1
testdb=# insert into pets values('Maize','cat',.5,'n');
INSERT 16981 1
testdb=# select * from pets;
   name    | type | age | fixed
-----------+------+-----+-------
 Amaranthe | cat  |   1 | y
 Raven     | dog  |   6 | y
 Maize     | cat  |   1 | n
(3 rows)

testdb=#
testdb=#
testdb=#
testdb=#
testdb=#
testdb=#
testdb=#
```

```
 🍎  Terminal  File  Edit  Scrollback  Font  Window  Help
                           ttyp1
(3 rows)

testdb=#
testdb=#
testdb=#
testdb=#
testdb=#
testdb=#
testdb=# select * from pets where type='cat';
   name    | type | age | fixed
-----------+------+-----+-------
 Amaranthe | cat  |   1 | y
 Maize     | cat  |   1 | n
(2 rows)

testdb=# select name from pets where fixed='n';
  name
-------
 Maize
(1 row)

testdb=#
```

8 Type **insert into pets values('Amaranthe','cat',1,'y');** and press Return.

9 Type **insert into pets values('Raven','dog',6,'y');** and press Return.

10 Type **insert into pets values('Maize','cat',.5,'n');** and press Return.

11 Type **select * from pets;** and press Return.

■ The database server displays the contents of your table.

12 Type **select * from pets where type='cat';** and press Return.

13 Type **select name from pets where fixed='n';** and press Return.

■ The database selects and prints the data you request.

ACCESS DATABASES FROM PHP

You can access data in your databases from PHP and include this information in your Web pages. While the setup required to provide information stored in a postgres database on a Web page is not intuitive, you can provide this functionality when you have the proper tools.

You need to install PostgreSQL on your server. You also need to use a Web server that supports PHP — for example, an installation of Apache that supports PHP dynamically or statically. In addition, your PHP build must support PostgreSQL; that is, you must build it with the `-with-pgsql` configuration parameter. Lastly, for a Web site to use PostgreSQL commands, the database must be running.

When you are sure that you have these prerequisites, you can create a Web page that incorporates information from your database. The first step is to identify the database that you are using, as follows:

```
<?
$host = "localhost";
$user = "postgres";
$pass = "dbacct";
$db = "testdb";
```

You can then open a connection to the database with a command such as `$connect = pg_connect ("host=$host dbname=$db user=$user password=$pass password=$pass");`. You can then determine if your connection is successful by testing the `$connect` value.

Next, you can create the query that you want to run — for example, `$query = "select * from pets";` — and execute that query with a command such as `$result = pg_query($connect, $query) or die("Query failed: $query");`. If your query is successful, the command stores the data that you just fetched in $result.

You can now decide how to process and display the data that the command returns from the database.

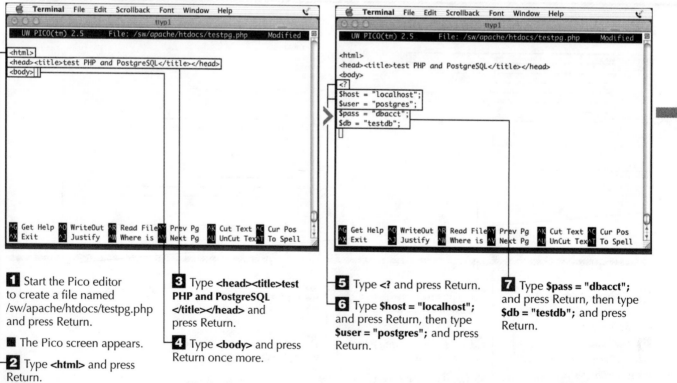

1 Start the Pico editor to create a file named /sw/apache/htdocs/testpg.php and press Return.

■ The Pico screen appears.

2 Type **<html>** and press Return.

3 Type **<head><title>test PHP and PostgreSQL </title></head>** and press Return.

4 Type **<body>** and press Return once more.

5 Type **<?** and press Return.

6 Type **$host = "localhost";** and press Return, then type **$user = "postgres";** and press Return.

7 Type **$pass = "dbacct";** and press Return, then type **$db = "testdb";** and press Return.

Extra

This example comprises the complete PHP
file for testing your database accessibility.

Example:
```
<html>
<head><title>test PHP and PostgreSQL</title></head>
<body>

<?
// database access parameters
$host = "localhost";
$user = "postgres";
$pass = "dbacct";
$db = "testdb";

// open a connection
$connect = pg_connect ("host=$host dbname=$db user=$user
password=$pass");
if (!$connect) {
die("could not open a connection to db server"); }

// generate and execute query
$query = "select * from pets";
$result = pg_query($connect, $query) or die("error in query:
$query" . pg_last_error($connection));

// get number of rows
$rows = pg_num_rows($result);
echo "There are $rows records in the pets db";
// close db connection
pg_close($connect);
?>
</body>
</html>
```

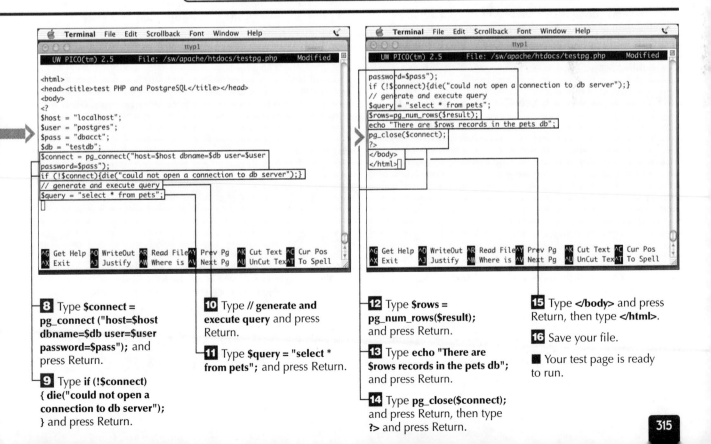

8 Type **$connect =
pg_connect ("host=$host
dbname=$db user=$user
password=$pass");** and
press Return.

9 Type **if (!$connect)
{ die("could not open a
connection to db server");
}** and press Return.

10 Type **// generate and
execute query** and press
Return.

11 Type **$query = "select *
from pets";** and press Return.

12 Type **$rows =
pg_num_rows($result);**
and press Return.

13 Type **echo "There are
$rows records in the pets db";**
and press Return.

14 Type **pg_close($connect);**
and press Return, then type
?> and press Return.

15 Type **</body>** and press
Return, then type **</html>**.

16 Save your file.

■ Your test page is ready
to run.

APPENDIX

WHAT'S ON THE CD-ROM

The CD-ROM included in this book contains many useful files and programs. Before installing any of the programs on the disc, make sure that you do not already have a newer version of the program already installed on your computer. For information on installing different versions of the same program, contact the program's manufacturer. For the latest and greatest information, please refer to the ReadMe file located at the root level of the CD-ROM as well as the manufacturer's Web site.

SYSTEM REQUIREMENTS

To use the contents of the CD-ROM, your computer must have the following hardware and software:

For Macintosh:

- Mac OS X v.10.2 or higher with a 400 MHz or faster CPU
- At least 256MB of total RAM installed on your computer; for best performance, we recommend at least 512MB
- A network card
- A CD-ROM drive

ACROBAT VERSION

The CD-ROM contains an e-version of this book that you can view and search using Adobe Acrobat Reader. You cannot print the pages or copy text from the Acrobat files. The CD-ROM includes an evaluation version of Adobe Acrobat Reader.

INSTALLING AND USING THE SOFTWARE

For your convenience, the software titles appearing on the CD-ROM are listed alphabetically. Some software provided on this CD may require additional components for installation. See the ReadMe file and links pages on the CD for additional information.

AbiWord

For Unix, Linux, and Windows. GNU Freeware/Open Source. Requires X Windows. AbiWord is a cross-platform word-processing program that enables you to perform the same task as Microsoft Word. From AbiSource c/o SourceGear Corporation, www.abisource.com.

Acrobat Reader

For Macintosh and Windows. Freeware. Adobe Acrobat Reader allows you to view the online version of this book. For more information on using Acrobat Reader, see the section "Using the E-Version of the Book" in this Appendix. From Adobe Systems, www.adobe.com.

Chimera

For Mac OS X. Freeware/Open Source. Chimera is a browser for Jaguar, Mac OS X v.10.2. From The Mozilla Organization, www.mozilla.org/projects/chimera.

Fink

For Mac OS X. Freeware/Open Source. Fink enables Mac OS X to import and fix open source Unix software. From The Fink Project, http://fink.sourceforge.net.

GIMP

For Unix, Mac OS X, and Windows. GNU Freeware/Open Source and Binary. Requires X Windows. The GIMP is the GNU Image Manipulation Program for photo retouching, image composition, and image authoring. From GNOME, www.gimp.org.

GNOME Core

For Unix and Linux. Freeware/Open Source. Requires X Windows. GNOME Core contains the core components needed to run the GNOME desktop environment. From GNOME, www.gnome.org.

GnuCash

For Mac OS X and Linux. GNU Freeware/Open Source. GnuCash is a finance software that enables you to manage your bank accounts, stocks, income, and expenses, and more. From The GnuCash Project, www.gnucash.org.

KDEbase

For Unix, Linux, and Solaris. Freeware/Open Source. Requires X Windows. KDEbase contains the basic applications that are used with the KDE desktop environment. From The KDE Project, www.kde.org.

KDElibs

For Unix systems. Freeware/Open Source. Requires X Windows. KDElibs contains libraries needed by the K Desktop Environment. From The KDE Project, www.kde.org.

Lynx

For Unix, VMS, Windows 95 and higher. GNU Freeware/Open Source and Binary. Lynx is a text-based Internet Web browser originally developed at the University of Kansas. http://lynx.browser.org.

Mozilla

For Unix and Linux systems. Freeware/Open Source. Mozilla is an open-source Web browser and toolkit. From The Mozilla Organization, www.mozilla.org.

OpenOffice.org

For all platforms. Freeware/Open Source. Requires X Windows. OpenOffice.org is an office suite that will run on all major platforms. From OpenOffice.org, www.openoffice.org.

PostgreSQL

For Unix and Linux systems. Freeware/Open Source. An advanced object-relational database management system (ORDBMS) with utilities needed to create and maintain the database server. From PostgreSQL, www.postgresql.org.

Screen

For Unix. GNU Freeware/Open Source. Screen is a utility that allows you to have multiple logon screens in a single terminal. From The GNU Project, www.gnu.org.

Vim

For Unix, Linux, and Mac OS X. Freeware/Open Source. vim (VIsual editor iMproved) is an enhanced text editor. From The VIM Group, www.vim.org.

XFree86

For Unix, Linux, Solaris, Mac OS X. Freeware/Open Source. XFree86 is an X Windows server. It provides a client/server interface between display hardware and the desktop environment, while providing both the windowing infrastructure and a standardized application interface. From The XFree86 Project, Inc, www.xfree86.org. For Mac OS X ports, go to sourceforge.netprojectsXonX.

Xmms

For Unix systems. Freeware/Open Source. X MultiMedia System (Xmms) is a multimedia player that supports MPEG, WAV, and AU formats. From 4Front Technologies, www.xmms.org.

TROUBLESHOOTING

The programs on the CD-ROM should work on computers with the minimum of system requirements. However, some programs may not work properly.

Many of the tools on the CD require that you first install an X Windows server, such as the XFree86 software included on the CD. The two most likely problems for the programs not working properly include not having enough memory (RAM) for the programs you want to use, or having other programs running that affect the installation or running of a program. If you receive error messages such as Not enough memory or Setup cannot continue, try one or more of the methods below and then try using the software again:

- Turn off any anti-virus software
- Close all running programs
- Have your local computer store add more RAM to your computer

Mac OS X requires more memory than previous versions of Mac OS. For acceptable performance, you should run at least 256MB of RAM.

Execution of programs that you install may depend on having the proper environment. Your search path should include the directory in which your software has been installed, for example, /sw/bin or /usr/local/bin. You may also have to adjust your dynamic library search path to enable these applications to find and use the runtime libraries they need. The environment variable DYLD_LIBRARY_PATH may have to be updated to include directories such as /sw/lib or /usr/local/lib.

In addition, any application that is not installed with an installer program will open slowly the first time it is run. This is normal.

If you still have trouble installing the items from the CD-ROM, call the Wiley Publishing Customer Service phone number: 800-762-2974 (outside the U.S.: 317-572-3994). You can also contact Wiley Publishing Customer Service by e-mail at techsupdum@wiley.com.

USING THE E-VERSION OF THE BOOK

Y ou can view *Unix for Mac: Your visual blueprint to maximizing the foundation of Mac OS X* on your screen using the CD-ROM included at the back of this book. The CD-ROM allows you to search the contents of each chapter of the book for a specific word or phrase. The CD-ROM also provides a convenient way of keeping the book handy while traveling.

You must install Adobe Acrobat Reader on your computer before you can view the book on the CD-ROM. This program is provided on the disc. Acrobat Reader allows you to view Portable Document Format (PDF) files, which can display books and magazines on your screen exactly as they appear in printed form.

To view the contents of the book using Acrobat Reader, insert the CD-ROM into your drive. The autorun interface will appear. Navigate to the eBook, and open the book.pdf file. You may be required to install Acrobat Reader 5.0 on your computer, which you can do by following the simple installation instructions. If you choose to disable the autorun interface, you can open the CD root menu and open the Resources folder, then open the eBook folder. In the window that appears, double-click the eBook.pdf icon.

USING THE E-VERSION OF THE BOOK

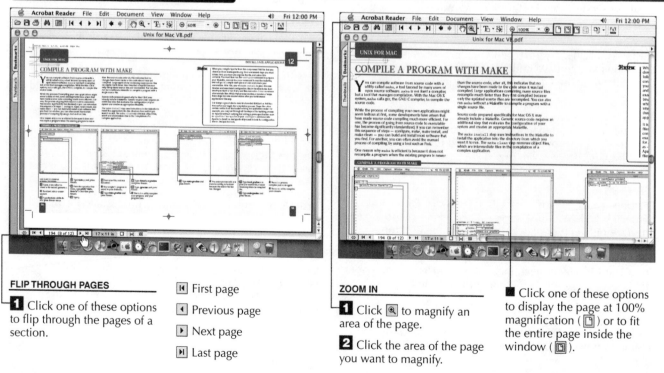

FLIP THROUGH PAGES

1 Click one of these options to flip through the pages of a section.

◄ First page

◄ Previous page

► Next page

►| Last page

ZOOM IN

1 Click 🔍 to magnify an area of the page.

2 Click the area of the page you want to magnify.

■ Click one of these options to display the page at 100% magnification (🗎) or to fit the entire page inside the window (🖾).

Extra

To install Acrobat Reader, insert the CD-ROM disc into a drive. In the screen that appears, click Software. Click Acrobat Reader and then click Install at the bottom of the screen. Then follow the instructions on your screen to install the program.

You can make searching the book more convenient by copying the .pdf files to your own computer. Display the contents of the CD-ROM disc and then copy the PDFs folder from the CD to your hard drive. This allows you to easily access the contents of the book at any time.

Acrobat Reader is a popular and useful program. There are many files available on the Web that are designed to be viewed using Acrobat Reader. Look for files with the .pdf extension. For more information about Acrobat Reader, visit the Web site at www.adobe.com/products/acrobat/readermain.html.

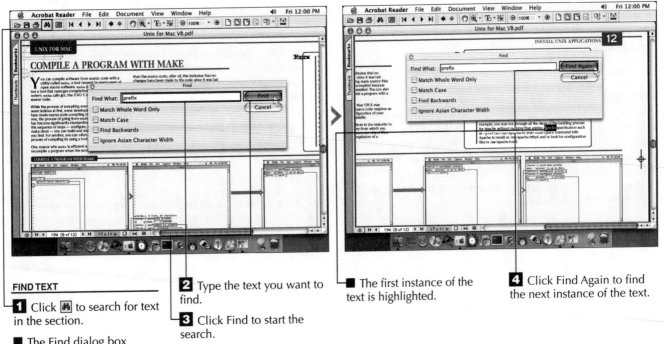

FIND TEXT

1 Click 🔍 to search for text in the section.

■ The Find dialog box appears.

2 Type the text you want to find.

3 Click Find to start the search.

■ The first instance of the text is highlighted.

4 Click Find Again to find the next instance of the text.

APPENDIX

WILEY PUBLISHING, INC. END-USER LICENSE AGREEMENT

READ THIS. You should carefully read these terms and conditions before opening the software packet(s) included with this book *Unix for Mac: Your visual blueprint to maximizing the foundations of Mac OS X.* This is a license agreement "Agreement" between you and Wiley Publishing, Inc. "WPI". By opening the accompanying software packet(s), you acknowledge that you have read and accept the following terms and conditions. If you do not agree and do not want to be bound by such terms and conditions, promptly return the Book and the unopened software packet(s) to the place you obtained them for a full refund.

1. License Grant.

WPI grants to you (either an individual or entity) a nonexclusive license to use one copy of the enclosed software program(s) (collectively, the "Software," solely for your own personal or business purposes on a single computer (whether a standard computer or a workstation component of a multi-user network). The Software is in use on a computer when it is loaded into temporary memory (RAM) or installed into permanent memory (hard disk, CD-ROM, or other storage device). WPI reserves all rights not expressly granted herein.

2. Ownership.

WPI is the owner of all right, title, and interest, including copyright, in and to the compilation of the Software recorded on the disk(s) or CD-ROM "Software Media". Copyright to the individual programs recorded on the Software Media is owned by the author or other authorized copyright owner of each program. Ownership of the Software and all proprietary rights relating thereto remain with WPI and its licensers.

3. Restrictions on Use and Transfer.

(a) You may only (i) make one copy of the Software for backup or archival purposes, or (ii) transfer the Software to a single hard disk, provided that you keep the original for backup or archival purposes. You may not (i) rent or lease the Software, (ii) copy or reproduce the Software through a LAN or other network system or through any computer subscriber system or bulletin-board system, or (iii) modify, adapt, or create derivative works based on the Software.

(b) You may not reverse engineer, decompile, or disassemble the Software. You may transfer the Software and user documentation on a permanent basis, provided that the transferee agrees to accept the terms and conditions of this Agreement and you retain no copies. If the Software is an update or has been updated, any transfer must include the most recent update and all prior versions.

4. Restrictions on Use of Individual Programs.

You must follow the individual requirements and restrictions detailed for each individual program in the What's on the CD-ROM appendix of this Book. These limitations are also contained in the individual license agreements recorded on the Software Media. These limitations may include a requirement that after using the program for a specified period of time, the user must pay a registration fee or discontinue use. By opening the Software packet(s), you will be agreeing to abide by the licenses and restrictions for these individual programs that are detailed in the What's on the CD-ROM appendix and on the Software Media. None of the material on this Software Media or listed in this Book may ever be redistributed, in original or modified form, for commercial purposes.

5. Limited Warranty.

(a) WPI warrants that the Software and Software Media are free from defects in materials and workmanship under normal use for a period of sixty (60) days from the date of purchase of this Book. If WPI receives notification within the warranty period of defects in materials or workmanship, WPI will replace the defective Software Media.

(b) WPI AND THE AUTHOR OF THE BOOK DISCLAIM ALL OTHER WARRANTIES, EXPRESS OR IMPLIED, INCLUDING WITHOUT LIMITATION IMPLIED WARRANTIES OF MERCHANTABILITY AND FITNESS FOR A PARTICULAR PURPOSE, WITH RESPECT TO THE SOFTWARE, THE PROGRAMS, THE SOURCE CODE CONTAINED THEREIN, AND/OR THE TECHNIQUES DESCRIBED IN THIS BOOK. WPI DOES NOT WARRANT THAT THE FUNCTIONS CONTAINED IN THE SOFTWARE WILL MEET YOUR REQUIREMENTS OR THAT THE OPERATION OF THE SOFTWARE WILL BE ERROR FREE.

(c) This limited warranty gives you specific legal rights, and you may have other rights that vary from jurisdiction to jurisdiction.

6. Remedies.

(a) WPI's entire liability and your exclusive remedy for defects in materials and workmanship shall be limited to replacement of the Software Media, which may be returned to WPI with a copy of your receipt at the following address: Software Media Fulfillment Department, Attn.: Unix for Mac: Your visual blueprint to maximizing the foundation of Mac OS X, Wiley Publishing, Inc., 10475 Crosspoint Blvd., Indianapolis, IN 46256, or call 1-800-762-2974. Please allow four to six weeks for delivery. This Limited Warranty is void if failure of the Software Media has resulted from accident, abuse, or misapplication. Any replacement Software Media will be warranted for the remainder of the original warranty period or thirty (30) days, whichever is longer.

(b) In no event shall WPI or the author be liable for any damages whatsoever (including without limitation damages for loss of business profits, business interruption, loss of business information, or any other pecuniary loss) arising from the use of or inability to use the Book or the Software, even if WPI has been advised of the possibility of such damages.

(c) Because some jurisdictions do not allow the exclusion or limitation of liability for consequential or incidental damages, the above limitation or exclusion may not apply to you.

7. U.S. Government Restricted Rights.

Use, duplication, or disclosure of the Software for or on behalf of the United States of America, its agencies and/or instrumentalities "U.S. Government" is subject to restrictions as stated in paragraph (c)(1)(ii) of the Rights in Technical Data and Computer Software clause of DFARS 252.227-7013, or subparagraphs (c) (1) and (2) of the Commercial Computer Software - Restricted Rights clause at FAR 52.227-19, and in similar clauses in the NASA FAR supplement, as applicable.

8. General.

This Agreement constitutes the entire understanding of the parties and revokes and supersedes all prior agreements, oral or written, between them and may not be modified or amended except in a writing signed by both parties hereto that specifically refers to this Agreement. This Agreement shall take precedence over any other documents that may be in conflict herewith. If any one or more provisions contained in this Agreement are held by any court or tribunal to be invalid, illegal, or otherwise unenforceable, each and every other provision shall remain in full force and effect.

GNU GENERAL PUBLIC LICENSE

Version 2, June 1991

Copyright © 1989, 1991 Free Software Foundation, Inc.

59 Temple Place - Suite 330, Boston, MA 02111-1307, USA

Everyone is permitted to copy and distribute verbatim copies of this license document, but changing it is not allowed.

PREAMBLE

The licenses for most software are designed to take away your freedom to share and change it. By contrast, the GNU General Public License is intended to guarantee your freedom to share and change free software—to make sure the software is free for all its users. This General Public License applies to most of the Free Software Foundation's software and to any other program whose authors commit to using it. (Some other Free Software Foundation software is covered by the GNU Library General Public License instead.) You can apply it to your programs, too.

When we speak of free software, we are referring to freedom, not price. Our General Public Licenses are designed to make sure that you have the freedom to distribute copies of free software (and charge for this service if you wish), that you receive source code or can get it if you want it, that you can change the software or use pieces of it in new free programs; and that you know you can do these things.

To protect your rights, we need to make restrictions that forbid anyone to deny you these rights or to ask you to surrender the rights. These restrictions translate to certain responsibilities for you if you distribute copies of the software, or if you modify it.

For example, if you distribute copies of such a program, whether gratis or for a fee, you must give the recipients all the rights that you have. You must make sure that they, too, receive or can get the source code. And you must show them these terms so they know their rights.

We protect your rights with two steps: (1) copyright the software, and (2) offer you this license which gives you legal permission to copy, distribute and/or modify the software.

Also, for each author's protection and ours, we want to make certain that everyone understands that there is no warranty for this free software. If the software is modified by someone else and passed on, we want its recipients to know that what they have is not the original, so that any problems introduced by others will not reflect on the original authors' reputations.

Finally, any free program is threatened constantly by software patents. We wish to avoid the danger that redistributors of a free program will individually obtain patent licenses, in effect making the program proprietary. To prevent this, we have made it clear that any patent must be licensed for everyone's free use or not licensed at all.

The precise terms and conditions for copying, distribution and modification follow.

Terms and Conditions for Copying, Distribution and Modification

This License applies to any program or other work which contains a notice placed by the copyright holder saying it may be distributed under the terms of this General Public License. The "Program", below, refers to any such program or work, and a "work based on the Program" means either the Program or any derivative work under copyright law: that is to say, a work containing the Program or a portion of it, either verbatim or with modifications and/or translated into another language. (Hereinafter, translation is included without limitation in the term "modification".) Each licensee is addressed as "you".

Activities other than copying, distribution and modification are not covered by this License; they are outside its scope. The act of running the Program is not restricted, and the output from the Program is covered only if its contents constitute a work based on the Program (independent of having been made by running the Program). Whether that is true depends on what the Program does.

1.   You may copy and distribute verbatim copies of the Program's source code as you receive it, in any medium, provided that you conspicuously and appropriately publish on each copy an appropriate copyright notice and

disclaimer of warranty; keep intact all the notices that refer to this License and to the absence of any warranty; and give any other recipients of the Program a copy of this License along with the Program.

You may charge a fee for the physical act of transferring a copy, and you may at your option offer warranty protection in exchange for a fee.

2. You may modify your copy or copies of the Program or any portion of it, thus forming a work based on the Program, and copy and distribute such modifications or work under the terms of Section 1 above, provided that you also meet all of these conditions:

(a) You must cause the modified files to carry prominent notices stating that you changed the files and the date of any change.

(b) You must cause any work that you distribute or publish, that in whole or in part contains or is derived from the Program or any part thereof, to be licensed as a whole at no charge to all third parties under the terms of this License.

(c) If the modified program normally reads commands interactively when run, you must cause it, when started running for such interactive use in the most ordinary way, to print or display an announcement including an appropriate copyright notice and a notice that there is no warranty (or else, saying that you provide a warranty) and that users may redistribute the program under these conditions, and telling the user how to view a copy of this License. (Exception: if the Program itself is interactive but does not normally print such an announcement, your work based on the Program is not required to print an announcement.)

These requirements apply to the modified work as a whole. If identifiable sections of that work are not derived from the Program, and can be reasonably considered independent and separate works in themselves, then this License, and its terms, do not apply to those sections when you distribute them as separate works. But when you distribute the same sections as part of a whole which is a work based on the Program, the distribution of the whole must be on the terms of this License, whose permissions for other licensees extend to the entire whole, and thus to each and every part regardless of who wrote it.

(a) Thus, it is not the intent of this section to claim rights or contest your rights to work written entirely by you; rather, the intent is to exercise the right to control the distribution of derivative or collective works based on the Program.

In addition, mere aggregation of another work not based on the Program with the Program (or with a work based on the Program) on a volume of a storage or distribution medium does not bring the other work under the scope of this License.

3. You may copy and distribute the Program (or a work based on it, under Section 2) in object code or executable form under the terms of Sections 1 and 2 above provided that you also do one of the following:

(a) Accompany it with the complete corresponding machine-readable source code, which must be distributed under the terms of Sections 1 and 2 above on a medium customarily used for software interchange; or,

(b) Accompany it with a written offer, valid for at least three years, to give any third party, for a charge no more than your cost of physically performing source distribution, a complete machine-readable copy of the corresponding source code, to be distributed under the terms of Sections 1 and 2 above on a medium customarily used for software interchange; or,

(c) Accompany it with the information you received as to the offer to distribute corresponding source code. (This alternative is allowed only for noncommercial distribution and only if you received the program in object code or executable form with such an offer, in accord with Subsection b above.)

The source code for a work means the preferred form of the work for making modifications to it. For an executable work, complete source code means all the source code for all modules it contains, plus any associated interface definition files, plus the scripts used to control compilation and installation of the executable. However, as a special exception, the source code distributed need not include anything that is normally distributed (in either source or binary form) with the major components (compiler, kernel, and so on) of the operating system on which the executable runs, unless that component itself accompanies the executable.

If distribution of executable or object code is made by offering access to copy from a designated place, then offering equivalent access to copy the source code from the same place counts as distribution of the source code, even though third parties are not compelled to copy the source along with the object code.

4.   You may not copy, modify, sublicense, or distribute the Program except as expressly provided under this License. Any attempt otherwise to copy, modify, sublicense or distribute the Program is void, and will automatically terminate your rights under this License. However, parties who have received copies, or rights, from you under this License will not have their licenses terminated so long as such parties remain in full compliance.

5.   You are not required to accept this License, since you have not signed it. However, nothing else grants you permission to modify or distribute the Program or its derivative works. These actions are prohibited by law if you do not accept this License. Therefore, by modifying or distributing the Program (or any work based on the Program), you indicate your acceptance of this License to do so, and all its terms and conditions for copying, distributing or modifying the Program or works based on it.

6.   Each time you redistribute the Program (or any work based on the Program), the recipient automatically receives a license from the original licensor to copy, distribute or modify the Program subject to these terms and conditions. You may not impose any further restrictions on the recipients' exercise of the rights granted herein. You are not responsible for enforcing compliance by third parties to this License.

7.   If, as a consequence of a court judgment or allegation of patent infringement or for any other reason (not limited to patent issues), conditions are imposed on you (whether by court order, agreement or otherwise) that contradict the conditions of this License, they do not excuse you from the conditions of this License. If you cannot distribute so as to satisfy simultaneously your obligations under this License and any other pertinent obligations, then as a consequence you may not distribute the Program at all. For example, if a patent license would not permit royalty-free redistribution of the Program by all those who receive copies directly or indirectly through you, then the only way you could satisfy both it and this License would be to refrain entirely from distribution of the Program.

If any portion of this section is held invalid or unenforceable under any particular circumstance, the balance of the section is intended to apply and the section as a whole is intended to apply in other circumstances.

It is not the purpose of this section to induce you to infringe any patents or other property right claims or to contest validity of any such claims; this section has the sole purpose of protecting the integrity of the free software distribution system, which is implemented by public license practices. Many people have made generous contributions to the wide range of software distributed through that system in reliance on consistent application of that system; it is up to the author/donor to decide if he or she is willing to distribute software through any other system and a licensee cannot impose that choice.

This section is intended to make thoroughly clear what is believed to be a consequence of the rest of this License.

8.   If the distribution and/or use of the Program is restricted in certain countries either by patents or by

copyrighted interfaces, the original copyright holder who places the Program under this License may add an explicit geographical distribution limitation excluding those countries, so that distribution is permitted only in or among countries not thus excluded. In such case, this License incorporates the limitation as if written in the body of this License.

9.   The Free Software Foundation may publish revised and/or new versions of the General Public License from time to time. Such new versions will be similar in spirit to the present version, but may differ in detail to address new problems or concerns.

Each version is given a distinguishing version number. If the Program specifies a version number of this License which applies to it and "any later version", you have the option of following the terms and conditions either of that version or of any later version published by the Free Software Foundation. If the Program does not specify a version number of this License, you may choose any version ever published by the Free Software Foundation.

10. If you wish to incorporate parts of the Program into other free programs whose distribution conditions are different, write to the author to ask for permission. For software which is copyrighted by the Free Software Foundation, write to the Free Software Foundation; we sometimes make exceptions for this. Our decision will be guided by the two goals of preserving the free status of all derivatives of our free software and of promoting the sharing and reuse of software generally.

NO WARRANTY

11. BECAUSE THE PROGRAM IS LICENSED FREE OF CHARGE, THERE IS NO WARRANTY FOR THE PROGRAM, TO THE EXTENT PERMITTED BY APPLICABLE LAW. EXCEPT WHEN OTHERWISE STATED IN WRITING THE COPYRIGHT HOLDERS AND/OR OTHER PARTIES PROVIDE THE PROGRAM "AS IS" WITHOUT WARRANTY OF ANY KIND, EITHER EXPRESSED OR IMPLIED, INCLUDING, BUT NOT LIMITED TO, THE IMPLIED WARRANTIES OF MERCHANTABILITY AND FITNESS FOR A PARTICULAR PURPOSE. THE ENTIRE RISK AS TO THE QUALITY AND PERFORMANCE OF THE PROGRAM IS WITH YOU. SHOULD THE PROGRAM PROVE DEFECTIVE, YOU ASSUME THE COST OF ALL NECESSARY SERVICING, REPAIR OR CORRECTION.

12. IN NO EVENT UNLESS REQUIRED BY APPLICABLE LAW OR AGREED TO IN WRITING WILL ANY COPYRIGHT HOLDER, OR ANY OTHER PARTY WHO MAY MODIFY AND/OR REDISTRIBUTE THE PROGRAM AS PERMITTED ABOVE, BE LIABLE TO YOU FOR DAMAGES, INCLUDING ANY GENERAL, SPECIAL, INCIDENTAL OR CONSEQUENTIAL DAMAGES ARISING OUT OF THE USE OR INABILITY TO USE THE PROGRAM (INCLUDING BUT NOT LIMITED TO LOSS OF DATA OR DATA BEING RENDERED INACCURATE OR LOSSES SUSTAINED BY YOU OR THIRD PARTIES OR A FAILURE OF THE PROGRAM TO OPERATE WITH ANY OTHER PROGRAMS), EVEN IF SUCH HOLDER OR OTHER PARTY HAS BEEN ADVISED OF THE POSSIBILITY OF SUCH DAMAGES.

INDEX

Symbols

Unix for Mac:
Your visual blueprint to maximizing
the foundation of Mac OS X

INDEX

Unix for Mac:
Your visual blueprint to maximizing
the foundation of Mac OS X

INDEX

Unix for Mac:
Your visual blueprint to maximizing
the foundation of Mac OS X

INDEX

Unix for Mac:
Your visual blueprint to maximizing
the foundation of Mac OS X

Q

question mark (?) wildcard, 26, 47
quit command, 74
quit Pico, 63
quotations marks in command line, 10

R

-R option, 37
-r option, 35
read access, file, 24
read files, Perl, 258–259
reboot command, 156–157
recall
   command history, 90–91
   shell commands, 8
redirect text to file, 48–49
regexps, 46
regular expressions, 46
relative pathnames, 21
remote access enable, 152–153
remote system
   reachable, 142–143
   secure access, 148–149
rename files, 22
repeat last command, 90
reply to e-mail, Pine, 225
resource forks, 128–129
restart computer, 156–157
restart process, 98–99
restore command, 165
rlogin command, 15, 144–145
rm command, 10, 23, 82
rmdir command, 23, 34–35
root account, 157
root user account enable, 160–161
rootless mode, start XFree86, 278–279
.rtf files, 293
Ruby applications, 306–307
ruler option, vi, 65
run from Terminal application, 15
rw-, 19

S

save file
   different name, vi, 74
   emacs, 78
   and exit vi, 75
   Pico, 63
   sorted text, 57
   vi, 74–75
   Window settings, 6
schedule scripts to run automatically, 120–121
Screen, 317
screencapture command, 124–125
screenshot
   capture, 124–125
   edit, 125
scroll bars, Terminal application, 5
search for text in files with grep command, 10
second prompt, 80
section of screen capture, 124–125
sed command, 118–119
selection of files with completion, 27
send
   e-mail, 218–219
   e-mail Pine, 226–227
sendmail, configure, 214–215
sequential commands run, 96
server
   Apache, 232–233
   X Window System, 268
set
   autolist command, 27
   prompt, 80–81
   value of shell, 85
   Window Title, 6
set command, 9, 82–83, 84
set environment variable, 94
set noclobber command, 49
setenv command, 86
setopt command, 95
sftp command, 148–149
shebang line, 253

Unix for Mac:
Your visual blueprint to maximizing
the foundation of Mac OS X

INDEX

Unix for Mac:
Your visual blueprint to maximizing
the foundation of Mac OS X

with these two-color Visual™ guides

Nov 02

"Master It" tips provide additional topic coverage.